KATHARINE LEE BATES

FROM SEA TO SHINING SEA

PRAISE FOR *Katharine Lee Bates: From Sea to Shining Sea*

"How I loved this splendid biography! Melinda Ponder brings Katharine Lee Bates to life as never before. And what a fascinating, remarkable woman she was—so much more important in the history and literature of our country than I had realized."

~Doris Kearns Goodwin, Pulitzer Prize historian

"Finally, a full portrait of the wise and witty woman who wrote the words that best express our love for America. Melinda Ponder's rich narrative is a timely reminder that intellect, integrity, and a rigorous respect for truth are the real pillars of patriotism."

~Lynn Sherr, former ABC News correspondent and author of
*America the Beautiful: The Stirring True Story
Behind America's Favorite Song*

"*Katharine Lee Bates: From Sea to Shining Sea* unfolds at long last the impressive life story and strikingly variegated career of the author of America's unofficial national anthem. A limit-bumping thinker ahead of her time, sometimes even at odds with it, Katharine Lee Bates also had a remarkable gift for reaching the broader American public."

~Lawrence Buell, Harvard University, author of
New England Literary Culture and
The Dream of the Great American Novel

"...[A] carefully researched and thoroughly entrancing life tale of a brilliant and accomplished woman whose many achievements have too long been eclipsed by the enduring success of 'America the Beautiful'.... Ponder wisely sets this triumph in the context of a full and richly lived life."

~Megan Marshall, Pulitzer Prize-winning author of
Margaret Fuller: A New American Life and
Elizabeth Bishop: A Miracle for Breakfast

"Melinda Ponder's ... beautifully written biography presents Katharine Lee Bates as, in her time, a "New Woman." Readers will find that this life story of a beloved poet, patriot, and social reformer has much to say about our own time."

~Barbara Kanellopoulos, *The Falmouth Enterprise*

"Congratulations to Melinda Ponder for telling the story of a poet who was also a true American hero.... This book is a stirring tribute to a brilliant and deeply patriotic American whose message we need to hear today."

~Stephen Kinzer, historian and author,
*The True Flag: Theodore Roosevelt, Mark Twain,
and the Birth of American Empire*

KATHARINE LEE BATES

FROM SEA TO SHINING SEA

MELINDA M. PONDER

WINDY CITY PUBLISHERS
CHICAGO

KATHARINE LEE BATES: FROM SEA TO SHINING SEA
© 2017 by Melinda M. Ponder

Windy City Publishers
2118 Plum Grove Road, #349
Rolling Meadows, IL 60008

www.windycitypublishers.com

Published in the United States of America

Paperback ISBN#:
978-1-941478-39-4

Hardcover ISBN#:
978-1-941478-48-6

eBook ISBN#:
978-1-941478-47-9

Library of Congress Control Number:
2017935596

WINDY CITY PUBLISHERS
CHICAGO

For Sophie, Zack, Natalie, David, Caleb, and Teddy

CONTENTS

*All quotations in chapter titles
are either by or about Katharine Lee Bates.*

PART TWO
WRITING PROTEST POEMS AND REVISING "AMERICA"
1893–1904

PART THREE
CREATING A GLOBAL COMMUNITY
1905–1929

WORLD WAR I AMERICAN FLAG OF THE "YANKEE" 104TH INFANTRY DIVISION

PROLOGUE

"TEARS ON THEIR FACES"[1]

I.

When Katharine Lee Bates—poet of "America the Beautiful," world traveler, social activist, foreign correspondent, mentor to Robert Frost, and Wellesley College English professor—went to sleep on Sunday night, November 10, 1918, American soldiers were still fighting in Europe's Great War. Only three days before, she had watched "the world and the college" go "wild" after a New York reporter mistakenly announced the war's end.[2]

But after four years of bloodshed and thousands of dead, wounded, and missing soldiers, when would Katharine and other Americans be able to celebrate the end of "the war to end all wars"? Would Germany finally agree to a cease-fire now that the other Central Powers had surrendered?

II.

November 11 had already arrived across the Atlantic on the hills above infamous Verdun, France. In drizzling rain American soldiers awaited the cease-fire that would end their exhausting days and nights of German shellfire, poison gas, ratholes, lice, and deep mud. Part of the massive Meuse-Argonne offensive line, at that time the largest American military operation ever attempted, the Yankee Division—National Guard troops from all six New England states—had been ordered to continue holding off as many German troops as possible and to attack night and day, without any letup.

In the previous two days of fighting, 2,454 American Army troops had died in Europe's bombarded villages and blasted fields.[3] Now, near Verdun, American artillery boomed along the entire front all night to show that the war was still on, in spite of the peace rumors.[4]

An ancient Roman garrison, Verdun had been a strategic military fortress for centuries, overlooking a long stretch of the Meuse River at the point where the historic highway from Rheims crosses toward Metz. By 1918, in this "modern" war, Verdun's battlefields were covered with more dead bodies per square yard than any others. In farmyards near field hospitals, corpses were sometimes buried with empty wine bottles in their arms, their names sealed inside to identify them long after their dog tags had rusted away.[5]

Katharine's friend, young Harvard poet Robert Hillyer, described the grisly job of driving wounded soldiers in his ambulance through one of the bloodiest battle areas, "Le Mort Homme" (Dead Man's Corner):

> Here is the crossroads where the slain
>
> Were piled so deep we could not pass.
>
> [....]
>
> *'Doucement, doucement!'* I hear
>
> The wounded gasping through their blood;
>
> The ambulance with grinding gear
>
> Lurches in shell-holes, sinks in mud.
>
> [....]
>
> The Mort Homme darkens all the ground.
>
> [....]
>
> With cracked and beaten lips that taste
>
> Commands like acid but obeyed,
>
> We still with leaden nightmare haste
>
> Convey our shadows through the shade.[6]

Although the armistice was signed at 5:30 a.m. that day, orders came to continue fighting until 11 a.m., the moment for the truce that would end the fighting to go into effect. Officers and doughboys alike were shocked: "Why snatch from some men the last chance they had of coming through the war safely?"[7]

Bedraggled soldiers grabbed their gas masks, helmets, and guns, and stumbled forward in the fog. Their boots falling apart, their uniforms tattered, their few remaining horses emaciated, and their equipment broken down, they inched forward through minefield craters of thawing mud, crawling over skeletons of soldiers still entangled in shreds of old uniforms.

Amid empty shell cartridges clanking onto the ground and pungent odors of gunpowder, poison gas, explosives, hot metal, and oil drifting up from the ravines, they dug in to mark their positions.

With only shell-hole water to drink, they were freezing cold, hungry, and wet from two days of rain that had soaked even their bread. Worse, frozen mist enshrouding the stump-filled underbrush had socked in their air support.

Deafening explosions and vivid flashes of German artillery assaulted them—shells whizzed over their heads and burst open with smoking bits of steel—and the Yanks sent their own deadly replies shuddering back through the dense air, their ear-splitting reports echoing across the ravaged hillsides and ravines.

But as the mist dissolved, the soldiers heard the faint drone of Allied planes flying northward toward them, and then, a few minutes before 11 a.m., shouts of "Truce! Truce!" came from the rear lines.[8]

While the gunners continued to shoot, counting the shells as the time approached, the infantry advanced, looking at their watches, and all along the front the batteries prepared for their final salvo.

The artillerists joined hands, forming long lines at the lanyards for their final blasts. Two hundred men each held five large firing ropes, waiting for a dropped handkerchief to signal the moment for their final shots of the Great War.[9]

Northeast of Verdun, just before eleven o'clock, American artillerymen wrote "Good Luck" on a ninety-pound shell and loaded it into a six-inch howitzer.[10]

After a few seconds of silence, a command rang out: "'Eleven o'clock! Fire!'"

The final shells exploded, "like a final thunder crash at the clearing of a storm…. As the barrage [of firing died], ending in a final husky rumble in the distance from the big guns, runners [sprang] along the firing line.

"Instantly comprehending, the whole line of doughboys leapt from the trenches, fox holes, and shell craters, splitting the unaccustomed silence with a shrill cheer."[11]

The armistice that the Germans signed that morning in General Foch's railway carriage command headquarters, hidden in a forest in France, had finally stopped the fighting.

On the battlefields, a bewildering silence fell. Like the two million other American soldiers in France, the Yankee Division stood speechless, staring at one another. And then they began to sing.

III.

Back in New England, when the sun rose on November 11, Katharine Lee Bates heard church bells pealing and the shrill whistles of the nearby Boston-bound train. After the peace rumors, the joyous noise "told the truth this time."[12] The nightmare of war was over.

Soon this short, matronly woman, dressed in the long dark skirts of the nineteenth century, climbed aboard a crowded train at the Wellesley station. Behind her spectacles Katharine's brown eyes may have characteristically twinkled as she joined the many Wellesley College students who were breaking "loose … without signing out" from their strict campus to join the throngs of people in Boston.[13] It was an ideal day for a celebration, with temperatures surprisingly on their way up to 60 degrees.

When her train pulled into the old Huntington Avenue Station in Boston's Back Bay, she was only a few blocks from where the Yankee Division had drilled before it left for France. She had recently submitted her poem, "Died of Wounds," about the heroism of a young American soldier who had dragged a wounded French comrade "from one / Grim shell-hole to another," to the nearby offices of the popular *Youth's Companion* magazine.[14]

Now, on the streets around her, Boston was "lifting its lid" with a bang—horns tooted, church bells rang out, and flag-waving crowds of ecstatic people surged toward Boston Common—"Every One Striving to Make the Most Noise"—beating tin-pan drums, blowing fish horns, and yelling themselves hoarse.[15]

The city's celebration had begun a few hours after midnight, when the Associated Press flashed the State Department's announcement of a peace agreement over its wires, and by 3 a.m. newsboys shouted out the headlines plastered on the windows in front of the excited crowds along Washington Street's "Newspaper Row," where printing presses rolled out extra editions.

They trumpeted President Woodrow Wilson's proclamation: "My Fellow Countrymen: The armistice was signed this morning. Everything for which America fought has been accomplished. It will now be our fortunate duty to assist … in the establishment of just democracy throughout the world."[16]

The *Boston Globe* declared it "THE DAY OF DAYS—THE GREATEST DAY IN THE HISTORY OF BOSTON."

Before sunrise, Boston's mayor had greeted elated crowds as he made his way from the docks up along the narrow winding streets, once seventeenth-century cattle paths, to stately City Hall. Factory whistles blew to celebrate this wondrous day.

A few hours later, bedlam reigned on Boston streets all around Katharine. But everyone was good-natured, "in everything except the sentiments expressed towards the Kaiser." Women, whose "hats were pulled to one side," smiled for happiness. [17]

Crowds pushed uniformed soldiers and sailors into automobiles, taking them for rides amid wild cheering. Boys and young women perched on "every conceivable part, including the engine hood" of the cars crawling along the streets. [18]

Girls waved flags with one hand, made noise with watchmen's rattles with the other, and blew horns gripped between their teeth. Along Washington Street, "staid business men" did snake dances that hinted of "past celebrations on college gridirons," grabbing up tin cans, sheets of metal, oil boilers, horns and rattles, anything that could make a satisfactory din.[19]

"The masses of people gone wild ... seemed to melt into one gigantic, hilarious, chaotic procession ... intent on making more noise than ever before," reported Katharine's newspaper, the conservative *Boston Evening Transcript*.[20]

Parades of workers marched past City Hall late into the afternoon in "almost an unbroken line" to the beat of a big bass drum a block away on Tremont Street, its "noise like the crack of doom."[21]

And on Beacon Hill, a minister exhorted his listeners to think of the starving victims of the war and quoted Katharine's words in "America the Beautiful"—to "confirm" America's soul "in self-control."[22]

She joined in this huge outpouring of relief at the war's end for as long as she could before returning to Wellesley. One student saw her waiting in the train station, "a little old lady perched on a suitcase, busy writing. It was our *famous* Miss Bates ... a dear, friendly and jovial person ... [who] was always stopping and talking to us as we walked on campus." She told them that she was "writing an Armistice Day poem."[23]

IV.

However, as Katharine later learned, she had received her greatest tribute as a poet earlier that day near Verdun.

On that morning of November 11 when the fighting ceased, a battalion of American soldiers—exhausted, wounded, and forever scarred, who had risked their lives to serve the country they loved—stood up and got themselves into military formation. With no official national anthem yet chosen, they began singing Katharine's words of "America the Beautiful," and "all came to life again and sang it with tears on their faces."[24]

Their voices were weak from poison gas and hunger, but soon many others joined their chorus.

Overwhelmed with shock, relief, and incredulous joy, they did not want a song about war. They wanted to celebrate the beauty and idealism of their own beloved country. In her words, they could picture it:

> O beautiful for spacious skies,
>   For amber waves of grain,
> For purple mountain majesties
>   Above the fruited plain!
> America! America!
>   God shed His grace on thee
> And crown thy good with brotherhood
>   From sea to shining sea!
>
> O beautiful for pilgrim feet
>   Whose stern, impassion'd stress
> A thoroughfare for freedom beat
>   Across the wilderness!
> America! America!
>   God mend thy ev'ry flaw,
> Confirm thy soul in self-control,
>   Thy liberty in law!
>
> O beautiful for heroes proved
>   In liberating strife,
> Who more than self their country loved,
>   And mercy more than life!

America! America!

    May God thy gold refine,

Till all success be nobleness,

    And ev'ry gain divine!

O beautiful for patriot dream

    That sees beyond the years

Thine alabaster cities gleam,

    Undimm'd by human tears!

America! America!

    God shed His grace on thee

And crown thy good with brotherhood

    From sea to shining sea![25]

Finally, they would be going home.

Later, hundreds of little fires, so long prohibited, flickered along the lines as soldiers thawed out their freezing limbs. That evening, while bells in Verdun rang out the victory, French and American soldiers marched to their bands under fireworks, and some soldiers kept singing.

When Katharine heard their story of singing her song, she said that it "made the tears come...."[26]

How had she journeyed to this moment? Born in 1859 on the eve of the Civil War, she had been "rock'd in a clamshell" on Cape Cod. How had that childhood village, and her trailblazing career as a writer and teacher begun as "Katie of '80" in Wellesley College's second graduating class, empowered her to write such a powerful national song that still resonates within us today?

How had Henry Wadsworth Longfellow inspired her to be a poet and to help create a national literature? How had his inspiration led her to become a mentor in turn, to such American poets as Robert Frost? Amid three romances—two with men and one with a woman—how had she changed the words of "America the Beautiful" at key moments in American history as she watched America grow from the rural country of her childhood into an urban industrial powerhouse and then an imperial power?

In her adventurous travels as a woman in Spain and Egypt, how did she become a global citizen who saw America as part of a world community? And how did the years after Armistice Day inspire her final surprising vision for all who sing her song?

An early committee of men searching for a less militaristic and more universal national anthem than "The Star-Spangled Banner" wanted a song that would "pervade and penetrate, and cheer the land like sunlight," words that would be "the national heart-beat set to music."[27]

This book is the story of how Katharine's tumultuous life and times enabled her to strengthen that national heartbeat, "from sea to shining sea."

PART ONE

Becoming the Poet of "America"

in a Changing Country:

1859-1893

The First Congregational Church,
Falmouth, Massachusetts

Chapter One

1859–1871
"Rock'd ... in a Clam-Shell"[1]

I.

On a cool Sunday morning in September 1859, a three-week-old baby girl, the future poet of "America the Beautiful," was the center of a heartbreaking scene. She awaited a poignant baptism in the picturesque Cape Cod village of Falmouth, Massachusetts, where sloops, schooners, and fishing boats bobbed in nearby Vineyard Sound while sheep and cows grazed in neighboring fields.

Her father, the Reverend William Bates, gravely ill, prepared to baptize his tiny daughter as his last official act, not in his stately First Congregational Church, on the Village Green, but in their home, where they were surrounded by family treasures—a wide three-paneled gilt-framed mirror from his prominent father, the Rev. Joshua Bates; his wife Cornelia's slender rocking chair; and upstairs, the highly polished maple bed from Joshua Bates's days as president of Vermont's Middlebury College.

Just the year before, families of oceangoing sailors and farmers had welcomed the forty-three-year-old Bates, who "loved his studies and his pastoral duties,"[2] and Cornelia, ten years his junior, with a simple beauty, dark hair, intelligent eyes, and a thoughtful and calm smile. They had chosen to come to Falmouth partly because it would offer financial security and good schools for their children.[3]

Although their first son had died before their move, their family of eight-year-old Arthur, a lively child with a determined look and his mother's dark hair; five-year-old Jane (later known as Jeannie), with her mother's pretty face; and their youngest son, two-year-old Samuel, with fair coloring, was growing again with their new baby, born on August 12, to be named for Cornelia's sister, the poet Catherine Lee.

Close to death from a tumor in his spine, William told Cornelia: "'You must compose yourself and be calm…. You must trust in the Lord and be reconciled to his will. He will provide for you. For your sake, for the sake of the children, and this dear people, I should be glad to live; but it is the will of the Lord that I should go now, and it is all right.'"[4]

That Sunday morning of the baptism, when he heard his church's huge Paul Revere bell calling parishioners to worship, although in great pain, he murmured, "How good that bell sounds! How often have I joyfully obeyed its call!"[5]

The Rev. Lewis F. Clark, officiating, described the poignant scene: "Very early in the morning of the sabbath, [the Rev. Mr. Bates] requested that the hymn, 'Thine earthly Sabbaths, Lord, we love,' might be repeated to him….

"Just before the sacred rite was administered, he offered a brief prayer [of] touching simplicity and pathos…. 'Blessed Saviour, accept the consecration which we now propose to make of this our last child to thee. Gentle Shepherd, make her one of thy lambs. Bless all the little flock, and bring them to thy kingdom. Amen.'"[6]

After six more days in great pain, William Bates died. For the first time, little Arthur wound the family clock, "symbolic" of his feeling of responsibility for a task "that he had taken from his father's hands" and "never thereafter neglected."[7]

At his funeral, Cornelia and her children sat in the "minister's pew," listening with nearly five hundred other bereaved parishioners to the Rev. Mr. Clark's words:[8]

> You have … lost a personal friend … a kind pastor, a wise teacher, an able and faithful preacher, [and] a judicious spiritual adviser….[9]

He urged the congregation to "remember that there is one family among you upon whom it presses with peculiar weight. It is not necessary that I should remind you of the sorrows of her whose dearest friend is now hidden from her sight, or of those little children, at this tender age, deprived of the care of him who was so fitted to be their guide and counsellor."[10]

WILLIAM BATES

CORNELIA BATES

ARTHUR BATES

JANE (JEANNIE) BATES

SAMUEL BATES

KATHARINE LEE BATES

II.

The congregation could offer its sympathy for the catastrophe that had befallen Cornelia and her four young children. But she would need all of her "indomitable industry and perseverance" to cope with the devastating loss of her husband and of their comfortable house, because the church's financial provisions for a minister's widow were meager.[11]

While relatives sent what money they could and offered to adopt Jane, Cornelia resolutely kept her family together and moved them to cheaper lodgings, the first of five moves during their next twelve years in Falmouth.[12]

Arthur knew that his father's illness had "used up all the money," so his mother "got along by earning what she could,"[13] by selling fruit, vegetables, eggs, and poultry to her neighbors, and even tagging merchandise with her children for a local manufacturing company.[14]

However, according to her great-granddaughter, Cornelia "was a proud and brilliant woman, and it was painful to be the object of charity and to work to make ends meet for her little family."[15] She was embarrassed to have to ask a neighbor for the seventy-five cents owed her for stitching that she needed for Arthur's geography book and to have to wait on summer visitors at the imposing Albert Nye house.[16]

While she had few "material resources," Cornelia drew on her spiritual and emotional resources to give her children a family life rich in love, hard work, imagination, and hope, one like that of her own childhood. Born in 1826 in Conway, Massachusetts, she came from a family of industrious yeomen farmers and craftsmen who valued education and books. Her father, Samuel Lee, treasured his copy of *The Dramatic Works and Poems of William Shakspeare* [sic], and when this book was later passed down to Cornelia's youngest daughter, she wrote inside its front cover: "Not in itself a valuable edition, but ... one of the few books remaining to us from the library of my mother's father, a 'tinsmith' of the widest reading and keenest intelligence."[17]

Samuel Lee was radically ahead of his time when he sent his intelligent daughters, Cornelia and Catherine, to one of the few institutions then in existence for higher education for women in America—the Mount Holyoke Female Seminary in South Hadley, Massachusetts. There they learned from capable intellectual women who unconventionally believed that girls possessed the same mental capacity as boys.

After graduating, Cornelia taught school in nearby Uxbridge, Massachusetts, where she was courted by the Rev. William Bates. When he asked her father for her hand in marriage, Samuel Lee advised him: "cherish [Cornelia] as your equal, she has a large and sound heart ... a soul not to be confined to this poor spot of earth, but that would be glad to grasp the universe ... as far as knowledge is concerned."[18]

In spite of losing that husband and having to worry constantly about their financial future, Cornelia lovingly sheltered her youngest child, now called Katharine ("Katie"), from the grim reality of their situation. To Katharine, she was simply an "audacious" mother,[19] who later wrote to her: "My dear Katie ... wherever you are on land or sea—in this world or in another you will always be my own cherished well-beloved child, who came to me when it seemed as if life's star had set, and who has been a sunbeam always since you came."[20]

III.

Cornelia gave Arthur the task of pushing young Katie in her carriage on Falmouth's unpaved, sandy, sometimes muddy, rutted dirt roads.[21] When a peddler jokingly put a pair of eyeglasses on her, she exclaimed, "'Why, I can see leaves on the trees!'"[22] She saw a Falmouth that was a timeless place of moss-covered rain barrels, wooden sinks, butter cooling in the cellar, and wood fires for heat, as well as fields, ponds, one part-time policeman, and neighborly side porches.[23]

A whitewashed split-rail fence enclosed the Green, surrounded by well-kept houses, as Katie remembered: "A gardened group of dwellings looking on / Each other neighborly, about the knee / Of the tall white meeting house, whose spire was key / To heaven."[24]

She grew up hearing its famous Revere bell ring at six every morning, at noon, and at nine in the evening; the church choir leader tuned his bass viol to its C-sharp pitch.[25] But to Katie, the bell was a living voice that rang out Falmouth's past, present, and future:

> Thou hast tolled from seed to fruit
> Generations three of life....
> Ring thy peals for centuries yet,
> Living voice of Paul Revere![26]

At the church, her mother joined other women, many of them also widows, to hold prayer meetings and organize help for the needy, including survivors and families of shipwrecked men. They established the Falmouth Seamen's Friend Society, furnished a room in the Boston Sailors' Home, and sent money for such a room in Honolulu.[27] In 1859, the year of Katie's birth, they stocked a library on a Falmouth ship, and filled barrels for the even more destitute families of Congregational ministers, first in Massachusetts, then in western states, and later in foreign countries.[28]

Katie, Jeannie, Sam, and Arthur attended the church's Sabbath School, where Cornelia was a teacher. On a warm day when the windows were open, they could hear the stamping and neighing sounds of horses hitched to various buggies, gigs, "carryalls," barouches, and farm wagons behind the church.[29]

The church was also where Cornelia gave her young daughter an unforgettable model of how women could take part in national events.

Katie had been born into a country at war with itself over clashing ideas about its ideals, economy, and future. Some Americans, shocked by the sadistic scenes of slavery in Harriet Beecher Stowe's powerful *Uncle Tom's Cabin,* wanted to prevent slavery from spreading or to abolish it. Henry Wadsworth Longfellow's good friend, the antislavery leader Senator Charles Sumner of Massachusetts, had been viciously caned, nearly to death, at his Senate desk. But radical John Brown's violent attack at Harper's Ferry in Virginia terrified slave owners about the fanaticism of northerners. Hardly had Abraham Lincoln been elected in 1860 when seven Southern states seceded from the Union. After the April 1861 Confederate attack on Fort Sumter, four more Southern states seceded, and war was declared.

During the next four years of Katie's childhood, battles raged, killing 620,000 men, dividing the North from the South and whites from blacks, and sometimes pitting families against families. It touched even Falmouth, far from the battlefields, which sent fathers and brothers to fight for the Union, seventy-one to the Army and Navy, nineteen of whom were lost.[30]

Between 1860 and 1865, her father's church contributed $1,100.50 to charity, along with three barrels of clothing for freed slaves and three barrels of "valuable supplies for Civil War soldiers."[31] At Falmouth harbor, coastal traders picked up the cloth made by one of the Falmouth mills for the Union Army.[32]

Finally, on April 11, 1865, celebratory bonfires blazed in the nation's capital, rockets exploded, and a band played while thousands of people crowded in front of the White House to hear Lincoln say: "The evacuation of Petersburg and Richmond and surrender of the principal insurgent army gives hopes of a righteous and speedy peace whose joyous expression cannot be restrained."[33]

Bostonians could almost begin celebrating the end of the war on April 14, Good Friday, when the morning headlines proclaimed: "REBEL LEADERS PROFESSING ALLEGIANCE.... OFFICIAL: THE WAR VIRTUALLY ENDED. NO MORE DRAFTING AND RECRUITING."[34]

But by that evening the headlines cried: "SHOCKING TRAGEDIES. PRESIDENT LINCOLN SHOT."[35]

"President Lincoln and wife visited Ford's Theatre this evening.... During the third act ... a sharp report of a pistol was heard.... The screams of Mrs. Lincoln first disclosed the fact to the audience that the President had been shot, when all present rose to their feet, rushing toward the stage, many exclaiming, 'Hang him! Hang him!'... There was a rush toward the President's box, when cries were heard, 'Stand back and give him air!' ... The President had been shot through the head ... some of the brain was oozing out."[36]

A special dispatch added: "A shock from Heaven, laying half the city in instant ruins, would not have startled as did the word that started out from the Ford's Theatre half an hour ago that the President had been shot. It flew everywhere in five minutes, and set five thousand feet in swift and excited motion on the instant."[37]

This was the news that suddenly burst upon five-year-old Katie and her mother. While shaking out a tablecloth, they heard the shrill voice of their neighbor, a Confederate sympathizer, shouting, "'They've shot Abe Lincoln, / He's dead and I'm glad he's dead.'"[38]

Katie long remembered seeing her mother stagger back into the kitchen, her face "all strange and blanched, / Her deep eyes filling, filling and brimming / With tears that the tablecloth, kept so sacred / From childish weeping, stanched." Hiding under the bare lilac bushes, she wondered, "And not one angel to catch the bullet! / What had become of God?"

Having lost William Bates as a father, husband, and minister, Katie and her family now grieved for the one man whose vision for the future might have been able to accomplish the nearly impossible task of bringing the battling sides of the country together after the war.

As the day became cold and wet, her "lonely village among the sand dunes" had to turn its thoughts to "how to honor our saint, our martyr, our hero evermore." Although isolated from Boston with "only its one scant store," Falmouth was part of the "stricken nation." On the Green, the flag flew "half-masted" for the first time in Katie's life. When she heard its bell tolling "upon the air / Lincoln, Lincoln, Abraham Lincoln," she imagined that even in his grave, her father could hear its clear voice from his "shadowy hill of sleep."[39]

When she later entered the hushed wooden church for Lincoln's memorial service, she saw black mourning cloth draping the wainscoting and the imposing pulpit.

Because the black fabric from whaling captain Thomas Lawrence, whose ship had been attacked by Confederate gunboats on its return home, had been insufficient, the widows of Falmouth had hung their own well-used symbols of loss and grief, their black shawls, around the church. As Katharine wrote sixty years later:

> Wonted to grief, the women of Falmouth
>> Hung the old church, pulpit and walls,
> With a simple mourning, a sacred mourning
> Already steeped in uttermost anguish,
>> Hung it with widow's shawls.[40]

Unable as women to speak from the church pulpit, the community of widows nevertheless helped their village voice its grief through their wordless contributions. Recognizing her own mother's shawl honoring her father, Katie understood that she too was part of the grieving country:

> The nation's sorrow I felt my sorrow,
> For my mother's shawl was there.

She never forgot this scene of women's collective power bringing a community together in a national crisis. Falmouth women, Katie knew, had "the tenderest hearts ... where sorrows sorest wring," living their lives "comforted and comforting" others.[41]

IV.

As she got older, Katie and her friend Hattie Gifford saw Falmouth history where they played, tramping on paths to Sider's Pond, pronounced "Sidder's," from "Consider's Pond," named for Consider Hatch, who had built his house on its shores in 1748. On the land between Sider's Pond and Salt Pond, the first white settlers, thirteen or fourteen people from Barnstable, Massachusetts, had settled the first "plantation" in 1660 in "Suckanesset," a name from the Indian word meaning "where the black wampum [polished shells] were found."

As the town grew, it acquired more land from the Indians. Indians still lived in Falmouth during Katie's childhood, many in nearby Mashpee, and although she understood the wrongs that had been done to them as a group, she wrote in her diary that she could see that not all Indians lived up to her expectations of them:

"Monday, March 26, 1866: Indians. I used to think indians were the ideal of eloquence, nobleness, firmness and integrity. Now 't is not so! One in my school, lies, cheats, and yet pretends to be a christian."[42]

Beyond the Old Burying Ground was Vineyard Sound, the waters that linked Falmouth with distant oceans and provided a common route around Cape Cod to Boston before the building of the present canal. With the frequent onshore wind at their sterns, all kinds of boats came into port with their sails stretched out "wing and wing" on each side.

Katharine later imagined a beloved minister who, much like her father, loved both the sea and the Bible:

> Ragged hats were lifted to him; grimy hands were ready with their greetings. There was not a rough fisherman along the shore who would not hurry in from his lobster-pots on a Sunday afternoon, when the muscular boy-preacher, who could handle a dogfish as well as a Greek Testament, might be seen standing on a pile of lumber at the end of Long wharf, beating time with his singing-book.[43]

Although the Rev. Mr. Bates's family called him "the saintly William,"[44] according to Arthur Bates, he used to "go into the cabin of the [schooner] *Emily Mac*, get into a bathing suit, sometimes not, and swim out in the Sound and float a long time: one day, men on a passing schooner saw him, thought he was drowning and tried to save him."[45]

Katie could watch schooners sail in to the Old Stone Dock with their cargoes of corn, flour, leather goods, textiles, lumber, or ice and then buy fish, salt, wool, glassware, and onions from Falmouth, part of the thriving coastal trade among seaports up and down the eastern American coast and Europe.[46]

Day fishermen mingled with men and boys going off for several weeks along the East Coast to fish for cod and mackerel to be eaten fresh or salted. Others harvested shellfish close to the shore.

Fishermen needed bait, and Sider's Pond gave Arthur a way to earn much-needed money for his family. One of eighty ponds in Falmouth Township, it was full of eels, herring, pickerel, and perch, just the right size for bait.

In the Sound, Arthur caught menhaden and bluefish, where "a good breeze and a fighting fish was great sport."[47] He and his pals might trick their schoolteacher in order to get in as much fishing as they could when the blue-fish were running. As he recalled, in "the afternoon some boy would get himself sent home from school for misbehaviour, and would go down and get some herring, and about sunset we would go down to the Sound bluefishing: our lines had weights and usually two hooks, half a herring on each hook and we swung the lines off into the water."[48]

When he caught a bluefish early in the day, Cornelia "would have it on the table within two hours from the time it was caught: that is the only way to really enjoy bluefish."[49] Younger brother Sam caught, on one famous afternoon, "more than fifty."[50]

Katie grew up among the boat-building sheds, sail-lofts, and stores necessary to this seafaring world. John Jenkins outfitted whaling ships with all necessary items—pea jackets, sea boots, tarpaulins, biscuits, canvas, matches, and ditty bags for their voyages, which could last several years.[51] Retired whaling Captain Hamlin kept a small store on Main Street where coconuts swung over the front door, and retired seamen gathered.[52] There she could inhale a mingling of exotic odors—salt herring in a barrel, ripe strong-smelling cheese, and strong tobacco.[53]

Nobska Light, Woods Hole, Mass.

NOBSKA LIGHT, FALMOUTH

When a ship just back from a long voyage entered Vineyard Sound, Nobska Light flashed the news down the line of Cape towers to notify the ship-owners waiting in the port of Boston that an important vessel filled with tea, silks, china, and spices might be arriving twenty-four hours later.

Looking back on her years in Falmouth, Katharine saw herself, despite her family's poverty, as having had a rich childhood. She had been "rock'd in a clam-shell"[54] by the saltwater, playing with children whose fathers sailed the sea and brought its treasures home.

V.

In the first half of the nineteenth century, sea captains headed about half of the three hundred households in Falmouth,[55] and it seemed to Arthur that "almost every man" was a sailor:[56] "The Captains often took their wives with them, on their four or five year voyages, and many ... schoolmates were born in foreign ports."[57]

Vineyard Sound's inviting waters were a gateway to global adventures, as Katie saw on the tattooed arms of her sea captain neighbors:

> That the world was wonderful and wide we knew,
>
> For we had watched the vanishing of sails
>
> On vague horizons, heard the vaunting tales
>
> Of bronzed old seamen whose adventures grew
>
> More terrible as pictured in tattoo
>
> On arms and breast....[58]

One of them, Captain Jones, "drove a horse as if steering a vessel." He awed Falmouth children because "hadn't he almost been eaten by cannibals in the Sandwich Islands on one of those ... whaling voyages?"[59]

Captain Lawrence and his wife brought home gifts of lusterware cups and saucers, an ivory pick made from a whale's tooth, ivory stilettos (small pointed tools) for embroidery work, and a calling card case exquisitely carved from ivory, with tiny figures of Chinese men and women in front of trees and boats.[60] He also brought back a gay pink and scarlet parrot with a salty vocabulary. When its words began to go "off on the wrong track," Mrs. Lawrence would throw a black shawl over its cage to silence it.[61] Perhaps Katharine remembered it years later when she acquired her own rakish parrot, Polonius.

Treasures from such ocean voyages surrounded her in Falmouth:

> In the spring the peach trees shone
>
> Pink as the lips of shells from coral isle
>
> Bordering our dooryard paths. Under the willows
>
> A rusty anchor rested on the grass,
>
> While peering over porch there watched us pass
>
> A carven mermaid that has stemmed great billows,
>
> A lonely mermaid with a fading smile.[62]

Distant worlds also came inside Falmouth houses—"sculpted teeth of whales" sat on mantels; the Orient's lustrous "shawls and veils / gold-frosted," and ivory flutes from inside a captain's sea-chest were "by us to be possessed [along with] the cocoanuts for which gray, chattering monkeys climb; / Tamarinds, and dates, and luscious sweetmeats pressed / Into blue jars of quaint pagoda dome!"[63]

Even more surprising, sea captains sometimes brought children from the South Seas to Falmouth for a few years to learn the English necessary for their families' trading businesses, and they impressed the Bates boys with their great hunting and fishing skills. Arthur recalled liking such boys, "who had beautiful bows and arrows and could hit a duck more surely than we could with our shot guns. They could swim all day: they enjoyed climbing to the cross-tress of a vessel, diving off and coming up from under other vessels."[64] Many years later, Arthur still treasured a bow he had been given by one of these South Seas boys, using it as a curtain rod in his Portland, Maine, home.[65]

VI.

As the first-born, Arthur understood his family's need for money, so he chopped the piles of necessary firewood, "drove cows, picked cranberries, caught herring" and, along with younger brother Sam, did all he could "to help out."[66] Once he completed his schooling in Falmouth, eight years after his father's death, he had to leave home to find work that would help support the family, and got paid only fifty dollars a year.[67] Nevertheless, he managed to send home what money he could.

One day, after Cornelia completed drying all the family laundry in the kitchen in bad weather, one of her endless tasks, she tallied up, in a little red diary, her earnings for quinces and stitching as well as her hopes for future egg production, with "Dido" for twelve eggs, "Lady Blessington" for thirteen, and "Jones" and "Princess" for eleven each.[68]

But she soon gave this diary to Katie, her imaginative child, who began her first entry: "I am writing, scribbling rather, just for fun. Not that I have anything to say. there is a charm in bright clean unfilled pages which I, for one, cannot resist. The lines are to short for good rhymes. Decent rymes that is. Storys take up two many pages so all I can do is to scribble. So I shall all over the book. Goodby, dear imaginary audience."[69]

In Falmouth, Katie read "everything she could get,"[70] works by Louisa May Alcott ("four novels"), Sir Walter Scott ("five novels"), Henry Wadsworth Longfellow ("The Song of Hiawatha"), and Charles Dickens ("fifteen novels"), as well as "others I've no room to put down."[71] In his laundry bag, Arthur sent her Dickens novels from his distant workplace.[72]

Dickens, with his novels about urban poverty and resilient children, became her "mental nurse. When I get tired of the world I live in, I run away into his world where I passed so much of my childhood and I grew up on his knee."[73] In her diary, with Dickensian details, she sketched the visiting ministers who had been "entertained at the home of Mrs. Bates," probably competing with her with for her mother's attention:

> Rev. Elijar Kellog: Very excentric. Writes stories for boys. Very fond of boys. Very quick in all his motions. Impolite and rude. Says very queer things. Dresses carelessly. Has dirty fingers, dirty hands, dirty nails.
>
> Rev. Mr. Fellows: A big, fat, surly, gruff kind of man. Laughs very loud, talks incessantly... Feels big of his sermons. Very powerful sermons. Talks and looks like a regular rowdy.... Such is my account of Rev. Mr. Fellows.[74]

At the Falmouth Primary School, Katie received all "5s"—denoting "faultless recitations and deportment" in arithmetic, geography, spelling, deportment, and reading.[75] She and Hattie became authors and publishers with their "Weekly Journal, Falmouth Grammar School," entering the burgeoning field of family periodicals that ran appealing illustrations of poetry, fiction, essays, and puzzles for all the age groups in a family—parents, adolescents, and children.

The girls modeled their "Weekly" after the Boston-based *Youth's Companion* and the Congregationalist Publishing Society's children's *Well-Spring*, and crafted their first issue to give their friend Abbie Moore a good laugh.

Their long poem, "Luckless Tommy," was the first installment of a poem about a young boy who, disobeying his mother, picks up a broom, and the reader must wait for the next issue to read what would happen next.

They lightened the tragic mood of "Home, Let Me Go," a ballad told in a dialogue between a captured boy and a diabolical "old lady," with "Puzzles 1 and 2 (An Enigma)" tucked in at the bottom of the page, following the family magazine model.

Katie's "Weekly" shows her wit, ear for language, and desire to entertain her readers. It anticipates precisely the type of publication that, ten years later, would launch her writing career.

VII.

The Bates family had a rich heritage of exploration, adventure, and humor, and a passion for intellectual, spiritual, and literary work. Katharine felt that her lifelong "sea-love" came partly from her Bates ancestors, "Sailors that steered for the misty Canaries, / Fishers whose feet loved the feel of the dulse [red seaweed]."[76]

Many had lived in Lydd, England, where "sea gulls sail over the broad meadows ... only four miles" from the English Channel on the Kent seacoast. She traced her family back to Thomas Bate, a chief magistrate of Lydd, who had died in 1485.

On April 6, 1635, his descendant Clement Bates sailed from London in the ship *Elizabeth* to Hingham, a seaport on Quincy Bay in Massachusetts. Clement's descendant Joshua Bates was born in coastal Cohasset, Massachusetts, in 1776, only three and a half months before the Declaration of Independence was written. As he humorously wrote, "I was born a subject of the royal government of Great Britain, but if my mother's account of my infantile character is to be taken as evidence in the case, I was not a very quiet and submissive subject."[77]

He grew up working on his father's farm, but after an injury, he was allowed to study Latin and Greek. To pay for Harvard College, he "procured" money by "teaching in a private school, trapping muskrats, and loaning the proceeds on sheep on shares."[78] He received Harvard's highest honor as valedictorian at the head of his class. According to Arthur, Joshua had a "commanding presence, great intellect and fine scholarship ... [and was] an earnest preacher" and "a prolific writer ... a strong man among strong men ... venerated by all who knew and loved him."[79] In his memoirs he comes across with a lively intellect and good sense of humor.

Although Katie never knew this grandfather, she saw his books in her family parlor, and she thought of him as a fun-loving man, comfortable with a joke, as she was.

Her grandfather and father, role models in their intellectual and religious vocations, gave Katharine a special sense of family pride and models of men who moved listeners with their words. Later she bought "tall bookcases ... in second-hand stores to match the old mahogany case" in which her grandfather and father had kept their sermons and books,[80] and wore a large mourning brooch with a lock of Joshua Bates's hair surrounded by three ovals of pearls.[81]

She was also proud of her female ancestors, writing a children's poem about how two young girls in her family had held off an attack by British warships, and telling Hattie: "Yes, Abigail and Rebecca really were of our clan and really did, by fife and drum, scare off the British attack. It's our one martial achievement."[82]

VIII.

Katharine's childhood in a female-headed household was typical of that of many girls during the Civil War, when the work of absent husbands had to be done by women. Many girls saw their mothers take charge, using their wits and energies to keep their families and communities afloat, and took them as models in their adult lives.

Both Katie's mother and aunt were serious readers and lovers of language. Catherine Lee was a published poet who gave her granddaughter homemade gifts, sending a scarf with a note of advice: "You will like to think that she made [this] for her dear little Kitty.... It is better to have good hearts and good manners than handsome dresses."[83]

Questioning the conventional gender roles of her time, Katie complained to her diary, "Girls. Some girls are dreadful flirts. It is them I speak of, not the virtuous ones, like me."[84] "Girls. Girls are a very necessary portion of creation. They are full as necessary as boys. Girls (excepting a species called tomboys) play with dolls, when young. Afterwards croquet.... Sewing is always expected of girls. Why not of boys. Boys don't do much but out door work. Girls work is most all indoors. It isn't fair."[85]

But she respected women, writing, "They are high spirited as a general thing and I am happy to say have become impatient under the restraint men put upon them. So the great question of women's rights has arisen. I like women better than men. I like fat women better than lean ones. Some women call themselves ladies."[86] "Women are / Vixens or / Ladies or / Old maids. / The worst is / an old maid. The vixen next / worst. / A ladie perfect."[87]

Boys were a mixed bag: "Boys are a very necessary portion of creation. In their place, very nice, too. they are general rough. As long as they will keep in their element, and swim, run, jump, fish, climb trees, skate, and slide, I like them. But when they kiss the girls, write love notes, can't talk sense, and hug girls, they are the greatest bores in existence."[88]

IX.

Perhaps, as French philosopher Gaston Bachelard has observed, one's strongest impulse as an adult is to recreate the spatial and psychological landscape of one's childhood.[89] For Katharine, Falmouth was both a homey refuge filled with hard-working women and books and a launching place for a lifetime of exploration and writing.

Beautiful, with narrow beaches bordered by beach plums, meadows of wildflowers, snug shuttered houses with kitchen gardens, low stone walls, and the sounds and smells of the sea, it gave her memories of an ideal time and place. Like her favorite writers, Dickens, who mined the London neighborhoods of his youth to expose problems of urbanization, and Scott, who placed his tales of local historical romance in his native Scottish landscapes, she set her early poems and local color stories in a Falmouth-like world of rural villages rapidly vanishing after the Civil War.

Like Longfellow, who gave American readers scenes set in a New England nostalgically familiar to him, and like Alcott, who centered her fiction on daily lives of energetic women in her own Concord and Boston, Katharine created characters who often hark back to Falmouth.

There, she remembered her young self as "a shy, near-sighted child, always hiding away with a book. It was in vain that unclothed dolls were given her to beguile her into sewing. She would promptly spin a romance that left them wrecked on a desert isle and obliged to wrap themselves in raiment of oak leaves secured by thorns and grasses."[90]

There, Hattie became her first loyal reader. For the next sixty years, whenever Katharine traveled to England and beyond, she wrote to her, as another friend recalled: "Vicariously then we, too, travelled Europe, entering old cathedrals, treading foreign streets and learning different customs. I am sure Miss Bates would have rejoiced had she known!"[91]

There, Cornelia impressed upon her children that in their community, it was "share and share alike,"[92] as Katharine later wrote: "I know how simple 'tis to bear / Each other's burdens, loving one another."[93] "Never were there friendlier folk / Than in Falmouth by the sea, / Neighbor-households [with] pride of pedigree."[94] At the end of her life she called it a "friendly little village that practised a neighborly socialism without having heard the term."[95]

Katharine's character Jim describes the big heart of a woman much like Cornelia:

> Indeed, it was not an uncommon occurrence for [peddlers] to run up to the house and ask for a doughnut, or piece of blueberry pie, which my mother, whose generous heart made all the world her neighbors, never failed to set before them in double measure, laying a fragrant slice of cheese upon the doughnut or pouring over the pie a river of creamy milk, cherishing perhaps a secret partiality for their frank manners and blue shirts, and certainly pleased with the compliment paid to her cookery.[96]

There, as both father and mother, Cornelia became Katie's intellectual mentor and ambitious companion. To this daughter she was "the mother-face, our star / Of home since life first read its calendar / Within her smiles."[97] With strength and courage she managed to raise her four children alone, showing Katie what a resourceful and determined woman could do.

With her own father gone, in Falmouth Katharine understood the grief of those whose fathers, uncles, brothers, and husbands never returned from their ocean voyages.[98] She had watched the "weepers ... bear / Their gifts of flowers ... To pale stones carved with a ship or anchor" because "many a Falmouth man lay dreaming / Under seas of dazzling blue / Mid the rosewhite coral." Some were "shrouded" in Arctic ice, and "The tomb of some none knew."[99]

There, her fatherless and impoverished family had been loved and nurtured, just as the Rev. Mr. Clark had hoped.

X.

By the time Katharine was twelve years old, Falmouth's population was decreasing because farming and fishing were difficult ways to make a living compared with the opportunities in industrial Boston and the West. In 1840 Falmouth had 2,589 people; by 1870, it had shrunk to 2,237.[100] Like many other Americans after the Civil War, Cornelia moved her family from a rural village to the outskirts of a city, to Grantville, Massachusetts (now Wellesley

Hills), west of Boston. In the rent-free cottage of friends, she could care for her sister, Catherine, now an invalid, and Arthur and Sam could commute to jobs in Boston.

In their new town her gifted youngest daughter could attend public schools that would prepare her for demanding college entrance exams, if only such a college for young women existed.

Katharine would always relish such moments of departure, later describing them in language she had absorbed in Falmouth: when the "tide is calling; the anchors lift."[101]

KATHARINE LEE BATES IN 1876

HENRY FOWLE DURANT   PAULINE FOWLE DURANT

CHAPTER TWO

1871–1880
"KATIE OF '80"

I.

Several miles from the Bateses' new home,[1] Pauline and Henry Fowle Durant looked out from the top of a hill at the three hundred acres of fields and woodlands, the "park" of their new college for young women. Red-tinged oak trees surrounded them, a breeze blew through evergreen trees, and below them a small lake glittered in the sun.[2] It had taken the Durants much prayer and planning to get to the morning of September 14, 1871, when their workmen broke ground for the cornerstone of gigantic College Hall, the future home of Katie and her Wellesley College classmates.

The workmen listened respectfully to Pauline Durant, slender and pale in a dark dress and bonnet, as she spoke a few words to each one. If a man was a Protestant, she gave him a King James translation of the Bible.[3] If a Catholic, he received the Douay translation, with a gold cross embossed on its black leather cover. In either case, there would be an inscription like the one in the Bible that went to one Walter Evans: "Presented to Walter Evans by Mrs. Henry F. Durant at the laying of the Cornerstone of the Wellesley Female Seminary."[4]

In a special brown leather Bible tooled in gold she had written: "This building is humbly dedicated to our Heavenly Father with the hope and prayer that He may always be first in everything in this institution; that His word may be faithfully taught here; and that He will use it as a means of leading precious souls to the Lord Jesus Christ."

She placed it inside a tin box that she put into the cornerstone of College Hall. From a family of well-educated women, Pauline had wanted to attend Cornelia Bates's Mount Holyoke Seminary, but her mother forbade it out of fear of losing her only daughter to the notorious wife-hunting foreign missionaries who visited it.[5] Thanks to her husband, Pauline now could help create just the kind of excellent college that she would have loved attending.

They saw the construction of College Hall, a building laid out in the form of a double Latin cross that would be 480 feet long, 166 feet wide in the wings, and 80 feet high atop the steep hill,[6] as a sacred undertaking that would help them refocus their lives after the deaths of their children.

Durant, a successful Boston trial lawyer from a well-established Yankee family, originally purchased their large farm property to be a country home for his young family. Then part of the town of Needham, it was next to the estate of Pauline's cousin, Horatio Hollis Hunnewell, who had named the property "Wellesley" for his wife's "Welles" family.[7]

However, the Durants' daughter died as an infant, and their son, Harry, died when he was eight years old. After these tragedies, Pauline, unable to have more children but with a strong religious bent, founded the Young Women's Christian Association. Her husband, meanwhile, experienced a dramatic religious awakening and became a lay preacher, and together they dedicated their lives and fortune to a special work for God that could reform America.

With his handsome features, "piercing black eyes," and flowing white hair, "worn rather long after the manner of some musicians,"[8] Durant became a popular preacher in western Massachusetts, using his courtroom rhetorical skills to move his listeners. When he preached at Mount Holyoke, then became a trustee, and oversaw the building of its new library, he imagined building his own school.

The Durants considered constructing a boys' school, a prison, and an orphan asylum before deciding to create a female "Harvard," a rigorous college for young women that could become an intellectual and aesthetically beautiful community for themselves and their students.

Katharine always remembered Durant's "erect, slender figure, [with a still] young face … a delicate determined face, alive with sensibility and stamped with will, the face of a poet and the face of a Puritan, [glowing] with spiritual light…. He knew no rest, no self-indulgence."[9]

For the next four years, he irrepressibly supervised every aspect of the building, promising his architect, Hammatt Billings, that, instead of using professional contractors, he would oversee his workers himself. Arriving at seven each morning, sometimes with his wife, he insisted that there be no profanity, loud talking, or quarreling among the mechanics, plumbers, and other workmen.[10] Every day local farmers watched, amazed, as eighteen cartloads of bricks arrived by train from Cambridge.[11]

As Katharine later wrote, "Eagerly, joyously, he flung himself into his task, daunted by no obstacles, deterred by no fatigues…. An eye-witness tells how … when a group of dull-witted laborers were making clumsy and unavailing efforts to drag an enormous iron pipe into place, Mr. Durant sprang into their midst and with one deft, impetuous thrust swung the sullen weight into position."[12]

He had already "improved" his acres of farmland into a picturesque campus of sloping hills, dells, and woodlands, in the English tradition of Capability Brown. College Hall would overlook Bullard's Pond, now "Lake Waban," the romantic name Durant chose because "waban" was the Algonquin word for "wind."

With enthusiastic confidence in women's abilities, he wanted to open new doors for them, explaining: "Women can do the work. I give them the chance"[13]—an idea which had begun with the brilliant women who had taught him.

The first was Mary Smith, his aunt, who had been a pupil of Mary Lyon, the founder of Mount Holyoke.[14] His mother, Harriet Fowle, was also a lover of books who understood Henry's childhood desire to have a library of his own.[15] Having awakened his love of learning, his mother and aunt sent him on to the remarkable Sarah Alden Bradford Ripley (1793-1867), to prepare him, under her "gentle yet enlivening instruction," to enter Harvard College.[16]

Although as a woman she was barred from enrolling or teaching at Harvard, for twenty-eight years Sarah Ripley was an extraordinary multitasker, raising her seven children and acting as housemother and teacher to the young men, such as Ralph Waldo Emerson, boarding and studying at her husband Samuel Ripley's preparatory school for Harvard. During his three years of study with her, Durant saw her "holding the baby, shelling peas, and listening to a recitation in Greek, all at the same moment, without dropping an accent, or particle, or boy, or peapod, or the baby."[17]

Her intellectual gifts were legendary in New England: "President Edward Everett of Harvard said she could have filled any professor's chair. And late at night she went on studying: botany, chemistry, theology, philosophy."[18] She was "'a Greek goddess in a Yankee wrapper, who washed the family clothes and scrubbed the floors and translated Klopstock and taught Homer and Virgil and Aristotle."[19] One historian has called her "the most diversely learned American woman of her age … one born before her time."[20]

If Pauline Durant had placed the Bible in the college cornerstone, many thought that it was the name of Sarah Ripley, "the most learned, brilliant and modest woman," that belonged on the outside of that stone because, "educating all the powers of mind and heart,"[21] she had inspired Durant to give that same experience to students like Katie Bates.

II.

At the time, very few Americans, mostly young men, attended college. Her brother Arthur, now working in Boston for fifty dollars a month, carefully saved $250 a year out of his salary to pay for Katie's college, and she would be the only child in the family who would attend college, an unheard-of opportunity, especially for a girl.[22]

In the East, women's colleges were just beginning to appear: Vassar opened in 1865, Wellesley in 1875 along with Smith, Radcliffe (the Harvard Annex) in 1879, Bryn Mawr in 1885, and Barnard in 1889. Mount Holyoke became a college in 1893.

Katie watched her college being built, "clambering, as a village schoolgirl, over the scaffolding of 'the college in the woods.'"[23] To prepare for its entrance exams, nearly as stiff as Harvard's, she attended Wellesley High School (then called Needham High School) with Emily Norcross, where they made up their entire class.

After Catherine Lee's death, Cornelia moved the family to nearby Newtonville, where Katie continued her advanced college preparations in Latin, mathematics, and science at Newton High School. She passed Wellesley's entrance exams in ancient and modern geography, physical geography, arithmetic, algebra, geometry, Latin, and possibly French and German, at the top of her forty-three classmates who would be the "Class of 1880."[24]

Then, with her brown hair pulled back into a knot and her face full and serious like her father's, in September 1876 she rode with her classmates in the horse-drawn "Barge" emblazoned with "Wellesley College" for the mile-long journey past the particolored granite pillars of the East Lodge Gate, modeled after those of an English gentleman's estate,[25] and on through the two pairs of large pylons that guarded the entry into the campus where she would be sequestered for four years of college work.

After riding past tall elms and copper beeches, then rattling down a shaded gravel carriage road that wound in a series of serpentine turns up summits and down into wild dells and passing through a stretch of trees next to Durant's rhododendron-filled hollow, Katie saw a spectacular panorama.[26]

A wide rolling lawn stretched to Lake Waban, and above it loomed the Durants' massive five-story College Hall, its towers and turrets silhouetted against the sky. With red bricks set into black mortar and brownstone trim, its upper windows in dormers below slate-covered mansard roofs, and asymmetrical bays, turrets, porches, and pavilions, it was a "bombastic" Victorian pile of a building, once called "Palace Beautiful."[27]

The college Calendar touted its "extensive grounds and costly buildings, the comforts and luxuries," as "usually found only in the abodes of the wealthy," as seen in a a sketch of a couple and their daughter, gazing across the mirror-like lake at College Hall, a fortress above a wooded shore.[28] Breathtaking in its ambitious style, it was meant to surround students and teachers with a sense of medieval beauty à la William Morris and the simpler values of the pre-modern Middle Ages.

At the top of the hill, as the horses pulled the Barge under the porte-cochère of College Hall,[29] their clattering hoofs echoed through the entrance.[30] Once inside, the girls saw the breathtaking central court where a colonnade of ten polished Hallowell granite pillars supported the five floors above.[31]

THE BARGE IN FRONT OF COLLEGE HALL

COLLEGE HALL

Durant wanted this spacious atrium-like court to evoke, even in freezing Massachusetts, an "airy" courtyard in a southern palace.[32] He had placed "rare exotics ... palms, banana plants and exquisite ferns" around the edges in a shallow marble basin to make his students feel that they were standing in a cloistered garden of a medieval convent, "the whole forming a scene which strikes the eye most pleasantly from the corridors and the open landings of the floors above, [shedding] a perennial influence over the College."[33]

This elegant pavilion was the heart of the building. One student recalled how she loved it, "with its towering palms and delicate tree ferns, its shining columns, its marble floor; the sense of space as one's eyes rose from floor to floor to the sunlit roof above; the surprises of beauty at every turn; the pictures, statues, beautiful aquariums flashing with goldfish in the great north windows of the upper floors."[34]

The reception parlor beyond had "walls of hard-wood wainscot and Pompeian red hung with pictures, including autographed portraits of Longfellow, Bryant, and Tennyson."[35] After Longfellow realized "the beauty of the situation of the building," he sent a larger and better likeness of himself along with his "best wishes for the prosperity of Wellesley College."[36]

CENTER, COLLEGE HALL

Beyond the parlor was the room that Katie would love best, the library, "the gem of the building ... arranged in alcoves, and superbly finished throughout in solid black-walnut ... with cozy nooks and corners ... sunny windows, some of them thrown out into deep bays; with galleries, reached by winding stairs, where the girls seem to have a keen delight in curling themselves away in such mysterious fashion [so] that you can only see above the balustrade a curly head bending over some book, doubtless found more fascinating than it could be if simply spread out on the table below."[37]

LIBRARY, COLLEGE HALL

The college library was built to hold 120,000 volumes, but when Katie entered Wellesley, it held only ten or twelve thousand volumes, many of them Durant's own books, which made it "rich and valuable for its size." The library included classics in English, Greek, Latin, French, German, and Italian as well as some rare old folios and many "choice editions."[38]

It was unforgettable; Margaret Sherwood fondly recalled "the brown of its carved woodwork, the tall, arched windows, the quaint charm of engravings and portraits ... that atmosphere of sheltered quiet, where the souls of old books seemed to steal out in fragrance."[39]

Adjacent to it, a sunny reading room, well supplied "with the periodical literature of the day," enabled students and teachers to have "every means of following the progress of modern thought in all its currents."[40] On the floor above was the chapel, "spacious and lofty."[41] Katie's room, at the top of the five floors, was a carpeted two-room suite, with black-walnut furniture.

Sixteen recitation rooms fitted with "appropriate photographic views, maps, charts, and other illustrations"; a laboratory "replete with every convenience," a natural history room, an art gallery, and music-rooms were interspersed among the suites. Even the hallways were lined with sculptures, etchings, drawings, and paintings, many that evoked the Hudson River School of American landscape painting.

One day before the college opened, Durant paused on a stairway landing and asked a friend: "'Don't you believe the girls, as they run up and down from one class to another, will enjoy drinking in at these outlooks an inspiration from the beauty of nature? I planned these windows for that very purpose.'"[42]

No wonder the prominent clergyman Edward Abbott could say that there was "no finer building of its kind in the world."[43] This was exactly what founder Durant intended when he spent one million dollars on it.[44] "'I hope,' he once said, with a touch of wistfulness, 'to make Wellesley so beautiful that the girls will forgive it the work and the prayer.'"[45]

III.

Katie's classmates soon christened her "Katie of '80" and elected her their class president, a position she held for her lifetime. They also chose her as their class poet, and when they suddenly had to come up with a poem for the planting of a class tree on a cold damp day, her verses pictured their future memory of that momentous day.

Her "Classical Class of '80"[46] then implored her to write their boat song, which won first prize. "Were they proud of her, that class of '80?"[47] They sang in the "sunset flush" to their friends rowing in their beamy wooden boats until "the chapel bell warned us to make what speed to shore our majestic crafts would permit."[48]

The "work" that Durant expected was either the "classical" courses of Latin, Greek, history, medieval history, essay writing, rhetoric, history of philosophy, history of literature, literacy and criticism, or the "science" courses of mathematics, chemistry, and physics; and the more modern subjects of English literature, mental and moral philosophy, and modern history.

As one student recalled, Durant, with a "dread of routine,"[49] enlarged the curriculum with his own ideas. He enticed, persuaded, and recruited the best students to sign up to learn Greek, a subject he had loved himself but one traditionally reserved for men. Katharine remembered how one September morning of her first year, "Mr. Durant addressed the college after chapel on the supremacy of Greek literature, urging in conclusion all who would venture upon Hadley's Grammar as the first thorny stretch toward that celestial mountain-peak, to rise…. Perhaps a dozen of us Freshmen, all told, filed in to Professor Horton's recitation-room that morning,—happy Freshmen that we were in so doing."[50]

Life in College Hall for the students and the faculty was rigidly regulated and supervised. On Mondays through Saturdays, a great Japanese gong awakened students and faculty at six a.m. They then had silent devotions, a chapel service, and a section meeting in which the students discussed Bible selections from the chapel sermon. Then it was on to fifty-minute classes throughout the day for the three semesters of the calendar year.

At one o'clock, sitting at one of the long tables covered with white linen tablecloths, Katie ate her main meal amid the din of talk and clatter of plates in one immense dining room. This midday dinner might be roast turkey or chicken, mashed potato, one vegetable, and oranges for dessert.

For her supper she had milk, bread, butter, and cookies, cake, or muffins.[51] Then she returned to the chapel for another service followed by silent devotions before the lights-out bell.[52]

Having successfully petitioned the state legislature in 1873 to grant that Wellesley Seminary be known as Wellesley College, Durant insisted that Wellesley students graduate "fully on a par in scholarship with the graduates of Harvard and Yale."[53] When he brought a little group of visitors to the window to show them the view from the top floor of College Hall, he emphasized that Wellesley was "Harvard University for girls!"[54]

Katie was "beaten up by his eloquence,"[55] understanding that he was "an impassioned poet in the stress of creation, alternating between raptures and despair, a Poet whose poem is Wellesley College."[56] His watchwords were: "'Aspiration! Adventure! Experiment! Expansion! Follow the Gleam!' He was the bugle and he, too, was the treasury."[57]

He expected each student to do one hour of domestic work each day, not to save expense, but to develop character:

> 'Devoting one's self entirely to study,' he used to say, 'is, in a way, selfish. But an hour of domestic work each day affords a much to be desired opportunity of doing something for the common good. Also … it teaches mutual interdependence. Each girl has a task in our little community….'[58]

To one student, "Wellesley was like a big family. We swept the corridors, dusted the library, set the tables and washed the dishes."[59] And when mothers tried to pay extra to have their daughters exempted from domestic work, Durant "invariably refused them, and would remark afterward that it was a good way 'to keep out snobs.'"[60]

He inculcated his students with a motto that he took from the New Testament: "*Non Ministrari sed Ministrare*," Not to be Ministered Unto, But to Minister, words that Katie read in the chapel several times each day.

"'Wellesley College,' he repeated, for the hundredth or thousandth time, 'is for poor girls…. One calico girl,' he declared, 'is worth two velvet girls.'"[61] The students knew that he meant that "one plainly dressed girl, willing to work, and anxious to succeed, was, in his thought, worth any number of the indolent, expensively clad young persons who cared for nothing but pleasure."[62]

A common argument at the time against sending girls to college was that hard study would destroy their health and make them unfit for childbearing, since thinking might divert blood to the brain from their reproductive organs. Durant believed instead "that hard study, properly directed and regulated, strengthens the body as well as the mind."[63] He wanted his girls to exercise one hour a day by taking "tramps" on the paths he laid out on the beautiful grounds or by rowing on Lake Waban.

He intended Wellesley "only for those young women who wish to become scholars in the very highest acceptation of the word … especially … those … who desire to become teachers."[64] He kept the tuition and board low in spite of the advice of the Board of Trustees, paying for its financial deficits with his own money. His mission was to "educate Christian women teachers" who could replace the men lost in the Civil War and reform the country into a better nation. [65]

To foster women's intellectual life and achievements, he declared that Wellesley would be the only college to have a woman president and a female faculty, difficult as that was at the time because few colleges awarded degrees, especially graduate degrees, to women.

He wanted Wellesley to outdo Harvard in science, and thanks to his friend Eben Horsford, a Harvard chemistry professor whose patent on Rumford baking powder enabled him to be a wealthy donor to Durant's classroom laboratories, it did. An early student recalled that while "Harvard University was still using the textbook method, Mr. Durant was equipping Wellesley with student laboratories in physics and chemistry, botany and biology, with extensive and expensive apparatus for independent research."[66]

Similarly, in Katie's other courses, such as literature, instead of teaching from textbooks, her professors required their students to engage directly with primary sources and supplemented them with lectures, recitations, and essays that Durant placed in the library.

Because of his own religious conversion, he was strict about the daily devotions of his students, as she understood: "He had given himself utterly to Christ.... There were those among us for whom his language held hard sayings, those who grew but slowly toward the light with which his spirit flashed and flamed.... It was not a perfect life, but it was a life of perfect aspiration."[67]

Durant wanted their rigorous daily schedule of work and prayer to teach the students that young women should not be passively subjected to the unpredictable "tradition and natural rhythms, ruled by the heart and the demands of the flesh" of most women's lives.[68] As he told students,

> The Wellesley College plan of education ... [embodies] the revolt which is the real meaning of the Higher Education of Women. We revolt against the slavery in which women are held by the customs of society—the broken health, the aimless lives, the subordinate position, the helpless dependence, the dishonesties and shams of so-called education. The Higher Education of Women is one of the great world battle-cries for freedom; for right against might. It is the cry of the oppressed slave. It is the assertion of absolute equality....
>
> Therefore, we expect every one of you to be, in the noblest sense, reformers.... You mistake altogether the significance of the movement of which you are a part, if you think this is simply the question of a College education for girls. I believe that God's hand is in it; that it is one of the great ocean currents of Christian civilization; that He is calling to womanhood to come up higher, to prepare herself for great conflicts, for vast reforms in social life, for noblest usefulness. The higher education is but putting on God's armor for the contest.

We have no time now to discuss woman's mission. One fact only, as we leave it: there are three hundred thousand women teachers in the United States. Who is to govern the country? Give me the teachers![69]

IV.

Katie, like Durant, was imaginative, brilliant, witty, and determined. In this handsome, intellectual, and charismatic man, she had found someone who could teach, mentor, inspire, and admire her for the next four years. And he saw that she was the kind of bright, curious, engaged, hard-working, and creative student that he wanted.

She recognized him as a pioneer, perhaps identifying with him in her own struggle to chart a new course: "No words can overstate the value to Wellesley of that teeming brain which mapped out her first pathways. A dreamer of splendid dreams is needed in the van of every movement.... Like the rest of the college, we stood essentially in awe of Mr. Durant, whose spirit was a changing flame."[70]

Katie basked in his high spirits, his mercurial personality, and especially his desire to create a new school of poets on the Wellesley campus with his thousands of "gypsy" crocuses and six snow-white English swans. He wanted Wellesley's English Literature Department, with students like her trained in the classics and in the poetry he had loved with Sarah Ripley, to become a unique kind of intellectual and artistic community, the first of its kind in the country, as she recalled:

> I can see still the shining of his eyes as he talked to me, one day in the old library, of that great English Department which should be deeply based on Icelandic and gothic works and yet so possess its students with the love of literature, so make them citizens of the Dominion of Dreams, that beside [Lake] Waban should spring up a new Lake School of poets, leaders in an American Renaissance,"[71] in his beautiful Wordsworthian landscape.

She understood his sensitivity to language and Sarah Ripley's methodical approach to appreciating it, evident in his spontaneous teaching:

> 'Now listen to this stanza!' he would exclaim, glancing up vividly from the reading of [Coleridge's "Remorse"]. 'Just listen to this: "Hark! The cadence dies away / On the quiet moonlight sea; / The boatmen rest their oars and say, / *Miserere, Domine!*"

> 'Do you heed that word moonlight? Why not moonlit? Because we want a long, slow, lingering word for the rays that lie on the quiet water through the long, slow, lingering night. Sunshine is bright and restless, belonging to the busy day. So the poets make a short epithet for that, sunlit, but what kind of a poet would he be who should write moonlit! I wouldn't have his works in the Wellesley library.'[72]

Also wonderful were the American writers Durant invited to the college: "Many were the poets whom he triumphantly brought out from Boston to face, as best they might, the welcome of our redoubtable three hundred ... then a very host of the Amazons. [William Dean] Howells, at that time editor of *The Atlantic*, surveyed us quizzically, and Oliver Wendell Holmes made so merry with us that he was voted an honorary member of one of the classes. I can still ... hear the silence that fell upon the chattering dining hall as Whittier, shy but benign, followed our stately president, Miss Howard, up to the head table."[73]

Fifty years later, Katharine would renew his practice and bring poets such as William Butler Yeats and Robert Frost to meet her own students, one of whom explained to me that, just as Durant had done, she "brought her friends, real live poets, to the campus to show us that real people had written what we read."[74]

Durant also introduced her to the publishing world, making James T. Fields, of Boston's famous Ticknor and Fields, "the genial publisher and author, a familiar figure at Wellesley in the early years."[75] Fields, "who always wore a red necktie when he came to Wellesley ... told us all sorts of interesting facts about famous people, with gusto and high good humor.... At frequent intervals one of the famous people [Durant] had told us about appeared on our chapel platform, and, what was better, supped with us in our big dining-room, which gave us further opportunities to study greatness."[76]

V.

Before her sophomore year, Katie and four friends with a "ruling passion [for poetry] from early childhood," formed a poetry club, calling themselves the "O.P." ("Other Poets"), and Durant advised them to forget their ambitious schedule and "Be a comet and come around when you like."[77]

"He assigned to each of us a poet for chief devotion—Milton to one, Wordsworth to another, Browning, Shelley, Morris. He often sent the choicest flowers of his conservatory to our meetings. He offered prizes for poetry to the college at large, but would be indignant if anyone outside our small band had taken them."[78]

Katie and her sister "O.P.s" began to star in Durant's brainstorms of surprise celebrations in which the campus became a giant canvas for unforgettable tableaux of live poets and talented students:

> We were just out from dinner one day in the early spring of 1878. In those heroic times the college dined at noon, all together in the capacious hall of the original building which then stood alone in that Arcadian woodland, where every girl of the three hundred had, as Mr. Durant put it, 'her own acre to whistle on.'

> As playmate he had no peer, and when, on this particular afternoon we saw the erect, slender figure coming with quick step down the other side of the grassy hollow, gladly we sprang up and went to meet him....

> 'It is spring.... and we must have a poet come out to tell us so.'[79] Inviting Longfellow, Durant envisioned dedicating a fountain in a small pond to him.

> 'Don't you see it all? We need a fountain here, at this upper end....Then the girls, all in white, shall march down from College Hall, singing songs. The songs must be original, and the music too.... And there must be all sorts of circlings and interweavings over the campus, a perfect maze of harmonious motions.'[80]

The pageant would climax with Fields asking what the fountain should be named and the O.P. girls reciting the answer in original poems, with one dressed as Minnehaha in feathers Durant would bring out from Boston, one as Evangeline, and one as Priscilla, all characters in Longfellow's well-known poems.

Katie and her sister O.P.s were "posted off to the attic floor to 'compose,' where for most of the night [they] sat in a wilderness of empty trunks, sympathetic or impertinent friends looking us up at intervals with relays of lamps, sharpened pencils, dictionaries and other supposed enticements for the Muse!"

Durant took the poems to the printer the next day, but because Longfellow was ill, the performance was cancelled, until he "came dashing into College Hall with the velocity of a bombshell, waving a telegraph above his head," calling out that Longfellow would come after all.

"How energy radiated from the sparkling figure that stood beneath the chandelier, the rain dripping from hair and coat!" The rheumatic President Howard was "bundled up" and "borne away" under Mr. Durant's "excited umbrella."

But Longfellow again telegraphed, this time with his regrets, and the pageant had to be cancelled.

However, for Katie, the episode was "more real than the most elaborate of all our campus spectacles" because Durant had turned to her and the O.P.s with his vision, fully expecting them to create poetry of interest to Longfellow, America's most popular poet.[81]

This support from Durant must have boosted her confidence. When she first began to submit her poems for publication, she did so under a male pseudonym. But while at Wellesley, Katie began to submit her poems to well-respected publications in her own female name.

VI.

As an approving, supportive father-figure, Durant enlivened the college in many ways with his ubiquitous energetic presence. He had big dreams for Katie that she understood: "He had been, in his own college days, no formal classman, but a hungry and passionate student, and when, here and there, now and then, he found among the Wellesley girls a genuine truth-lover, he could not do enough to further her opportunity. His sympathy was bracing, demanding more of her than she had believed possible to herself."[82]

Durant mentored Katie, introducing "some of us to well-known authors and publishers who visited the college, giving them private recommendation of which we knew not till long after, that they should lend us a hand in the fields of our chosen endeavor, if we proved worthy of it and it became practicable to them."[83]

She had first seen her name in print in her high school days, when her story, "Three Newton Girls on Vacation" with its female protagonists writing their version of Longfellow's *Evangeline,* ran in her hometown newspaper, *The Newton Journal.* Like many other hopeful writers, she had submitted her work where it had a good chance of getting published—in the burgeoning newspapers and magazines of Boston and New England.

After her first year at Wellesley, Katie saw her Wordsworthian poem, "Ballad of the Three Sisters," a fairy-tale story of the "rainbow steed" of death that comes to take each sister away, published in the widely read *Boston Evening Transcript.*

In her second ballad, "The Sea Father," she described the feelings of a child whose father has died at sea before she knew him.[84] In Poe-like rhythms and with details of the Falmouth seacoast, her speaker tells of her desire to finally meet this dead father who she believes still calls her from the sea.

As more of her poems and stories appeared in print, she saved and glued each clipping into a scrapbook, carefully fitting them onto each page and sometimes writing little comments on them. In her scrapbook pages she could see her literary career growing.

Her poetry, fiction, and essays began to ask how an artist develops without sacrificing human love, perhaps her own dilemma. Such a concern may have vanished when she received a letter with exciting news from Howells. As the editor of the highbrow *Atlantic Monthly*, he consciously championed women writers because "the new age of readers was mainly an age of women readers, and his mind was naturally in harmony with this obvious condition."[85]

In a letter on stationery imprinted "Editorial office of *The Atlantic Monthly*," Howells wrote to her: "I am glad to accept your poem ['Sleep']: it is both fresh and subtile [sic] in its qualities, and clear too." She kept his handwritten letter until her death.[86]

Katie could feel justified in thinking that she was on the verge of a professional writing career and perhaps destined for national fame when she saw her poem in the pages of the *Atlantic.* In 1879 it reached serious readers who were willing to plow through its two-columned pages of small print without any illustrations or advertisements for articles on English and European history, culture, politics, and economics as well as some poems and fiction. It canonized such New England writers as Nathaniel Hawthorne, Longfellow, Harriet Beecher Stowe, Rebecca Harding Davis, Henry James, and Sarah Orne Jewett.

The October 1879 issue of *The Atlantic Monthly: A Magazine of Literature, Science, Art, and Politics* must have been a special one to her. Howells gave her poem a good placement, twenty-four pages into the one hundred forty-three pages, with only one other poem in front of it: "Ah, Dawn, Delay," by Celeste M. A. Winslow, a vapid plea that dawn "Delay, till my tired heart grow stronger." The twitterings of this unremarkable poem fade away with the subsequent majestic organ tones of Katie's poem "Sleep," a lyric description of the experience of a sleepless night in a romantic poem that speaks with classical authority.

As she knew, the Latin poet Horace advised, "If you want me to weep, you must first feel sorrows yourself."[87] So she depicts a subject that she unfortunately would know well all her life, the agonies of a sleepless night.

In the first stanza, her speaker laments that she is unable to enter the "rustic gate / That opens on the shadowed land" of the personified sleep, "weary for its dews" and impatient "to hear its rivers flowing, drowsy-deep." She describes the "circling thought" beating blindly through her brain, "With dull persistency of empty pain." The "withered" grasses outside sleep's gate contrast with the "crimson-dotted mosses" and "shining grape-vines" whose clusters "droop low" on the other side. Then the speaker suddenly halts her melodic description of sleep's allegorical kingdom and begs: "Take me in!"

With that dramatic moment, Katie emphasizes the speaker's interior consciousness of pain, fear, confusion, and frustrated anger. Horace may have inspired her final stanza as well: in it she lifts her poem to a symbolic level above its story of the landscape of a sleepless night and of her own tormented thoughts into a new level of meaning. Moving from the ordinary to the profound, she suggests that sleep's regenerative powers can be symbolic of a spiritual awakening, not just of a new day, but of a new life, her soul restored.

Her vivid details portray each stage of sleeplessness: her initial desire to fall asleep easily, her increasing "doubting and distress," her demanding anger, her bargaining for any kind of sleep, her cry to be sound asleep, "in thy grotto." She is so desperate that she wants to forget even language and have her senses be made "deaf and blind," unthinkable desires for a poet who needs words and sensory images to create her poem.

These layers of contradictory but simultaneous meanings make Katie modern to us, a complex thinker adept with wit, playful with a reader when she wants to be. This early poem suggests what would be an ongoing quest for her—how to convey the tension between the complex human, social and later, national, problems she experienced and her own voice as an idealistic poet trained to give satisfying closure in the final words of the poem.

"Sleep" drew a special commendation in a small clipping that she pasted onto the review page in her scrapbook: "The poem by Miss Kate Lee Bates, of the senior class, Wellesley, is a charming one."[88]

Durant would be as thrilled as she was about her debut in the *Atlantic* because, as she knew, "any small magazine success that came our way was sure to bring ... some special indulgence against which a scandalized faculty might protest."[89]

VII.

He had one more surprise—a visit for Katie and her club to famous "Craigie House," the Brattle Street home of Longfellow.

Western writer "Bret Harte ... justly said ...'Why, you couldn't fire a revolver from your front porch anywhere [in Cambridge] without bringing down a two-volumer [a book in two volumes]!' Everybody had written a book, or an article, or a poem; or was in the process of expectation of doing it."[90]

Elm trees and lilac hedges surrounded Longfellow's imposing pale yellow three-story house, and a white balustrade encircled a terrace.[91] Two white pilasters flanked the large front door set between tall windows that gave hours of daylight to the spacious rooms within.

Durant and Katie's little club climbed the stairs of the welcoming side porch to the famous house, built in 1759 by the Tory Colonel John Vassall, Jr., occupied by George and Martha Washington in 1775-76, and then owned by the Craigies.

When Longfellow had first come to Cambridge to be Harvard's young Professor of Modern Languages, he was intrigued by the house and rented rooms in it.[92] Then when Fanny Appleton accepted his marriage proposal after a seven-year courtship, her wealthy father gave the couple the house "where Washington dwelt in every room."[93]

Of course Katie had seen Longfellow at Wellesley, where he had been rowed on Lake Waban, "stoutly splashed about," and forced to walk up the steep hill to College Hall through the double line of students under "a trium-

phal arch" of crossed oars, "panting a little ... but smiling back to the beaming faces of the girls who had so thoughtlessly forced him to suffer their athletic homage."[94]

By that time he had a white beard and hair, "leonine, but mildly leonine."[95] His voice had a "mellow resonant murmur, like the note of some deep-throated horn ... very lulling in quality.... He did not talk much himself.... But he always spoke both wisely and simply, without the least touch of pose, and with no intention of effect.... [H]e cast the light of a gentle gayety."[96]

He had become an international celebrity, one of the most famous men in the country. Even in 1857, two years before Katie's birth,

HENRY WADSWORTH LONGFELLOW, C. 1880

Longfellow's books had sold astonishingly well: *Voices of the Night*, 43,500 copies; *Ballads and Other Poems*, 40,470; *The Spanish Student*, 38,400; *The Belfry of Bruges*, 38,300; *Evangeline*, 35,850; *Seaside and Fireside*, 30,000; *The Song of Hiawatha*, 50,000.[97] The next year, *The Courtship of Miles Standish and Other Poems* sold 25,000 copies in two months.[98]

As a young man, he had understood how important American writers were to the young nation. When he gave a speech on "Our Native Writers" at his graduation from Bowdoin College in 1825, his classmate Nathaniel Hawthorne listened to him say: "Yes!—and palms are to be won by our native writers!"[99] Historian Van Wyck Brooks thought that "Europe had taught him: a poet was the poet of his country.... [A]nyone could see that Longfellow's poems, what-ever their subjects were, expressed the young American state of mind."[100]

For Longfellow, America, important in itself, was also part of the larger world of books, languages, art, architecture, and European travel, and he wel-comed people from all over the world into his home. As one visitor noted: "His work is interrupted by frequent visitors.... And speaking fluently French, German, Italian, Spanish, and Portuguese, having also a knowledge of Danish, and of Dutch, it may be supposed that there seldom comes a traveler with whom the poet cannot … hold forth in his own tongue."[101] One Englishman "came to see him because there were no ruins to visit in America."[102]

With its high ceilings, long windows, marble fireplaces, and spacious dimensions, his house was probably the grandest Katie had ever seen, and one that the poet and his family enjoyed. Every room was full to the brim with books. Even in the dining room, he had squeezed books into hanging bookshelves between the gold silk damask floor-length draperies.

The revered Gilbert Stuart's portraits of Fanny's parents, Maria and Nathan Appleton, as well as a portrait of Longfellow's three daughters, familiar to his readers from his poem "The Children's Hour," hung in the dining room.

Below an early portrait of Fanny hung a small painting with vivid colors by the famed painter of the American West, Albert Bierstadt, that portrayed the famous scene that Longfellow described of Hiawatha's departure into a blazing sunset:

> And the evening sun descending
> Set the clouds on fire with redness,
> Burned the broad sky, like a prairie,
>
> …
>
> Westward, westward Hiawatha
> Sailed into the fiery sunset,
> Sailed into the purple vapors,
> Sailed into the dusk of evening. [103]

Fourteen years later, at the top of Pike's Peak, where she was inspired to write her own poem for America, Katharine would think of this Longfellow poem.

But it was the study where he worked—reading, thinking, writing, correcting proofs, visiting with friends and family, and smoking cigars—that probably held the most interest for Katie and her friends. With its red patterned rug, long red draperies, brown wallpaper with faux bamboo molding—all set off by the white woodwork of the wainscoting and white paneled fireplace wall—it overflowed with books in tall cases and stacked on the desk and center table.[104]

There he wrote with "smooth, regular, and scrupulously perfect handwriting."[105] There stood his quill pen and inkstand, the fireside armchair made from the "spreading chestnut tree" and presented to him by the children of

Cambridge right before their visit,[106] his old-fashioned folding writing desk and the standing desk by the tall front window from which he could look across the meadows at the Charles River.

In his study, he was surrounded by busts and statuettes of poets—the Italian Dante, the German Goethe, and the English Shakespeare—and by crayon portraits of his friends, important American writers and thinkers who had stood in this very room: antislavery senator Charles Sumner, transcendentalist Ralph Waldo Emerson, Harvard Greek Professor Cornelius Felton, and Bowdoin College classmate Nathaniel Hawthorne.

Longfellow wanted Americans to appreciate their own culture and see themselves as a nation with their own rich and wide history, even in his house. In this study, General Washington had held his military conferences, met with Benjamin Franklin and a committee from the Continental Congress, welcomed Quakers and Indians, and "decided that the best solution for the American colonies was to separate from England."[107] Beyond his study was the "library," music room and party space, with a grand piano, white-paneled walls, oriental rugs, long red draperies, oak library table, gold upholstered settee, gold highlighted Japanese screen, marble fireplace, and window seats. It was where he had hosted balls, banquets, and children's parties. It held treasures of Longfellow's many trips to Europe, where he had met such artists as the composer Liszt, whose portrait was on the wall, along with those of Dickens, Alfred, Lord Tennyson, and John Ruskin. If Katie had looked carefully, she would have seen a statue of Sappho, an early woman poet whose volumes of poetry were on Longfellow's shelves.

His home was full of memories for him—both wonderful and terrible. He was a young widower when he married Fanny. They had filled the house with their friends and children, but in 1861 Fanny had burned to death when her light summer dress with hoop skirts caught on fire, and he could not save her.

In spite of this personal tragedy, Longfellow for Katie was a model of a living poet who was beloved by Americans for making their history unforgettable and suggesting that their ordinary lives could be the subject of heartfelt writing, and for giving Americans a sense of their own native culture and history. In *The Song of Hiawatha* he celebrated old Indian legends to show the romance and humanity of the first Americans. In *The Courtship of Miles Standish* he brought early Pilgrim history to life, and to remind Americans of their common ideals during the Civil War, he wrote "The Midnight Ride of Paul Revere," the tale of how the American Revolution began.

The appealing rhythms and simple language of his poems encouraged Americans to read them aloud by their firesides, and his poetry created a sense of American identity in those who read it, heard it, memorized it, and sang it at a time when many immigrants were bringing their foreign cultures to the country.[108] A music lover himself, he saw hundreds of his poems set to music and published by the burgeoning sheet music industry for everyone to enjoy in their homes.

Longfellow believed that the United States was similar to his home—a gathering place for people of many nationalities, like his *Tales of a Wayside Inn*, with storytellers from around the world. Katie could see that he was immersed in foreign languages, cultures, and literatures; and his travel mementoes kept those experiences alive, both for himself and his visitors, a good example for her.

When he singled her out to tell her "that he had read" her poem "Sleep" in *The Atlantic Monthly* "and had liked it,"[109] it was an extraordinary compliment from him to her.[110]

Howells had probably shown the poem to Longfellow, both men happy to please their friend Durant. According to Howells, "No new contributor made his mark in the [*Atlantic*] unnoted by him…."[111] Longfellow always felt "a kind of reverence" for a young writer's first work, because it held "so much aspiration … so much audacious hope and trembling fear, so much of the heart's history."[112]

Perhaps he put Katie at ease, as once he did the young Howells, who recalled, "Longfellow always behaved as if I were saying a succession of edifying and delightful things."[113]

More important, by congratulating Katie on her poem, Longfellow encouraged her to follow him as a poet for America. It was almost as if he were anointing her to be his literary heir and inspiration to the next generation of American poets.

VIII.

Before her graduation in 1880, Durant and his friend Horsford gave Katie and her classmates a special gift, transforming the Latin recitation room to celebrate the most famous woman poet at the time, Elizabeth Barrett Browning. The room was decorated to evoke her "sojourn" in Italy, the panels on its frieze were scenes from her poem "Aurora Leigh,"[114] and her marble bust was lit with a "carefully adjusted light illuminating her features."[115]

In the center of the room stood "the exquisite statue of 'The Girl Reading,'"[116] whose significance Durant emphasized, as one student remembered: "When this statue was being set in its place between the front windows, Mr. Durant turned, with one of his rare smiles, to the girls who were looking on. 'She is not intent upon light reading,' he said, 'for it requires twelve men to lift her. And observe, she wears no bangs!'"[117] Bangs, a new fad, were frowned upon by Durant and others because they obscured the full forehead, thought to be a sign of a large brain, important in a college-educated woman.

He tried to dispel his students' fears, prevalent at the time, that they might lose their appeal to men if they developed those brains. Katie valued his "lofty conception of women's life…. He would cut away at the root that world-old, pernicious distinction between the training of boys and girls, —that boys should be trained to be, and girls to seem,—boys to do right and girls to make themselves agreeable."[118]

With his enthusiasm for literature, his dream of building his own school of Lake poets, and his love for the "calico girls" whose minds and hearts he could inspire, Durant challenged Katie's intellect and encouraged her ambitions. In spite of Wellesley's demanding work and rules, she blossomed as a student and found her calling as a poet under his warm praise, enjoyed her life in this community of women with their productive professional lives, and enlarged her circle of readers to include serious writers and publishers.

Trained as rigorously as a Harvard student, she now was in a peculiar position. While her intellect and talents were not restricted by her gender, her professional and social life were, as she learned one "beautiful June afternoon" during her graduation festivities when her class went to Mrs. Claflin's home in Boston.[119]

Mrs. Claflin had to "say to some unfortunate youth, 'Mr. So-and-so, please take Miss Bates to such-a-place,' as if she were a bundle of dry goods quite incapable of locomotion."[120] Wellesley College had not prepared her for this—"It was something to which we had been so entirely unaccustomed for the greater part of the last four years, that the novelty struck us as almost amusing."[121]

Katie was even less prepared for the difficult financial realities she would soon face, and her college years ended on a sad note: Wellesley barred her brother Arthur, who had unselfishly paid for her Wellesley education as well as her black silk graduation dress, from attending her graduation since he was neither a parent nor guardian. Shocked, he disappointedly wrote on her dress bill that, although Mrs. Durant had included some Harvard students as her guests, she couldn't make room for him.[122]

Now, with most professions closed to her, even as a college graduate, Katie had few channels of work open to her brilliant mind and imagination and did not want to lose the "new life" of a writer that the Durants had nurtured in her, no matter how hard it would be.

In his poem "Possibilities" Longfellow wondered who would inherit his mantle as a beloved poet of America,

> some dreamy boy.../
> Who shall become a master of the art,
> An admiral sailing the high seas of thought.

Little did he know that Katharine Lee Bates might be that "dreamy boy" about to sail forward, as she had from Falmouth to Wellesley, "fearless and steering ... For lands not laid down on any chart."[123]

CHAPTER THREE

1880–1885
"A LITTLE MONEY, A LITTLE FAME"[1]

I.

Like Longfellow, Katharine had to support herself after she graduated from college, and so, like him, she became a teacher. The Teachers' Registry of Durant's Wellesley College advertised its "reliable teachers" to high school superintendents,[2] and she took "the first chance that came"—to teach Latin, algebra, and English at nearby Natick High School.[3]

But she soon lamented her job in "The Schoolroom":

> Come to my aid, Oh ye Gods & ye Muses!
> Must I describe what my soul loveth not??
> Blackboards and figures my vision confuses.
> Chained to a schoolroom—how bitter my lot.[4]

She had to squeeze her writing projects into the end of her tiring days of teaching, and confessed to her former professor Mary Sheldon, "I came home from school one Monday night, tired from head to foot, feeling as if that suffocating atmosphere of a winter schoolroom, the atmospheric compounded of chalk, mathematics and mischief, was clinging to the very soul of me."[5]

Fortunately, Durant again changed the course of her life by appointing her to be a teacher the next fall at his new Dana Hall School. It was his official preparatory school for the college, several miles down the hill from it in the village of Wellesley.[6] The Eastman sisters, Julia and Sarah, formerly Wellesley College teachers, would be its associate principals, guaranteeing that its pupils would be admitted to the college without further examinations.[7]

Longer on his visionary ideas than on their practical application, Durant had accepted the vacant building of Wellesley's Second Congregational Church as a gift from his friend, wealthy East India trader Charles Blanchard Dana, and hastily remodeled it into a classroom and dormitory building.

When Katharine moved in, the former New England meetinghouse was almost unrecognizable, with its attic spaces expanded into dormered bedrooms for its students and teachers. She joined three other teachers—all Wellesley graduates—to greet the eighteen students at the new school that would be her cramped home for the next four years.

She needed her famous sense of humor for the school's makeshift beginnings when she welcomed the students to the "coziest" of rooms, rooms "bedecked with classical pictures, kerosene lamps, tidies, and bricabrac."[8]

While she taught Latin and Greek, she could hear Martha Bennett teaching English, Marie-Louise Reuche teaching French, and Virginia Smith teaching mathematics because their "dumpy, little one-roomed schoolhouse" had been divided into spaces by partitions that did not reach the ceiling so that "a Babel of education floated cloudily overhead."[9]

Katharine's students "recited Geometry in a denuded parlor and read Homer in a chamber where the mice, excited by the tales of ancient valor, used to race across the floor as if it were the windy plain of Ilion."[10] Each morning the Dana Hall dog (first Shot, a water spaniel, and then Don, the Eastmans' black Newfoundland), joined in the required morning prayers, "nipping the heels of the kneeling girls,"[11] where the house was "afrisk" with cats.[12]

Her students were in "the smallest of classes" and did "most of the speaking themselves."[13] Although she knew Greek and Latin grammar and literature well, she confided years later to her eldest great-niece, "I'm sure I don't know what I taught in the geometry class!"[14]

The village of Wellesley looked much like a wealthy version of Falmouth. With grassy paths along meandering brooks, the land around Dana Hall was a place where Katharine could roam, enjoy birdcalls and wildflowers, and dream up poems and stories.

Just as she was moving into a new chapter of her life, Wellesley, like many villages across America, was also growing. In the beginning of the nineteenth century its farms grew produce and livestock for the slaughterhouse in Brighton, just a few miles away, and Boston's Quincy Market. Some industry, such as the shoddy mills manufacturing fabric from reclaimed wool at Newton Lower Falls, had sprung up, but with each decade, the town became more noted for its healthy air and inviting landscapes.

By 1881, the village of Wellesley was home to a growing number of country houses for Boston's elite families who wanted to commute by train to work in an urban Boston increasingly crowded with immigrants and tenements. Roads, sidewalks, and bridges replaced paths and muddy lanes, and the town spent its tax money on schools and streetlamps.[15]

With only 2,500 residents on approximately 6,664 acres of land, and an average school enrollment of 500 children per year,[16] it had a charming "refined rural atmosphere" with its "pleasant homes ... delightful drives and its beautiful landscaped scenery."[17] To make commuting to Boston appealing, the town commissioned the famous Boston architect Henry Hobson Richardson to design its new railway station on grounds landscaped by Frederick Law Olmsted, of Central Park fame.

Soon Wellesley had a water and park commission as well as a fire department. Disgruntled resident Fletcher Abbott immortalized its new identity. When asked how he liked living in the country, he replied: "'Country? Do you call this country? This isn't country any more, it's only a damned suburb.'"[18]

II.

Henry Durant died suddenly during her first fall at Dana Hall, but he had given Katharine a new mentor and friend in her employer, Julia Eastman. She had been an informal writing tutor at Wellesley, teaching essay writing as a sort of extracurricular activity, and was a successful published writer who could give Katharine inside knowledge of the literary marketplace and the encouraging support of a role model.

As she learned, Julia's father, a Congregational minister, treasured a clipping of her first published poem in his pocketbook, much as the Bates family saved every piece of Katharine's writing. Julia first published in the popular *Springfield Republican*, "'one of those magnanimous sheets which pay liberally and honestly for everything that is deemed worth publishing.'"[19] Her "animated contributions were for years among its most attractive features."[20]

Its first editor, Samuel Bowles, was much like Durant—intense, vigorous, and conscious of social issues, especially women's rights. He argued that women were capable of far more than men gave them credit for, envisioning "a common brotherhood" in which "it is both desirable and necessary that woman should assume her place as an integral unit in life, and take a larger and more independent share in all its duties and responsibilities."[21] Bowles wanted to see the day when reform would open "all these duties, all this work of life, to woman equally with man."[22]

He championed women's causes and mentored promising young women writers, publishing many East Coast women from Colette Loomis to "Fannie Fern" (Sarah Willis Parton).[23] Known for his "partiality for women of spirit and brains,"[24] he wrote encouragingly to one beginning woman writer: "I think you can do it. Go ahead and try.... I shall be glad to give you welcome."[25]

Writing in *The Boston Evening Transcript*, Katharine expressed hope that American writers would portray the true qualities of American girls: "The Yankee smartness and cuteness ... the quick tact and intuition, the dry humor and love of fun, the restless, eager curiosity ... the spirited independence ... the sparkle and gleam that play over the surface of earnestness and energy, thoughtfulness and devoutness, passion and intensity.... The best types of our country girls have their bright eyes open, their natures full of life, their character written in a score of blended colors, not one dull blank of white simplicity ... for the predominant stamp of heroism must be activity. [They should be] of all women the most daring, intelligent and forceful."[26]

III.

The *Republican* began publishing Katharine's stories with just such female characters. She aimed "A Story of Christmas Eve" at both young and old readers, telling how Mrs. Santa Claus rescues a brilliant professor of Latin before his work consumes him at the cost of his child's love. Mrs. Claus had appeared in the work of other nineteenth-century writers, but Katharine was the first to give her a major role.

The professor's study is dismal on Christmas Eve, a setting to make its young readers cringe: "The ... windows, which looked out upon the happy, lighted street, looked in upon a large, somber, simply furnished room, whose only adornments consisted of high cases stuffed with fat, pompous books in dull black and brown covers, and of a few pallid, unhealthy-looking busts...— gentlemen to whose acquaintances Harry [the child] looked forward through a dreary vista of Latin grammars and blotted exercises."[27]

LET ME GO AND HOLD THE REINDEER.

"LET ME GO AND HOLD THE REINDEER."

Harry's father has made "himself over from a man into a professor ... [groping] deeper and deeper among the pitfalls of syntax and etymology," and such work has become "dearer" to him than his late wife.[28]

After her death, he is given one last chance to learn the error of his ways. He permits his young son Harry to hang up his crumpled stocking while he warns him that Santa Claus does not exist.

But late at night while the professor works at his desk, Santa and Mrs. Claus do arrive. While she darns the stocking of the now motherless Harry, Santa miraculously presents the professor with all his childhood Christmas stockings, reminding him how loving and generous his own father had been.

Guiltily, the professor dashes out to buy his son things to "make him glad"—"a pair of skates and a story-book and such a double runner as I had when I was a little shaver," and vows to change his strict ways and not ask him "a single question on Latin grammar through all the holidays."[29]

Katharine took elements from her own life for the plot—the professor teaches the classics, his books and scholarly life threaten to destroy him, and a life devoted solely to the intellect needs correction; and she made her female character, Mrs. Claus, the most original and essential character. As she darns the professor's stocking under his eyes, he looks ridiculous telling her she is not there. And Santa cannot do his job without her.[30] In such a story, Katharine surprised her readers by giving an intelligent activist wife to the legendary Victorian bachelor Santa Claus.

Editor Bowles also wanted fiction that reflected events and issues in the daily lives of its readers, the kind of realistic fiction that Howells championed.[31] While Longfellow looked back to America's history for his poems, Katharine pictured her own very different times. She could see her country changing from rural villages to industrialized cities, and emphasized the hardships that faced factory workers:

> A sinking sun … was flinging its last gorgeous rays of orange and red down upon the dingy streets of a large manufacturing town in New England. Streams of operatives were pouring out of the long brick factories, like bees from the hive, many of them nearly as black as bees, truly, but with little suggestion of honey in their fretful and dogged looks.[32]

Although American home industries were seeking new markets abroad, the influx of immigrant laborers competing with native workers led to conflicts and strikes. Katharine's next editor, the second Samuel Bowles, stated that it was his ideal to promote "earnestly and persistently the public good" in his newspaper.[33] For her, the public good included understanding the complex values and cultures of immigrants entering the United States.

In "Miriam's Choice," her young male narrator, "just plain Jim Grump," is a well-meaning but uninformed farmer who tells the story of his surprising discoveries about the young Jewish immigrant woman he loves. Miriam, after her mother's death, has agreed to marry Jim if she is unable to find her brother Abraham, from whom she has been separated for eight years.

Katharine describes them leaving their sleepy pastoral village on a train, a "one-eyed, flame-breathing monster [that] rushed shrieking up and down our quiet corner of the earth."[34] Railroads had enabled cities to grow into an industrialized urban nation populated by a variety of religions, cultures, and ethnic groups. The 1880 national census listed fifteen million immigrants in the United States, out of a total population of fifty million; in 1885, over 63 percent of Boston's population was classified as "foreign by birth or parentage."[35]

When Jim, a stand-in for the similarly ignorant reader, accompanies Miriam to Boston, they explore the little-known Hebrew religion and the big city, an urban world they have never seen. Horrified at the price of food in restaurants, they shrink from the "throng of passers-by, the line of noisy vehicles and the brilliant arrays in the shop-windows."[36]

Jim sees that in the congregation of Ohabel Shalom, a Reform congregation in Boston at the time, the men and women sit together, small boys run around, and the adults walk in and out, chatting during the service.[37] Miriam knows that her devout brother would never worship with such a congregation, and so she and Jim explore a second synagogue, the more traditional congregation of Shaaray Teifila, which bears within "in various small features, the stamp of its more ancient and Hebraic spirit."

Miriam does find her brother there and chooses to stay with him rather than marry Jim, explaining, "'I was not born a Gentile.... I must go with my mother's people.'" As their names imply, Abraham and Miriam are a living part of a long Hebrew tradition.

Jim has assumed that it would be a simple matter for Miriam to renounce her people in order to marry him, a Yankee farmer. He is surprised, as many of Katharine's readers might have been, to learn that Miriam does not want to abandon her birthright, even to join Yankee society.

Showing that a single stereotype of Judaism does not take into account the variations of worship and philosophy among Jews, Katharine created a believable tale that asks how two cultures with differences that cannot be easily abandoned can best live together in a changing country.

IV.

By the summer of 1883, after living for seven years surrounded by girls and women, and now nearly twenty-four years old, she finally got away, to spend the summer in Amherst, Massachusetts, with its classical architecture and abundant gardens, to study advanced Latin and German at the Sauveur Summer School of Languages.

Emily Dickinson would become Amherst's most famous citizen, but she was then fifty-three, reclusive, and three years away from her death. But both she and Katharine published work in the *Republican* (which Emily Dickinson read daily),[38] and so could have read each other in its pages, and Dickinson could have read Katharine's poem "Sleep" in *The Atlantic Monthly*.[39]

Katharine, wrote to her friend and Dana Hall student, Annie Beecher Scoville, granddaughter of Henry Ward Beecher and great-niece of Harriet Beecher Stowe, that, unfortunately, her summer school, with "reformed" ideas about teaching languages, had its problems:

> The work is of a dilettante, showy, hothouse order that continually exasperates me, and the actual performance falls far short of their promises.... Dr. Sauveur ... is a strange man ... a little, vivacious, vain weather-cock of a Frenchman, who usually has his pupils take this Caesar class, while he chatters French with the ladies on the back seat.... There is another, a Belgian, who has an advanced class of three or four of us, in which we talk Latin entirely [and] his class is the only one I heartily enjoy, although I have one German class which is entertaining, —a sort of cross between a singing-school and a circus.... The school is great fun, of course, as soon as you accept the first disappointment and give up expecting to learn much....[40]

But Katharine enjoyed the male camaraderie and portrayed it in her lively short story, "The Unknown Tongue," which ran in the *Republican* that summer.[41] Set mostly in the train station of nearby Palmer, Massachusetts, the story has the kind of "local color" prized by readers who wanted American writers to immortalize the rapidly disappearing small town life.

"The Unknown Tongue" is one of her funniest tales, based on the still prevalent premise that since men and women speak essentially different languages, one's native "tongue" may be unintelligible to the other. A female narrator, whose nickname, "Pop," suggests how little she embodies traditional female traits, tells how her stay at a summer language school helped her realize how much she loved John, "this apostle of the commonplace," even though he did not speak her "language" of enthusiastic poetry, elegant metaphors, or romantic sentiment.

Pop goes off to study French, German, Latin, and Greek and to board where "languages are spoken at table." After her six weeks' course, she takes the train home to Palmer.

Much to her surprise, John welcomes her home in the railway waiting room and asks in "his old, cool fashion: 'Well, Pop, now that you can add Latin common-sense to your French graces and German taste in cookery, I don't see as you need anything else but a good Yankee heart. Have mine?'"

Although Pop thinks that John should have had more regard "for the poetical fitness of things than to propose in a railway station," when he kisses the muddy toe of her boot, she sees that he has learned "the unknown tongue" of sentiment after all.

Katharine tells this tale of romance in a tongue-in-cheek tone, inviting the reader to join with Pop in laughing at her attempts to understand and appreciate John's language. With its positive portrayal of a romantic relationship full of realistic problems solved with warmth and understanding, Katharine's story suggests that she learned more than Latin and German at her summer school.

It gave her a chance to attend classes with men, to be taught by men, and to board with men and women in an adult world rather than in an all-female environment. Her letters suggest that she enjoyed it, perhaps even having a romance with one of the other participants. A year later, she wrote to Annie that she was getting her "body and temper in good position, all poised for the scholastic tournament," and that in a week she would see "Richard himself again,"[42] probably her "beloved Professor."[43]

V.

At Dana Hall, Julia Eastman acquainted Katharine with another market, the fast-growing field of family magazines. Growing up in the 1860s and 1870s, Katharine had been able to enjoy the burgeoning of children's literature, where Nathaniel Hawthorne and Louisa May Alcott, two of her favorite writers, created fiction for intelligent and imaginative children. Katharine learned from Hawthorne's "respect for children's intelligence" and his grasp of "their desire to get at the essential truth of things ... [and] their quickness to comprehend the poetic—as opposed to the literal—method of stating truth."[44]

A generation later, advances in printing technology and shipping networks, along with low commercial postal rates, enabled all kinds of periodicals to become financially successful and compete for popular writers and their readers. Especially during the Civil War, Americans began to turn for "escapist" reading to "sensational" stories, stories of "blood and thunder," crime, the Western frontier, and mystery, in the pulp weeklies and cheap "dime novels."[45]

Alcott earned her first money from such sensational publications as *Frank Leslie's Illustrated Newspaper* and *Flag of Our Union*. Garishly illustrated, these inexpensive pulp fiction periodicals had huge circulation numbers. One publisher put out 7,500 novels, and there were 250 million copies of the Horatio Alger stories in print.[46]

Such publications in post-Civil War America were an alarming development of popular culture to many educators, ministers, and parents who objected to their lack of moral values in images of egotists, physical strength, and material wealth. Worst of all, their stories showed that luck and disguise could bring financial gain, instead of showing how good living and the Golden Rule would bring happiness. Equally appalling to many readers, the female characters were often criminals or victims, or simply absent from the plot.

In Boston, the Yankee literati, editors, and publishers joined forces with Protestant ministers in denouncing the sensational weeklies and knew they must improve their own publications in order to compete with and counteract the lowbrow papers.

Protestant Sunday schools began to create libraries for young readers of books and periodicals that fostered Yankee "American" values of fair play, honesty, and a sense of community in a recognizable everyday world of villages full of schools, churches, families, and nature. Astute publishers realized that there was a huge market just waiting to be filled in the empty shelves of these church and home libraries.

When Louisa May Alcott decided that she wanted to stop writing under pen names to hide her steamy stories from her parents, she began writing for family magazines under her own name, and created Jo March, who made the same decision to write the truth unashamedly, from her heart.

It was a new era in American children's literature, and Katharine became part of it. She described to Annie her excitement at seeing her work published: "When the editor accepts your manuscript, then forget it. Fix your mind on something new, and one day the Post-Man will bring you a check and then you can steal out to the nearest book-stand and lock yourself in your room with your maiden journal. For the paper will not seem to you to contain much but your own article."[47]

Editor Lyman Abbott helped advance Katharine's career in this field, as she told Annie: "I have found [Dr. Abbott] invariably the gentlest of critics and promptest of pay-masters."[48] His *Christian Union* paid well ($10 as compared with the *Well-Spring,* which paid only $5), "altho' if Dr. Abbott condenses the paragraphs enough, he may cut it down quarter of a column. Isn't it funny to write by the inch and be paid accordingly?"[49]

Then *The Congregationalist*'s editor, Asa Bullard, awarded Katharine a hundred-dollar first prize for her children's poem, "Sunshine," publishing her two columns of twenty-one four-line stanzas inside a delicate vine-like border.

Her voice in the poem is whimsical and inviting. Illustrated with a charming miniature kingdom by the root of a tree, evoking a fairyland setting and a curious young girl, its lesson is simple: "Bless God, the Giver of all delight!" "Sunshine" gives a sermon that nature is the true minister to the human world. It was so popular that Boston publisher Daniel Lothrop republished it as a gift book.

Having surveyed the publishing field, Lothrop foresaw the huge market in Sunday school libraries throughout America and created three family magazines aimed at children of different ages, *Babyland, Pansy,* and the attractive *Wide-Awake,* all designed to "Crowd out the Evil in the world with the Good"[50] and to make American children "broad-minded, pure-hearted, and thoroughly wide awake."[51]

Since he wanted his young subscribers to find their magazines full of both beautiful language and beautiful illustrations, Lothrop commissioned such American artists as Maurice Prendergast, Childe Hassam, and Winslow Homer to illustrate his spacious pages. *Wide-Awake* invited the imaginative child to enter an irresistible world of poetry, fiction, and art, and the *Transcript* stressed its excellence: "'It is the king of the juveniles'…."Neck-and-neck with the best periodicals in the world"…."Foremost among the most elaborate and attractive publications of its kind."[52]

Lothrop gave Katharine good exposure, publishing her children's poem "Slumber Fairies" in his *Wide-Awake.*[53] In a two-page spread, drawings of graceful fairies on their way up to sleep entwine its stanzas. A mother could read the poem to her sleepy children, lulling them and perhaps herself to sleep with Katharine's slow rhythms and delightful images of dreamland.

VI.

To reach adult readers, Katharine submitted her poems to the highbrow *Boston Evening Transcript*. In 1881, Edward H. Clement, known for his elegance and intellectual mind, became Katharine's editor there. A former abolitionist, he supported reformist causes, and advanced the newspaper's already well-established coverage of the arts and literature.[54]

Although Boston had eight daily papers and four weeklies, most located on Washington Street's "Newspaper Row," only the *Transcript*'s office gave serious writers a welcoming sanctuary in downtown Boston.[55]

Ensuring that her name would reach educated and influential homes in the Boston area and beyond, it provided a platform for new writers like Katharine to reach 50,000 readers in its daily editions.[56] They could rest from its long columns of tiny print with the eye-catching "Brilliants" feature—a group of short poems at the top of the "literary" page. It was a good way for a young poet to get attention, with her poems placed next to those of more prestigious poets.[57]

Katharine's poem "Fate" appeared with a Walt Whitman poem, "Spirit That Formed This Scene."[58] Whitman would eventually rival Longfellow as the most important nineteenth-century American poet, so Katharine was in good company.

Later that year her poem "A Plea for Rhymesters" appeared at the top of another group of "Brilliants," which concluded with a sentimental poem by popular Hoosier poet James Whitcomb Riley:[59] "Our fortunes! Oh, we need not waste / Our smiles or tears, whate'er befall; / No happiness but holds a taste / Of something sweeter, after all!" Katharine was more serious in her poem, envisioning the poet as important to humanity for the music he or she gives it.

However, as she and Julia Eastman both knew, no matter how appealing her poetry and short stories were, they would not bring her significant fame or money without being published as books. Fortunately, Julia's own publisher was the enterprising Lothrop.

His company eventually published 1,600 titles and sold 1,500,000 books, many by the same women who published in his magazines.[60] Working on a smaller budget than some of the well-established larger publishers, Lothrop found new writers to publish by running contests with large cash prizes for manuscripts.

Katharine knew the exciting story of how Julia had submitted her young adult novel *Striking for the Right* to a prize contest just when her family's finances were in trouble, and Lothrop himself walked up "their grassy path with a thousand-dollar check in his pocket."[61] Tucked in with the thousand-dollar prize was a statement from the publisher that this was the best book he had "ever seen for a Sunday School library."[62]

Lothrop had a successful line of books with attractive bindings marketed as special gifts at the holidays, and he asked Katharine to contribute several poems to *Through the Year with the Poets*, a collection of poems for each of the twelve months. And so she would finally see her name on the table of contents page of an attractive book for a big audience.

An anonymous but complimentary "puff," pasted into her scrapbook, singled out her poems for praise: "A dainty bound volume ... as dainty within as without, for its pages are sweet with the fragrance of the dreamy days of July, and the summer tourist who has this book to help him while away on his vacation will find that the days pass most pleasantly [with one] of the Cape's fair daughters, Miss Katharine Lee Bates."[63]

Lothrop next published a full book of poetry for each month. His "September" volume included another poem by Katharine, similarly anonymously praised: "September ...What exquisite things the poets have written of this month!... One noticeable thing in the volume is the space that is given young authors, especially young authors. We find ... the [name] ... of Katherine [*sic*] Lee Bates ... and others who are beginning to make their influence perceptibly felt in American literature...."[64]

Lothrop then employed Katharine to select poems for an entire volume. Published in 1882, it is a small green book, its cover adorned with an elegant garland of flowers and a gold-lettered title. A sketch of Cupid ready to shoot his arrow at two lovers announces its theme, *The Wedding-day Book*, inside the front cover. Other illustrations of Cupid introduce each month's poems.

In Portland, Maine, her brother Arthur may have felt that his financial support of his sister's education was bearing fruit when his local newspaper noted the first book bearing her name on its cover: "A handsomely bound and neatly illustrated volume, containing for each day of the year, three passages from the poets, one appropriate for the bridegroom, one for the bride, and one for both. Each month has its picture and its poem. There is a good deal of work well bestowed in this compilation."[65]

Katharine's *Wedding-day Book* would prove so popular that Lothrop commissioned her to revise it in 1895 in a fancier edition, with gold-edged pages, a border design of hearts and birds with wedding bells dangling among them, and a white ribbon to bookmark the date of the couple's wedding. And although she had little personal wedding experience, with her selections of appealing poetry and the book's attractive layout, she hit another bulls-eye with the reviewers.

The *Transcript* praised its appearance "in beautiful holiday dress" and its editor: "Miss Bates has a wide and appreciative knowledge of English poetical literature, and there are few who could, with so large a space to fill, have made so many happy selections." The *Congregationalist*, always her mother's favorite, noted that the volume was "decidedly attractive" and her selections "remarkably apt."[66]

Just two and a half years out of Wellesley College, with her wit and knowledge of poetry, Katharine could be pleased that the *Transcript* described her as a young author "beginning to make [her] influence perceptibly felt in American literature."[67]

VII.

By the spring of 1883, she began to look for other teaching jobs, perhaps because of her successful writing and her frustration that the Eastmans did not require her students to conform to the high standards of college preparations that Katharine knew Durant had expected for his Wellesley College entrants. She wrote to her old friend Emily Norcross of her dilemma:

> Although I love and honor Miss Julia, she and Miss Sarah have so little notion of strict intellectual work that they are always interfering most seriously and unconsciously with my scholars, for whose progress they nevertheless hold me responsible.... I can't, however, keep on advising that certificates be refused to poor scholars and having my advice disregarded, only to be indignantly upbraided when the College finds fault with these same pupils....
>
> You know what a scrimble-scramble mind Miss Sarah has. And our blessed Miss Julia, altho' a noble woman at heart, detests the higher education, which is certainly a complicating circumstance in a fitting school.[68]

In her short story, "The Red Tassel,"[69] Katharine's character Ralph Rainford tells of how he came to choose a career unlike those of his ancestors. Injured as a baby, Ralph has grown up unable to walk, an "incessant reader" with a head full of romances and the "ideal world" of his imagination. His ancestors are famous sea captains, and his imposing grandfather, Captain Rainford, laments that the family traits of proud courage and action do not seem to be alive in Ralph. Yet one day, despite his crippled body, Ralph is able to rescue his beloved schoolteacher, as well as his grandfather, from being attacked by a vicious bull by grabbing the schoolteacher's red-tasseled cloak, engulfing himself in it, and luring the bull to follow him. His grandfather then decides to give him the money he needs for medical training so that Ralph can devote his life to caring for the sick.

Katharine's portrait of "Skipperville," a fictional New England coastal town in the 1840s, is rich with details from Falmouth. Like travel essays in which the writer takes her reader to a place that exists only in her memory or on paper, such fiction was thick with realistic factual detail and local voices and settings—nostalgic and elegiac of a place and time vanishing from the United States.

Ralph sounds like Katharine, a voracious reader, dreamer, poet, and writer, a child who had felt the "Rainford energy" go to his "brain" so that "many a romance" had he spun out of the cobwebs in his head. Although he is physically unable to follow in his patriarch's footsteps, he is far better equipped as a doctor to live in the world forty years later when schooners were being replaced by steamships and the globe colonized for its economic riches, and as the urban populations of an increasingly industrialized nation were in need of doctors.

Ralph's rescue of his teacher and his grandfather is also a rescue of his future when he decides to develop the family talents in new directions. Katharine showed that Ralph's own realization of how he could be most useful and best live out his Rainford heritage is to seek a future career different from those of his illustrious ancestors, one that is appropriately realistic, a future that he can create for himself.

As he says, "I have a little money, a little fame, a little goodwill up and down the street, and a profession that gives my intellectual activities and my human sympathies equal play." Katharine's story shows her realization that although as a woman she could not follow her male ancestors into church pulpits or publish sermons, she could use her pen in other useful ways to make her family proud.

At twenty-six, she had outgrown living in a boarding school as a kind of daughter in the Eastman family of girls, and accepted the invitation of Alice Freeman, Wellesley College's dynamic new president, to become an Instructor on its faculty in the fall semester of 1886.[70]

She remained close friends with the Eastman sisters throughout her life. Their "tranquil home whose broad Colonial porches were screened with 'white foam flowers' of clematis" welcomed her often. They later adopted Laddie, the brother collie of her beloved Sigurd. As the brother dogs romped wildly through Wellesley's fields and streets, their mistresses conspired together, an extended family worried about their unruly young ones.

Julia would continue to encourage and mentor Katharine's creative writing, giving her diaries and advice with which to pursue her writing dreams, and significantly for American poetry and Robert Frost's career, taking her to the first meeting of the Boston Authors Club.[71]

Katharine's frequent pieces in New England newspapers and magazines showed that, if she had the time to write, she was skilled enough to publish with the best writers of her time, as one of the new generation of women writers.

This was a good time for a young writer to become nationally known. Her marketplace of periodicals and readers was growing. During 1885 there were 3,300 periodicals in addition to newspapers in circulation in America, and the total number of such periodicals would increase by more than a thousand between 1885 and 1890.[72]

Before she started teaching at Dana Hall, Katharine had published six stories and thirty-two poems. While she taught there, although busy with her students, she managed to publish an impressive eleven stories, fifty-eight poems, two essays, and one anthology of edited poetry, and fill all the pages of her first scrapbook.

Once she joined Wellesley's faculty, her scrapbooks would have to wait as she entered an exciting new world, joining her own young generation of women making Wellesley College an "Adamless Eden."[73] They were American heroines like those she had envisioned, "the most daring, intelligent and forceful," and they would plunge her into a "vita nova" far more exciting than anything even Durant had imagined.

ALICE FREEMAN (BETWEEN PILLARS, IN WHITE RUFFLE) AND STUDENTS

CHAPTER FOUR

1885–1890
"NEW LINES OF THOUGHT
AND PURPOSE"[1]

I.

K atharine worked hard to prepare to teach at Wellesley, telling Annie Scoville, "And then hurrah for my twenty-two lecture topics! Meanwhile two hours a day must go to elocution and gymnastics."[2] And she still wanted "to let loose one or two rhymes that are buzzing like bees in my bonnet."[3]

But as the fall drew nearer, she confided to Annie, "I'm dreading next year horribly. I'm a regular coward and I would like to take to my heels and run for it…. And when I try to imagine myself deliberately and impressively reading aloud my own manuscript [of lectures] to a crew of staring youngsters, I blush up to my eyebrows in the solitude of that dismantled schoolroom and my tongue becomes really numb from fright."[4]

She thought of her return to Wellesley as "an experiment, to which I look forward with many misgivings. I have never thought … that it would be possible for me to work in the College at all…."[5] She dreaded "the peculiar strain attaching to that life,"[6] but returning to enormous College Hall to live and teach was a move towards a more professional career and financial security.

In September, President Alice Freeman welcomed Katharine back to the college, proudly celebrating the growth of its first ten years. In 1880 Katharine had graduated with forty other young women, but now there were 353 collegiate students and 156 non-degree students. When she had entered in 1876, there were twenty-two teachers on the faculty, but now she would be joining a faculty of forty-seven.[7]

It was flourishing under the youthful Freeman, just twenty-six when she became president. Before his death, Durant, "the Great Heart" of the college,[8] had wisely handpicked his successor, choosing "the most magnetic and sympathetic woman"[9] who made her work at Wellesley "'creation, not imitation.'"[10]

She was "hardly more than a girl, with her slight figure, her abundant brown hair, and her wonderful eyes, also of a deep velvet brown…. The college classes … and the whole atmosphere [were] full of a delightful buoyancy of youth and vigor, led by this young and charming president. The eager young women about her, the professors and the girls were pioneers, for, in those days it was the girl who really wanted to study who went to college."[11]

"Her own vivid personality … her setting, so to speak, in the beautiful great hall, as she stood against College Hall center with its masses of palms and tropical foliage, —all this made a picture which fired the imagination."[12]

Caroline Hazard, a later president of the college, thought that Alice Freeman "quite literally set Wellesley on its feet…. [She was] able to recognize clever people and people who could help, and welded the whole together, so that what had been a chaotic endeavor soon became a solid achievement."[13]

Freeman recruited Katharine to be one of a young group of women who had graduated from intellectually rigorous colleges and universities. Little by little, she was replacing Durant's teachers, like Louise Manning Hodgkins, the head of the English Literature Department, with her new hires, who could establish Wellesley as a first-rate serious college.[14]

An appealing leader and role model, Freeman showed that a woman president could plan her own course of action and take it; she once left a tedious college faculty meeting to watch a rehearsal of a French comedy at nearby Dana Hall. She drove "gleefully" there, "flashed in at the performance, laughed steadily for half an hour, and came back to the tired Faculty, blithe and breezy, to swing the discussion on to a prompt conclusion."[15]

Katharine was soon reading first editions of important literary works and periodicals in the library and the Browning Room to prepare for her fifteen hours a week of lectures in which she taught students to understand and analyze great writers.

But by Thanksgiving, she confessed to her brother Arthur's wife, Gertrude, "I live in a terrible scramble from one week's end to another…. I like the study and the work. I like my classes, too, and the scenery. [But my] Professor [probably Miss Hodgkins] is a trial to me, as I dare say, I am to her, and I don't like a quarter-of-seven breakfast, especially when I have to ask the blessing over it."[16]

By the next fall, Miss Hodgkins's illness gave Katharine the opportunity to teach Shakespeare. She assured her that if she would entrust her "precious little Shakespeare" class to her, she would "handle them as if they were bubbles, each crossed by a rainbow of literary promise.... It would be only a pleasure to read Macbeth with the class...." Perhaps recalling her grandfather Lee's pride in his own volume of Shakespeare, she added, "I could not spend my time more profitably or more pleasantly than in studying my Shakespeare."[17]

One student happily responded to her: "I want to ... tell you a little bit of the help you have been to me this year in our Shakespeare work. I have enjoyed all of it ... the outside work as well as you in class, who are an inspiration to us all.... [O]ne thing I am sure of—that I have only begun to get acquainted with the great poet."[18]

Katharine would ask a "running fire of questions," to "prick" into life the students' "sluggish perceptions,"[19] questions "that lead the student to recognize and define in [her]self the emotions aroused by one passage or another in the poem ... [that] mould the student's mood into sympathy with that higher mood, sensitive, eager, impassioned, in which the singer first conceived the song."[20]

As a poet herself, she felt that great literature was alive with ideas, emotions, and images conveyed in song-like language, and she wanted her students to hear that song. She agreed with Longfellow: "It is the poet himself, who, arresting the attention by song, holding it by vision after vision, can best impart ... the truth he has to tell, can alone inspire ... a sympathetic passion for that truth."[21]

II.

In her third year back, Katharine moved from stressful College Hall into the smaller Stone Hall, where she could more easily befriend and mentor students.

One recalled Katharine humorously asking, "'Do you happen to have a picture of the President?'

"'Why — no,' I answered, a little shy and bewildered, staring at my unknown questioner with wide-open eyes.

"She laughed. 'I mean, do you have a postage-stamp?'

"I ran to my table and got it for her.

"'Thank you,' she said and affixing it to her letter, went on down the hall to the mail-box. I stood at my door looking after her in wonder—at her youth, her quick, light steps, her cheerful self-possession."

She remembered how Katharine's "windows looked out through the trees to the lake, and her walls were lined with books.... I visited her often ... she sitting in her armchair, and I on a stool at her feet. She taught me poetry.... I took many long walks with her, down about the lake and through the woods. She always talked of poetry, in one way or another, even when she might seem to be talking of the stars. Her life was poetry."[22]

While Katharine might have been content to think only of poetry, Alice Freeman had flung open Wellesley's gates to the larger world beyond. She "reached out her hand and spanned the distance between Wellesley and Cambridge. We were no longer sufficient to ourselves, shut away from the larger life at our doors, narrow, constrained, dogmatic, exclusive. At a bound our infancy was left behind."[23]

Durant had envisioned an army of Wellesley-trained teachers re-forming the United States, and Freeman hoped that an army of Wellesley social and political activists could also re-form the country and still live by his motto. Instead of a safe asylum for young women, the college could be the training ground for radical idealists.

She looked beyond Wellesley for some of her next recruits to the faculty, young women like her friends who were graduates of the University of Michigan, one of the few schools that granted women advanced degrees. While Katharine's closest friendship had been with the younger Annie, it was time for her to be challenged by her new colleagues, women who were truly her peers, thrilled to be at Wellesley and determined to use their excellent educations to change the country.

First, the gifted and radiant Katharine Coman, from Ohio, arrived. A brilliant and charismatic teacher interested in applying her scholarship to pressing social and economic issues of the day, she attracted both students and faculty to her. She had "that wonderful halo about her; was it the arrangement of her hair or its color, or was it something invisible?"[24]

KATHARINE COMAN

VIDA SCUDDER

Then another imaginative young woman, Vida Scudder, a Smith College graduate, joined them. With a direct gaze, firm jaw, and light-brown hair pulled to the top of her head except for the few tiny curls on her forehead, she liked the idea of being a writer but wanted a more practical career. She lived with her widowed mother in Boston's fashionable Back Bay and came from a distinguished family: one uncle was writer Horace Scudder, editor of *The Atlantic Monthly* (1890-1898), who was appointed a Wellesley trustee by Alice Freeman later in the year; another uncle, E.P. Dutton, was a publisher in New York City. Unlike the Bateses, Vida's family could pay for her to travel abroad and study at Oxford University with philosopher and art critic John Ruskin, where she learned how to use "thorough analysis, especially linguistic" in studying English writers.[25]

Vida brought her breezy energy and genius to Wellesley, a college her mother had rejected for her as a student, ironically, because all the professors were women. She later wrote that when Wellesley paid her the "munificent salary of five hundred dollars a year" to be an instructor, that seemed "a great deal of money; I was scared, amused, and a little ashamed, when told that I was to earn it."[26]

But Vida was a born teacher who left her classroom "walking on air. It was a little class, made up of a few rather reluctant girls, scratched together to present to an unknown young teacher. It glowed to me with promise. I had found my vocation."[27]

Katharine Lee Bates, "bubbling over with poetry, fun, and affection" and already the "pride and joy [of the college] ... took the young colleague from Smith under her wing,"[28] and the two shared many adventures. Vida remembered how they "talked incessantly, especially at night, pacing to and fro by Longfellow pond; for she lived in Stone Hall, and I spent one night a week in the awe-inspiring Minister's Room of old College Hall.... But how gay she was, how much we had to share!

"Up and down by the pretty walk we would saunter, talking—naughty school girls rather than sober instructors—till all hours of the night.... Now and again, I shamefacedly summoned the night watchman; on one occasion Katharine boosted me in through one of the Gothic windows, left unfastened, of the library...."[29]

They talked of "English poetry ... Wellesley, Smith, Oxford ... people, people, people, from her background or mine. Gossip, exciting, sublimated;

and it was through her that I came to know most of my new colleagues, especially her fellow alumnae. But more than all ... we talked of a great idea of mine, a nascent aspiration."[30]

Vida's "great idea" was a desire to create fellowship among all people by working to achieve social justice. She told Katharine how Cambridge and Oxford university students were using some of John Ruskin's ideas to solve the problems of the poor in the slums of London's East End. Young Oxford men had established Toynbee Hall, a settlement house, to "provide education and the means of recreation and enjoyment for the people of the poorer districts of London," and young women were beginning to plan a similar residence where college women could live and help neighborhood families.[31]

Katharine introduced Vida and her ideas to Katharine Coman. Vida thought that Coman had "a lovely mature dignity, somewhat awe-inspiring, but alluring,"[32] and they both championed the English social reform movement.

Urban poverty was growing in American cities, along with bankruptcies, as the *Transcript* began to note: "Business Troubles—Heavy Failures in the West."[33]

So many workers were demanding fair wages and going on strike for them that the *Transcript* had to create a new column, "Labor Troubles," to keep its readers informed about such disturbing news as the weavers who stopped working in Andover[34] and Fall River,[35] Massachusetts, and the workers who went out on strike at the Weymouth Iron Company and at Brockton's forty-two shoe factories.[36]

As more and more immigrants arrived in America in search of better lives, their willingness to accept low wages threatened native-born workers in places like the Connellsville, Pennsylvania, mines where a "howling mob of Hungarians" attacked them.[37]

Native-born workers began joining together in labor organizations like the Knights of Labor, "an important and ever-growing power in the country," with 500,000 members in 1886. Its mission was "to protect the interests of labor, to elevate the wage-worker, to promote cooperation and mutual aid, mainly, to act as an organization, with authority and power, whenever the interests of labor and capital come into conflict."[38] Their boycott could be "a powerful weapon," but they went on strike only "as a last resort, when peaceful compromise has been denied."[39]

Alice Freeman wanted the Wellesley community to understand the brewing national crises, and so she invited famous activists to the campus to speak. One lectured on "the study of man and his relation to the community," and General Samuel Armstrong of the Hampton Institute of Virginia "lamented the present policy of the government with the Indian."[40]

American Indians came to the college in the next year, including Bright Eyes, who made students care about the "Indian question." The African-American statesman Frederick Douglass spoke, along with Dr. Phillips Brooks, an urban activist and later minister at Trinity Church in Boston, and President Freeman lectured on "Industrial Education" and on "The Education of Pauper and Criminal Children."[41] Meanwhile Pauline Durant celebrated the twentieth anniversary of her Young Women's Christian Association in Boston, which served the urban poor.[42]

By the Christmas holidays of 1887, Katharine could be pleased with the way her life was developing. Although Alice Freeman surprised many by marrying Professor George Palmer of Harvard and resigning the presidency of the college, as one of the last acts of her administration, she recommended to the trustees that Katharine be promoted to Associate Professor of English literature.[43] With her future at Wellesley almost secure, Katharine could begin to enjoy trips away from the campus, as she explained to Arthur's daughter, her one-year-old niece, "Tot":

> Did you think your Aunt Katharine was very bad not to thank you earlier for her sweet photographs? It is only because she is a very busy Aunt Katharine this vacation, lunching out and dining out and carrying on generally. I am afraid she is a very worldly Aunt and you mustn't take after her. I am just now on the point of starting off for Boston, where I expect to ... dine in Newberry St., meeting Mrs. Horace Scudder, and sleep and breakfast there, lunching tomorrow at the Bristol.[44]

Then, in a turn of events too improbable for the plot of one of her stories, when Katharine visited Annie Scoville's Connecticut home during their Christmas vacation, she was exposed to smallpox, an event that would change her life.

III.

Katharine shared her colleagues' desire to educate students and people beyond the campus about the roots of the social and economic problems facing America, and she wanted to write fiction that would do this, if only she had the time.

But after her Christmas visit to Annie's, she was suddenly given that necessary uninterrupted time when she had to go into smallpox quarantine for several weeks in a little rented attic room in Boston. She "roasted" in the sulfur fumes that fumigated her clothes, but she began to use her forced isolation to write a young adult novel for the market she knew best—the Congregationalist Society's Sunday school libraries—and a big cash prize.

While the coals glowed in her little stove, she encouraged Annie to write such a novel too, and excitedly described her plan:

> I've mapped out mine, —24 chapters of 20 pages each, and I've put a title to each chapter, and decided on which of my friends I would model the characters. The heroine is to be drawn partly from you and partly from Clara Jones. In fact, all my characters are composites.... The hero is partly Willie Denton and partly—Dear Teach [Katharine herself] —What do you think of that for a combination? The title is 'Rose and Thorn,'—they're twins, Rosamund and Thornton Maynard. And the plot is wildly improbable, with small-pox in it.... I'm going to write a chapter a day, so I shall have it half done when I go back to Wellesley.[45]

Although her hand often became too chilled to write, and she had to "sneeze pathetically in the cold half the morning" to induce her landlady to make her fire,[46] Katharine immersed herself in her project, exhorting Annie: "Try, as I do, to throw yourself into your work, to be its various characters one by one and think out their life-puzzles instead of your own."[47]

Five days later she urged: "Dig away at the book, Dear. I've done nearly a hundred pages and hope to do another hundred before I go back to Wellesley."[48]

Dreaming of the prize money, she hatched a plan of going to England, confiding to Annie, "This is probably all moonshine, but if a Professorship were assured me on my return, I would go even on borrowed money."[49] Such a trip to Oxford would enable her to do the kind of scholarly work necessary for an eventual book and for Wellesley to award her a master's degree, an essential step before she could be made a full professor and department head to replace Miss Hodgkins.

When her quarantine was over, she began hobnobbing with well-known Boston writers, some of whom had appeared in the *Transcript*'s columns with her, at a Wellesley benefit Authors' Reading.[50]

The gathering was a success in bringing in over three hundred dollars, "and in the way of enjoyment, too, for that portion of the audience who could hear.... Naturally, Mrs. [Alice Freeman] Palmer presided, and Col. Higginson,[51] Mrs. Julia Ward Howe, [and] Mr. Howells meant to come, but was detained, and Dr. [Oliver Wendell] Holmes failed us on account of his wife's death."[52] These writers and publishers were a significant part of the Boston literati network, and Katharine wanted to become one of them.

In spite of Wellesley's demands on her time, she bragged to Annie about her growing popularity as a writer for the family market, "The *Wide Awake* is asking for poems, the *Republican* is asking, work is pressing on every side, and I'm good-for-nothing."[53]

Meanwhile, the nation's economic and social crises were worsening. The *Transcript* tried to calm its readers' fears about the declining stock market, the growing threats of violence by anarchists, and the increasing membership in labor unions. Workers marched in the New York Elevated Railroad strike and businesses were being foreclosed. Conflicts were erupting throughout the country, including in Chicago.[54]

Katharine's Wellesley friends, with their concern for families of the poor, threw their energies into teaching about the underlying causes of poverty, as she wrote to Annie: Vida was "bringing a strong intellectual stimulus to bear upon my life ... new lines of thought and purpose,"[55] and she urged Annie to read her article in the latest *Christian Union* about London's Toynbee Hall.[56]

Soon Vida's question, "Why could not we young women start something of the same kind in our country?" ignited Katharine Coman and Katharine to plan such a settlement house in Boston.[57] Her Wellesley friends' talk about their vision of a world with better social and economic treatment of everyone, especially working women, became the heart of Katharine's novel, which she completed just before the contest deadline, announcing, in Falmouth language, "I am resting on my oars after the S.S. bk. [Sunday school book] pull."[58]

IV.

She wanted her readers to see the very real problems around them on the streets of Boston and New York, and so opened *Rose and Thorn* a few days before Christmas on a cold day in downtown Boston:

> How the wind blew! It hooted up and down the stately avenues on the Back Bay; it roared across the Public Garden and the Common; it shrieked a flying greeting to the great gilded dome of the State House; it whistled the length of Tremont Street; it pinched intellectual noses; it sent erudite eye-glasses spinning through the air, and all the good citizens of 'the Hub' shivered inside their great-coats, and said hoarsely to one another, with blue lips and chattering teeth:—
>
> 'Fine day! A little windy, to be sure, but genuine Boston weather. Very fine day!'[59]

We meet her heroine, Rose, unaware of how privileged she is: "Rose lingered for a moment in the doorway of Fera's, where she had just made her customary purchase of half a pound of chocolate creams, to watch the crowd stream by."[60]

When Rose gets out of the wind in a doorway, she notices the condition of a shabby man, a vender of toy watches with "a downcast and disheartened look curiously out of harmony with the festive season. There was a droop in his back, his seedy garments were peanut-colored, his long arms mechanically waved the bundles of dangling watches to and fro, and his voice wheezed like a pump run dry."[61]

A model for the reader, Rose ponders how people from different economic and social classes can come together on Boston's streets and yet remain almost invisible to each other: "'It seems queer for people to be so near in—in geography, and so far apart in happiness.'"[62]

After buying a toy watch to cheer up the shabby man, a singing-top from a one-armed man, and a wooden cow from a lame man, Rose gives money to a child selling matches.

"PLEASE, PARDON ME," FALTERED ROSE. "I'M SO VERY SORRY."

When the child she intended to help turns suspiciously away from her, she realizes that she does not truly understand how to help: "The trifling incident saddened Rose's winsome face, and the shadows there grew deeper."[63]

She decides to give all her purchases, even the chocolates, to a small child with his face pressed against the window of a great toyshop, "as ragged as he was dirty … but the smile shining so luminously through the dirt shed a luster down over the grimy little jacket that many a broadcloth coat might envy."[64]

Empathetic and intelligent, Rose shows readers how to learn the same lessons that she does as the story unfolds. Adopted by a wealthy uncle when her parents died, she has a good heart, but she has not had her own parents' guidance. Her custodial uncle, Mr. Thornton, has spent his large inheritance only on creating a beautiful Back Bay home, "a marvel of the decorators' art … a luxury of color."[65] He did not believe in giving money to beggars because such charity kept "pauperism in existence…. Taste was his morality."[66]

The tension between the values of humanitarian Rose and her self-centered uncle grows as she begins to learn her true identity and develop her own values. Since we have already been told what Rose does not know—that she had a deformed twin brother whom Mr. Thornton did not want to adopt—when she accidentally knocks down a humpbacked boy her own age whose eyes are as blue as hers, we sense that he could be her less fortunate brother, Thorn.

Rose is Katharine's "American heroine," an active, lively, and compassionate girl who discovers startling truths in Boston's streets.

Her plot is Rose's coming-of-age story, but all her characters keep us turning her pages. Katharine knew a novelist must know how to create "a group of people involved in some exciting situation which swiftly rises to crisis and therefore inevitably falls to catastrophe."[67] To make her characters "alive" she had to manage to "coalesce" their elements of "all the human complexities of temperament, environment, talent"[68] into what the reader experiences as believable characters.[69]

With her good ear for a variety of expressive phrases and speech, Katharine could write lively dialogue. Her characters from various classes, regions, and generations, especially the wittily named "Dr. Killem," remind us of Dickens, and she similarly used humorous touches to keep her readers involved in a serious consideration of urban poverty and misused wealth.

Rose helps unite Thorn with their uncle and aunt, and their young son, Jewel. Smallpox, in a special nod to the novel's genesis, enters when Rose and Thorn travel to New York City at Easter time, significantly the season when Christians celebrate the Resurrection. The twins enjoy a cozy Easter eve, but, "a few miles from them, within the limits of the same huge, life-teeming city, a group of haggard women, but newly aroused from heavy slumber, were beginning their fourteen hours of work with needle and machine."[70]

To emphasize the scene's ongoing horror, Katharine shifted the narration into the present tense, a technique to make a scene seem to unfold before our eyes in our present experience, much as a cinematic scene does, and she accelerated the pace of her sentences as she piled up the horrors for her reader:

> For [the haggard women] there is no day. From dawn unto nightfall the dense shadow of the Brooklyn Bridge shuts them off from the blessed sunshine; from night-fall unto dawn the cold electric light glares in upon their labors; and when the city wakes to the busy stir of morning, these pallid, joy-forsaken creatures grope their way to miserable beds and sink into that leaden sleep again.
>
> For them there is no Sabbath. How should they have time to praise their Maker? They have no time to mend their dingy garments; no time to wipe away the foul, unwholesome damp from the reeking walls; scarcely time to dull the hunger-sickness by eager swallows of the rank, boiled tea, which stands to them for food and stimulant at once; scarcely time to mourn or remember the babies who died of the fever, and the girls who went astray.
>
> For them there is no Easter—not for them nor for their daughters nor their daughters' daughters. In that dreary, tenement house they are as the dead and buried.[71]

Their job is to sew fancy clothes for small children born into wealthy homes, in spite of losing their own babies because of the dreadful living conditions created by capitalists not yet restrained by more humane labor laws.

Katharine makes clear who is to blame for the poor but hardworking women's misery, squeezing out every drop of symbolism from her Easter morning setting:

> Their blood is on the skirts of the heedless, greedy city. The selfishness of the rich, the cruelty of the strong have rolled the stone to the door of their sepulcher. The angel of the Easter

shall yet find and deliver such as these—but how long, O Lord, how long![72]

Although the women's "attic closet, bare and grimy and malodorous" is bad enough, below them are the "vile, hideous, indescribable basement-dens … where men, women, and children herd together like ill-kept beasts … [where] the air was noisome with a poisonous stench, the walls dripped with filthy water, and the stamp of bitter, grinding poverty was over all."[73]

Regardless of their terrible working environment with the "deafening clatter" of the "hurrying machines" and "drunken shouts" from below, and their own appearance in rags, "blue circles beneath their eyes, the sunken cheeks and the hopeless droop of the mouths," the women are nevertheless virtuous, sketched by Katharine to be intrinsically good: "honest, patient, kindly, [they] worked on swiftly and silently, for rent must be paid, and coal must be bought."[74]

Taking a cue perhaps from Annie's great-aunt, Harriet Beecher Stowe, with her direct entreaties to readers in her best-selling *Uncle Tom's Cabin*, Katharine asks her readers to admire these hard-working impoverished women and to see the hypocrisy of comfortable American "Christians":

> Now and then one would turn suddenly from her machine for a feverish gulp of the black tea, but instantly after the noisy wheel would be whirling with redoubled haste, striving wildly to overtake the lost minute....
>
> Oh, what righteousness has there been in those happy years of yours, cherished, cultured, sheltered daughter of the rich, to entitle you in heaven to a seat at the feet of the least of these who chose in youth this strenuous virtue, so ill-rewarded on earth, rather than easy and luxurious vice, and who still, in their premature gray hairs, the past, the present, and the future alike dark, blank, and miserable, trust blindly in the goodness of God and do the duty that they see? The martyrs of our boasted civilization, these are the reproach, and yet the exemplars, of nineteenth-century American Christianity.[75]

The "stout and ruddy" man, the "'sweater'" who pays two of the women paltry wages, "had been to church the day before, had listened to the Easter music and looked into the white hearts of the lilies; but he … gloated in thought over the profit that was his."[76]

On their return from church the women find that one of their group has collapsed onto an old blackened mattress, fatally stricken with the dreaded smallpox. Thus a garment, a child's sailor suit, created, as it were, out of poverty's dreadful conditions, will physically link the poor and the rich together, when young Jewel wraps himself in the little sailor suit invisibly soiled with the sweat of exploited labor and its plague of smallpox.

Katharine shows her reader the effects of this catastrophe on the Thorntons. Rose's twin, Thorn, unselfishly risks his own life to nurse little Jewel through the near-fatal smallpox that he contracts from the contaminated sailor suit. Thorn and Rose become truly brother and sister in their shared awareness of economic realities and their love of beauty and sensitivity. Forced to learn about the true conditions of the poor whom he has always dismissed, Mr. Thornton, a stand-in for Katharine's most resistant reader, grows into a caring man who feels a sense of connection with others, seen and unseen, rich and poor.

Her final scene takes place on a Falmouth-like New England seacoast, a fitting place in her imagination for the formation of a loving community. Its concrete details, as well as those of Boston and New York, anchor her novel in the social reality of her times. Narrated in an inviting style at a brisk pace that moves her readers along, her novel effectively showed all kinds of readers that serious problems in America needed fixing.

Rose and Thorn had a good chance to win a prize from the Congregationalist Society, with its pitch to ministers, when Rose wonders where practical Christianity is on Boston's streets, asking, "'But if Christ came to the world nearly two thousand years ago to teach us to love each other, why is the world so wrong today?'"[77]

Katharine knew that the prize committee was looking for more than a Sunday-school book that could teach its youthful readers about true Christianity and the working conditions of the poor. Its characters and style would have to captivate its audience who would love it for its zest and humor, and mostly for Rose, its plucky "American heroine."

Sensitive to sharp satire aimed at "women's pioneer adventures in the far land of culture,"[78] Katharine always wanted to create "effectual [female] banner-bearers…[because through] immemorial time women, living under paternal and marital authority maintained by physical force and economic advantage, have had such a thorough training in deceit that it is a wonder there is any candor left in us."[79]

Thus, Rose desires to do loving deeds; the poor women in the slums under the Brooklyn Bridge personify how the powerless are exploited and destroyed by the sweatshop system, and Katharine's own character of capable Mrs. Santa Claus even appears in a bedtime story Rose tells about how she saved ten children by knitting them stockings of snow.

Mr. Thornton's English wife points out: "'Are you an American and do not realize that in this land of the free, the more a woman knows of any thing or every thing, the more of a woman she is?'"[80] And Rose (we hear her creator chuckling) will become a student at …Wellesley College after she brings all those around her into true community.

V.

While Katharine anxiously waited to hear if she had won the prize money for *Rose and Thorn*, she learned that the college had promoted her to be an associate professor of English. This was good news, but it came with strings: she would have to be the faculty editor of the expanded College Edition of *The Wellesley Courant*, a weekly publication.

She knew, as her character Thorn had explained, that sometimes a creative person had little choice "between drudgery with a decent living and an aesthetic pursuit with slow starvation."[81] She needed her job at Wellesley to support herself, but now, instead of being able to devote time at her "writing desk" to working on her poems and fiction, she would have to devote that time to revamping and editing the college paper.

Helen Shafer, the new college president, intended it to be a public relations tool that would give Wellesley more visibility throughout the country and abroad, at other colleges, and especially to the alumnae who helped recruit students and whose financial support was essential to its future.

This was not a responsibility Katharine wanted, but her co-editor, Wellesley graduate Edith Souther Tufts, gave her sympathetic and practical help. Proving to be a good businesswoman, Katharine called the shots with Mr. Howard, her printer, at the beginning of the year, withstanding his notion of changing the paper's name and insisting that he provide a better quality of paper, better proofreading, and twenty-five free copies for contributors.

Delegating various columns to faculty members and college clubs, she mused, "I don't think we shall lack for material—but as for good material, —hmm." With a good sense of marketing, she wanted to whet the readers' appetites by announcing future articles because "that would excite almost as much interest as the [article] itself."[82] While the *Courant* did report on college activities, because of the serious articles by the activist faculty members, it also showcased the college in the larger context of current national social and political questions.

Katharine's *Courant* became a lively weekly newspaper full of provocative news and stimulating ideas. One column, "The Wide, Wide World," summarized international news notes of interest. One article reported Dr. Phillips Brooks's speech on the need for foreign missions; Julia Ward Howe explained why she thought women should register to vote (for school committees); and staunch college feminist Ellen Hayes's column, "Our Outlook," covered news of women's rights events.

In little space-fillers, Katharine raised her readers' awareness of women's lives and issues by squeezing in tidbits of information such as the fraction of English women who worked outside the home (60 percent) and notices of forthcoming addresses on women's suffrage.[83] Women's rights were becoming newsworthy in national newspapers as well, with the *Transcript* running frequent articles on women's suffrage meetings, the growing Women's Christian Temperance Union, and women's activities in community organizations.

The *Courant* also gave Katharine a place to publish pieces by several of the students she had mentored. She ran a travel essay, "A Voyage Through the Wilderness," by Annie after spending considerable time editing it, and wrote to her, after apologizing for her corrections, "It has flashes and gleams of picture in it that I value exceedingly, and the diction is good and racy."[84]

But the proofreading problems with Howard, along with his tardiness and sloppy work, demanded strong tactics from Katharine. In her letters to Edith she let off steam and turned her trials and headaches into scenes from a melodrama, with Howard as its chief villain.

She recounted to Edith how on one Saturday morning she had to take an early train to the neighboring town of Natick, "cold as cold could be. Walked sternly into office.

"'Good morning, Mr. Howard.'

"Hat on. Slinky appearance.

"'Goo'-morning.'

"'Are your presses frozen up here this cold morning?'

"'N-no, they aint.'

"'Then where's our proof [pages to review]?'

"'Well! Willy was just goin' to bring it over to you.'

"'Oh! was he? And when do you expect to get out the paper?'

"He scratched that hoary head which isn't a crown of glory and pulls his hat down over his nose to render the process more thorough.

"'Well! Not till Monday <u>this</u> week.'"

"'You know that with the Christmas work and all, the result will be that the paper will reach our subscribers nearly a week behind time.'

"'The Blower' [Katharine] waxeth far sterner than before. The Delegate of the Massachusetts Press [Howard] wisheth 'The Blower' were in Mexico or even a warmer place.

"'Well! We can't get out that paper till Monday.'

"Doggedly on the part of Delegate.

"'What was your reason for the delay?'

"'Oh! oh! Christmas advertisements.'

"The Blower reflected. The Delegate eyes her from under his hat-rim.

"Saith The Blower: 'May I speak to Mr. Reardon [Mr. Howard's superior] a moment?'

"Apparently the full force are assembled behind the door to hear The Blower blow. 'Don' promptly appears ... unabashed.

"'Good morning, Mr. Reardon.' Responsive and amiable growl in the throat of him.

"'If I sit down here and correct this proof lying on the table, handing you the shrifts as fast as I correct them, would it be possible for you to get our paper printed and down to Wellesley by half-past three?'

"'Yes'm.'

"'We could do that,' puts in the dear reprobate Boy suddenly advancing to the front.

"'If she should correct the proof right now, you know,' adds 'Charley,' likewise emerging from eaves-dropping obscurity.

"'Eh? O yes, yes, O yes ... sit right down, Miss Bates. Sit right down. She has saved you a good cold job, Will. Is that chair easy for you, Miss Bates?'

The Blower gloomily draweth off her gloves, regarding with much disfavor the wet proof and dusty, conglomerate table-top before her.

"'It is all right, thank you. Have you any mucilage here, Mr. Howard?'

"'Say, Will! Get Miss Bates the—the silver chalice, you know.'

"The tin sauce-pan of paste is duly presented.

"Blower sitteth and readeth proof—in order. Charley talketh volubly, with the sleeves rolled up to the shoulders of him ... grimy and black with the badge of noble toil. Dan laboreth right valiantly. Will waiteth on the Blower ... for copy-box, scizzors etc. All these ... with hats on their gallant brows, come and go noisily.... Task finished."[85]

In spite of her irritation, Howard continued to miss his deadlines, and Katharine replaced him for the following year with two young printers in the town of Wellesley.[86] But she was tired of the *Courant's* demands on her precious time and energy, writing to Miss Hodgkins that she had to withdraw as editor because "it has entrenched far too much on my time and strength and yet it seemed necessary for someone to give herself up to it for the first year, when the character of such a paper is being determined."[87]

She happily told Edith: "My dearest of Co's, I read my last *Courant* proof, five pages of it in Mt. Auburn [Cemetery] yesterday, resting under the shadow of a tombstone [possibly the Durant memorial]. Then I spent an hour with our amiable Old Slouch [Howard] in his untidy sanctum."[88]

Katharine may have felt like her character Goody (Mrs.) Santa Claus, who has done all Santa's work for him and exclaims, "Joy-bells ring in every steeple,/ And Goody's gladdest of the glad. I've had my own sweet will."[89]

This unwelcome *Courant* job did enable Katharine to see firsthand how an editor chooses material for a periodical and copes with deadlines, space limitations, layouts, and the necessity for creating a balanced mix of material appealing to the interests of different readers. She saw how diplomatic editing comments were sometimes necessary, and how the ultimate responsibility to one's employer was for the content. She used good executive ability in her organization and delegation of work, and in her negotiations with Howard, she showed that an articulate and strong woman could capably make a lazy man meet her deadlines before she replaced him.

And she had learned from being an editor how to write for particular editors and publications so that they would reach her growing number of readers.

She began to move onto a national stage when Smith College offered her a job and the poetry-reading public showed interest in her. Proudly, she wrote to Annie, "I've told President Seelye I wouldn't go to Smith, and a man who is going to start a Magazine of American Poetry has written to me for my works (!), address of my biographer (!!) and my portrait (!!!) That's all that's happened to me this week."[90]

VI.

In January 1889, Katharine finally heard from M. C. Hazard in the Editorial Department of the Congregational Sunday-School and Publishing Society in Boston:

> My Dear Miss Bates:—
>
> It gives me great pleasure to say that to 'Rose and Thorn' was awarded the first prize, and hence, in payment for the same, I enclose a check for $700.00.
>
> Now if that isn't cheerful, what is?[91]

Somewhat ironically, Katharine's determination to keep going in her career as a popular writer for the humble family market with *Rose and Thorn* would give her a year in England at Oxford University where she could do the advanced scholarly work on medieval drama that would enable Wellesley to promote her to the rank of full professor.

Her work as the *Courant's* editor also paid off with her increasing success in popular periodicals, as she told Annie, "I've had unusual luck with writing this fall. I've taken in about $60.00, all but $5.00 for verses. My account for 1890 opens with $25.00 for a moral tale from *The Youth's Companion*. They wrote a little while ago to know if I would scribble for them, and they took this performance and would like more."[92]

The Youth's Companion, whose motto was "None but the Best," was the most widely read and best-paying of the family market. By 1886, it had two million readers every week;[93] by 1896 it would have 14,000 submissions a year and a circulation of 500,000 all over the United States, a larger readership than *Harper's* or the *Atlantic*.[94]

Before they left for England, Katharine wrote a second young adult novel that she published with her old friend Daniel Lothrop, who, she felt, had always generously encouraged her.

He made her second novel, *Hermit Island,* attractive with an olive green cover embossed along the top and left side with a design of pine branch clusters that suggests its Maine seacoast setting. Although it lacked the successfully realized main characters of *Rose and Thorn*, its appealing setting along the rocky shores near Old Orchard, outside Portland, Maine, was one that Katharine often enjoyed with the growing family of her brother Arthur and his wife, Gertrude.

Like the American artist Winslow Homer (1836-1910), whose studio at Prout's Neck was only a few miles up the shoreline from Old Orchard, she wanted her audience to see that American artists could celebrate American landscapes in their art, and opened her novel with a painterly description of the Maine seacoast at sunset:

> It was a tranquil summer evening, and the long waves of the Atlantic broke gently, even caressingly, on the sandy shores of Hermit Island. The moon, almost at the full, slowly climbed the sky, which was still flushed with the last faint colors of sunset.... A few film-like sails glimmered on the horizon, and between the island and the mainland a dory was in sight, but so far away that it seemed to lie motionless on the water.[95]

In *Hermit Island* Katharine tells the story of a group of individuals, young and old, who eventually come together after each one comes to understand the others better. Two sisters have been rescued from the urban rat race by their father, who has served prison time for tampering with bank books in order to support his wife's expensive tastes. To keep his daughters ignorant of such extravagance, he has taken them to the island to separate them by water from the mainland's temptations.

On the island the families appreciate natural beauty away from cities and must learn to create a future based on loving friendship, a kind of alternative America. They value education for women: just as Rose was rewarded with a future education at Wellesley, Del and Dolo achieve their dream of attending a girls' school.[96]

While she could earn necessary money from such novels, with her Wellesley promotion looming, Katharine had to buckle down to finding a more appropriate topic on which to write a scholarly book for Wellesley before her departure for England.

She turned to ballads, the oldest narrative poems in the language. Originally intended to be sung, they had strong rhythms, repetitive rhymes, and vivid language. And as she explained to Miss Hodgkins, her "actual experiment [teaching the ballads] in the class-room ... would add to the value of the book."[97]

To help Katharine do necessary research, because as a woman she could not use Harvard's libraries, Wellesley trustee Eben Horsford arranged a meeting for her with the famous authority on and collector of English and Scottish ballads, Professor Francis James Child of Harvard. He assured Miss Hodgkins that Professor Child "is very ready to do any thing for the ladies."[98]

Katharine worked away on her *Ballad Book*, reporting that it was "fast getting into shape.... I'm having no end of fun."[99] With Miss Hodgkins pressuring her to give up writing for the family market, Katharine was pleased when the prestigious *Century* magazine accepted her serious poem "The Ideal" for its April 1890 issue.

Reprinted on the front page of the *Transcript*, and then in *The Wellesley Prelude*,[100] Katharine's ambitious poem received many compliments. Her eight stanzas, each with three rhyming lines, dramatize "The Ideal" as a living force that strongly exhorts a "recalcitrant dreamer" to follow his or her dream, in spite of temptations to sleep, to socialize, or to give up.

The "Ideal" is "a burning fire" kindled within the dreamer herself, reassuring her that she will be able to attain her distant goals, just as the acorn will surely develop into an oak tree. The voice of the Ideal cries, moans, and resounds; it is also compassionate and understanding, offering the dreamer a "sudden embrace" as consolation for her necessary solitude. If the dreamer hesitates or loiters, the Ideal will keep her moving forward on the "crag-path chosen" to the "crest" where finally, "shall rest be sweet." The strong and consoling Ideal explains to the dreamer that while human pain and desires may perish, the quest for the Ideal will always remain:

> Call me thy foe in thy passion;
>> claim me in peace for thy friend;
>
> Yet bethink thee by lowland or upland,
>> wherever thou willest to wend,
>
> I am thine Angel of Judgment;
>> mine eyes thou must meet in the end.[101]

In her eloquent poem Katharine articulated her struggle to remain committed to her dream of being a creative writer in the midst of all the other demands in her life,[102] and it may have helped her lay out her own goals. To Miss Hodgkins she could say: "I'm glad you like 'The Ideal.' It has no lack of faults, but it stands for the order of work I want to do. These stories [for the family periodicals] are only stepping-stones."[103]

One admirer, Richard C. Cabot, wrote her a letter that she kept throughout her life:

> Your poem the 'Ideal' has come to occupy such a place in my life that I have for some time wanted to thank you for it, to try to make you feel how it comes home to all the thinking and feeling of one who knows nothing of you and has no reason except the intrinsic worth of the poem, for feeling deeply thankful that it exists.
>
> Every line in it is an experience of mine or has helped to create one; it rings true and pure on our deepest life and makes our hearts beat quick. I say 'our' because I have showed it to many friends in many stages of development and have found that my appreciation of it is [not] due to anything peculiar to my needs and experiences. It has rung in my head unexpectedly at all kinds of times, the more constantly since I have been trying to put music to it, and I would to God I could bring to you the happiness that would surely come with the sense of having done such a service to the world as your poem has done.
>
> Graduates of Harvard especially if, as in my case, they choose medicine for their life work are probably not associated in your mind with an over-expression of feelings and so I hope that you may not have to take any salt with what I say....
>
> I am very gratefully and sincerely yours,
>
> Richard C. Cabot[104]

What a sweet triumph for Katharine to hear that her poem resonated with a Harvard graduate, even a Cabot of Boston. It helped her think of herself as what she had first wanted to be, a poet "of service to the world," whose words might be set to music.

She chose it as the title poem in the collection of poetry she was assembling for Katharine Coman.[105] Identifying herself as a serious poet and voice in American literature, she wanted to show her friend that she had the kinds of creative and intellectual gifts that would make her a fitting companion for the woman who was already inspiring her with her energy and passion for learning all she could about the world in order to improve it.

Unfortunately, in the spring of 1890 Katharine became so seriously ill with an inflammation of her lungs that the plans for her year abroad were in jeopardy, and her mother was reluctant to have her "cross the ocean and leave her, just after an illness which has frightened her so." [106] But President Shafer urged her departure, and Horsford sent her a check for $350.00, a loan that, on top of her book prize money, would pay for her trip.

As her health improved, Katharine began packing for her first sea voyage and a year at Oxford that could give her a promotion to a tenured and permanent Wellesley professorship and a welcome increase in her salary.

KATHARINE LEE BATES, C. 1890

CHAPTER FIVE

1890–1893
"THE LOVE-LIGHTS BURN FOR YOU"[1]

I.

On a Brooklyn pier crowded with well-wishers on a windy and warm day in May 1890, brothers Arthur and Sam Bates saw Katharine and Annie off on the *State of Nebraska* bound for Glasgow, Scotland.

Katharine marveled at her *bon voyage* gifts—a portfolio from Katharine Coman, a steamer rug from the Eastmans, a monogrammed silver flask, roses, a dressing-case, slippers, a medicine case, and a pen from other friends and family, and "more letters than the agent, so he said, had ever seen for any one person."[2]

Thirteen days later, in pouring rain, she and Annie climbed into a small dory that ferried them to the harbor near Glasgow.[3] Excited to be on foreign soil, on the picturesque island of Arran, off Scotland's southwest coast, they began their adventures before Oxford's fall term. They read, took walks in this "land of color," pressed flowers between pages of their books, and wrote stories which would help finance their trip.

In Lamlash, Mrs. McIntosh was an ideal landlady: not only did she cook and clean for them while they wrote, she could speak the dying language of Gaelic and recount fairy-lore stories that Katharine transcribed. She was impressed that Katharine was an "hauthoress,"[4] keen to see where her writer heroes had lived.

At the home of Scottish poet Robert Burns, Katharine enjoyed just standing "in the little stone kitchen where he was born and reared."[5] Then at Dumferlaine, she could picture the scene from the old ballad, "where the old King, who sent Sir Patrick Spence out to sea, once took his royal ease."[6]

The settings of Sir Walter Scott's popular poetry and fiction—Stirling Castle, Dumbarton, Ballock, Loch Lomond, and Loch Katrine—captivated her. At Abbotsford, Katharine imagined Scott in his study with its worn black leather-covered armchair and small writing-table.[7]

On they went to Bristol, Bath, and Gloucester, and enjoyed the impressive ruins of Wordsworth's Tintern Abbey in the moonlight. Katharine used a copy of Nathaniel Hawthorne's travel essays on England as her guidebook and frequently compared her reactions with his. Like him, she was disappointed in Shakespeare's Stratford, where there was "little enough of the spirit — Shakespeare, there the ashes of his body—what are they beside the living fire of his soul, still burning his words upon the heart and conscience of the two great hemispheres?"[8]

After London,[9] Salisbury, Stonehenge, and Exeter, she and Annie began a thirty-mile walking excursion in southwestern England. With her excellent writer's ear, she was delighted with the local dialect: "Man saying about a lost glove — 'It's nought to we, but it's summat to they.'"[10] And "We asked a woman smiling in her vine-wreathed doorway how near we were to Hartland. 'Win the top of yon hill,' she said, 'and you'll soon slip away into it.'"[11]

Missing America, they celebrated the "glorious Fourth" of July in Scotland by singing "My country 'tis of thee," to America.[12] With relations between England and the United States frosty, Katharine felt that many English people regarded themselves as "the conquering race."[13] Although they asked her about "Niagara and the Yosemite,"[14] she was irritated with their condescension:[15] "When I happen upon the more intelligent English people they try to conceal their compassion for one born outside the hallowed circle of their fogs and usually ask me if I intend to return to America.... And at the entrance of a park, — a city park, not private— I usually encounter the British lion in bronze, nonchalantly rolling the round world under his paw."[16]

Always interested in women's lives, she was appalled at York Cathedral's "absurd [monument] in the choir of a kneeling family, the father having had himself and children done in marble and his wife in limestone," a less permanent stone,[17] and she imagined her mother's "righteous indignation" at how the monument immortalized the man's rank, higher than that of his wife.[18]

She wanted to know if America's labor problems existed in Britain, and heard, in a remote cottage on the moors, that local wages were too low, and had "a good talk with [the landlady's] husband that evening over the peat fire about English laborers and socialism and the like and found that the signs of the times were to be as clearly read in that secluded farmhouse as in any Chicago anarchist assembly."[19]

In contrast, when she went to Llandoff Cathedral in Wales, she felt the "beautiful" thing about it was that the whole community had "labored, lovingly and zealously, to restore their old Cathedral…. The men who worship in it are … the men who have labored for it, with head or hands or both."[20]

II.

Renting lodgings in Oxford's Walton Street,[21] Katharine and Annie made themselves cozy on this "long, gray street. Our parlor, which is also a study, dining room, reception-room and anything else that comes handy, is on the second floor. We have a red rug over a green carpet, two great mirrors, dining-table, writing-table, bookcases, lounge, easy chairs, uneasy chairs, open fireplace and various ornaments more or less ornamental.

"Over this foundation we have scattered books, photographs, china, our very remarkable minerals and other trophies of our summer wanderings, and the stars and stripes are draped from the little chandelier. Upstairs we have two comfortable chambers."[22]

The Tower, Magdalen College, Oxford University, England

Wandering about "the picturesque old town," Katharine began exploring the "bewildering … twenty-two colleges and some four halls … besides all sorts of historic old buildings."[23] Beginning at Magdalen College's graceful ancient tower, she enjoyed the beautiful riverside walk around Christ Church Meadow where the river, "a mere ribbon," was "lined with handsome barges, belonging to the Rowing-Clubs of the various colleges and fitted up as club-houses … with newspapers … for loafing."[24]

She could imagine Oxford's medieval past when she went to hear the "glorious" music of Evensong, the Church of England's music-filled prayer service late in the afternoon, in candlelit Magdalen College Chapel.[25]

Another evening she and Annie went to Christ Church Cathedral, where they were impressed to see, in the dim light after the service, "white-surpliced figures flitting about it and vanishing into the dark doorways."[26] Katharine was glad to learn that its eighth-century history began with a woman, St. Frideswide, "a princess with a pronounced vocation for the religious life who had erected a nunnery where she was the first abbess."[27]

Oxford University's wealth astounded her—its annual income was around two million dollars—and she understood its effect: "No wonder English students and English books so far outrank us poor, breathless, over-busied Americans.

"We have no kings to tax the commons and endow colleges, and I'm glad of it, but still Oxford is a place to make even the least bit of a scholar envious [of the] old books and the rare old manuscripts!"[28]

She plunged in to work in famous Bodleian Library, established by Humphrey, Duke of Gloucester, son of Henry IV, and built in 1445-88. Later despoiled, the library was then restored and enlarged by Sir Thomas Bodley, who began in 1598 to add to its holdings of books and manuscripts.

Katharine basked in its beauty, admiring its emblazoned oak ceiling and "treasures" of illuminated manuscripts.[29] But she missed her brilliant mother, so often her intellectual companion and unlikely ever to see Oxford University: "All the time when I'm not doing something else I'm pegging away at Anglo-Saxon, and wish I had my mother to peg with me."[30]

Since women and American men could not receive graduate degrees from Oxford, they attended special lectures. For the first time in her life, Katharine's professors were all men. Once a week she listened to their lectures on poets Edmund Spenser, Lord Byron, and Wordsworth; twice a week she could attend the coeducational "University lectures" on her specialties of Middle English, the history of Anglo-Saxon literature, and Old English.

She was initially shocked at the attitude of these men. Dr. Wright, her Old English professor, was "trained in Germany and very rough and gruff, and he hates American students, especially women, — says they have no ability, anyway, only a little shallow enthusiasm...."[31]

But she found his course "interesting and [it] wakes up all the student in me again, and I have been impatient with my own students too often to feel that I am getting any more than my fair recompense when this choleric gentleman wants to throw the table at me.... I silently protest against his theory, but ... I am very glad to get it."[32]

Katharine found "a likable honesty about him, but what a savage!... Said he never looked at modern literature, anyhow."[33] Even worse, she felt, was that to him, "philology is everything and the literature nothing."[34] He was "vastly disgusted at my preference of literature to philology. He says he used to read poetry himself, — yes, used to <u>write</u> poetry, — but all that was pure ignorance. He would rather read a page of the dictionary any day than a page of Browning or Shakespeare. 'Poets, — why, they don't even know the meaning of the words they use.'"[35]

One day she went on a special outing to see the famous James Murray's workshop, the Scriptorium, "one of the sights of Oxford," where he was overseeing the assembling of the groundbreaking multivolume *Oxford English Dictionary*. He was "an old, old, very wise gentleman, with benevolent face and flowing, snow-white beard. The University has engaged him to write a Dictionary that shall be worthy of the attention of the enlightened English people. Common dictionaries they scorn...

"But Dr. Murray is making and has for many years been making, with a large staff of assistants, a mammoth dictionary, which shall be in many volumes and give fullest etymology and history of every word, with copious illustrations in chronological order. <u>They are now working on C.</u> This Herculean labor is carried on by gaslight in a long, low, narrow room, without windows, the walls lined with cubby-holes full of papers. The Clarendon Press has offered him large, well-lighted and well-ventilated rooms, but he clings to his little den, tho' many of his workers sicken and have to leave him....

"Well! We entered Dr. Murray's sanctum late in the afternoon, and the air was almost unbreathable. He very courteously began an explanation of the whole long process. I was vastly interested at first, then I became aware, to my horror, that his voice was getting further and further away and the room was turning black and beginning to swim. I clutched the table and held out a moment or two longer, thinking how awfully illiterate it would look to the English mind if an American should faint away at the mere sight of their dictionary, — but it was no use.

"I had to make a hurried excuse and just succeeded in getting to the door, where the open air, fog and all, was blessedness. The assistants sprang for a chair and a glass of water and the like with very suspicious alacrity, and I've since been told that nothing pleases them so much as to have a lady turn faint in their dreadful little prison-hole.... Dr. Murray, tho' I returned in a few minutes, regarded me with sorrowful disapproval and cut his explanations short."[36]

Clearly, American women should stay away from dictionaries in Oxford.

III.

Meanwhile, American men were seeking out Katharine and Annie in Walton Street. Some may have known of Katharine's writings, and Annie attracted others because of her famous and notorious Beecher family. Her great-aunt Harriet Beecher Stowe was, as Lincoln had quipped, the "little" woman whose radical portraits of slavery in *Uncle Tom's Cabin* had started the big Civil War. Her novel had sold more than a million copies in Britain, more than three times as many as in the United States. In addition, Annie's notorious grandfather, Henry Ward Beecher, was a world-famous preacher and possibly an adulterer. In 1887, at his death, the British press had recounted the salacious details of his scandal-filled life.

Katharine and Annie hosted their new friends with "at homes," informal times, "only fussing our pretty little maid, Rose, whose face is always smiling and whose hands are never clean, [to get] in a few flowers and [have] chocolate and little cakes on hand. We have bought some Oxford teacups and saucers, with the College crest on them, and mean to present them with much tenderness to our friends, when we get home."[37]

One afternoon, two of their "countrymen, a Princeton man ... and an instructor in English at the University of Minnesota, off on a two years' fellowship ... [stayed] an hour and a half.... Come to count [the American men studying at Mansfield College], there are certainly eleven. We invite only a very select few, — otherwise our cups and saucers would not go around."[38]

Oscar Lovell Triggs, that "instructor in English," was six years younger than Katharine, had graduated from the University of Minnesota the year before, and was taking Wright's course with her. With an oval face and a look of intellectual intensity in his eyes, in his photograph he appears poised to begin an energetic and lengthy discussion. He was the only man whose name she underlined in her diary.

Katharine enjoyed such socializing, one day chatting with a Mr. Smith in his "cozy study," going home to tea with him before a "cocoa party" at the all-women Somerville College, and "then to Mansfield again, for [a] lecture on Matthew Arnold. Such a Sunday! We were eating most all day, but it was so cold we didn't care."[39]

OSCAR LOVELL TRIGGS

Mansfield College was opened in 1889 by Congregational churches for the education of their ministers, but offered evangelical teaching, "without insisting on the adoption of particular theological doctrines,"[40] a good place for the free-thinking Oscar.

Katharine and Annie's outings involved both history and men. Once they "wandered through a dim old library, and in and out of silent, grassy, chrysanthemum-bordered, gray-walled quadrangles," and then had tea, "very elegantly served, but strong enough to break the cups, and … went to take supper with Mr. Smith, a Mansfield tutor, who reads four American papers a week. His mother presided and another Mansfield man [probably Oscar] was there and everything was charming."[41]

One rainy day she walked to the nearby village of Iffley, frankly noting in her diary what she did not write to her mother, that she was indeed happy with so many men around: "Came and went by towing path and greatly enjoyed the beauty of the misty, many-towered landscape. Enjoyed the sight of the University men pulling too, while others ran with the boats."[42]

Oscar talked with her about social reform, including William Morris's circle of artist and reformer friends who wanted to revive the traditions of English medieval handicrafts, in which the individual workman was valued. Katharine went with Oscar to see their work in Exeter Chapel before they explored Christ Church Cathedral, where they were so busy "delighting" in the Sir Edward Burne-Jones windows that they forgot to look at anything else.[43] At Keble College she marveled at Holman Hunt's painting, *The Light of the World*, but could barely see it because of the fog.[44] Keble's costly chapel reminded Katharine that, as Virginia Woolf would later point out in *A Room of One's Own*, men could generously donate money that they had inherited or earned to their sumptuous male-only colleges: Keble was "new ... built very magnificently.... The chapel is superb, — cost five hundred thousand dollars. I thought of Wellesley, struggling somewhere in the fourth thousand of her chapel fund, — and labor so much cheaper over here."[45]

She listened to a discussion in the Town Hall on trade unions and "on the best remedy for the social problem of the poverty of the many and the over-wealth of the few," Oscar's big concern.

> Mr. Courtney, [from] the House of Commons, presided, and first a representative of the tradesmen ... spoke, claiming that co-operation would do it all. Then a gentleman of the Fabian society, the non-Christian socialists, spoke, — a very winning young fellow — expressing his socialistic dream of an ideal society, but urging the working-men to be patient and wait for legislation.
>
> Then a very rude but effective speaker, secretary of the Iron Founders' Union of Lancashire, defended strikes, and an angry-faced young orator, president of the great London dockers' union, voiced the misery of East London, and finally one of the directors of the dock company, a most disgusted old gentleman, spoke for the capitalists.
>
> Then the audience, who had not been quiet a minute, always cheering or groaning, peppered the speakers with questions, the chairman summed up, awarding praise and blame in an impartial, parental fashion and urging technical education and the Golden Rule. A Professor gave thanks, our under-graduate seconded the motion, and we got home by midnight, too much excited to go to bed.[46]

At such events the injustice of English class system was clear.

Near the end of the fall term, Oscar came to call on her more frequently, on one occasion spending "three hours discussing the relation of art to nature."[47] As she and Annie prepared to depart from Oxford to visit London and the continent for their winter break, he stayed all evening.[48] She was careful to refer to him in letters to her mother as her "Yankee brother," and downplayed her feelings for him ("He's good for his age, but young"), while assuring Cornelia how homesick she was for her.[49] Even so, she spent much of her free time with Oscar and accepted his offer "to come flying" to her aid if she fell "into a den of thieves on the Continent."[50]

She had never been so flatteringly pursued by a man of her own educational background who shared her interests in literature and idealistic social reform. Oscar and her other male friends in Oxford helped Katharine start thinking about a life apart from her mother's dream for her of a professorship at Wellesley, where she could not have remained on the faculty as a married woman expected to devote her life to her husband and family.

IV.

Because of Oscar's courtship as well as Wellesley's rule that faculty must be church members, she warned her mother on Dec. 23, "I hope you will not feel disappointed or troubled to know that I seriously contemplate breaking my connection with Wellesley."[51]

When Katharine embarked for her year in England, she had expected her scholarly Oxford work to result in Wellesley's award of a master's degree and promotion to full Professor and head of the English Literature Department and a secure income. When she had first been hired at the college on a trial basis, the trustees had temporarily waived Mr. Durant's original statute that "every Trustee, Teacher and Officer should be a member of an Evangelical Church."[52] If she wanted this more lucrative promotion, she would need to join a church, or the statute would have to be changed.

Katharine refused to be ordered to join a church for this reason, feeling that her religious life was a private matter between herself and a divine power.[53] Now, if the College wanted to promote her, it would have to accommodate her firm stand against what she saw as the college's forcing faculty to publicly join a church for the sole sake of keeping their jobs.

After her good times with Oscar, it was not just the church issue that weighed on her, as she explained to her mother: "I have spent almost all my adult life in the village of Wellesley and I am very tired of girl-problems and girl-judgments. I do not think I could maintain my health there many months, for girls here in Oxford … tire me more than anything else…. I hope you will not be sorry about this. I am almost sure such a change would be best for me in every way."[54] Still with no permanent home or income herself, Cornelia must have been reluctant to see her daughter risk leaving her academic job that could provide income, housing, and a distinguished career.

But when Miss Hodgkins wanted Katharine to assure her that she grasped "the eternal verities" and would "maintain the divinity of Christ,"[55] that was the last straw. She feared that even if Wellesley accepted her and promoted her, she would never succeed as a writer if she returned to "that narrow, absorbing, timid, nerve-wearing life."[56] If she wanted to devote her life solely to her writing career or to a man, this would be the time for her to cut loose from Wellesley.

Unresolved, she bundled up in her steamer rug on a train to London with Annie to spend Christmas with English and American friends and took some rooms amid Bloomsbury's terraced rows of townhouses with their wrought-iron balcony railings and small private squares.

Because women were allowed to use the nearby British Museum's extensive library, many women of interest to Katharine had lived in this neighborhood to use its books. The pioneering feminist Mary Wollstonecraft, writer of the revolutionary *A Vindication of the Rights of Women*, had lived on Gower Street. The Pankhurst daughters, leaders of the English suffrage movement, grew up in Queen Square, where novelist Fanny Burney had lived. Writer Mary Russell Mitford had hosted Wordsworth in Russell Square, and Katharine liked to stay in poet Christina Rossetti's Torrington Square. Virginia Woolf would make this neighborhood her future home.

Soon Katharine and Annie were happily working away at the British Museum's famous Reading Room, "a beautiful great rotunda, full of concentric circles of books, with a large force of attendants to bring volumes to the readers, with comfortable seats at well-furnished desks and everything — except a little more oxygen, — that the heart of [a] student could desire.

"I didn't work hard, — simply loafed around and learned how to use the catalogues and took notes…. Many more men were reading than women, — some colored men, Africans and East Indians, among them, some Chinamen, many Frenchmen and Germans. A few of the men, even the librarians, kept their hats on. You know even the little boys wear tall silk hats over here."[57]

Its walls were cream and azure blue, and its structural ribs were gilded, as were the moldings and lines of the dome, panels, windows, and pilaster caps. With electric reading lights, it could stay open until 8 p.m. and welcomed over five hundred readers a day.

Katharine and Annie sat on mahogany chairs at long padded black leather-covered tables divided by tall partitions fitted with book rests and folding shelves for extra books, and warmed their feet on the tubular foot-rail filled with a current of warm water that ran end to end under each table which radiated out the from center enclosure occupied by the superintendent and his staff.[58]

Earlier in the century, Ruskin, Dante Gabriel Rossetti, poet Matthew Arnold, novelist George Meredith, and political theorist Karl Marx had worked at its tables. A.C. Swinburne, a favorite poet of Katharine's, had fainted from its lack of oxygen. Waiting for her books to be brought to her table, she might have caught glimpses of novelist and poet Thomas Hardy, of Leslie Stephen (literary critic and father of Virginia Woolf), of India's Mahatma Gandhi, of anarchist Peter Kropotkin, or of dramatist and Fabian Society reform activist George Bernard Shaw.

Its large catalogues, full of thousands of handwritten entries, required some strength to hoist. Even William Butler Yeats, the Irish poet whom Katharine would later invite to the Wellesley campus, recalled that when he used the library to compile Irish folklore legends, he was so delicate that he delayed consulting a necessary heavy book because he did not want to lift the heavy volumes.[59]

Katharine read in the great rotunda even though fog seeped in from outside and dimmed the electric lights, lunched in the lunch-room "(6 [pence] for chocolate and rolls, 2 [pence] for fee to waiter)," and strolled in the galleries after lunch admiring "Cleopatra's mummy and other pleasing objects."[60]

She loved it: "Spent the day in the reading-room of the Museum, making notes for summer work. Beautiful place. Warmed the book-worm heart of me."[61]

Then, she found her own prize-winning novel whose money had brought her to England in "the largest library in the world [among] a large number of grandfather Bates' discourses, one or two pamphlets by Uncle Joshua, Uncle Sam and Aunt Mary.... *Rose and Thorn*, published by Nelson and Sons, of London, [was] in a gorgeous binding of lavender with green-leaved, very red roses running all over it, inscribed on the outside: *A Story for Boys* and, within,

A Tale for the Young. My name is brilliantly printed on the cover, but no credit is given to the Cong. Pub. Soc. or to America."[62]

Although distressed that her "American" novel had been pirated by a London publisher (although an international copyright law had not yet been enacted), and billed in green letters as "a story for boys," she was heartened to see her own work shelved among her illustrious male ancestors' sermons.

Her little lavender clothbound book, with its "very red roses," is still in the British Library today. Its delicate cover decoration of little green tendrils and leaves with small red roses branching up the left side and across the top gives her book a romantic and medieval look, emphasized by the *R* in *Rose* set in a purple-outlined rectangle with a red background, like a medieval illuminated manuscript letter. By 2000, the British Library would contain fourteen more of her books published later in both London and the United States.

Nevertheless, Katharine was incensed with the English publishers who had pirated *Rose and Thorn* for their own profit. She "walked calmly" into Thos. Nelson and Sons publishers, 35 Paternoster Row, and had an interview with the manager, "a white-haired old Englishman, who squirmed in his chair" under her "rebuking gaze, for he knew they had stolen the book out and out, tho' he couldn't own it.

"He said: 'Ahem! Really can't remember just now the — ah — the precise terms of that arrangement.' Anyway, he gave me to understand (very politely) that even if I could prove they had stolen it, I couldn't under the former copyright conditions do anything about it. And I gave him to understand (with equal politeness) that I knew that as well as he did."[63]

V.

On her winter break from Oxford, Katharine got busy writing several pieces that reveal her quandary as a single woman. She pointed out that for a Norman lady, "there were open two possible destinies and only two. She might be nun or wedded dame; there was no middle path ... it [was] the duty *of* the wife to suffer all things in silence, letting her lord speak the words and be the master."[64]

Then, in "Woman as Scholar," she hoped, that if she remained a woman scholar, she could find new "heart-space" in academic work.[65]

But Oscar, later probably a free love advocate, may have suggested a different path for her—that of returning to Wellesley as a writer, a scholar, and his lover. She could be someone as independent as the novelist George Eliot (Mary Ann Evans), a woman criticized for living unmarried with a married man. Katharine described her as a brilliant thinker and intellectual, refusing to condemn her for her shocking personal life.[66]

To her mother, no doubt worried about her daughter's financial future, Katharine played up her hopes for a writing career, pleased that Miss Hodgkins suggested that she drop teaching and write juvenile literature, and pleased that the American Press Association wanted to publish her picture.[67]

But she had made no firm decision about her future and pressed on with Annie to Canterbury and Dover and then across the English Channel to Rouen, Paris, Cologne, Aix-la-Chapelle, Amsterdam, Leiden, and The Hague, before going to Rotterdam, Antwerp, Ghent, and Bruges. By the end of February, she was back in London where, probably pursuing Oscar's interest in social reform, she went to East London to visit "with joy of heart, the People's Palace."[68] This was Toynbee Hall, the famous pioneering settlement house that she would now be able to describe in detail to Vida and Katharine Coman.

Finally Katharine heard that Wellesley's Board of Trustees would simply now require "every Teacher [to] be of approved Christian character and influence, and in sympathy with the Evangelical views."[69]

This change, along with the many letters from her mother and colleagues and perhaps no word from Oscar, forced Katharine to make the decision she had been avoiding, as she wrote to her dear friend Katharine Coman: "I probably shall go back to Wellesley if I am well enough.

> I love Wellesley — love her so much more than ever now that she is <u>right</u> — and I think work at Wellesley as urgent and rich and noble as work anywhere in the world. Still, there is such a thing, with no disrespect to a square hole, as its not fitting a round peg, and when I am most a Wellesley teacher I always feel least myself.
>
> I think I should make a horribly bad Professor — honestly I do. I can't speak well, I dread to face even a class-audience, I'm sinfully bored by critical works on literature, I would

like to hold my peace instead of always having to talk, and a
crowd of people takes all the magnetism and life-enterprise
out of me. I don't mind the essential teaching, tho' I abominate
'lecturing.'...

And so I have slipped along at Dana Hall and College, year after
year, never really meaning to settle down into College work.[70]

In this letter, one of the few between them she did not later destroy, she
then revealed to Coman her new reason to return to Wellesley: "You are always
in my heart and in my longings.... It was the living away from you that made,
at first, the prospect of leaving Wellesley so heartachy ... and it seemed least of
all possible when I had just found the long-desired way to your dearest heart."[71]
Katharine could at least look to Katharine Coman for companionship and the
emotional stability of a deep friendship.

But it was her old friend Julia Eastman who understood the sacrifice Katharine
would have to make: her only "literary salvation" if she wanted to devote her life
to her writing would have been "a prompt withdrawal" from Wellesley.[72]

VI.

In March when Annie went back to the United States, Katharine returned
to Oxford. Oscar called on her before leaving for several months, and she
began spending time with other men, although she assured her mother that
she nipped "these frivolities in the bud...."[73] Even the Bodleian expanded her
social life when she met "an ex-Harvard tutor, a man of some Greek reputation," working in her alcove, and they became friends, "each having come to the
decision that the other was too free and easy to be English."[74]

She finally received Mrs. Durant's official letter: "...salary to begin at
$1200.00 as is the custom, and increase $100.00 a year till it reaches $1500.00."[75]

She confided to her diary, "I wish I knew what was right,"[76] and twelve
days later wrote to her mother, "I have not yet answered Mrs. Durant, but
since no light opens on any other path, I expect to write her my acceptance
in a few days."[77]

Since no "other path" such as a commitment from Oscar appeared,[78] she
accepted the Wellesley professorship.[79]

When he finally returned, she recorded his frequent calls in her diary but not in her letters home, now that they were unchaperoned in the flat without Annie: "May 16: Mr. Triggs in the evening. May 18: Mr. Triggs (lunch). May 19: Mr. Triggs in the evening. Long discussion of aesthetics. May 25: Triggs." On May 30, he walked her to Bagley Wood to hear the nightingale. "A beautiful walk, tho' we didn't hear the nightingale, but we heard an inspired blackbird and a far-away cuckoo."[80]

She was happy with him back—birds chirped in Exeter's garden, and even the blue emblazoned ceiling looked beautiful to her.[81]

The ideas of Oscar's William Morris occupied her when she concentrated on his "Defence of Guinevere,"[82] about the queen who chooses to love a man who was not her husband. Morris was a free thinker against Victorian conventional ideas of marriage, feeling instead that sexual relationships should not be possessive.[83]

She recommended that her family read Morris's *News from Nowhere*,[84] a utopian novel about brotherhood and individual fulfillment with radical views of women and sexuality, a novel where in "all sexual liaisons the partners are free to come and go."[85]

Oscar probably discussed his feelings about such ideas in their many long evenings and riverside walks. Later, at the University of Chicago, he published on William Morris and edited works on Walt Whitman, also known for his unorthodox views of sexuality.

With no apparent future plans with Oscar, by mid-August she was ready to come home from her "long exile."[86] Although she had enjoyed Oxford's hallowed manuscript collections, as a woman and American in Oxford, she had felt like an outsider.

However, that year Katharine had become a serious scholar and a woman whose company men desired. She received male callers, was invited on walks and to evenings of debate and lectures, and spent hours with Oscar. He would remain in Europe for one more year, but his enthusiasm for cutting-edge ideas of social reform and idealistic solutions to very real problems of poverty, class conflict, and workers' rights educated her. He gave her both a romance and a desire to take action to change the world.

She had been able to see her own country from the perspectives of Oxford's riches and its parochial attitudes towards Americans, especially women, and become increasingly aware of the fragility of the American ideal of democracy, now challenged by the growing gap between social classes.

As she had learned from Oscar, English medieval culture was present in 1890 not only in Oxford's Gothic architecture but also in the humanistic and shared community ideals of Morris's group. Like the families in her Falmouth village, who created their own "socialism" in her childhood, English social activists in the 1890s wanted to use communal values to eradicate the growing urban poverty and excesses of unregulated capitalism and imperialism.

Increasingly enthusiastic about the early English drama performed by the common laborers which was so valued by Morris and which she would soon teach, she wrote to her mother, "I've read all our English Miracle Plays and I think you would enjoy reading them, too. I'm full of plans for courses and that sort of thing."[87] Determined to get the maximum professional mileage possible out of her Oxford year, she began to plan the book that would take her to Colorado and on to fame.

VII.

Katharine knew that returning to Wellesley and taking Miss Hodgkins's place as the head of the English Literature Department would mean "a long goodbye to any original writing,"[88] and her diaries and letters from England sat waiting for her "story pen." But her students had missed her, as "friend and teacher," and they were delighted to have her back, showering her with "the warmest welcome which love and honor can give."[89]

She wrote to Miss Hodgkins that the department felt "rather waify and as if we were playing school," an "orphan department" without her,[90] but she took up the department reins, happy to see her three colleagues, after her year of listening to Oxford men.

Vida Scudder would be emphasizing social issues in the literature she taught and wrote. Margaret Sherwood, a new member of the department, with her wavy hair piled up on her head and engaging smile, taught a reduced course load so that she could write her fiction. Under a pseudonym she wrote popular novels with serious current themes.

Also new was Sophie Jewett, with dark, large pensive eyes and a delicate expression below her brown hair pulled loosely up. She was a poet and translator. With an "unerring sense of excellence, exacting standards of scholarship [and] her rich stores of English, French and Italian reading" she "lavished her full strength on class work, spending herself as a teacher with unstinted generosity."[91]

Like Katharine, these three lively and creative young women taught literature with the special insights and enthusiasm of writers, infusing their writing, scholarly work, and classrooms with their passion for social reform.

SOPHIE JEWETT

As Vida recalled, "The Department [was] an unusual group. Sophie Jewett, Margaret Sherwood, and I were the nucleus, working under the genial, witty, and resolute leadership of Katharine Lee Bates. Scrupulously she left us free in handling our courses, [but] ... her mind held firm control."[92] All close in age, they were also a congenial and supportive group of friends.

More students elected their courses than any others,[93] and Katharine soon was busy teaching eighty-six students, including juniors, seniors, and those pursuing master's degrees, while running her department and explaining the special mission of women's colleges that could best satisfy women hungering for the "intellectual bread" in their "single-minded pursuit of knowledge."[94]

Without a college education, she wrote, wives and mothers might remain "ignorant, narrow in view, stunted in mental growth and morally bewildered." Nearly 40,000 women had already graduated from American colleges, and so she looked forward to the next fifty years of reaping a "harvest of women, sound of body and of mind, frank and free and capable, beautiful in face and soul...."[95]

But by the end of her year as full professor and department head, Katharine was frustrated by the problems faced by the women faculty at Wellesley. At the Commencement Dinner in 1892, an evening when the beautiful campus grounds were illuminated with lanterns and an orchestra was waiting to serenade all the celebrants, "Miss Bates, in her usual happy manner, spoke on behalf of the faculty."[96]

She described the stressful competing demands on the faculty women to the Trustees: "We are scholars by consecration, educators by profession, and life to us fundamentally means labor."[97] She asked: "How shall the same individual devote herself effectively to the three vocations of woman, teacher, and scholar?"[98]

Then she wittily made her case: "For it is still a profession in itself to be a woman. We may read Hebrew, or Sanskrit, but we are not exempt from making calls, entertaining, chaperoning; we may calculate eclipses, but we are not set free from the tyranny of the needle. Even blue stockings [the traditional symbol of intellectual women] have to be darned. We have not better halves to keep our gloves mended for us and our bonnets in repair…. We live in our workshop. We eat with our apprentices off the bench. We sleep on the shavings."[99]

Good teaching required time and reflection: "How can we communicate the passion for truth unless we are ourselves in very deed truth-seekers and truth-finders…. Nothing in the Wellesley life, sweet and beautiful in so many of its aspects, wears our hearts out like this daily, weekly, yearly disappointment in our incessant struggle to secure the essential time, the essential quiet, the essential liberty of soul for genuine, fruitful study."[100]

Using English universities as her model, she argued that the faculty should have separate specializations in teaching or researching rather than all being overworked in both areas with no time to be "a woman," a suggestion the college never implemented.

VIII.

Hard financial times were still causing American workers to demonstrate for better working conditions. In Michigan 3,000 miners demanded an eight-hour shift for night work,[101] in the spring and early summer of 1891 Pittsburgh coke workers rioted,[102] Illinois coal companies ordered a lockout when the legislature passed a law for better working conditions,[103] and Seattle striking miners were replaced by scabs.[104]

Massachusetts workers wanted "fair" wages as well. Striking tanners in Woburn submitted to the state board of arbitration in hopes of getting a pay raise,[105] hod (cement) carriers in New Bedford went on strike for $1.75 a day, and the stonecutters in Springfield were locked out by their employers.[106]

On July 4, 1891, in Boston, the Central Labor Union "elucidated" Americans about "the truth that eight hours [a reduction in the working day] means high wages and better conditions … [and] by demonstrations in favor of the new declaration of economic independence."[107]

The country was heading toward a severe economic depression. Some farmers in the West were living in poverty, crop failure had brought famine to

South Dakota,[108] and the business climate of 1891 was uncertain.[109] Businessmen throughout the country called on Congress to create a new bankruptcy bill.[110]

The competition of immigrants with native-born workers for the dwindling number of jobs raised tensions. In 1887 the New American Party had proposed restricting immigration and naturalization of foreign-born people.[111] By 1890 Congress was considering legislation to shut out foreigners from doing business in the United States.[112] After nearly six million immigrants arrived in the 1880s, in 1890 the federal government established the Bureau of Immigration and selected New York's Ellis Island to be the country's first federal immigration station.[113]

The shortage of jobs helped cause racial, ethnic, and religious persecution. Californians wanted to make "Eastern people understand that the real and substantial sentiment of the Pacific coast" was "anti-Chinese";[114] Washington state citizens vowed to drive out Chinese workers;[115] and in Massachusetts, Italian "workingmen" were called "hoodlums."[116]

With racist lynch mobs and Jim Crow segregation growing,[117] Congress wanted to encourage African-Americans to move to Africa by giving them financial aid.[118] The *Transcript* ran news stories about Indian violence in the American West and the likelihood of "a prolonged war with the now fully roused savages," while presenting the Indian Rights Association's plea for more schools so there would be "a new generation of English-speaking people with scarcely a vestige of the Indian tongue or Indian customs remaining," [119] insisting that the Indians "must accept our civilization or cease to exist."[120]

The rich seemed to be growing richer on the backs of the poor. The Populist Party of 1892 asserted: "Corruption dominates the ballot-box.... The fruits of the toil of millions are boldly stolen to build up colossal fortunes for a few, unprecedented in the history of mankind; and the possessors of these, in turn, despise the Republic and endanger liberty."[121]

Railroad companies continued to form alliances with each other, enriching their millionaire owners. In Massachusetts, the wealth of railroads far surpassed the treasuries of the state.[122]

Monopolies of the "early oil, lead, sugar, leather, whiskey and beef combines with $15 and $20 million capitalizations" joined the railroad monopolies.[123] These giant corporations were accused of colluding with the government, of killing the American ideal of paying workers what they deserved, and of using them to devalue labor in order to "produce new fortunes of unprecedented size and power."[124] Professor Richard T. Ely, whom Katharine would soon meet, and other young economists established the American Economics Association, which called the corporations' laissez-faire economic approach "unsafe in politics and unsound in morals."[125]

At Wellesley, as speakers described these growing social and economic problems to the campus, Katharine supported attempts by Vida and by Katharine Coman, now a professor of political and social science, to find practical solutions to the country's growing problems. When asked about her own "philanthropic activities," Katharine replied, "I 'belong' to all the reform associations of all my philanthropic friends!"[126]

As Vida recalled, "Every one in those days was curious to see what girls who had had a college education would do with themselves, and it … forced us to be curious too."[127] In a settlement house, they could help those suffering in crowded city tenements, and give themselves an alternative to returning after graduation to living with their families as spinsters or to agreeing to unhappy marriages.

Katharine helped her friends create such a unique place in Boston, and Wellesley cheered, "A house has been secured on Tyler Street … in the midst of various classes of the working-people…. [T]his Settlement will give much careful attention and systematic study to social problems, and they hope that the intimate acquaintance with the working people, which ought to be gained through a life among them, will throw much light on the grave questions that are facing American society to-day, and will greatly aid in their solution."[128]

In December 1892, Boston's women's college settlement, Denison House, opened, with Coman elected chairman.

Vida described their inspiring vision of creating model communities: "The College Settlements Association is a real fellowship. The chapters … are full of intellectual and moral earnestness, awake to the social issues of the day, and capable of doing good service by helping to keep such interest [alive] in their college communities."[129]

IX.

In spite of the economic depression, Americans in Chicago were gearing up to celebrate the 400th anniversary of Columbus's "discovery" of the New World at their World's Columbian Exposition that would showcase American achievements—past and present—on a grand scale.

To draw the nation's attention to the Chicago Fair's dedication, patriotic words and poems filled the air on October 12, 1892. Alice Freeman Palmer, on the stage platform, excitedly looked out at 150,000 people listening to the "grand bands playing the Star Spangled Banner, everybody ... shouting wildly."[130]

Harriet Monroe heard her poem, "Columbian Ode," read to the huge audience.[131] (As the editor of the innovative *Poetry* magazine, she would later become a friend of Katharine's.) Schoolchildren across the country simultaneously recited the Pledge of Allegiance, newly adopted by Congress, partly because of a campaign Katharine's *Youth's Companion* had spearheaded. The magazine had sent a flag to fly over each schoolhouse that joined the recitation that October day.

Nations, states, cities, industries, artists, and colleges throughout the world had prepared exhibits for the millions of Fair visitors. To display its strong academic work, Wellesley sent exhibits from each academic department, like the one that Katharine prepared, because Alice Freeman Palmer, still a Wellesley trustee though now dean of women at the new University of Chicago, recognized the enormous visibility it would give a woman's college.

Meanwhile, Katharine hopefully waited for Oscar's letters. Until her year at Oxford, Katharine had only a few male admirers. In 1888, she confided to Annie her discomfort when she lived in a single room at Wellesley and entertained a Mr. Rodman:[132] "We had a horrid time. He wished to come again the next morning.... I have a reverence as well as compassion for him, but I don't like to have him hold my hand and shut all the doors and slip into 'Dear' and talk about 'the glorious liberty in purity permitted to the children of God.'... He teased to come ... to my room, but he made me so uncomfortable that I refused."[133]

Spending much time in Oxford with Oscar, she had experienced how buried passion could flare up:

> I deemed this ravening grief long since was slain,
>
> But yesterday, as I went forth to reap,
>
> Soft in his covert stirred mine ancient pain
>
> And rose upon me with a tiger-leap.[134]

With similar intensity, in "Heart of Hearts" she asked her lover to enter her innermost being:[135]

Will you come to my heart of hearts? 'Tis a path o'ergrown
with rue,

> Where rarely a footprint parts the mosses or dims
> the dew;

Yet there in the thorntree cloven her nest hath a song-bird
woven,

> And deep in my heart of hearts the love-lights burn
> for you.

The poem's images of an untouched virginal space inhabited by a song-bird, often a metaphor for a poet, suggest Katharine's own unfulfilled desires and a heart still radiant with memories: "When we builded with rustic arts a roof for the storm to mar. / Only the wind at the latches, but in through thy broken thatches, / O shrine in my heart of hearts, gleams a glory-tinctured star."

But by the fall of 1892, she had heard nothing from Oscar, even though he had completed his fellowship abroad, and she suffered more losses with the deaths of several of the brilliant and creative men who had valued her work and her career dreams, possibly as her own father would have. In December, Daniel Lothrop, her stalwart publisher and longtime friend and mentor, died. Then, during the next month Eben Horsford, who had assumed Durant's special role as a supporter of her work as a poet, died.

At thirty-three, Katharine was already past the age when most young American women married, but she may have still hoped for a man's romantic love. She described the pain of loving in a poem originally illustrated with a Cupid figure crying from a thorn prick on his thumb:

When it befortunes us, who love so dearly,

> To hurt each other, let us haste to wring,

This joy from our remorseful passioning;

The wound is witness that we love sincerely.

So slight a weapon, word or silence merely,

> Would scarce effect surprisal of a sting,

> Were't not my word, thy silence, for we cling

> One soul together. Life allots austerely

Unto the rose of love, the thorny power

> To tear the heart....[136]

In Oxford she had also written "To Truth," which portrays the bitter struggle of someone trying to escape the power of a deceitful lover. She is

> enmeshed and clouded so
>> In multitudinous error....
> For subtle filaments of falsehood blight
>> The pattern fair whereto my deeds would grow,
> And still their fruits are bitter in despite
>> Of all this groping of the roots below.

Her speaker commands Truth to rescue her:

> Melt thou these glooms and set the spirit free,
>> For save thou aidest, all my toil is vain,
> From deeps of darkness straining still toward thee,
>> Immortal only by the power to strain.[137]

In spite of what Katharine might have hoped for, her relationship with Oscar was over, perhaps for the best. An ambitious man, he would eventually marry the beautiful and well-connected Laura McAdoo, from Georgia, in 1899. She, however, later became involved with the cultural critic and womanizer Thorsten Veblen, who was dismissed from a university professorship because of his involvement with his female students. Oscar and Laura eventually divorced.[138]

THEOPHILUS HUNTINGTON ROOT

When Katharine used the word "roots" in her poem about truth, she may have been thinking of Oscar as well as Theophilus Huntington Root, another nice-looking mustachioed young man, who had come back into her life.

She probably met him through his sister, Elizabeth ("Lizzy") B. Root, in her Wellesley Class of 1880.[139] Two years younger than Katharine, he had first worked in a bank for three years before deciding to apply to Harvard. To prepare for its demanding entrance exams, he needed to review his Greek and Latin.

Katharine was then teaching high school in Natick, and he was in nearby Framingham working "assiduously" at his studies.[140] She would have made an ideal tutor for him, and his entry in his Harvard class book describes a romance that could have been with her:

> That year I worked harder than I ever did, before or since. But when spring came on, a factor ... now proved a source of much disturbance judged from the point of view of study. I was, to tell the truth, in love. Study had a strong rival. My interest in Greek and Latin flagged. Many hours which should have been devoted to them were spent in rides and rows and walks. My excuse was the reflection that after so many hours of close application cracking and trying to crack the hard dead shells of the classic languages, I needed the relaxation afforded by intercourse with a congenial friend.
>
> This youthful love ripened into a strong friendship which has continued with increasing strength to the present time ... because with its sincerity and earnestness it has been one of the pleasantest features of my recent life.[141]

In his long class entry, Theophilus comes across as a chatty, fairly entertaining young man, who describes his bicycle-riding, running, and humorous adventures trying to sell books, door to door. But he decided that he "could accomplish more good in the ministry than in business or medicine,"[142] and so did enroll at Harvard.

Sadly, in the spring of 1888 Katharine probably saw him at the funeral of his sister Lizzy in Framingham,[143] which she described to Annie as a "bleak morning, already beginning to howl," in which to "carry their classmate to her rest."[144]

Theophilus graduated from Yale Divinity School in 1890 and studied at Harvard Divinity School in 1891-92, Katharine's first year back from Oxford. Ordained as a Congregational minister in 1892 in Framingham, he accepted a position as a tutor in New Testament subjects when the University of Chicago opened.

On the rebound from Oscar, Katharine welcomed Theophilus into her life, noting significant moments with "T.H.R." in her new "Line a day" diary.[145] When she left this diary for future biographers, she left his initials in it, a sign of his importance to her.[146]

That February Katharine published "Valentine" in *The Independent*. Her speaker says, "Good-night, True Heart!" before hoping that St. Valentine will assure her of her beloved's presence for another twelve months, having had him always with her in her dreams: "I awake to the grace of thy visioned face, / My soothfast morning-star."[147]

Unfortunately, Theophilus, in spite of all his academic degrees and compatible family background, would have been unable to support Katharine, let alone a family, had she married him. He was just beginning his career while she was already a popular professional writer, a respected literary scholar, and professor at a top women's college, a job she could not duplicate in Chicago.[148]

Feeling that she must tell him goodbye, Katharine wrote mournfully in her diary, "Classes. The last letter fr. T.R. that I will ever read."[149] The next day she spent in "Much weary meditation on T.H."[150] Then: "Meditation on T.H. Wrote last letter to him. Did up his to return."

Depression—"Blues deepening to indigoes"—enveloped her.[151] Three days later: "Physical and moral nausea, but think I'm a little better." He was not making it easy for her: "Letter from T.H.R. wh. returned." The next day she was suicidal: "Nerves on edge. Episode of the carving knife. Ill."

She had faced serious depression earlier in her life, as she had confided to Annie in 1888: "I am as near the thought of suicide as it is safe for me to be. The labor seems to call to me day and night, and it is hard to eat or sleep … but whether I can endure the summer or not, I can't yet tell."[152]

Again desperate, on April 1, 1893, she went to Boston to see a doctor for help, "like an April fool," noting in her diary, "Returned two letters from T.H.R." But then, "More letters fr. T.H.R. Wrote note."

She taught her classes but "Went to bed with neuralgic headache."[153] And she noted, perhaps with ambivalent feelings, that "Katharine [Coman is] back…. Wretchedly weak. Disastrous evening." Then she talked "T.H.R. thro' with K.C.," who wanted her own special relationship with Katharine. A week later, "Blue. Conquered myself in part."[154]

Katharine Coman had exciting plans for them—both women would teach summer school in Colorado Springs and stop in Chicago to visit Coman's parents and sister. But Katharine was not over Theophilus, when once more on a Sunday, she admitted: "Pitiful effort for 'a Spring vacation.' Heat, wind, dust. Drove to Mt. Auburn [Cemetery]. Saw beautiful purple [flowers]."[155] And perhaps T.H.R.

She was determined to recover, noting, "Mr. Smith [perhaps from Mansfield College] to dinner. Pretty new dress."[156] Keeping busy, Katharine chaperoned three Wellesley students to Worcester, Massachusetts, for the new intercollegiate press association banquet. The Amherst Glee and Banjo Club sang and played, and male colleagues attended—perhaps Oscar or Theophilus.

Coman took her to a dinner at Denison Settlement House in Boston, where they listened to the "Anarchist. — Mr. Swift — in evening."[157] In Hamlin Garland's "Under the Lion's Paw," Katharine heard the story of how hardworking farmer Haskins cannot believe his ears when he realizes that all his hard work will only give land speculator Jim Butler more profit: "Haskins sat down blindly on a bundle of oats near by, and with staring eyes and drooping head went over the situation. He was under the lion's paw. He felt a horrible numbness in his heart and limbs. He was hid in a mist, and there was no path out."[158]

Perhaps Katharine identified with him.

X.

Chicago had worked feverishly to rise from the ashes of its 1871 fire as a modern city, a gateway to the western two-thirds of the country. By 1890, with one million inhabitants, Chicago was second in population only to New York among American cities, and was at least briefly among the most populous cities in the whole world. As pioneering settlements expanded westward, it presided over America's western territories at the moment of their greatest population growth.[159] The "windy city," so-called because of all the hot air in the voices of its booster citizens, seemed to embody the future of the West and of the nation, with all the world its empire.[160]

**"THE COLUMBIAN ILLUMINATIONS ...
THE SPLENDORS OF THE ADMINSTRATION BUILDING"**

Chicagoans wanted Americans to see that their city was the result of America's growth and to celebrate America's "discovery" by Columbus with a spectacular fair.[161] They constructed more than two hundred buildings on two square miles of grounds, an area nearly more than three times the size of the 1889 Paris Exposition. With its elegant white classical buildings illuminated by electricity—a first for a world's fair—its "White City" was stunning, especially when seen from the unique Ferris Wheel, built to surpass the engineering wonder of the Eiffel Tower in Paris.

Katharine was one of many Americans thinking about Chicago. Promotional letters, pamphlets and articles, perhaps 50,000 to 60,000 pieces, inundated Americans that spring,[162] many urging them to visit the Chicago Fair and then head west.

Nearby stood the revolutionary new University of Chicago, which now employed both Oscar Triggs and Theophilus Root. Its young and brilliant president, William Rainey Harper, had received his Ph.D. from Yale University at the age of eighteen and persuaded the Baptist John D. Rockefeller to invest one million dollars in the University of Chicago, which would rival Congregationalist Yale.

Harper "shamelessly" robbed Yale, Harvard, Cornell, Hopkins, and others of "their best men" for his faculty, envisioning his school as the "University of the West."[163] Oscar was beginning his Ph.D. work at the University of Chicago, where his interest in social good fit right in with Harper's desire for his school's activist professors to influence public policy through their "laboratory" courses and community outreach.[164]

Then Harper hired Theophilus as a Tutor in his own field of Biblical studies, a big compliment, and made him his assistant on *The Biblical World*, the scholarly journal that Harper personally edited.[165] Proud of his name in a first-rate scholarly publication, Theophilus mailed the issue with his article to Katharine.

Also, Harper had employed Alice Freeman Palmer as his dean of women to help him shape his new school to attract the number of female students necessary to fill up its new classrooms. In exchange, he agreed to accept women into his graduate schools so that more women would be qualified for college faculty positions, like those at Wellesley.[166] (She spent much of her time, though, back in Cambridge with her Harvard professor husband.)

With Theophilus and Oscar in Chicago, Katharine Coman's invitation, and her romantic life in shambles, Katharine hurriedly wrote up lectures on early English drama for her Colorado Springs summer school students. Now an authority on pre-Shakespearean drama, she could draw on her Oxford research and her talent of telling a good story to invigorate a dry topic.

She rushed to prepare for the job that would pay for her train ticket west: "May 22: Made a start on the Colorado lectures.[167] May 27-29: Worked on Colorado lectures. May 31: Finished first Colorado lecture. June 5: Ground away on Colorado lecture. Would rather play. June 7: Wrote all day. Finished 2nd Colorado lecture. June 9: Hard scratching at lecture. June 11: All day long at lecture. June 14: Worked on lectures. June 15: Worked hard finishing lecture III. June 17: Worked all day. June 18: Clouded the whole beautiful Sunday with lecture IV. June 19: Worked to exhaustion on that everlasting lecture. June 20: Finished lecture."[168]

Theophilus still courted her with letters. On June 21, she gave herself a day in Cambridge at Harvard, probably with him. In spite of her resolve to end things, she admitted, "Alumnae Day, Harvard Fishpond. Lovely time all day."[169]

She finished her lectures just in time to board her train for America's West, where prairies and mountains awaited her.

CHAPTER SIX

1893
"AN ENCHANTED SUMMER"[1]

I.

Exhausted from weeks of frantic lecture-writing and heartache over Theophilus Root, Katharine boarded her train heading west from Wellesley to Chicago.

With her auburn hair pulled up in a bun, she exuded both warmth and dignity. Her brown eyes, intelligent behind little spectacles, must have shone with good humor and a ready wit, and although short in stature, she carried herself with the erect posture and attentive expression of an accomplished professional woman.

Her train's steam engine hissing and coal dust flying above her, she was on her way to see the young and huge America west of Boston, thanks to her summer school salary, which would pay for her trip. Her first stop was the remarkable American sight of Niagara Falls whose "glory and … music" thrilled her.[2] Then it was on to the bustling city of Chicago, where Katharine Coman welcomed her and whisked her off to Chicago's World's Columbian Exposition, the majestic fair that commemorated America's first four hundred years.

Although Katharine would be able to thoroughly explore it on her way home later in the summer, she was dazzled by its "White City," sparkling fountains, ponds, and lagoons reflecting buildings the color of alabaster—a scene she called a "thing of Beauty."[3] Brass bands played marches by John Philip Sousa, sightseers crunched on Cracker Jack, and the surprising new Ferris Wheel lifted its passengers above the exotic Midway to view Theophilus's brand-new University of Chicago in the distance near the shores of Lake Michigan.

THE SOUTHERN VISTA

But just what defined "America"? Was it the Liberty Bell display made of oranges, the horse statue made of California prunes, or the thousand paintings by American artists such as Winslow Homer and Mary Cassatt? Was 1893, full of serious economic and social problems tearing the country apart, really the high point of American progress?

Katharine had plenty of time to think about her country aboard her Colorado-bound train on the Fourth of July, 1893. As the fertile fields and prairies of Illinois and Missouri rolled by her window, her "New England eyes" delighted "in the wind-waved gold of the vast wheat-fields."[4]

She was fortunate to be going to a paying job as part of the progressive and idealistic young faculty of Colorado's Summer School at a time when many other Americans were jobless, hard hit by the fast-spreading financial crisis.

She would be teaching in the new (as of 1876) Centennial State of Colorado in a special kind of frontier town, where the civilized polo-playing "little London" of Colorado Springs met the untamed wilderness at the foot of Pike's

Peak. While she taught Chaucer and early English drama, other faculty would be teaching how to prospect for gold in the boomtown of Cripple Creek, just a stagecoach ride away.

"PIKE'S PEAK AT SUNSET—THE MOUNTAIN SHADOW IN THE EASTERN SKY"

In a *Harper's Weekly* illustration, "Pike's Peak at Sunset,"[5] armchair travelers could see how tiny the new town of Colorado Springs looked from the summit of Pike's Peak. Giant boulders sit at the top of the mountain, far above the timberline, curving across the foreground. Two adventurous hikers perch on a large rock to admire the view below, while other hardy climbers stand near the rustic summit house looking at the town below on the edge of the prairie stretching to the horizon. In the corner of the engraving is an oval insert of the view looking at Pike's Peak from the east, with Colorado Springs nestled in its foothills, the sun setting behind it in the West—an irresistible destination.

Rather than sail to Europe to see the vastness of the Alps, Americans had begun to discover their own sublime landscapes, from the picturesque White Mountains of New England to Colorado's dramatic Rocky Mountains.

Katharine's Summer School "Prospectus" assured her that she would be living in "the most beautiful spot in the Rockies … a charming city of about 13,000 inhabitants, situated on a plain 6,000 feet above the sea level and just at the base of the foothills. Its environs are grand in the extreme … and its social and intellectual life compares favorably with that of the most cultured city in the East."[6]

How could she resist such attractions for her summer adventure in the exciting West with the vibrant Katharine Coman? When her train rounded the bend that brings the magnificent Front Range of the Rocky Mountains finally into view, Katharine was delighted.

The towering blue, green, and purple mountains rose out of the flat golden plains, filling her with a sense of "sublimity."[7] She would be teaching "under the purple range of the Rockies, which looked down with surprise on a summer school."[8]

Her train chugged along between Fountain and Monument creeks, and with its bell clanging, nosed into the impressive Denver and Rio Grande Western Railroad Station. With a tile floor, walls of Colorado "glass stone," and a twenty-foot ceiling of Colorado spruce, it had been built for $16,000 to welcome the tourists who often generated $30,000 in ticket sales a day.[9]

Katharine made her way through the crowd to the wide oak doors. About to begin her Colorado summer, she was sure that her journey had made her a "better American" on that Fourth of July.[10]

II.

To the northwest of the Colorado Springs train station, across Fountain and Monument creeks, are the remnants of the original settlement, the "old" town of Colorado City created by fur trappers and mountain men, and then by silver and gold prospectors. A supply town in 1859 while Colorado was still part of the Kansas Territory, Colorado City briefly became the Territory seat in 1862.

In 1871, the romantic and energetic General William Jackson Palmer began buying up land on the other side of Fountain Creek for the elegant town of his imagination. Self-trained as an engineer, inventor, and planner, he was a problem solver who thought and lived unbounded by things as they were, and like Henry Durant, dreamt of creating a unique community.

He was born into a family of Pennsylvania Quakers in 1836, but at the coming of the Civil War, despite his religious beliefs, he joined the Cavalry of the Union Army. At the war's end he left for the West, vast enough to provide his talents and energy the scope they needed, where Kansas, Colorado, and Mexico became his new "theaters" of command, campaigns, and triumphs.

He decided to build his own railroad, the Denver and Rio Grande. Unlike other railroads, his would use a narrow gauge track to scale the rugged mountainsides and run south from the silver mining center of Denver through the southwest to the rich mining areas of Mexico City. He planned to buy up the lands surrounding his railroad lines, build towns whose property sales would finance the railroads, and return good profits to his Eastern and English investors.

Then General Palmer fell in love, appropriately, on a train, with a beautiful nineteen-year-old woman, with large eyes and wavy hair, Mary Lincoln "Queen" Mellen, from the East. A month later they were engaged.

He charmed her into sharing his romantic dream, writing to her: "Just before sunset we came in sight of the mountains, Pike's Peak, Spanish Peaks and Greenhorn Range. A thunder-storm came on and the clouds threw themselves into grand and fantastic shapes, blending with the mountain peaks so as to scarcely be distinguishable. Riding as usual on top of the coach I got wet, but what of that?"[11]

He was awakened, he wrote, "by the round moon looking steadily into my face when I found the magnificent Pike's Peak towering immediately above at an elevation of over 14,000 feet, topped with a little snow. I could not sleep any more with all the splendid panorama of mountains gradually unrolling itself, as the moon faded and the sun began to rise, but sleepy though I was, I sat up and drank in, along with purest mountain air, the full exhilaration of that early morning ride."[12]

Breakfasting near spectacular red rock formations, Palmer knew he had found the "enticing scenery" necessary to attract visitors and settlers, writing to Queen: "The scenery is even finer South of Denver than North of it, and besides, the grass is greener, there is more water, a little forest of pine occasionally, and the sight is gladdened by the rude but comfortable farm-houses.... Down in the valley of Monument Creek will be the farms of industrious ranchers that will supply this Eden with what it requires."[13]

Palmer pictured his friends joining them in this paradise: "They would be glad to make their summer homes here ... where the air is fraught with health and vigour, and where life would be poetry—an idyll of blue sky, clear intense atmosphere, fantastic rock, dancing water, green meadow, high mountain, rugged canyon, and distant view of the kind that gives wing to the imagination and allows no foothold for it to halt upon, short of infinity."[14]

Even the winter landscape was a tonic to him, a landscape to transform all who saw it: "The day has been one of those crisp winter days, cold and bright, with the ground just covered with snow, which are so beautiful in a mountain country.... Pike's Peak, Long's Peak and the higher peaks along the whole range of the Rocky Mountains looked in an instant down upon us, as though, like the sun or moon, they had just risen above the horizon. They were covered with snow to the base and looked in the clear sunlight so exquisitely pure and serene, that I could imagine a glance at them would calm the most excited and troubled mind; all stormy passions and jealousies, angers and fear, would surely be exorcised and driven out by the grand calm beauty of these Heights."[15]

Queen agreed to make their home in the West. Palmer wanted his colony to be a place "where Republican institutions will be maintained in pristine purity,"[16] to appeal to like-minded families with sufficient incomes as well as to investors from the East who brought their New England village concepts and money. With its warm springs, his town began to lure visitors to its spa-like atmosphere created to rival such resorts as those in Saratoga Springs, New York, and Newport, Rhode Island.[17]

He was eager to attract English people, to create an ambience of culture and encourage Anglophile imitation.[18] One such was British investor William Blackmore, who christened one of the springs "Manitou" to associate the area with the great Indian deity in Longfellow's best-selling *Song of Hiawatha,* which had popularized legends of America's earliest people.

A year before Katharine's arrival, in June of 1892, American writer Richard Harding Davis described the English rituals there of afternoon tea, riding the hounds (with a coyote substituting when necessary for a fox), and polo playing on the grounds of the Broadmoor Casino in his series, "The West From A [Train] Car Window." He wrote that in Colorado Springs, the "Eastern man and woman ... are much more in evidence than the born Western man [recognizable by] the smartness of their traps and the appearance of their horses."[19]

Palmer reportedly had told the surveyors platting the house lots, wide streets, and parks, "Take your center line from here to the summit, reverse your instrument, and you have Pike's Peak Avenue."[20] *Harper's Weekly* showed fashionably dressed ladies and gentlemen strolling along that wide avenue to the newly built first-class Antlers Hotel under the snow-capped mountain range, as well as four slender young men guiding their well-behaved horses over the prairie polo field, gracefully swinging their mallets at the ball.

Nevertheless, while its English traditions might have been the reason Katharine had been hired to teach courses in Chaucer and English religious drama, it was, just as Palmer had hoped, the spectacular Colorado setting that entranced her. She joked that her classes on centuries-old literature, perhaps in contrast to other up-to-date courses on local geology and socialism, "seemed incongruous enough under that new and glowing sky."[21]

Palmer believed that the sublime Front Range of the Colorado Rockies, "all covered with snow, [arising] pure and grand, from the brown plains" could transform those who gazed at them: "As I looked I thought, 'Could one live in constant view of these grand mountains without being elevated by them into a lofty plane of thought and purpose?'"[22]

Katharine certainly could not. Under those grand mountains that summer, she would rise into such a lofty plane and find her voice as a poet.

"PIKE'S PEAK FROM COLORADO SPRINGS"

III.

She settled into her rooms in the newly opened (1883) state-of-the-art Antlers Hotel.[23] Gables, turrets, towers and balconies, Gothic furniture, billiard rooms, gas lights, hydraulic lifts and indoor bathrooms made it "the foremost hotel of the Pike's Peak Region ... one of the most delightful hotels in all our land ... substantially built and elegantly furnished."[24]

But it was with an aching head that Katharine, dizzy from the 6,000-foot altitude, joined other women sweltering in corsets, petticoats, long skirts, high-collared shirtwaists, and hats, promenading amid the dust clouds from bicycles, and the horses and buggies, with their flies and manure smells.[25]

Colorado Springs, in its flat open rawness and red soil under the deep blue sky and breathtaking mountain backdrop, was a still a work in progress. Its newly planted telegraph poles and spindly young saplings lined wide unpaved streets daily watered down by horse-drawn sprinkler wagons.

At Queen's suggestion, the street names celebrated Western landscapes, with the east-west streets named for rivers, and the north-south streets, for mountain ranges and canyons.[26] Their names told Katharine of the state's historic Spanish and French explorers. How far away from the New England street names of "Main" or "Elm" were the exotic "Vermijo," "Cimarron," "Tejon," "Sierra Madre," and "Cache la Poudre."

Grand rambling three-story Victorian homes marked the way to Colorado College on mostly empty North Cascade Avenue, where Palmer envisioned shade trees, green lawns, and gardens full of roses, irises, and lilacs from the East lining his gracious parkway.

From her hotel, Katharine could walk to dressmakers, tailors, a cigar store, two railway stations for the five railroad lines, several livery stables with carriages of all sizes to hire, new office buildings for 141 mining companies,[27] and the fancy Opera House.

She could also pore over the daily *Colorado Springs Gazette*'s broadsheet pages with eight columns of small print crammed with national and local news, gossip, notes on travel in England, national baseball scores, reviews of current literary magazines, and mining stock quotes, as well as advertisements for shoes, hats, neckwear, underwear ("an excellent line of summer novelties"), portrait photographers, banjos, laxatives ("Syrup of Banana ... Nature's Laxative"), and sightseeing expeditions, as well as railroad timetables with special fares to

Chicago's Columbian Exposition and its daily attendance numbers. Of special interest to her, it ran good coverage of the main attraction that summer: the Colorado Summer School, created as an important element of Palmer's ideal frontier community.

The wealthy citizens of Colorado Springs welcomed its faculty, especially the women, to the West, where men far outnumbered women, as Katharine recalled thirty-five years later: "When we were not actually lecturing we were beset by the most generous and varied hospitalities."[28] She was soon listening to banjo concerts and riding in the moonlight with her escorts Will Coffin, a mining broker, and Atherton Noyes, a Yale University graduate and secretary of the Summer School.

Somewhat of a celebrity as a female scholar and professor, with all-female Wellesley's academic grind miles away, Katharine began to enjoy the swirl of teas, receptions, "hen parties," carriage outings, and dances. On her first evening a carriage brought her up the imposing circular driveway to the wide two-story Broadmoor Casino with its long colonnaded veranda and Palladian windows, a hotel resort built in "the grand European manner."[29] Set in the foothills of Cheyenne Mountain on a $30,000 lake created for boating,[30] it served full-course dinners and employed a Hungarian band to play frequent concerts as well as for ballroom dances.

But not even waltzing with Will Coffin could take Katharine's mind off Theophilus. She wrote dejectedly in her diary, "Homesick. Listless."[31] She did rally for "Boys and banjos,"[32] and was "better" the next day when Will took her to see one of Colorado Springs' most famous sites, the Garden of the Gods.[63] Its forest of giant coral-colored sandstone rocks, stunningly rising up out of green scrub and evergreen trees below the progressive greens, blues, and purples of the distant mountains, stood in sharp relief against the vivid blue sky.

In her working notebook she wrote: "red as with memories of sacrifice ... gorgeous   cliffs—furrowed—labyrinth—buff—lilac—orange—brown—pillars and obelisks and colonnades— ... vermilion crags ... Mountains—gorgeous. Earth has 'dipped her cliffs in sunset.' Palisades. Palpable splendor."[34]

A few days later Katharine Coman arrived, and they began their adventures: "We were driven to Manitou, to the Garden of the Gods, to the grave of Helen Hunt Jackson, to canyons, lakes, glens, bluffs, and cascades innumerable, all so marvelous that our stock of exclamations gave out. An enchanted summer! We loved it all."[35]

Near Manitou Springs, they hiked in their long skirts up to the famous Ute Pass in the Pike's Peak foothills where, in the 1820s, the Sioux and Arapahoe on the Plains and the Utes had lived on the land that Palmer later appropriated as the site of Colorado Springs.

The two Katharines did not meet Palmer, who was in England, but they did visit Glen Eyrie, the first home that he built for Queen in 1872, in the mouth of a great canyon on seventy-five hundred acres of ravines, huge round hillsides, and rock pinnacles.[36] Constructed of wood with several pointed roofs and towers repeating the shape of the rocks and hills around it, Glen Eyrie celebrated its grand mountain setting with large windows and viewing balconies.

They then set off for popular poet, novelist, and Indian rights activist Helen Hunt Jackson's Cheyenne Canyon, where bubbling waterfalls cascaded down the creek-bed between rosy and gray colored granite crags. Hearty walkers, the two Wellesley professors would have laughed at the female picnickers who arrived later in the afternoon and "espied a piece of phosphorescent wood, decided that it was the eyes of a wild animal shining in the darkness and became hysterical [and] were brought down with considerable difficulty."[37]

Katharine Coman began to fill Theophilus's void, organizing their sight-seeing outings, hikes, carriage rides, and excursions, and strengthening her own loving relationship with Katharine, who began to understand "KC"'s "Westering Heart, Restless Heart, Heart of the Pioneer /...Lover of far horizons, eager to bring them near, / Journeying Heart, Yearning Heart, rover of land and sea"[38] and her "mountain look, the candor of the snow,/ The strength of folded granite, and the calm / Of choiring pines, whose swayed green branches strow / A healing balm."[39]

A fascinating companion, Coman enthusiastically embraced her life as an independent woman.

IV.

Their "Colorado Summer School of Science, Philosophy, and Languages," was overseen by Palmer's Colorado College. A self-educated man of wide reading who could quote Elizabeth Barrett Browning's poetry to Queen, Palmer believed a college should encourage lifelong learning for all, and in 1873, set aside twenty acres of land for it,[40] and a strong town-and-gown relationship began.

The 1893 summer school welcomed anyone who wanted to participate in a kind of Chautauqua experience of intellectual enrichment with the students to its lectures, concerts, and field trips. Katharine found herself once more a distinguished faculty member at a young college created by a charismatic idealist, this time with strong ties to her father's Congregationalism.

Each of its early presidents helped shaped the college. Thomas Nelson Haskell had attended Oberlin College in Ohio, the first college in the United States to admit women (1837), and the first major northern college to educate African-Americans. He wanted Colorado College to be modeled after Oberlin, and it opened as a co-educational college with a woman on the faculty.

Its second president, Edward Payson Tenney, a graduate of Dartmouth College and a Congregational minister, conceived of the "New West," the Rocky Mountain region, "as both the last frontier and the last opportunity to found educational institutions to promote religiosity and morality on that frontier."[41] He wanted a nonsectarian college to include Mormons, Mexicans, Indians, "and the heterogeneous border population."[42]

And, eleven years before Katharine stayed in Colorado Springs, Tenney predicted what was happening to her: "One of the best of God's creatures is the Yankee enlarged by coming west!"[43]

The next president, William Frederick Slocum, another Congregational minister, assembled the 1893 Summer School faculty. A man committed in his own career to finding solutions to troubling social issues, especially urban poverty, Slocum recruited like-minded professors from Amherst College, Wellesley College, the University of Chicago, and Oxford University, brilliant scholars and teachers committed to social and economic reform.

Its summer school offered public school and college teachers "higher professional training" and the experience of "receiving the new ideas that always come from [associating] with others pursuing similar lines of work." In it "students and teachers in the West [could have] an opportunity to come personally in contact with the brightest minds and most progressive spirits of the country," and "weary with the year's work in the college or school room, [they could] pursue the course of study most congenial, amid the most charming surroundings."[44]

The school would furnish the "most delightful courses in every department of Science, Philosophy, and Modern Languages,"[45] and its teacher-students could economize by sleeping in tents.

Katharine taught her courses on the college campus a mile north of the city in Palmer Hall, built earlier that year of rough-hewn gray stone in a classical Boston Gothic style of architecture. It had two symmetrical peaked wings balancing the three-peaked center section, long rectangular windows, and narrow columns flanking the deeply arched central doorway. Strong Colorado winds blew around it, and instead of seeing green trees and the shores of blue Lake Waban below her classroom in Wellesley's College Hall, Katharine looked out on a treeless prairie.

Now she had to do what she dreaded most—lecture to an audience of all ages and educational backgrounds, some arriving for one afternoon lecture with no preparation and others enrolled for serious college-level work, along with town visitors, many of them from England, who demanded both a scholar and a good speaker for their teacher. Anyone could buy a ticket to her lectures, with no obligation to prepare the readings suggested in the school's "Prospectus."

To lecture to such a mixed audience, to the best-prepared students as well as to the visitor who wandered in off the street, Katharine needed energy, careful preparation, and good humor in the July afternoon heat. She taught the "Origin and Development of English Drama" and Chaucer, topics she knew well from her graduate work at Oxford.

She also had to welcome her faculty colleagues into her classroom and visit theirs. Dr. William J. Rolfe, a Shakespeare authority from Cambridge, Massachusetts, who often lectured at Wellesley, and was familiar to the many high school and college students who used his numerous editions of Shakespeare,[46] was her supervisor.

Even he had trouble at first in satisfying his keen Colorado Springs students, with one complaining in the *Gazette* that he should not be so "elementary. His class is altogether capable of assimilating stronger mental diet."[47]

In the West, Katharine could teach alongside male professors, a professional position almost impossible for her anywhere else, and she was paid third on the salary scale.[48] Her pay was a sign of both her rank and the demand for her courses.[49]

Katharine found herself right at home in a town used to such creative women as Queen Palmer, and such free-spirited writers as Rose Kingsley and Grace Greenwood. Colorado Springs women had helped create their coeducational college and assumed women's leadership roles in the many women's clubs and committees, making the previous Summer School a success.[50] Englishwomen in Colorado Springs had even generously founded the Tuesday Club to correct the grammar and pronunciation of local townswomen.[51]

Women's participation in civic affairs was on the front burner in Colorado politics that summer because of the upcoming November statewide binding referendum on the issue of women's voting rights in state elections. While Katharine was teaching her students how to pronounce Chaucer's Middle English, the Equal Suffrage League meeting was discussing women's voting rights, "a subject of great interest."[52] A few months later, a cartoon in the *Denver Republican* reminded its male readers: "Don't Forget the Women When You Vote on Tuesday."[53] Colorado would be the first state where women won their suffrage rights by a direct vote of the male voters.[54]

President Slocum's young but distinguished faculty, progressive thinkers like Katharine, would help shape the social, economic, and cultural future of the United States. President Andrews of Brown University taught political economy; Richard T. Ely lectured on socialism's nature, strength, weakness, and practicality; and Dr. Edward W. Bemis of the University of Chicago addressed the growing national economic crisis in his lectures.

Katharine Coman taught the "Industrial History of England," and even Mr. Ryley from the English Department taught "The Evolution of Freedom," culminating in a lecture on "The Social Ideal." His course, said the Prospectus suggestively, was "designed to afford a basis for the right reading of our own history."[55]

Such courses attracted students from throughout a state hit hard by layoffs in the mines, currency inflation, and the threat of violent labor conflicts, and they immersed Katharine in the real-world problems on the streets around her.

She was a hit with her students, the *Gazette* calling her courses "most delightful."[56] The Western respect for women and her own success in a challenging co-educational faculty line-up, as well as the flattering male camaraderie and socializing, were new to her. Her high-powered colleagues' attention on the nation's problems and the reforming of national values necessary for the health of the country in the new century ahead focused her thoughts on contemporary America; Theophilus was far away.

V.

When President Andrews of Brown gave the summer school's kickoff address on "The Re-monetization of Silver," he characterized the financial crisis as a conflict between Eastern and Western America, blaming the 1873 demonetization of silver for causing the "rupture of the world of commerce into two opposing hemispheres...."[57]

The financial depression familiar to Katharine in Massachusetts was worse in Colorado, where the national move to change the silver standard to gold threatened the entire state economy. Eastern investors, however, feared that the demand for silver would create an inflationary economy and diminish government gold reserves, so they strongly opposed the Western silver campaign.

In June 1893, days before her arrival in Colorado Springs, India's cessation of the coining of silver caused the price of an ounce of silver to fall from 83 cents to 62 cents, a drop which closed the silver mines. As banks gave shaky loans to shore up commercial failures, and speculators tried to dump their holdings, the crisis deepened.

Katharine's evenings at the Casino epitomized the impending economic disaster: on its elegant dance-floor, couples whirled to the Casino orchestra's waltzes and cornet solos, apparently oblivious to the dangers of speculation and risk of bankruptcy threatening its owner, who, only a week later, lost his property.

Concern grew in Boston, Baltimore, Philadelphia, and Pittsburgh, and as people in Colorado began to feel the lack of available currency, the *Gazette* kept its readers apprised of Washington's update on the gold reserves necessary to keep the country running. Then banks closed in the Colorado towns of Leadville and Pueblo, and local railroads began lowering their prices.

The Sherman Silver Purchase Act and the West's silver industry were becoming national scapegoats for the depression whose real causes were much broader. The West felt overpowered by Eastern banks, financiers, powerful capitalists, and monopolists, and by a Congress controlled by the wealthy East. People in Colorado saw themselves in an unfair struggle between the little man and powerful Eastern interests, between poor and rich, agriculture and capital, native-born populists and immigrants.

On July 12, while Katharine and the entire faculty spent the evening with "fully one hundred townspeople" at "a pleasant" and "enjoyable" reception given by Mr. Dexter with refreshments at the "tastefully decorated" Alta Vista

Hotel, a dreadful "howling mob," 1,000 men strong, was erupting at the Denver Silver Conference.[58]

There Colorado Governor Davis H. Waite, a populist reformer who felt that railroad monopolies were to blame for the monetary crisis, urged the assembled silver delegates to defend civil liberties and used a phrase that was unfortunately paraphrased as "bloody bridles." His lack of cool judgment soon brought him in for much criticism from the *Gazette* for encouraging an "anarchist gathering."[59]

People in Colorado Springs feared that the East would begin to pull back from investing in their town. The financial crisis was beginning to blow up more violently than the fireworks set off by a tightrope walker "from his airy perch above the lake" at the Casino.[60] The Summer School went bravely on, helped by "the press of the city ... standing by,"[61] when the *Gazette* had to squelch a rumor that the famed Antlers Hotel was closing because of tourists rapidly departing or failing to arrive.

Meanwhile, the Denver panic created anxiety in the New York stock market, wheat prices fell, wages dropped, jobs vanished, and union workers began to strike. Such strikes became violent when companies brought in non-union workers to work for decreased wages.

Men began to band together to support their unemployed fellow workers: "Railroad men report that the trains are besieged by men who cannot pay to ride and ... are beating their way out of the mountains. The train men are inclined to let them ride when they behave themselves...."[62] Westerners saw these jobless family men as victims of the Eastern financial powers who kept their wages low and opposed silver currency. Katharine could follow it all in the *Gazette*: "Hard Times." "Cotton Mills Closing." "Industrial Distress Not Confined to Colorado." "A Serious Conflict at the Kansas Coal Pits." "Penniless Colorado Emigrants Capture a Burlington Train."

Then a hundred starving Colorado men commandeered an eastbound train to showcase their plight to their fellow Americans. Hoping to "get to friends in the East," the Colorado men carried cards "from different trade unions [saying] that they were laborers and honest men" to show their willingness to work at any job.

As their train rumbled across the prairie into neighboring Haskins, Nebraska, the townspeople showed their solidarity with them by handing them "several hundred loaves of bread and cases of butter which were devoured with the rapacity of savage beasts," and sent the men on their way.[63] Soon "Coxey's

Army" of such desperate men would march up the steps of the United States Capitol to publicize their plight.

VI.

The nearby Manitou Bank closed, although the *Gazette's* even more shocking story was that local families needed help. The "great many men begging in ... the city," not "regulation tramps" but "decent looking" men, with destitute and suffering families appealed to all generous citizens who "would not [hoard their] last penny rather than know that there was a hungry person hereabouts."[64]

Meanwhile Katharine was still in personal turmoil. When her "studious morning" was interrupted by a letter from Theophilus, she became "Ignominiously ill."[65] Fighting depression, she went for an evening carriage ride through the moonlit Garden of the Gods, where she heard her first coyote howling nearby,[66] and prepared for an early start the next morning for the trip of her lifetime, to the top of Pike's Peak.

The *Gazette* had pumped up just such a trip as an escape from thinking about earthbound financial realities: "Why stay at home and worry over the silver question and breathe an atmosphere which is constantly reminding you of an unstable currency, when you can take the Colorado Midland's early morning California Flyer, reach Cascade [canyon] eleven miles from Colorado Springs ... and spend the time ... in that beautiful resort ... air laden with delightful and invigorating odors from the pine, fir, and spruce trees ... the finest climate for toning up the system...." After all: "The grandest mountain drive in the world, the Pike's Peak carriage road, is now open...."[67]

Katharine drew one of the faculty's twenty-six lucky straws for a place on the trip up the mountain range that looms over Colorado Springs and left at dawn on the excursion train to Cascade. There, at 6,000 feet above Colorado Springs, the temperatures began to drop, and the air grew thinner in the dense pines with Pike's Peak above them at 14,110 feet. At Cascade, they climbed aboard a prairie schooner, a large covered wagon pulled by horses for the second leg of their trip, its tailboard emblazoned with the traditional slogan, 'Pike's Peak or Bust.'"[68]

They hoped that the halfway house near the timberline where the road began to rise steeply and "where the horses were taken out and sturdy mules put in,"[69] would be a good place for lunch.

But eating would have to wait: "We had all brought basket lunches, but our astronomer, Professor Todd of Amherst, warned us so solemnly of the danger we incurred in eating above the clouds that we meekly passed over our baskets to him. As a seasoned abider in the upper spaces, he proposed to remain a week on the summit, where the observation station was more famous for its view than for its food."[70]

The last long stretch of the road climbed through more dramatic scenery. Below groves of quaking aspen, the plains grew dim in the distance below. Then the road seemed to climb vertically.

At 11,500 feet, the land was a frozen glacial moraine of earth and stones like arctic tundra. Mules tugged their "cumbrous chariot up and up through a waste of dead white stems, a ghostly forest,"[71] until they finally reached the summit.

Katharine never forgot the excursion: "My memory of that supreme day of our Colorado sojourn is fairly distinct even across the stretch of thirty-five crowded years.… An erect, decorous group, we stood at last on that Gate-of-Heaven summit, hallowed by the worship of perished races."[72]

She felt it was a place consecrated by an Indian legend, "the awful abode of the ancient Manitou," which Longfellow described in his *Song of Hiawatha*, evoked in the painting by Albert Bierstadt that she had seen in Longfellow's home as a Wellesley student fourteen years before.

As she knew, the poet's great Manitou was "the mighty … the Master of Life" who calls "the nations…the tribes of men together to "subdue their stubborn natures," and asks them, "Why are you not contented? / Why then will you hunt each other?" Manitou, their creator, then angrily chastises them: "I am weary of your quarrels, / Weary of your wars and bloodshed, / Weary of your prayers for vengeance, / Of your wranglings and dissensions" and instructs them: "All your strength is in your union, / All your danger is in discord; / Therefore be at peace henceforward, / And as brothers live together."[73]

When Katharine "gazed in wordless rapture over the far expanse of mountain ranges and sea-like sweep of plain" in "one ecstatic gaze" she looked at endless horizons like those beyond her childhood shores, "the sea-like expanse of fertile country spreading away so far under those ample skies."[74]

To the south and west, mountains stretched to the horizon—the Sangre de Cristo ("Blood of Christ") range to the south and to the west, below Pike's Peak, the gold mining town of Cripple Creek.

The dome of the sky overhead can be a deep brilliant blue, perhaps because of the thin transparent atmosphere, a blue that grows lighter near the horizon. In spite of its fierce winds, the summit puts its visitor far above the man-made world below, creating a sense of peace and freedom from human cares. All seems possible with endless pathways over each succeeding range of mountains suggesting limitless opportunities for starting over, for bringing new visions of Utopias into existence.

Standing on Pike's Peak, Katharine saw the majestic "Gate-of-Heaven summit" of America's beauty, and, as she recalled:"It was then and there that the opening lines of 'America the Beautiful' sprang into being," floating into her mind.[75]

In the summit house, a low stone building with several chimneys and a telegraph station amid piles of rocks, she wrote a breathless telegram to her mother back east of her mountaintop joy: "Greetings from Pikes Peak glorious dizzy wish you were here." [76] Well she knew how much Cornelia Bates wished it too.

But her stay was "brief—barely half an hour. Professor Todd himself fainted and we were all unceremoniously bundled into the big wagon."

She had been to the top of the world, looked around, and brought back memories of both physical beauty and a transcendent experience, as she wrote in her diary, "Most glorious scenery I ever beheld."[77]

She knew that for many poets in the Bible, mountains had been a source of sacred inspiration. Now this descendant of Congregational ministers had much to reflect on, especially her view from the rocky summit where Longfellow imagined the great Manitou bringing warring people together.

VII.

In her last week of teaching, when a letter from Theophilus arrived, Katharine could not go with her friends to a ranch outing, being "wretchedly sick all day."[78] Meanwhile, around her the financial crisis worsened. Desperate men were caught stealing, making Colorado Springs like the legendary Wild West: the infamous train-robbing "Starr gang" was caught and prosecuted in Colorado Springs, thieves frequented the taverns and tents, and a man was robbed of his gold watch on a street car.[79]

Violence against non-union men who took the jobs of striking union miners erupted first in Kansas and then in Leadville. Unemployment grew, cash-starved homesteaders rushed to stake their claims on the suddenly opened "Cherokee Strip" in Oklahoma, and the *Gazette* proclaimed "A DAY OF PANIC": "BANK FAILURES IN MILWAUKEE AND LOUISVILLE…. PANIC IN STOCKS, PRICES REACH THE LOWEST POINT FOR MANY YEARS." "A DECREASE IN [RAILWAY] TRAFFIC THROUGHOUT THE WHOLE COUNTRY…. FINANCIAL WRECK…. MONEY IS TIGHT: FINANCIAL TROUBLES FROM THE ATLANTIC TO THE PACIFIC."[80]

Westerners put all the blame on the East for their labor violence, unemployment, and bank failures. William Jennings Bryan, then a Congressman from Nebraska, urged the Western Democrats to take their stand for silver and democracy, the *Gazette* criticized the Eastern-controlled Congress for locking up property and money, and the Summer School presented Professor Edward W. Bemis's talks on monopolies.

At Dr. Richard T. Ely's special free lecture to members of labor unions,[81] one hundred and fifty men crowded in to hear him say about socialism: "Forty years ago … there were few millionaires…. Now … enormous fortunes [are] due to such industries [now] monopolies, the railroads and the telegraphs…. The remedy for this concentration of wealth [is] in the governmental ownership and operation of such industries."[82]

Having squeezed men like Palmer out from their railroad empires, Eastern financiers now owned Western communication systems, telegraph lines, and the railroad transportation system, while Eastern banks held mortgages and loans on Western farms, ranches, mines, and commercial investments.

The little man in the West with his family to support felt helpless. With no income tax and no antitrust laws regulating monopolies, people could see that, as Dr. Ely suggested, social Darwinism's "survival of the fittest" philosophy had encouraged the enormous greed of capitalists who essentially owned a nation beginning to collapse into destructive factions, warring regions, and starving families.

The one bright spot was thirty miles away over the Rocky Mountains, in the gold mines and boomtown of Cripple Creek, and Katharine wanted to see where prospectors had found gold only three years earlier. So a week after going up Pike's Peak, Katharine boarded a stagecoach for the rugged thirty-five mile journey up through Bear Canyon to Seven Lakes and on to Cripple Creek over the mountains (only eighteen miles as the crow flies).

Her stagecoach rattled up the Cripple Creek Stage Road through the North Cheyenne Canyon, where the red clay and sandstone dirt road was carved into the steep hillsides of Cheyenne Mountain, before it plunged down around sharp gullies and dramatic rock overhangs with frightening drop-offs. Even today, park rangers advise any automobile drivers afraid of steep roads without guardrails to take a safer route.

Then the dark canyon suddenly widened so that she could see the breath-taking vista of miles of snow-capped mountain ridges stretching along the horizon, the same mountains she had seen looking west from the top of Pike's Peak. It was a route that Theodore Roosevelt once described as "the trip that bankrupts the English language."[83]

The Gold Camp Road continued up and down gullies, through cuts blasted out of the coral-colored sandstone and dusty granite and over the narrow paths hugging the hillsides, where the previous summer a stagecoach driver had been injured when his team of six horses reared up, crashed the coach into a huge boulder, threw him out, and ran over his leg.[84]

While Katharine bumped along the five miles of "terrible roading," disaster struck her own stagecoach journey, but, as she remembered: "We loved it all, even when the road by a precipice caved in almost before we had passed, obliging us to spend a night at Cripple Creek, then in its first fierce develop-ment as a gold-mining center."[85]

Cradled in the rim of an old volcano crater base, Cripple Creek sat above the miles of hillsides stretching toward the distant mountain ridges. Its story was a romantic tale of the triumph of American persistence, when Bob Womack, a ranch owner and prospector who refused to listen to experts, found gold in unpromising pastureland in 1890.

Katharine might have been especially interested to know that the first woman ever to register a mining claim in her own name, Mollie Kathleen Gortner, had done so in Cripple Creek in 1891. She had spotted a "rich out-cropping of wire gold" while out on a "hiking adventure."[86]

Men flooded in as more gold strikes were made; thirty street blocks were laid out in a grid, and in 1892 electricity, telephone, and telegraph lines were built when there were fifty active mines producing $500,000 in gold a year.

By 1893, with the arrival of unemployed silver miners from Aspen, Leadville, Creede, and Central City, several hundred shacks crowded the surrounding fields, spilling up into the barren hillsides, while its gold mines were producing two million dollars' worth of gold.[87]

With hastily erected clapboard hotels, saloons, and brothels lining its dirt streets, as well as workingmen sporting wide thick dark mustaches and short beards beneath their homburgs, derbies, or cowboy hats, Cripple Creek showed Katharine a West very different from Colorado Springs.

Plate-glass windows adorned the false-fronted wooden buildings under their galvanized tin roofs. A "fair meal" could be "had" for between twenty-five and fifty cents, and horses stood with their wagons and droppings along the dirt streets.[88] Katharine would have found her long skirts hazardous as she navigated her way along plank sidewalks past the open gutters, mud, and litter.

It was no place to spend the night. But with "no baggage along but a volume of [poet Robert] Browning," she had to "rough it" at the "Wolf" Hotel for four dollars a night.[89] Little did she know that close to where she slept that night, a gang of robbers broke into one of the gold mines around 3 a.m., tying up the guards in one mineshaft and stealing sacks of gold ore from another, choosing, unfortunately for them, the sacks with the least ore in them.[90]

Her unexpected night in Cripple Creek cost her more than a Colorado Springs hotel room and one dollar more than its miners were making in a day's pay. But it gave her the chance to visit a real boomtown where she could see and hear gold mines working amid the excitement of American enterprise and energy creating a vital frontier town with streets scratched out of scrub pastureland. Now Katharine's "West" was proper Colorado Springs with its wide boulevards, churches, afternoon teas, Victorian mansions, and waltzes at the Casino as well as primitive, thriving, hardscrabble Cripple Creek, where everyone had a chance to strike it rich.[91]

VIII.

Two days later, feeling so ill that she was cross with Katharine Coman, perhaps over Theophilus, Katharine saw callers, packed, and "pulled up" her stakes in Colorado Springs to start her trip back east toward Chicago and the Fair.

Once more, on her hot and bumpy train ride, with engineers pulling the whistle cord for each country road crossing in Colorado, Nebraska, Missouri, and Illinois, she could think about how her summer had given her new visions of America and the confidence to define it.

Her summer adventures—her glimpse of the World's Columbian Exposition celebrating America's first four centuries; her exploration of steep canyons and waterfalls; her moonlit carriage rides in Colorado Springs; her experience of the worsening financial depression of 1893 and her growing friendships with Katharine Coman and other faculty thinkers and activists; her firsthand view of Cripple Creek-in-the-making, and the energetic Western women valued for their ideas and words—converged in her memory of the 360-degree view from Pike's Peak.

Could a word portrait of Colorado's breathtaking landscape—its natural beauty, sublime and endless—bring its readers together and symbolize a place of new possibilities for the troubled nation? What truly defined "America" and its people, and what did the West have to contribute to it?

On July 12, 1893, while Katharine nervously taught Chaucer under Dr. Rolfe's eye, another young professor, Frederick Jackson Turner, was describing "The Significance of the Frontier in American History" at the Chicago Fair.[92] His ideas would have made their way into the heady discussions swirling around Katharine that summer, since his teacher at the University of Wisconsin was the summer school's Dr. Ely.

Seeing the "Great West" as the "true point of view in the history of this nation," Turner examined the enormous national implications—philosophical, societal, economic, political, and cultural—of the statement by the Superintendent of the Census in 1890 that a "frontier line" no longer existed. The frontier line, said Turner, is the "meeting point between savagery and civilization," the place where America has been continually reborn as primitive conditions have given way to new social development. It has created a "new product," an American, not European, independence.

Unfortunately, in some places, a "new kind of Americanism arose," and the "West and the East began to get out of touch of each other." But the frontier promoted the "formation of a composite nationality for the American people," decreased dependence on England and Europe, and encouraged nationalistic legislation supporting railroads, protective tariffs, and "the disposition of public lands." Like Katharine, Turner saw the West as the "least sectional" area of the United States, a possible place for family-based individualism and democratic cooperation.

Colorado Springs and Cripple Creek, young towns built where the prairie literally meets the mountains, symbolized Turner's frontier as a place where civilization meets the wilderness. Both towns had been built by individual enterprise, creative invention, and frontier energy.

In Palmer's town, Katharine had enjoyed its atmosphere of a family enterprise, a kind of participatory capitalism and a slightly paternalistic socialism. It was like her two earlier communities built around ideals of community—Falmouth, where she remembered everyone practicing "a little neighborly socialism"[93] and Wellesley College, a school to improve the nation.

Chicago's World's Columbian Exposition suggested how American artists could create various forms of art, including poetry, out of the America they saw. In the Fair's enormous Palace of Art, the paintings of such American artists as Winslow Homer, Thomas Eakins, John Singer Sargent, and Frederick Remington showed all kinds of American men, women, and children at work and play, fishing, hunting, and relaxing.

Although its fountains and white buildings symbolized a European ideal that looked back, not forward, its classical Beaux Arts architecture evoked Greek democracy and the Roman Republic's participatory government, a model for America's future. In the West, Katharine had seen a more modern populist spirit in the pioneers of both "Little London" Colorado Springs and the gold boomtown where adventurous men and women were creating new communities.

Also in Colorado, as in Falmouth, Wellesley, and Chicago, she saw women taking action to create a better future for all the people, even the poor, around them. She had already helped her Wellesley friends design and establish the first settlement house in Boston, a new kind of community like Jane Addams's Hull-House in Chicago. For the Chicago Fair, her English department's display, part of Wellesley College's prize-winning exhibit, showed how it was educating young women to reform the nation.

The country needed to come together around a shared vision of its best self. Longfellow's "frontier," the summit where Manitou brought his warring tribes together in brotherhood, might be such an image and ideal. Now perhaps she too could inspire Americans with the power of that same landscape to lift them above the alarming scenes of rioting, starvation and greed on their streets and think of their legacy of noble national ideals. And so she wrote the original words of "America the Beautiful," which she called simply "America."

She opened her poem with images of her view from Pike's Peak, describing the Colorado skies as "halcyon" (peaceful, golden, happy, and prosperous), from the name of a Greek legendary bird thought to calm ocean waves during incubation. Perhaps such skies in the West could calm the storms of American life as new hope was born. The grain, a life-giving plant of the Western plains, was "amber," the color of the gold of Cripple Creek, in "waves," like those of her childhood seashore. The mountains below Pike's Peak were "purple," a royal color.

The flat expanse of the American prairie below was a place of surprising beauty when sunlight "enameled" or decorated its surface:

> O beautiful for halcyon skies,
>> For amber waves of grain,
> For purple mountain majesties
>> Above the enameled plain![94]

Just as her mother had joined with the other widows in Falmouth to bring healing to the congregation gathered in her late father's church after Abraham Lincoln's death, she prayed for God to "shed" his grace on the nation, lifting it above its financial and social crises to a more ethereal realm, like that at the top of Pike's Peak:

> America! America!
>> God shed his grace on thee
> Till souls wax fair as earth and air
>> And music-hearted sea!

Her two "Wests" of Colorado Springs and Cripple Creek, both young settlements, represented the pioneering spirit moving forward, like the Pilgrims, celebrated at Chicago, America's founders striding together on the same path toward the future:

> O beautiful for pilgrim feet,
>> Whose stern, impassioned stress
> A thoroughfare for freedom beat
>> Across the wilderness!

She hoped that divine grace would be "shed" on America long enough for such new paths to be made through the tangled "wilds of thought" pulling the country apart:

America! America!
God shed his grace on thee
Till paths be wrought through wilds of thought
By pilgrim foot and knee!

But Americans also needed to remember the sacrifices that had been made in the past by men for the greater good of the whole country:

O beautiful for glory-tale
Of liberating strife,
When once and twice, for man's avail,
Men lavished precious life!

As long as a few powerful men built huge financial empires on the backs of underpaid workers, the nation could not fulfill its hopes of "liberty and justice for all" voiced in the new Pledge of Allegiance. It was the "selfish gain" made by a few that was "staining" America, a stain so deep that only divine grace could cleanse it:

America! America!
God shed his grace on thee
Till selfish gain no longer stain
The banner of the free!

To envision a reborn America, Katharine pictured the Fair's celebration of the "patriot dream" of an earlier America of hearthsides, farmyards, and villages. And Chicago's White City, with its beautiful buildings, fountains, and statues unified by its miraculous electric lights into one grand design of classical harmony by its master architects, gave her another image of ideal community for her final stanza:

O beautiful for patriot dream
That sees beyond the years
Thine alabaster cities gleam
Undimmed by human tears!

Chicago's "alabaster" city, reflected in the waters of the Fair's lagoons and fountains, both in the sunlight and in the striking evening spotlights, offered another image of community. There, on muddy swampland, thousands of workmen and artists together had built acres of stunning buildings, bridges, gardens, and enormous sculptures of "Columbia" and America's native elk, bears, bison, and moose.

Although she knew it was a temporary creation, the Fair symbolized the ideal of American art, ingenuity, engineering, and individual cooperation coming together to create some new vision of American possibilities that could shine "undimmed by human tears."

Perhaps such an ideal could help Americans remember what their best selves should be like, "nobler" than the behavior of many in 1893:

America! America!
God shed his grace on thee,
Till nobler men keep once again
Thy whiter jubilee!

Katharine found her voice as a national poet that summer. She had taken a personal journey with feminist Katharine Coman away from a future with Theophilus into a new part of the country that empowered her to begin fulfilling her original dream of becoming a significant writer. She now had something to say.

By the time she left Colorado Springs, she had penciled the four stanzas in her notebook, but little did she realize their significance. Once she was back home, she admitted to her diary: "Consider my verses. Disheartening."[95] Nevertheless, they were a start.

PART TWO

Writing Protest Poems

and Revising "America":

1893-1904

CHAPTER SEVEN

1893–1897
"ON THE KEEN JUMP ALL DAY"[1]

I.

"Disheartened" by her verses, Katharine left them closed up in her note-book for months, and in spite of being a nationally recognized scholar who had danced in Colorado Springs with interesting men, she was still in love with Theophilus. In Chicago on her way back east, when a friend told her that Theophilus was married, she was so shocked that she wrote his initials as "T. H. S." in her diary and forgot to record her visit to the Fair that day.[2] It was actually another Rev. Mr. Root, Theophilus's cousin and close friend, Edward Tallmadge Root, who had married in 1893. Even though she knew her Theophilus could not support her, she was stunned that he might have married someone else.

In her poem "Ruby Heart," she told the sad story of a woman who arrives in Heaven, followed by the "dark Angel Pain."[3] "Sorrows" and "savors of dust" "encompass her," as "vainly for peace she sighs." Ruby Heart is "flaming" with Pain's "Smart upon stinging smart," and, even when she has reached heaven, she is unable to escape the "sound like rain" of Pain's engulfing "plumes."

Although there could be no happy future for their romance, Theophilus continued to write to her, and she marked his birthday with a dried flower in her diary.[4]

When he sent her copies of *The Biblical World* with his articles on "The Self-Consciousness of Jesus," Katharine felt "wrong" in her "temper" and "meditated on [poet Robert] Browning," another longsuffering lover, who waited many years to be with his beloved Elizabeth Barrett.[5]

The next night she lectured to a Boston Browning Society meeting where she could have seen Theophilus. Afterwards, she felt "especially used up," was "melancholy," and so severely upset that she "alarmed" the family.[6]

He was not well either and had taken a leave of absence from the University of Chicago. A few days later she went to Worcester, Massachusetts, possibly to see him, where her day was "Beautiful. Sorrowful." The next day she was "alarmed" and "tired" after her "errand."[7]

MARGARET SHERWOOD

Katharine was also upset by the news that the lover of her colleague Margaret Sherwood had drowned.[8] Although she had turned to Katharine Coman for advice over Theophilus, it was Margaret, the newest member of the department, with whom she shared a desire for romantic male companionship and intimacy.

When Katharine tried again to end their relationship that year, Theophilus suffered a severe nervous breakdown.[9] "Finding that an indefinite period would be necessary for recuperation," he resigned his position at the University of Chicago in January 1894,[10] and he came to see her on January 3, 1894, when she "Enjoyed my belated Christmas. T. H. R."[11] Three months later, "Card from T.H.R. Shall keep it."[12]

II.

Katharine Coman, who wholeheartedly embraced her life as a pioneering woman activist, teacher, and scholar, now offered Katharine an alternative role model. As Coman knew, in Chicago, as in Colorado, capable women were creating powerful new roles for themselves. Running the Fair's authorized "Board of Lady Managers" was the wealthy and charismatic Bertha Honoré Potter Palmer, determined to make the Chicago Fair do far more for women than had Philadelphia in 1876.

She hoped that the Chicago Exposition would create "a well-defined public sentiment in regard to [women's] rights and duties, and ... their becoming not only self-supporting, but able to assist in maintaining their families when necessary."[13] Echoing the new Pledge of Allegiance, she exhorted women to step down from their pedestals, because "Freedom and justice for all are infinitely more to be desired than pedestals for a few."[14]

At the opening ceremonies she reminded the huge audience that a woman, Queen Isabella of Spain, had enabled Christopher Columbus to make the journey they were celebrating.[15]

She insisted on a special building to highlight women's achievements and organized a unique architectural competition for it.[16] Sophia G. Hayden, a twenty-five-year-old graduate of Boston's Massachusetts Institute of Technology, won its $1,000 prize and the chance to design the first such Woman's Building in the world.

Although the male directors banned Julia Ward Howe's "Battle Hymn of the Republic" from the official opening because they associated it with women's reform and suffrage campaigns, 1,500 women defied them and sang it when the Woman's Building opened.[17]

It presented women as subordinate to none, and showcased women's achievements, "an exhibit [to] clear away existing misconceptions as to the originality and inventiveness of women ... [who] were the originators of most of the industrial arts, and ... not until these became lucrative ... were appropriated by men, and women pushed aside."[18]

Inside its elegant arches were gold inscriptions of the names of women activists—Susan B. Anthony, Lucretia Mott, Elizabeth Cady Stanton, and Dr. Caroline Winslow—whose statues encircled a large fountain. High above them, colorful murals by Mary Cassatt and Mary MacMonnies showed women pursuing fame and picking the fruits of Knowledge and Science.

Katharine and the Comans could also marvel at the paintings, etchings, needlework arts, and demonstrations of women's labor that honored the handicrafts of women produced "in factories, workshops and studios under the most adverse conditions and with the most sublime patience and endurance."[19]

Katharine Coman might have been particularly interested in the Records Room's statistics that women had gathered for the first time from every American state and countries abroad on women's work. With wall charts, albums, and exhibits all testifying to the terrible working conditions and the inadequate wages of women, data hitherto invisible to the public, it was meant to bring about reforms.

The Woman's Building Library held 70,000 books by women, the first such American collection.[20] While Katharine and the Comans did not need a Woman's Building to show them the abilities and skills that women possessed, this building was a symbolic step to other determined women who created and visited it.

Orchestras performed three large works by women composers commissioned by women patrons. Nathaniel Hawthorne's daughter Rose spoke out: "Oh, woman, the hour has struck when you are to arise and defend your rights, your abilities for competition with men in intellectual and professional endurance, the hour when you are to prove that purity and generosity are for the nation as well as the home."[21]

EASTERN VERANDA OF THE WOMAN'S BUILDING

Nevertheless, some satirized what the Woman's Building might suggest to its female visitors with its dedication "to every propaganda that modern woman has seen fit to espouse…. [They] paid a dollar each for Isabella quarter-dollars with a crowned head on them; looked at Marie Bashkirtseff's last picture; drank Ceylon tea, inquired for Mrs. Potter Palmer; got dinner on the roof-garden … or, better yet, heard some famous woman lecture on the needed reforms of the age."[22]

But popular author Kate Field wrote: "If all the world were enlightened, the Woman's Building would have been a wasteful endeavor, but the least understood being on earth is woman even to her own self. She needed a revelation and has had it."[23]

Wellesley's exhibits were in the enormous Manufactures and Liberal Arts Building, "the largest building … constructed by man … The Greatest Building That Ever Was"[24] because Alice Freeman Palmer had insisted that women's colleges exhibit where they could compete with men for the judges' medals.

Eighteen-year-old Wellesley did win one for the excellence of its equipment and of work of undergraduates and graduates. In a case of its all-women faculty publications, Katharine could see her English Literature Department report in the College Scrapbook.

But most startling for visitors was probably the little booklet of eighteen small photographs for visitors to take home.[25] On the first pages were Wellesley's beautiful campus and College Hall. But in the gymnasium photo young women wore controversial Bloomers, the wide-legged pants associated with suffragist Amelia Bloomer.

They were a sure sign of how Wellesley students were happily becoming the kind of "New Woman" beginning to raise eyebrows, new women just like Katharine and her friends—capable women engaged in the world beyond the expected sphere of female domesticity as wives and mothers, who could become creative artists and social activists, and so push against the limits of conventional society.

One such was Jane Addams, creator of the famous Hull-House, her idea of combatting poverty in the poor tenements of Chicago by creating a community of people from all backgrounds, and Katharine Coman took Katharine to meet her. Sitting at the head of one of the long tables in the dining hall, Addams would encourage her guests to discuss the important issues facing the nation.[26]

Back in Boston, the two Katharines then took Cornelia Bates to see Wellesley women's version of Hull-House, Denison House, also dedicated to making a new kind of inclusive community in Boston's South End, where families squeezed into wretched tenements among the many saloons. With no public bathhouses, people bathed in the Charles River, full of sewage and horse droppings. During the coldest weeks of the winter, landlords could shut off all water (cold) to the unheated tenements.

What could be done? At Denison House, Wellesley College women discussed socialism's belief in equitable pay and hosted the monthly meetings of the Federal Labor Union, Local 5915. Coman was quoted in the *Boston Herald* blaming the widespread depression on reckless financial speculation of wealthy investors because the "present system does not secure to the worker the fruits of his labors, and some are obliged to accept charity instead of the rightful return of their industry."[27]

That winter unemployed people crowded the streets around the State House on Beacon Hill in Boston, and Coman took Katharine in to see the largest-ever gathering of unemployed people in Boston, seven thousand of them. Members of the Central Labor Union of Boston, activists who wanted more rights for working people, mingled in the crowd. A delegate from Wellesley's Denison House had joined the Central Labor Union along with the remnants of the Knights of Labor, communist anarchists, populists, Fabian socialists, single-taxers, and their supporters.

The next summer Coman took Katharine off to England for work and fun, where she could encourage her to think of all she could do to reform her country, not as a union organizer, but as a writer.

III.

Nevertheless, even in Oxford, Katharine was still trying to forget Theophilus, with "Love" on her mind, feeling "Heartache,"[28] perhaps because he and his mother had moved to distant New Orleans for his long recuperation. She spent a sleepless night listening to a nightingale from "2:30 to 6:30 [a. m.],"[29] and inquired in her letters to her sister whether there was any mail for her.[30]

Like other trailblazing women, she wanted to try propelling herself forward as fast as possible. While adventurous Katharine Coman "perched" on a bicycle riding down English lanes, Katharine stuck to the safer large tricycle with its two giant rear wheels, then popular with women, and wrote to her mother:

You should have seen your daughter last evening tearing over the more retired roads of Oxford on a tricycle, with a breathless boy running after to give dire instructions:

'You'd better not go on all sides of the road, 'm. Uf! Uf! You should keep to the left, 'm, and turn to the left, 'm. Uf! Uf! Why, 'm? Sure I couldn't tell you, 'm, only that's the way we do it, 'm. Uf! Uf!'

You should have heard me sound my warning bell and whiz madly by, with my poor boy scrambling desperately after.[31]

When Coman bought a pattern for making Bloomer-like bicycling trousers, Katharine playfully sent her mother a clipping that asked fathers and brothers to decide what women should wear.[32]

Their glee at cycling soon gave way to happily applauding other independent women. They went unchaperoned to London to see the famous Sarah Bernhardt in *Fedora,* "a wicked play and a tigerish actress, but frightfully artistic and true to bad life."[33]

Katharine began to realize how married life might restrict her. After a visit to a newly married friend, she mused, "I suppose [Mrs. Vrooman] looked at me and tho't it was grievous not to have a husband. I looked at her and tho't it was grievous to sit alone in a strange land before a basket containing forty-nine stockings to be darned, while the husband was off tasting the joy of lectures with his peers."[34]

She enjoyed being a female scholar amid men when she was researching Shakespeare's *The Merchant of Venice.* She told her mother that in Oxford's Bodleian Library, Professor Stoddard "works right beside me and gives me the benefit of much lively conversation."[35] She was, she joked, "enjoying my job so much that there's no telling when I shall finish it."[36]

She liked even the strenuous parts of library research, noting in her diary, "On the keen jump all day ... slinging these tremendous volumes about."[37] She was such a Shakespeare expert that schoolteachers turned to her for help, one imploring her:

My Dear Miss Bates,

I'm in trouble here in my efforts to teach Shakespeare. I have a very large class, all bright and enthusiastic, and my wits are at a loss to know <u>how</u> to teach climaxes, incentive moments, catastrophe and tragic moments! Can you help me? Will you?... I know I am taking a great liberty in writing you in this strain, but in my despair I turn to you as an authority on everything Shakespearian.

Please do pardon the liberty and give me a little light in my darkness![38]

With confidence, Katharine debated Oscar Triggs in the pages of *Poet-Lore* over how and why literature should be studied.[39] Coman encouraged Katharine's political activism, inviting her to hear William Morris speak to a socialist meeting, and then taking her inside the Houses of Parliament to hear Irish home rule debated:

One policeman stopped us after another, but we showed our card, and were driven into the sacred enclosure. There we were passed up countless flights of stairs, until a sergeant at arms received us and led us over crooked steps into blackness of darkness. We finally emerged in a little iron cage, through whose gilded grating we could catch faraway glimpses of galleries full of listening men, and feminine bonnets dimly visible behind other gratings, and, far below, the speaker in flowing wig upon his throne, the three wigged secretaries writing at the head of a long table before him, and on his right the Government benches and the Radicals and Union-Liberals and Labor Men, and on his left the Conservatives and the big, black-headed Irishmen.

One Irish member was naughty about his question, and the Speaker sprang to his feet calling 'Order!' in thunder-tones and gave the cowering member a schoolmaster reprimand.[40]

The United States also faced revolutionaries and debated keeping four hundred Anarchists from entering the United States, a proposal Katharine found "all fair enough. No house can receive as guest the man who comes to burn it down."[41]

IV.

But what could bring Americans together? It was the same question she had asked herself on Pike's Peak. Was it time to send off the draft of her poem still in her notebook and hope for publication?

The financial crisis had worsened. "The Nation's Unemployed. Eight Hundred Thousand in the Great Cities. Two Million Dependent Upon Them for Support."[42] At the end of 1893, 5,000 men out of the thirty thousand out of work in Boston had registered in the Citizens Relief Committee headquarters looking for work.[43]

New York bankers had to loan the U.S. Treasury $50 million to prevent a complete crisis: "Total failure might have brought about most disastrous consequences to industry in all its branches."[44] Even the book trade was hit by the depression, and Katharine's loyal publishing house, D. Lothrop and Company, failed, a failure that would "bring to very many a feeling of regret. The company … has brought pleasure and profit to a multitude of homes."[45]

In London, Katharine worried about rumors that Chicago was being burned and looted by strikers.[46] Chicago's Pullman strike raised issues at the heart of what America stood for. The courts ruled that a boycott or strike restrained interstate commerce and was therefore a violation of the Sherman Anti-Trust Act, a ruling reaffirmed by the U. S. Supreme Court.

Was it right that workingmen be paid wages too low to live on while owners and investors lived on the profits from other men's labor? Could Katharine's poem "America" somehow remind Americans of their country's true values? She had seen how all kinds of artists at the Chicago Fair portrayed America's vitality. In the Palace of Fine Arts, on five acres of over 140 rooms, the paintings and sculptures of a thousand artists, such as Winslow Homer, James A.M. Whistler, John Singer Sargent, Thomas Eakins, Childe Hassam, William Merritt Chase, George Inness, Howard Pyle, Frederick Remington, and Daniel Chester French pictured America from Maine's rocky coast to the western prairies.

Hamlin Garland had urged writers to focus on the American landscape.[47] Inspired by the Fair, Czech composer Anton Dvorak had created his *New World Symphony* to celebrate Longfellow's poem of America's beginnings, *Hiawatha*.

Vinnie Ream Hoxie's large sculpture had depicted "The West" as a tall woman with a rather brief flowing classical gown draped over one breast. Her bare feet stood on broken hatchets and bows and arrows; sheaves of corn waved over her head and her forehead was decorated with a star of empire.[48]

Illinois's "Grain-Picture," a huge mosaic of grains and grasses framed by corn-ears, as well as the patriotic Liberty Bell made of oranges, in the Horticultural Building, showed America as the land of plenty.

But Katharine had also seen two far more provocative depictions of her country's identity.

In Chicago, at the Wild West show of Buffalo Bill Cody, Katharine and the Comans watched a triumphalist celebration of American whites subduing primitive Indians—Manifest Destiny dramatized. Along with 18,000 spectators, they heard "The Star-Spangled Banner" announce 100 former U.S. Cavalry soldiers, along with Cheyenne, Kiowa, Pawnee, and Sioux Indians, with fifty Cossacks and Hussars, 180 horses, many buffalo, elk, and mules.[49]

Annie Oakley shot bulls-eyes from her horse before Buffalo Bill himself rode by, his gray hair flowing out under his big white cowboy hat trimmed in silver to match his jacket as he fired into the air and cowed savage Indians with none of the dignity of Longfellow's Hiawatha.[50]

Then on her last night in Chicago Katharine and hosts, along with 4,500 other spectators, gazed at "America," a "Grand Historical Spectacle" dramatizing the progress of four centuries of American civilization produced by impresario, choreographer, director, and dancer Imre Kiralfy on a 7,000-square foot-stage.[51]

"IN MAGNITUDE AND POMP UNPARALLELED,"[52] "THE ENTIRE GIGANTIC PRODUCTIONS, THE BALLETS, PROCESSIONS, AND MISE-EN-SCENE, CONCEIVED, CREATED, AND DESIGNED BY IMRE KIRALFY,"[53] enthralled its sold-out audiences for two and a half hours, as electric light bulbs created a glowing palace full of colorful dancers moving like a kaleidoscope.[54]

Audiences saw tableaux of Washington crossing the Delaware and accepting the British surrender at Yorktown, as well as Peace and Liberty triumphing with a pealing of bells and the support of the entire corps de ballet.[55]

After scenes of "The Early Pioneers of the Far West, 1845" and "The Close of the War of Secession, 1865," the show climaxed with "The Triumph of Columbia" and a "Congregation of Nations, and Grand Cortege of the States and Territories of the Union." The Queen of Asia rode onto the stage on a live elephant along with the African Queen on a camel, while South American "countries" joined them on horseback.[56]

Dancers wearing national costumes saluted from the towers and balustrades of this "White City" while others knelt in homage to the Goddess of Chicago and to Liberty, who waved in reply from her pedestal. As the nations of the world acknowledged America's excellence, a rousing march brought the hand-clapping audience to its feet with its words, "O Columbia, the gem of the Ocean ... a world offers homage to thee.... Thy banners make tyranny tremble, When borne by the Red, White and Blue."[57]

But where were America's ideals of community and hope?

When Katharine had written a poem about the Chicago Fair, she stressed that beyond the Fair's "circle of glistening domes," when a cry went up from the nearby "hunger-smitten homes" that were "staining" Chicago and the nation, no one heard it.[58]

After the collapse of Chicago's Pullman strike, *The Congregationalist* hoped: "A new sense of the <u>interdependence of all the people</u> has been awakened.... Patriotism has been rekindled and sectionalism thrown down ... in defense of a common country.... Injustice cannot be done to one class without harm resulting to all classes.... Finally let us trust God and trust the people. God has a great work for this nation to do."[59]

Empowered by Katharine Coman's support and picturing her Pike's Peak epiphany of how America's landscape of amber waves of grain and purple mountain majesties could symbolize national unity, she finally sent off "America," the early version of "America the Beautiful," for publication in *The Congregationalist*.

V.

Katharine was typical of many women who grew up after the Civil War and wanted futures different from the domestic lives of their mothers. A college degree increased a woman's chances for good employment, but women's colleges like Wellesley began to face declining enrollments because of the national depression and the growing number of coeducational colleges accepting well-qualified female students.

To attract more students, new president Julia Irvine wanted Wellesley student life to be more appealing. Students would no longer be required to do domestic work or attend chapel every morning, and they could study in the library on Sundays—and she required faculty to teach more elective courses while building their reputations as scholars. Katharine's books on English literature were just what Irvine wanted because they put Wellesley's name before teachers and students throughout the country.

At the same time, Wellesley needed to assure parents that it would not rob their daughters of their femininity, and Katharine got pressed into service to write a light article to be "as finely illustrated as possible" to stress this for the *Century* magazine. Editor R.W. Gilder wrote her: "In the colleges for women—especially those devoted solely to women—there seem to be … certain games and celebrations which are as different from those in vogue at men's colleges as women are different from men,"[60] and could she please write about the feminine Wellesley "call," a contrast to Harvard's masculine "yell"?[61]

For this popular magazine of current arts and culture, Katharine explained: "Wellesley was founded by a poet … who built his poetry into a women's college."[62]

She described a recent "Float" night, when thousands of spectators on Lake Waban's shores heard "the silver note of a bugle" and then the chant of youthful voices calling out their class cheer:

Who's alive? Who's alive?

Wellesley! Wellesley! '95!

New, bold, gaudy stars shot up into the dove-colored heavens [and the] college flotilla clustered in the form of a star near the bank…. For an hour the unwearied crews sang on, chorusing new songs and old, while the musical response from the land waxed more and more tumultuous in merriment.[63]

"THE FLOAT, WELLESLEY COLLEGE"

And then Katharine wrote out the "feminine" Wellesley "call": —"Tra la la la, tra la la la, tra la la la, la la la, W-e-l-l-e-s-l-e-y. Wellesley," delightfully illustrated with tiny musical notes.[64]

She was probably happier to represent Wellesley with her essay, the only one by a female professor alongside those by eighteen prestigious male English literature professors in *The Dial*'s series promoting the "Teaching of English at American Colleges and Universities."[65]

It was a time of change for young women and men. As "A Daughter at Home" explained, "This is a transition period—the old and the new are balancing—both men and women demand more of each other."[66]

Was college education for women causing them to marry later or not at all? "A Western College Graduate" wrote: "To the women of today marriage is not what it was to the women of earlier generations—the only loophole out into the world."[67]

Another writer thought that "college education makes women demand much from marriage, and the men who might otherwise have satisfied them no longer seem suited to be their life companions.... [W]omen are not obliged to marry for a home, since they can earn one, or for a career, since they can make one."[68]

Single women could turn to each other for the "kindred tastes, aims and sympathies" that they could not find in men: "[T]hese resources make life full and happy if the right marriage never comes in her way."[69]

However, a single woman who chose women as her friends and supported herself in a career that utilized her talents could also be seen as aberrant and threatening to society. The Rev. Dr. Charles Henry Parkhurst would label "Women Who Ape Men" as "Andromaniacs."[70]

In response to such views of women and perhaps to inspire herself, Katharine began to promote the careers of women writers who were both appealing and accomplished, inviting best-selling author Kate Douglas Wiggin, author of the bestselling *Birds' Christmas Carol* and *Rebecca of Sunnybrook Farm*, to speak at Wellesley.

Although Wiggin had helped develop free kindergartens in the slums of San Francisco, she did not have a college degree; but students crowded in to see her, and then enthusiastically repeated the college cheer three times for her.[71]

She wrote to Katharine about how "bright a spot" her visit was in her memory[72] and sent an autographed copy of one of her books and a "little picture of myself that you may hang in any unobtrusive corner where there isn't room for a greater light."

She asked for "a more lasting souvenir than the hundreds of bright eager faces that met mine…. [Will] not the girls send me a cap & gown to hang among my previous relics?…. I should value it greatly."[73] So significant was Wellesley to this successful writer.

Katharine pointed out such women to Annie: "And do you notice that Eliz. Stuart Phelps Ward is opening a story in the new *Atlantic*…. And will you see the article in the new *Century* … whereto I contribute the Wellesley column? And will you keep a sharp lookout on the coming *Centuries* for my Miss Jewett's poem 'The Pilgrim,' signed Ellen Burroughs?"[74]

Since only a few of Emily Dickinson's poems had been published during her lifetime, Katharine eagerly read Emily Dickinson's letters, published by Mabel Loomis Todd, wife of the Professor Todd on Pike's Peak.[75] In these letters to her friends, lovers, publishers, mentors, and teachers, Dickinson was a good example of a woman devoted to her art.

Katharine wrote to the English female poet she and Coman loved, Christina Rossetti (1830-94), whose brother William replied to her, on a sheet of stationery bordered in black, that Christina was dying and "will soon have passed away from us."[76] When he read Katharine's letter [to Christina], "It ought to have pleased her and it did please her."[77]

Katharine began to promote Christina's poems, and nearly twenty years later, she would use them as models for her own sonnets on Coman.

As a New Woman, Katharine was also free to nurture her male friendships. Her Oxford friend, Francis Stoddard of New York University, came to lecture at Wellesley, probably at her invitation. Ten years older, he was "a brilliant lecturer, a wit … and a personality of great vividness, spice and charm."[78] His work as the editor of a series published by Macmillan may have helped her get a job offer and book contracts there. He later wrote to her:

> Dear Miss Bates, You were very good to send me the interesting story of Judge Sewall's stay in Northampton with my Grand-Father. I would I had been there. The old chaise in which his grand-son and perhaps the Madame and he also used to ride abroad was still in use in my boyhood in Northampton. How I … should take joy in asking you to ride with me, swaying on

its leather suspensions, high in air the much observed of all the much observers…. Seeing your gracious handwriting brings me back to the Bodleian and those leisure hours when we thought we were working…. with minds at ease we read and smiled. Alack, alack, if we were back in [Oxford].[79]

Katharine kept up some kind of relationship, however limited, with Theophilus. On Christmas Day of 1894, she told her diary: "Stocking fun. T.H.R." Then she added ominously, "Came home to bed and chloroform."[80] A few weeks later, she received a calendar "from my poor boy."[81] He was still living in New Orleans.

VI.

The Congregationalist finally published her poem "America" in its special patriotic issue for July 4, 1895.[82] Its cover page, with a large half-page illustration of "The First Prayer in the Continental Congress, Sept. 7, 1774," told how, at the opening of Congress, with news of bloody battles in Massachusetts and Connecticut, George Washington had unified Congregationalists, Presbyterians, and Episcopalians in prayer, "as if heaven itself was uttering its oracle."[83]

Katharine's "America," the newspaper said, had "the true patriotic ring."[84]

The country had been looking for a national hymn or anthem since 1861, when a committee offered a prize of $500 for a poem that better expressed the country's ideals than did "The Star-Spangled Banner." In a book that Katharine owned, *National Hymns: How They Are Written and How They Are Not Written*, Richard Grant White explained that "The Star-Spangled Banner" is "so utterly inadequate to the requirements of a national hymn"—its words are too descriptive "of a particular event … they do not embody a sentiment … [and its lines] tax the memory" when they should aid it.[85]

Such a new hymn should be "adapted to the whole country—not a war-song,"[86] because any "truly patriotic national hymn is … the great peace song and … fits every emotion of the national heart. It is the national heart-beat set to music."[87] Its words must "express or suggest some strong sentiment common to the people among whom they are sung, or … bring up vividly some cherished association" in a "glowing and lively" style.[88]

The all-male committee would have been amazed that Katharine, a woman, had written it. Women, they wrote, from "the soil whence sprout Bloomers and Women's Rights Conventions" could not write a national hymn because they have "such an inability to guide [themselves] by the rules of right reason, that if the control of affairs should pass into [women's] hands, the world would rush headlong into barbarism in a single generation."[89]

But Katharine's themes of fertility, peace, and community did answer the female contributor to the contest who asked, "What is the use of a National Hymn? Is it to be sung in the churches or is it to be sung when Men are going to Murder (war)?"[90]

Although the 1861 committee had not found a new American hymn at the time, Katharine's "America" was like what they had hoped for, a poem that "must of all things proclaim, assert, and exult in the freedom of those who are to sing it … [with] its allusions … to our fathers' struggle for national existence, and its spirit … that of our nationality"—a hymn that would "pervade and penetrate, and cheer the land like sunlight."[91]

For Katharine, "Poetry is the most practical thing in the world [because] it helps us in the doing of our nobler and more difficult deeds."[92] And, as if answering the committee's beliefs about women, she explained, "It feeds the dream, without which the achievements even of the lunch-table and sewing room are incomplete."[93]

While Francis Scott Key wrote "The Star-Spangled Banner" as a song to be sung and saw it published as sheet music set to the melody of an English drinking tune,[94] Katharine wrote "America" as a poem to be read. She would be galvanized by the tumultuous events of the next ten years into revising the words into the beloved song we sing today.

But on July 4, 1895, the day she should have been celebrating its publication, Katharine saw Katharine Coman off on her sabbatical year abroad and agonized in her diary, "God strengthen us!" and the next day she was more depressed: "Almost ill with parting-pain."[95]

Without Katharine Coman's companionship in the year ahead and without any other close relationship such as that Theophilus might have given her, Katharine's future seemed bleak. Her college teaching did not sufficiently fulfill her intellectual, creative, or emotional needs, and did not give her enough income to accumulate savings to support a writing career. So she did what her mother had done long ago in similar emotional and financial straits. She acquired a new "Poems Account Book," where she could focus on and track each of her publication payments, tallying them up yearly just as her mother had tallied up her earnings from asparagus and quinces in Falmouth. Such pages, where she added up all her earnings from her salary, her writings, and her lectures, gave her visible proof of her successes and of her professional intentions as a writer.

She turned then to her work as a literary scholar. She had a good track record with her first book, *English Religious Drama*, so popular that it was reprinted five times.

Her edition of *The Merchant of Venice* had established her credentials as a Shakespeare scholar, with one critic writing to her of his "genuine admiration and delight ... [in] the thorough conscientious scholarship and wide reading."[96]

Katharine now tried to complete a classroom edition of *A Midsummer Night's Dream*. But by the end of the summer of 1895 she was "such a tired annotator" of Shakespeare, writing so "hard in my wrapper [robe] all day" that she was in "...a state of despair."[97] Working hard to finish it before classes began, she was "Still at it, but tired ... Want some fun."[98]

Although this book was received "very favorably,"[99] each time she produced such a book during a break from teaching, she realized how much she enjoyed writing without the stress and interruptions at the college, and with Coman now away, Katharine again thought of getting a job as an editor and leaving the college.

Worse still, Wellesley life was not what she wanted, "mainly consumed by college mechanisms.... Unremitting office hours and Board of Examiners."[100] As department chair she served on the "idiotic Council"[101] and admitted, "Rude to a student."[102] "Heavy-hearted," she even "Tried Salvation Army" to fortify herself before attending a wedding.[103]

Did she want to devote the rest of her life to Wellesley and its women? She knew that the education of life was "richer than the education of books."[104] And she admitted: "Who doubts that the happy wife and mother has won a wisdom, as well as a blessedness, that honorary degrees cannot bestow?"[105]

Worst of all, she was not even doing what she loved most, writing poetry and fiction, as her reading public noticed: "Miss Katherine [*sic*] Lee Bates [was] the most gifted worker in the [Wellesley] department of poetry and fiction" but she, like other graduates of women's colleges, had "not been a conspicuous figure in the creative literature of the past two decades."[106]

Miserable, she took herself to New York City for "an interesting talk" with Mr. Brett, an editor at the Macmillan press who offered her a job.[107] Back in Boston, "'T is a weary life."[108] Two weeks later, she had a "scrap" with the college president, perhaps over leaving Wellesley.[109]

Two days later she wrote to *The Independent* in New York, "I am so sorely harassed by the pressure of professorial duties on one side and the allurements of literary opportunities on the other that I am thinking very seriously—it's a secret—of resigning my Wellesley chair and betaking myself to a New York garret.... I am, of course, a tyro at editorial work, but I'm fairly well disciplined to general working habits, and I wondered if *The Independent* had any tags or shreds of regular employ that I could learn to do."[110]

Hearing nothing in reply, Katharine "[c]lasped hands with Mrs. Irvine. Agreed to stay by the ship."[111] But the next day her friend Hamilton Mabie, literary critic and assistant editor of New York's *The Outloook,* sprang "his earthquake. What now?"[112] She traveled to Smith College the next day "in a dream and talk[ed] in a fog."[113] This new job proposal prompted more intervention from Wellesley's president: "Mrs. Irvine says I am bound to stay. We'll see."[114]

When Mr. Brett wrote to her again, her dilemma grew. This chance to move to New York City and earn her living as an independent woman away from Wellesley College made her feel "Almost ill."[115]

Nevertheless, Katharine understood why she needed to chart a new course for herself: "I have chanced, in the last two years, to have several editorial opportunities and may yet drift away from what is to me nevertheless the dearest college in the world.... Nothing ever told me to teach classes and marshal a great department of girls and instructors. Something has always told me to sit at a desk and splash in ink. Not very sensible reasons, are they? But you see I am a rather sensible person, for I listen to warning voices and pause upon the brink."[116]

She wondered in her diary, "Is life worth living?"[117] A month later: "Awfully tired of everything. Go to work on a story."[118] The next day, she had finally resolved her future for the time being: "Ill.... Will stay one more year at Wellesley."[119]

But she had signed a contract with Macmillan to write a book about American literature, a topic with little written on it at the time, for which she would need to make many research trips into Boston, only a quick train ride away. There, as a New Woman, she could become a "Bohemian" while she used her perspective as a woman and a professional writer to create a groundbreaking book that would help build the new academic field of American literature.

VII.

Boston, a city experiencing its own renaissance, was growing on land created by the filling in of tidal flats and becoming known as the "Hub of the Universe." Yankee money—invested in banks, mines, and the many railway lines that ran across the country, and in the manufacture of textiles, shoes, and iron—was building libraries, museums, and churches.

One guidebook admired its "stately avenues and well-improved streets... [that] every year advance... [making] Boston famous for taste, elegance, refinement, and prosperity."[120] It was the ideal place for Katharine to flourish in a renaissance of her own.

She turned to her friend Margaret Sherwood, who wanted to work part-time at Wellesley and so be free to write popular novels and live wherever she chose. Katharine began reading her new novel about a "Bohemia" for women and shared "a delightful Bohemian tea" at Margaret's. [121]

Her novel, *A Puritan Bohemia*, portrayed a romance between a young man and woman, Anne Bradford, in 1890s Boston, a city of female reformers. Anne refers to her "Rembrandt Studios" as "Bohemia" because they were "a woman's Bohemia in a Puritan city.... For this is a land of quest. One does not come to rest or stay, only to search for that which one has not yet found.... Life is earnest, sad, ascetic." [122]

It may have strongly resonated with Katharine. Margaret, who had mourned for her own lover, wrote: "The shadow of grief rests over it, <u>for women whom life has robbed</u> come here to forget their sorrow ... in philanthropy or art. The little black bag that the Bohemian carries is a symbol of an aim in life. It may hold books, or manuscript poems, or comments on Aristotle ... art that ... recognizes the claims of human brotherhood."[123]

Anne's apartment was "odd and picturesque, with its irregular nooks and angles" and its Turkish coffeepot.[124] She and her guest talked by the fire, perhaps as Katharine and Margaret did: "Bohemia had cast its spell on Miss Wistan [Anne's guest]. She reveled in the waywardness of her new life. Lunching every day at a restaurant; breakfasting when she chose in her studio; exploring at her own will the irregular streets of the old city—this was freedom, this was reality."[125]

Inside the studio building there is even more freedom, with mysterious gender roles and sexuality: "Queer things happened in this queer building:

theatricals, concerts, art exhibitions. Monks and satyrs and long-trained queens wandered through the corridors on the evenings of masquerade balls. College boys in feminine costumes laughed in corners between the acts of the plays they gave."[126]

Anne refuses a marriage proposal because "Bohemia is no place" for a man who does not understand women's aspirations.[127]

Tired of suffocating in "a great department of girls and instructors," Katharine was soon dashing "into slippery Boston for the libraries"[128] and meeting other creative people. Oscar, still unmarried and perhaps now more of an intellectual companion than a suitor, came to Wellesley to lecture on "Some Phases of Modern Art,"[129] and attended Boston Browning Society meetings, perhaps with Katharine.

She joined the Walt Whitman Fellowship[130] and the folklore society, saw Henry Irving and Ellen Terry in *King Arthur*,[131] heard "Mr. Gates on Blake" and "Mr. Black on 'Burns' in the evening,"[132] went to a William Morris symposium,[133] and, on Beacon Hill, met with the editors of *Poet-Lore*.[134]

Then she boldly rented a room—a Bohemia of her own—in the Back Bay, where wealthy Bostonians were building high-ceilinged brownstone townhouses like those in the novel of her old friend William Dean Howells, *The Rise of Silas Lapham*.[135] In this private space, she could work and entertain visitors like Oscar and Theophilus.

Her room was down the street from Copley Square—the new center of Boston's life of the arts, the soul, and the mind. She could walk to the 1876 Museum of Fine Arts, a massive three-story Venetian Gothic building decoratively capped with peaks and turrets, and wander through its rooms of Greek and Etruscan vases, antiquities from Egypt, Cyprus, Athens, and Rome, and galleries of paintings.[136]

Adjacent to it was Trinity Church, a striking Romanesque building designed by Henry Hobson Richardson, the most distinctly "American" architect,[137] for its rousing preacher Phillips Brooks.

With rich Pompeian red walls, accented with soft greens and golds, gilt-leather upper walls, and painted scenes of Old and New Testament figures, carved wooden furniture, oak timbering, and luminous stained glass by John La Farge, the church was an exciting change from pristine white New England meeting-house interiors, and gave Brooks an ideal setting in Boston to advocate for the ideals of community and social justice of the early Christian church.

Katharine could cross Copley Square to research her book on American literature in the new Boston Public Library, the first such in the country in size and importance, where its triple-arched entrance with Saint-Gaudens sculptures welcomed her into a pink marble vestibule.

When she climbed the grand stairway, two huge lions of Sienna marble on towering pedestals marked the way to the great barrel-vaulted hall lined with tall arched windows, the long Bates Hall reading room, where she could delve into its 628,297 volumes. Nearby she could enjoy the wall paintings by John Singer Sargent beneath the vaulted ceiling and chapel-like space.

After a day of researching in old books and magazines, she could stroll past women's studios, art schools, and galleries for like-minded creative New Women. At Copley Square's School of the Museum of Fine Arts, 82 percent of the 116 pupils were female.[138] In nearby Park Square, American artist William Morris Hunt taught art classes for women.

On Boylston Street was the Lily Glass Works, the studio of Sarah Wyman Whitman, who had designed stained glass windows and more than three hundred Houghton Mifflin book covers. Nearby were studios of photographer Alice Austin, painter Lilla Cabot Perry, bookbinder Mary Sears, silversmith Elizabeth Copeland, and painter Laura Coombs Hill.

Katharine could also explore the nearby Copley Hall Studios, where Gertrude Fiske, Marion Louise, and Marion Boyd Allen worked, and near her Back Bay train station was the Cowles Art School, where many women studied. Women exhibited their paintings on fashionable Newbury Street at the Boston Art Club and the Copley Society, created by the first women graduates of the Fine Arts Museum School.

On her way up to Beacon Hill, she could walk through the Public Garden on its gracefully curving paths past botanic trees, flower beds and a charming lagoon with a picturesque swan boat propelled by the pedaling of a young man dressed in trousers, a waistcoat, shirt with arm garters, stiff collar, bowler hat, and pipe.[139]

When Katharine trudged up the Boston Common to Beacon Hill, she could see more growth—workmen were digging cavernous tunnels for the first leg of the first subway in the United States to help relieve the gridlock of trolleys and horse-drawn cabs, carriages, and wagons on Boston's busy streets.

Down the street from the domed State House was the Boston Athenaeum, a private library open to scholars. Built with prosperous Yankee China trade money, the Athenaeum's tall Palladian windows and bronze front doors exuded elegance. Katharine could work in the book-lined alcoves along the sides of the eighty-foot-long library room and climb up iron spiral staircases to the books in the long balcony galleries. There she could read ensconced among books, other readers, paintings, sculptures, mahogany tall clocks, and antiques.

Poet Amy Lowell described it well:

> How often in some distant gallery,
>
> …
>
> Far from the halls and corridors where throng
>
> The crowd of casual readers, have I passed
>
> Long, peaceful hours seated on the floor
>
> Of some retired nook, all lined with books.[140]

There Katharine forged ahead on her history of American literature, escaping Wellesley to be a New Woman in Boston Bohemia.

VIII.

Having seen much American art at the Chicago Fair, she would establish the new field of "American literature" to show how both male and female American writers were also constructing America's identity. At the time, American literature was not regarded as a serious field of study, so she had first created a unique course on it, a workshop for her ideas, and asked women for their help.

One of her favorite American writers was Nathaniel Hawthorne, partly because of his portrayal of complex female characters, like Hester Prynne in *The Scarlet Letter*. Katharine invited his younger daughter, Rose, a published poet who had written articles on her father's literary methods, to come to her American literature class at Wellesley.

Rose replied that she would be "very glad to be present … at the discussion" of her father's writings and to answer "certain questions that are apt to come up…. It is very nice to have you think of letting me be present, as you cannot be sure that I might not be a drag upon your spirit and thought!"[141]

She explained that she would come because of the students: "It will interest me greatly; I wish I could hope to add at all to the light that will be playing about, but I am not good at saying anything just when it is needed. However, if in any way I can be of use to the girls I shall be glad, & they will certainly interest me."[142]

According to the *Boston Evening Transcript*, Rose "gave many delightful reminiscences of her father and described his methods of working,"[143] and in spite of her misgivings, "gave a delightful talk in the chapel."[144]

After they met, Rose sent some sonnets by another woman writer to Katharine, explaining, "I have an almost fierce enthusiasm about the fine work of women. Please tell others what you find here. With loving thoughts of your ... light."[145]

When Katharine later saw a photo of Rose, who by then had become "Mother Alphonsa," receiving a medal for her service to humanity in founding a Catholic home for women with cancer, she wrote a sonnet, which recalled Rose's visit to her Hawthorne symposium:

> I who remember still across the blurred
>
> Thousands of folk your golden hair, your grace
>
> Of greeting, laughing sparkle of a face
>
> Seen only once....
>
> None the less
>
> You are Rose Hawthorne, Rose that blossomed by
>
> Our rarest door of dreams.[146]

After Rose's death, her nephew Manning Hawthorne wrote Katharine: "I'm sure if Aunt Rose could tell us, she would show how delighted and honored she was to have such a beautiful piece of poetry written for her."[147]

Katharine's contact with Rose renewed her connection to Hawthorne, whose fiction was often set in early America. Because she wanted her readers to understand how their literature was "an outgrowth of American life,"[148] in her American literature book, she suggested that teachers use "whatever the neighborhood affords in the way of old houses and old portraits, old furniture and old china" to bring American history to life for their students.[149]

This history surrounded her in Boston. Walking down to the old cobblestoned lanes of Boston Harbor, she imagined the *Arabella*'s arrival and Puritan Governor John Winthrop preaching about making Boston an inspiring "city on a hill."

Nearby, she could see Paul Revere's gabled house near Fanueil Hall, where the Sons of Liberty had planned the Revolution. In the early "national" period, Beacon Hill, named for the original tall beacon that was a landmark for ships, became a stylish neighborhood just as Boston was becoming "the Athens of America." Poet Phillis Wheatley had arrived as a slave from Africa in Boston's South End near Denison House before being taken to live near Beacon Hill.

Many of the American writers Katharine wrote about—her old friends Longfellow, Holmes, and Howells as well as Emerson, Hawthorne, Thoreau, Lowell, and Stowe—had visited their publishers, Ticknor and Fields, in the Corner Bookstore on Washington Street's Newspaper Row, which she knew well from her Daniel Lothrop days.

Katharine toiled away on her manuscript: "At work all day.... In the libraries all day long.... At the library morning, noon and night.... Getting ready for Revolutionary Period.... Blue as indignant about the Book.... All day in library ... Should think my pen had been dipped in glue.... On my back, revising Amer. Lit.... Cooper, a weary world of Cooper. Like Cooper.... Only there is too much of him."[150]

Frantically trying to complete her book before the 1897 fall semester began, she felt exhausted and depressed: "I don't know why anybody should read or write.[151] ... Life isn't worth living when it's making an index.[152] ... All day in busy labors over that weary appendix.[153] ... Substantially finished the book today. Ah me![154]

Katharine was the only woman at the time to place her views alongside those of the few male scholars, like Oscar, who were beginning to teach courses in American literature. Few of them authored books on it.[155]

For her, as for her friends Vida and Katharine Coman, her work, in this case, her book, was the place to start practicing a kind of inclusive democracy by unconventionally writing about a wide range of "American" writers—women and other outsiders.

She began by placing American literature in the framework of famous literary works familiar to her readers: The "Pilgrim Fathers and Gentlemen Adventurers" of Massachusetts were "like [Virgil's] Aeneas, a great part of the wonderful tale they told."[156] Her readers should picture the first American colonists as transplanted Englishmen: "Graduates of Oxford and Cambridge, gallants of royalist houses, gentlemen and scholars, accustomed to the best in art, in thought, in society, lived in the log cabins of Jamestown and Plymouth Plantation."[157]

Plymouth's John Smith published his first book "in 1608, the year of Milton's birth" and Boston poet Anne Bradstreet, of "English birth ... was four years younger than Milton."[158] Thomas Gray's "Elegy in a Country Churchyard" was a model for poems by Americans John Trumbull and Phillis Wheatley,[159] and Susannah Rowson's novels were "after the manner of [British novelist] Richardson."[160]

Which writers should be considered the "true" American writers? Brander Matthews of Columbia University, who would not let women attend his classes and was a close friend and literary advisor to Theodore Roosevelt, emphasized only "manly" male American writers in his books.

In his *An Introduction to the Study of American Literature* Matthews lists only male writers from Benjamin Franklin to Francis Parkman, and models his book on "the father telling the son, and the son, in turn, telling the grandson."[161] As a recent critic has noted, Matthews's own novels "were Rooseveltian at the core, their subtexts promoting Roosevelt's belief that plutocrats, anarchists, and 'liberated' women were leading the country to ruin."[162]

In contrast, Katharine's *American Literature* readers learned of the many other possible plots written by and about outsiders in America.

She praised previously obscure American women writers, making them visible in this new territory: Madam Knight, a Puritan who journeyed on horseback in 1704 from Boston to New York, "wrote a lively narrative of her adventures"[163]; Mercy Warren wrote with a "graceful turn."[164] She further observed, "A refreshing tartness pervades Mrs. Tabitha Tenney's *Female Quixoticism*" and "Mrs. Hannah Webster Foster ... made ... a sentimental sensation with *The Coquette, or the History of Elisa Wharton: A Novel founded on Fact.*"[165]

Catherine Sedgwick's *Hope Leslie* "ran through edition after edition."[166] Louisa May Alcott joined male writers lamenting the Civil War with her "tearful-smiling *Hospital Sketches.*"[167] Katharine wrote that Harriet Beecher Stowe, "in the excess of indignation roused by the Fugitive Slave Law, penned the most tremendous of Abolition tracts, *Uncle Tom's Cabin.*" To show readers the face of the woman whose book outsold all others, except the Bible, in the nineteenth century, she included a print of the portrait of her owned by Annie's relative, Mrs. Samuel Scoville.

Katharine described other women now studied in standard undergraduate and graduate courses: Margaret Fuller, Lydia Maria Child, Mary E. Wilkins Freeman, Sarah Orne Jewett, Celia Thaxter, Helen Hunt Jackson,

Emily Dickinson, Lucy Larcom, Louise Imogen Guiney, Elizabeth Stoddard, Elizabeth Stuart Phelps, and Emma Lazarus, author of the poem ("Give me your tired, your poor") that adorns the Statue of Liberty.

Besides opening the American literary field to women, Katharine also welcomed two writers considered of dubious worth then, Henry David Thoreau and Walt Whitman. At the time, Thoreau was little known or respected. Katharine, alone among her contemporaries, characterized Thoreau as our "poet-naturalist"[168] who made "the American aspects of nature ... at home in prose."[169] She caught his essence with her novelist's eye: "With his deep-set gray eyes under the shaggy brows, his beak-like nose, his wary glance, his swinging gait, his weather-stained garb, he was a man to note."[170]

A seeker of the ideal herself, Katharine recognized Thoreau's similar search for the world beyond the "farm-lot and roadside tangle ... Thoreau's literary art, the end and aim of all that ceaseless note-taking and journal-keeping, was to speak the truth...."[171]

In her portrait of Walt Whitman, "a looming, rugged figure,"[172] she praised his Civil War *Drum-Taps*, with its "gleams of pure imagination, throbs of sonorous music, and a tone of noble passion, culminating ... in the marvellous Lincoln elegy."[173]

Although she believed that Whitman's delight in "the physical and the sensuous" limited his subject matter,[174] to her credit, she could see the importance of this poet so different from herself, a poet now regarded as one of America's best:

> His long, unrhymed lines, sometimes falling into measures of natural grace and power, suggest the careless postures, now majestic, now a sprawl, of the grand old gypsy himself. But he loved the big show of America, he had faith in the wholesomeness of common life and common folk, he filled his daydreams with the trooping figures of our industrial pageant, he gloried in our basal idea of human brotherhood.[175]

She used Longfellow's words as her touchstone: If "'we want a national literature altogether shaggy and unshorn, that shall shake the earth like a herd of buffaloes thundering over the prairies,' we come near getting it in Walt Whitman."[176]

American writers had a special calling: "America has long realized that she stands pledged ... to demonstrate the power of democracy, with its free schools, free ballot, and free religious thought, to elevate mankind."[177] By reading about her inclusive group of American male and female writers, Americans could come together to better understand each other. With her engaging writing style, Katharine was an entertaining and well-informed guide to the new field she had helped create.

Before she left Wellesley for her 1898-99 sabbatical year in Europe, the reviews of this book, done so exhaustively and exhaustingly, began to arrive. She was hardly prepared for the responses to her trailblazing book.

KATHARINE LEE BATES

CHAPTER EIGHT

1898–1904
"AND CROWN THY GOOD
WITH BROTHERHOOD"[1]

I.

Katharine's American literature book took her right into the battle over who should define America and who the true Americans were. With large numbers of immigrants changing the ethnic and racial makeup of the United States, and more women obtaining advanced degrees, many male literary critics wanted to see the "manly" white Anglo-Teutonic "race" assert itself, partly through "manly" writers like *The Virginian*'s Owen Wister.[2]

One such critic objected to Katharine's inclusion of Whitman and Thoreau, "names that do not deserve a position … in our only academy of letters."[3] And as a female scholar, Katharine also came under fire—she had "simply undertaken a task beyond her attainments … [with] a feminine charm in the insight that springs from affection."[4]

This kind of criticism really was about what men thought about women's abilities and what roles they thought were appropriate for women in America around 1900. According to the "race suicide" theories of Roosevelt and others, Anglo-Saxon women should keep their "race" in the majority by having more babies than immigrant women of other races. Roosevelt believed that "the greatest duty of [Anglo-Saxon] womanhood, able and willing to bear, [was] to bring up … children … numerous enough so that the race shall increase and not decrease."[5] Even though women should have "ample educational advantages," they should not "be trained for a lifelong career as the family breadwinner."[6]

To such men, Katharine was a threat to the nation's future, because she educated young women who would be able to support themselves and remain single, if they chose to.

Meanwhile, she was becoming more famous in the hallowed male field of English literature with her books on Shakespeare and the poet John Keats. Prominent scholars such as Albert S. Cook at Yale University told her, "You have done an admirable piece of work.... Do not hide your light under a bushel; give this sort of work to the world.... You will be extending the fame of Wellesley College, and doing a service to thousands."[7]

The University of Chicago's A. H. Tolman wanted to buy more copies of her publications,[8] Harvard's George P. Baker referred students to her work, and Bliss Perry took "great pleasure [in the] thoroughness and convenience [of her] admirable handbook."[9]

Her book earnings would help Katharine pay for her 1898-99 sabbatical year in exotic Spain, a journey that would open her eyes, as Colorado had done, to a wider world, this time to the world far beyond America's shores. She would follow such American writers as Washington Irving, Longfellow, Hawthorne, Howells, and Louisa May Alcott to soak up European literature and culture.

Wellesley had a special connection to Spain in Katharine Coman's friend Alice Gordon Gulick, founder of the International Institute for Girls in Spain, dedicated to remedying "the intellectual poverty" of Spanish girls who were married off or sent to a convent at a young age.[10] Wellesley and other women's colleges supported it with books, money, and their professors. Through its network of Spanish families, Katharine would be welcomed into local homes where she could converse with ordinary Spaniards and experience a Spain otherwise closed to Americans.

As her departure drew close, Spain was suddenly front-page news because Theodore Roosevelt, assistant secretary of the Navy, was pushing for America to expand its territorial possessions—both in the Caribbean (Cuba and Puerto Rico) and in the Pacific (Hawaii and the Philippines), and the sensationalist, anti-Spanish "yellow press" newspapers of William Randolph Hearst and Joseph Pulitzer supported him.

America would define itself by how it saw its future. Should it opt for what some would call the prudent course of action and resist rushing to war? Or should America change from a self-contained, inward-looking nation into an international imperialist for military and commercial reasons since Asia could provide vast untapped markets and refueling bases?

U.S. warships, including the battleship *Maine*, steamed toward Cuba. Then on February 16, 1898, the *Maine* exploded in Havana harbor, killing more than two hundred. Was it an attack? An accident? More Navy ships were sent from Key West to Cuba. By the next day, "Whole World Sympathetic with America."[11]

In Boston rumors spread that Spain would attack the Eastern seaboard, so Boston harbor's Fort Warren prepared for war. Although Spain began to seem innocent of the *Maine*'s destruction, American jingoes in favor of a belligerent American foreign policy were "On the Jump. Driven from Pillar to Post in Their Efforts to Prove the Explosion an Act of Treachery."[12]

American cruisers at Hong Kong were ready to start for Manila, in the Philippines, if war broke out with Spain over Cuba. One Spanish newspaper threatened that if the United States menaced Manila, "Spain Will Menace New York—Means to Be Ready."[13] When a Spanish cruiser arrived in Havana, American extremists clamored for war.

But was war inevitable?

When Congress granted fifty million dollars for the defense of the United States, McKinley called it a "peace appropriation,"[14] but as the *Transcript* noted, "It arms the President with a power he did not previously possess."[15]

The United States, "Not Looking for Trouble," bought two Brazilian warships.[16] Then, with such American military expansion better able to protect its Pacific interests, there were "Good Chances for Investors in Hawaii."[17] By the end of March, Americans began enlisting in the Navy, and the United States bought designs for torpedo boats.

When Spain refused to "sell" Cuba to the United States to avert a war, Britain sent gold from Africa to New York City to help finance one. The Spanish fleet of torpedo boats and torpedo destroyers left the Canary Islands for Puerto Rico, and McKinley reluctantly conferred with Roosevelt and John Davis Long, the secretary of the Navy, about battle plans.

The next day the United States contemplated a peaceful resolution with Spain, offering complete self-government to Cuba,[18] but as Katharine wrote in her diary, "War in the air,"[19] because of the hotheads in Congress.

Many Americans, remembering the bloody Civil War, opposed another one. Fifty Massachusetts Civil War veterans, traveling through the South, saw a new "national unity," and were "filled with the breath of hopes for peace. All spoken with confessed to having had enough … of the horrors of war."[20] But others, like Roosevelt, saw a war as an opportunity for their generation of younger men to be heroes in what would be the first American war in thirty-three years, and Katharine worried, "War cloud dark."[21]

Conservative Bostonians hoped that war talk would achieve peace. *The Boston Herald* called a possible war a "terrible alternative,"[22] and Katharine wrote "Let Me Be Blessèd for the Peace I Make" to remind her *Transcript* readers that the American "stars and stripes" should not be used as a banner for "might and power."[23]

Concerned about her upcoming trip to Spain, she read "the message on Cuba"[24] from the House of Representatives, but in the Senate, the pro-war Lodge justified the war to his Yankee constituents because of their superior race—their English and Dutch blood—saying that history demanded it:

> We are not brought here by chance, by clamorous politicians and yellow journals.... [If] we of English and Dutch blood meet Spain in battle array it will be no accident but because we stand for those who followed William the Silent and sailed with [Sir Francis Drake].[25]

Such race talk alarmed other countries: "Instead of the 'Sweep of the Yellow Race' It Is Feared That the Anglo-Saxon Energy of the United States Will Overwhelm European Civilization."[26]

Katharine watched her country move closer to war, with all "human interest in newspapers."[27] On April 20, President McKinley unenthusiastically signed the congressional war resolution against Spain, and on Boston's Newspaper Row, where crowds waited for the news, a "ringing cheer went up.... Uncertainty over."[28]

She exclaimed, "Excitement over war makes it hard to attend to work.... 'Cuba Libre!'"[29] How would Spain respond?

A few days later, crowds lined Boston streets to watch the 762 men of the First Massachusetts Regiment depart "in heavy marching order.... Cheer upon cheer was given the troops as they passed along the streets, flags and emblems were displayed, women waved their dainty handkerchiefs and tears stood in the eyes of many a veteran as he recalled the similar departure of troops from Boston almost four decades ago."[30] Boston became "one brilliancy of banners."[31]

Meanwhile, at Roosevelt's urging, Commodore Dewey led U.S. warships into the Pacific to defeat what was left of the Spanish Navy in Manila's huge harbor. Katharine kept a close watch: "Greatly occupied with war map.... Busy with my paper fleet and map."[32] Katharine was not alone in making a war map. Even President McKinley was not sure exactly where the Philippines were.[33]

The American fleet started bombarding Manila, but "Spain Has No Idea of Surrender as Yet."[34] When her brother Sam enlisted, she felt even closer to the war.

With no news from the Philippines, she felt "Anxiety over Dewey's silence." Then: "Dewey heard from at last. Boston wild with joy..." and Katharine "praised God for Manila."[35] As more details of Dewey's overwhelming victory came in—"Entire Spanish Fleet Sunk or Burned"—and Americans wanted an invasion of Cuba.[36]

A call went out for an additional one hundred thousand volunteers to fight Spain in a war that began to unify the American South and the North: "'One flag, one country, one destiny. Brothers forevermore.'"[37] The United States military called for 75,000 more volunteers. At the end of May, the "Fighting Ninth" Regiment of Massachusetts left for the battlefront, and the invasion of Santiago, Cuba, began. With most of its fleet at the bottom of Manila harbor, Spain was helpless.[38]

By the middle of June there was an "Imperial Policy. Many Congressmen Outspoken for Colonization. Favor Retention of Land Seized in Conflict.... Thus More Ports Are Opened to American Goods."

But the *Transcript* noted sarcastically, "The House would have voted last night to annex the Sahara Desert if it [had] met that question."[39]

Like others across the country, many of Katharine's friends were so distressed by the prospect of the United States conquering and ruling over other countries that they eventually formed the Anti-Imperialist League in Boston. They believed that imperialism "is hostile to liberty and tends toward militarism," and that because "governments derive their just powers from the consent of the governed ... the subjugation of any people is 'criminal aggression' and open disloyalty to the distinctive principles of our Government."[40]

America was in a new position: "Momentous Issues Raised by Capture of Philippines. Senate Never Will Consent to a Restoration. The President Fears Imperialist Fever.... Had Not Intended This to Be a War of Conquest."[41]

Intended or not, this "War of Conquest," made America a major international power, and Katharine would soon see how her nation looked from Spain. Her Spanish teacher in Boston was "eloquent (in French)" over the war,[42] canceling her lessons and telling her, "'Madame, c'est fini.'"[43]

At the end of June, with the war still imminent in Cuba and European nations competing for power in the Pacific, Katharine bravely boarded her ship to England alone. She faced the "hard goodbye. Mamma so brave at home, Jeannie so plucky, [Annie] so sweet, Katharine [Coman] so steadfast—everybody so dear…. Could not bear steamer letters—hardly steamer packages—as yet…. watched the widening sea."[44]

Meanwhile 3,500 U.S. troops occupied Manila, and raised the American flag over the Ladrone and Marianas islands in the Pacific.

On her ship, Katharine followed the war news. Roosevelt had resigned his Navy position to enlist in the Army and was leading his "Rough Riders" up Cuba's San Juan Hill to the astonishment of the reporters he had brought along.

Even *The Congregationalist* reported, "It is impossible to read the accounts of the valiant fighting of our regulars, the Rough Riders and the Second Massachusetts and Seventy-first New York Volunteers last week, in which not less than 1,000 were killed or wounded, without a thrill of pride in their valor and desperate energy."[45]

To *The London Chronicle* the United States was "a new America … an America standing armed, alert and exigent in the arena of the world struggle…. By the seizure and retention of territory … the United States becomes a colonizing nation and enters the field of international rivalries."[46]

Another correspondent worried that the annexation of Hawaii "means that America … does not yet grasp the full significance of her colonial policy [because]… the change in the great republic from a self-contained nation to one exercising sway over colonies and dependencies is scarcely appreciated as being what it is—a supreme event to be ranked with the greatest world changes of the last three centuries."[47]

Katharine's mother sent clippings that warned against being swept up by the fervor of expansionists: "Let the nation's demand be, Stop this war!… From the moment that peace is possible jingoism means wholesale murder."[48] Anti-imperialist Senator George Hoar of Massachusetts saw the bloodshed as "a sad thing for the country … a sad thing for mankind, if the people of the United States come to abandon their fundamental doctrine."[49]

The war also raised questions of how "great masses of people, aliens in birth, of strange language, of different religions" would change America.[50] With its startling military victories in Cuba and the Pacific, the United States had become a global imperialist.

II.

Since it was too dangerous to proceed directly to Spain, Katharine went to London to wait out the peace treaties being negotiated in Paris.

For her thirty-ninth birthday and future travels she bought herself a green parasol to match her green silk dress and bonnet and began attending the Berlitz School to brush up on her French, Italian, German and Spanish. She enjoyed the British Museum, lunching there "in pleasant company, — there are always people there I know."[51]

After a few weeks of Spanish lessons, she reported that she was able to quarrel with her Spanish teacher in his own tongue, "his favorite amusement,"[52] but "my endurance of books is drawing to an end. High time I was up and off."[53]

Once in Paris, she enjoyed her boat ride on the Seine to the Convent of the Assumption for more Spanish lessons. Her new teacher was "the dearest little sister from Manila, wan and big-eyed, speaking no English and almost no French, but chattering Spanish like a hundred squirrels in one."[54] Katharine admired the "fire, vigor, vitality, intensity, that lay stored like so much electricity behind the tranquil convent look."[55]

She learned how "we have given these poor Spanish cause to mourn many dead,"[56] and listened to how this nun had suffered during the battle in Manila harbor: "All that Sunday morning ... the nuns maintained their customary services, hearing above their prayers and chants and the solemn diapason of the organ, the boom, boom, boom of our wicked American cannon ... when suddenly ... a pirate fleet bore down upon her and overthrew at once the Spanish banner and the Holy Cross."[57]

Newly aware now of how American military power felt to those it crushed, Katharine wrote her mother: "Poor Spain! The papers say to-night that el Señor Rias consents to the Treaty of Peace. But my little Spanish nun doesn't! She told me in very emphatic Spanish this afternoon that she was 'indignant, indignant, indignant.' All these years the Spaniards had been working in the Philippines, Christianizing the heathen, and then we came with a terrible big fleet and took their islands away."

Katharine confessed: "I did not try to explain our new Imperialism in Spanish. It troubles me not a little to understand it in English."[58]

Once she got to Spain, she was the first American woman correspondent to report from vanquished Spain, and she contracted with *The New York Times* to write a "worthwhile" series of "Letters from Spain" for five hundred dollars.[59] Not only would her payment help with trip expenses, her columns might give her material for future books.

In the middle of January, 1899, Annie Beecher Scoville joined her in the seacoast border town of Biarritz, France, where Alice Gulick's International Institute for Spanish Girls had been "spirited" over the border from San Sebastian, Spain, at the outbreak of the war.[60]

Katharine exclaimed, "Adorable Biarritz! Happy day. Like the people and love the sea…. Chills and fleas! Life cannot yet be Paradise, but I've had rather a pleasant day of it, after all."[61] She enjoyed her adventure of "a moonlight walk and the lullaby of the surf…."[62]

After giving a talk in her newly acquired Spanish to the students, Katharine joked, "Christian Endeavor Society this afternoon. I posed as [a] missionary."[63]

Her first "Letter" to the *New York Times* appeared on Sunday, Feb. 12, 1899, surrounded by international news: "GERMANY AND AMERICA: Imperial Attitude Announced in the Reichstag…. Prince Bismarck Praises the United States," and the *Times* highlighted her unique perspective: "An American Woman's Observations in Biarritz. SCARS LEFT BY THE LATE WAR. Oppression of the Spanish Middle Classes."

Katharine wanted her readers to see Spain through her eyes, to meet its people, experience its complexity, and so observe the "enemy" up close. The love of the Spanish for their country, in spite of its problems, was a theme she would develop throughout her letters.

Spanish workers were still grieving from the war: "the 80,000 Spanish dead of Cuba, the prisoners in the Philippines, the wretched *repatriados* landed, cargo after cargo, at ports where some have been suffered to perish in the very streets…. Every household has its tale of woe."[64]

When her friend in Paris had asked families in Spain to host her, one Spanish mother replied, "'I would gladly oblige you and receive your friend, but you will pardon me when you read that my only son, my precious Andrés … for whom you ask so kindly, fell at Santiago. How can I see an American and not feel the pang of the American bullet that killed him?'"

Another potential host wrote: "'My brother—living or dead—God knows!—is in the hands of Aguinaldo [in the Philippines]. Our whole province is plunged into mourning. Nevertheless, such hospitality as it is still in our power to offer we cannot refuse to any friend of yours, especially a lady who is a stranger in our land, but I must insist that she come to us only as a guest. I could not force myself to touch American money."[65]

Explaining that the "industrious middle class," that "stratum of the nation in which lies the best hope of Spain" was suffering greatly, Katharine wanted her readers to see them as she did, "kindly, honest, hard-working, self-respecting people."[66]

Dispelling the yellow press's negative stereotype of Spaniards as "densely ignorant,"[67] she described low-paid factory workers, energetic children, and an industrious female teacher who also taught night school.

Taking her readers into places such as Cordova's stunning mosque, which "well-nigh makes Mohammedans of us all,"[68] she also educated her American readers about Spain's history and beauty:

> Entering by the studded Door of Pardon into the spacious Court of Oranges, with its ancient trees and sparkling quintette of fountains, one passes … under the Arch of Blessings into a marble forest of slender, sculptured pillars. The wide world, from Carthage to Damascus, from Jerusalem to Ephesus and Rome, was searched for the choicest shafts of jasper, breccia, alabaster, porphyry, until one thousand four hundred precious columns bore the glory of rose-red arches and wonder-roof of gilded and enamelled cedar.
>
> More than seven thousand hanging lamps of bronze, filled with perfumed oil, flashed out the mosaic tints, — golds, greens, violets, vermillions, — of ceiling, walls, and pavement….[69]

For a month in Grenada, Katharine and Annie stayed where Washington Irving had, roaming about in the "ruined fortress" where they had their "favorite courts and corridors in the magical maze of the Moorish palace … and its far outlook over what is perhaps the most entrancing prospect any hill of earth can show … of sweeping plain with wealth of olive groves, vineyards, orange orchards, pomegranates, aloes, and cypresses, bounded by glistening ranks of snow-cloaked mountains."[70]

Katharine wandered in "these wonderful old ruins," passing through "peasants' tumble-down kitchens into beautiful old walled gardens with Moorish fountains" in the enchanted halls of the Alhambra.[71]

Observing Spanish children, she found models for the young brother and sister for the book she would write for American children about Spanish children's fear when their father was called up to fight in the war.[72]

Alhambra boys asked her about America, but knew that it "was not the ladies that made the war.... When America fought us it was as a rich man, fed and clothed, fighting a poor man weak from famine. And the rich man took from the poor man all that he had. Spain has nothing left—nothing."[73]

However, Katharine quoted one man's criticism of his country's corruption: "'You admire the Alhambra? I suppose you have not palaces in America because your Government is a republic. That is a very good thing. Our Government is the worst possible. All the loss falls on the poor. All the gain goes to the rich. But there are few rich in Spain.'"[74]

Her hosts' son believed that Spain had sold the American victories in Santiago and Manila for sums of money now hidden "deep down in official pockets.... We, the people, are always the bone to be gnawed bare."[75]

To illustrate the war's effect on ordinary Spanish people, she told the story of a young Granada man, an orphan, who offered to enlist in the army in place of his friend whose mother could not stand for him to leave. She collected sixteen dollars, as much she could, to repay him, but when a second mother asked him to serve in her son's place, he gave her the sixteen dollars to pay for a substitute.

This Granada man died in Cuba and never saw the welcoming crowd the two mothers had gathered for him. The lesson, Katharine said, was that "this young Spaniard, in his obscure Cuban grave, only one out of the eighty thousand, will promptly be forgotten. 'No importa.' There must be something better than glory for the man who does more than his duty."[76]

Katharine also wanted to experience Catholic traditions during the week of Palm Sunday, Seville's big "Striking Spectacles Relating to Christ and Mary," successive scenes from the life of Christ Jesus.[77] She was eager to see it all, "on the balcony from four o'clock till ten,"[78] fortified with the "Andalusian version of twisted doughnuts ... crisp dainties,"[79] much like those still enjoyed there today.

The next day, Good Friday, "twenty thousand people were massed in the 'plaza,' and ... over one hundred thousand waited along the line of march.... The Spanish colors floated out from city hall and courthouse, but the great concourse below was all in hues of mourning, the black mantillas often falling over dresses of plain purple,"[80] reminders of their war dead.

Katharine relished being a tourist in Seville, where sightseeing was "no brief matter. You must climb the Giraldo, walk in the parks … shop in 'Las Sierpes,' buy pottery in Triana, see the gypsy dances in the cafés…. You must lose your heart to the Alcázar … a storied palace, embowered in fountain-freshened gardens of palm and magnolia, oranges and cypresses, rose and myrtle, with shadowy arcades leading to marble baths and arabesque pavillions…. Beauty, mystery, sublimity."[81]

**KATHARINE WROTE ON THIS POSTCARD,
"PLEASE OBSERVE WHAT NICE WALKING WE HAVE!
SIDEWALKS ARE THE EXCEPTION, NOT THE RULE."**

And she loved its food—"cold soups like melted salads, home-made fig marmalade, cinnamon pastes of which the gypsies know the secret, and sugared chestnuts overflowed by a marvellous syrup wherein could be detected flavors of lemon peel, orange peel, and a medley of spices!"[82]

So used to frozen New England, Katharine gave her readers a warm and fragrant Spain. She felt that she would always grow "homesick for Seville, for her palm trees and orange gardens, her narrow streets like lanes of shadow, her tiled and statued patios, with caged birds singing answer to the ripple of the fountain, the musical midnight cry of her 'serenos,' her black and burning eyes like beacons in the dark,' her sighing serenaders, 'lyrical mosquitoes,' outside the grated window or beneath the balcony, her fragrances of rose and jessamine, her poetic sense of values…. What more does a mortal want?"[83]

But Spain was not so beautiful when she went to see a bullfight in an effort to learn how it could appeal to Spaniards.

She saw how the picador plunged his pike deep into the shoulders of the bull, "but could not hold him back. He plunged his horns, those mighty spears, into the body of the helpless, blindfolded horse, which the 'picador,' whose jacket was well padded and whose legs were cased in iron, deliberately offered to his wrath. The poor horse shrieked, plunged, reeled, and fell, the 'chulos' deftly dragging away the armored rider, while the bull ripped and trampled that quivering carcass, for whose torment no man cared, until it was a crimson, formless heap."

Sickened, she watched "two bloody masses that had once been horses" disfigure the arena, and the bull, "stuck all over like a hedge-hog with derisive, many-colored darts," that had gone down under Guerrita's steel…. Horse after horse crashed down before his furious rushes, while the [audience], drunk with glee, shouted for more victims and more and more. It was a massacre.

"At last our hideous greed was glutted, and the 'banderilleros' took their turn in baiting the now enfeebled but undaunted bull…. But even before a blow was struck the splendid, murdered creature sank to his knees, staggered up once more, sank again with crimson foam upon his mouth, and the music clashed jubilantly while Fuentes drove the weapon home."[84]

After she had watched the killing of six bulls, she picked her way "through pools of blood and clots of entrails."[85] Her host was "disconcerted" by her nausea, reminding her that "'animals are only animals; they are not Christians.'

"'Who were the Christians in that circus?' I asked. 'How could devils have been worse than we?'

"He half glanced toward the morning paper but was too kindly to speak his thought. It was not necessary. I had read the paper, which gave half a column to a detailed account of a recent lynching, with torture, in the United States."[86]

While Spaniards cheered at their bullfights, Americans were murdering black citizens.[87] It was how Spain saw America.

III.

As an unmarried middle-aged woman in Spain, Katharine frequently received condescending treatment. She had come to Spain to study Spanish drama but found her male professor a "whimsical old philosopher,"[88] who declared that "ladies always had a distaste for useful information," and said he had never read Calderón [her subject] himself...."[89]

While she could study the dramatists on her own, she was almost prevented from fondly reenacting the grand journeys of early male Spanish explorers by sailing down the Guadalquivir River from Seville to Cadiz, the "silver road" of Spain's "silver fleets,"[90] because her Spanish host was horrified by her plan to travel without a male chaperone. But for Katharine, "That was not the way Columbus went, nor Cortés.... I did not feel called upon to bow a New England bonnet beneath the Moorish yoke."[91]

Barely escaping, she hurried onto a small steamer. Although the boat was dirty and smelly, she imagined herself "sailing on a treasure ship of the Indies, one of those lofty galleons of Spain, rowed by thrice one hundred slaves and gay with streamers, banners, music, that had delivered [its treasure] at the Golden Tower ... and was proudly bearing back to the open roads of Cadiz...."[92]

As the boat floated through the salt marshes, Katharine saw gulls and ducks "flashing" in the sunshine "which often made the winding river ... sparkle like liquid gold."[93]

On her trip back to Seville in a railway carriage, talk turned to America's war. A German man declared, "'The Spaniards deserved to be beaten ... but the Yankees don't deserve to beat. They were conceited enough before, heaven knows, and now they expect all Europe to black their shoddy shoes.'"[94]

But Katharine enveloped herself in her memory of entering Cadiz from the sea, as if she had been part of the Silver Fleet, a successful female explorer, a woman who had escaped Spain's imprisoning gender roles for one glorious day.

Katharine's readers liked her articles and sent "pleasant letters" to the managing editor of the *Times,* who told her that the praise of one man, originally from Spain, "is undoubtedly the opinion of many of our readers, including those in the *Times* office:[95]

> 'Dear Madam: I must congratulate you.... one of the most accurate descriptions of 'things Spanish' I have ever read coming from the pen of a foreign observer.... certain passages ... reveal a very unusual degree of intuitive perception and a very keen power of observation and comprehension.... [The] appearance of an interesting, breezy and truthful narrative like yours, is quite a treat to be enjoyed and appreciated by all educated Spaniards and by all those interested in "la bella Andalusia."
>
> 'Could you not write something else about your Spanish trip? You must surely have other notes and recollections and you ought to write them down.'[96]

The letter writer helped convince the Macmillan press that Katharine could write a successful book on Spain for them,[97] and she later asked him to comment on her manuscript.

He replied: "I see that you are inspired in your writings by such commendable spirit of justice and fair play—and that you are striving hard and earnestly to fathom the depths and strange phases of Spanish life [and] it will give me keen pleasure & satisfaction to help you."[98]

Having witnessed the human suffering caused by America's war with Spain, Katharine wrote "A Private" to protest the deaths of ordinary soldiers from the poorest families:

> [....]
> His comrades scaled the splendid heights;
>> But for his only deed
> He proved the bullet how it bites,
>> The wounds and how they bleed.[99]

She came to see during her year in Spain that war declared by heads of states could result in blood shed by the helpless people forced to fight. Without "war fever," diplomatic negotiations might have avoided war and given the United States the territories so desirable for expanded trade.

But men like Roosevelt felt that a just war was good for a man's soul.[100] Just as American Indians had been demonized as the "enemy," an evil force that deserved to be obliterated, in 1898, the yellow press had made Spain the devil.

Katharine replied to such ideas by saying on her book's first page, "Rough Riders may be more pictorial, but hardly more heroic" than "the gallant little band of American [women] teachers spending youth and strength in their patient campaign for ... truth."[101]

Her months of exploring the recently defeated enemy country as a woman writer paid off. As Franklin Ware Davis wrote after he interviewed her, "Miss Bates has pictures of more interesting things from Spain than would have been dreamed of in our American philosophy a year ago."[102]

Determined to combat the criticism that she was unable, as a woman, to write an important textbook on American literature, she had spent her sabbatical year adventurously plunging in to a little-known part of the world, learning a new language, and challenging its patriarchal culture.

IV.

Once back at Wellesley, Katharine found a new era beginning. If college-educated women were going to help reform the nation as the generous Durants had hoped twenty-eight years earlier, women's colleges needed new ways to survive financially.

With their coffers getting empty, the trustees had looked outside academia to choose as the new president of Wellesley College Caroline Hazard, a woman from the New England network of wealthy Yankee families.

Former president Alice Freeman Palmer's husband told Caroline that in her,

CAROLINE HAZARD

Wellesley would gain "the greatest President she has had since my robbery [of Alice], & you have insured for yourself a rich & happy life.... You will have a crowd of eager & needy young people below you, & a band of exceptionally intelligent & disciplined women by your side."[103]

October 3, 1899, was the crisp autumn day of the inauguration of Wellesley's fifth president. Guests watched the long winding line—trustees present and past; delegates (other college presidents); senior faculty, including Katharine and her colleagues; junior faculty; alumnae; and students—proceed slowly downhill from College Hall.

It was a colorful sight with presidents Eliot of Harvard, Hadley of Yale, Angell of Michigan, Seelye of Smith, Taylor of Vassar, Thomas of Bryn Mawr, Warren of Boston University, Slocum of Colorado, and Mead of Mount Holyoke arrayed in their academic regalia. The procession strode past Lake Waban and passed through two lines formed by the undergraduates, dressed in white, in front of the newly built classic gray stone Houghton Chapel, large enough to seat 1,300 people under John La Farge's stained glass windows.

After a prayer and a brief address welcoming Caroline Hazard into her office, Pauline Durant presented her with the charter keys "with a few fitting words and with deep feeling."[104] Hazard then entered the pulpit and "read her address in a winsome, unaffected manner," saying that because she believed in women, she would take her part in this great work.[105]

The next speaker, President Eliot of Harvard, must have astonished many in the audience, especially the Wellesley faculty, when he questioned why women should go to college when they are not as intelligent as men, stating that it "would be a wonder, indeed, if the intellectual capacities of women were not at least as unlike those of men as their bodily capacities are."[106] Therefore, a college for women should find the best methods for becoming "a perfect school of manners ... [teaching] bearing, carriage, address, delicate sympathy, and innocent reserve."[107]

Fortunately, the next speaker, Durant's old friend James B. Angell, president of the University of Michigan, challenged such ideas: "No better fortune has come to American women than the ... well-organized college.... How much our life has been enriched by the thorough education of so many women as our colleges have graduated, many a delightful home can bear witness....

"[It] would be difficult to name any single influence which has contributed more to the elevation of the schools of the country than the contribution of thoroughly trained teachers which the colleges have furnished to the ranks of teachers.... Formerly, very few [women] could find an opportunity to gain an education comparable to that which their brothers received in college.... But now they know, and others know, that they have a training substantially as extended and as thorough as the men [and] ... bring to their work as teachers a vigor and power which were formerly unknown to women.

"So throughout the country the beneficent influence of this institution has been felt in hundreds of schools and in the instruction of thousands of pupils."

And he wished "new prosperity to the College. May large-hearted bene-factors to it be multiplied!... [And] make it memorable by enlarging the resources and multiplying the power of Wellesley College."[108]

Katharine knew that she was able to do far more with her "intellectual capacity" than teach manners. Her time in Spain had made her a global thinker, part of the world beyond the Wellesley campus.

Although she found it hard to get back into the grind of lecturing to her 103 students after her year away, she enjoyed talking about Spain: "A busy tired day. Lectured badly, but had a delightful evening with the Spanish Club."[109] She began to illustrate her talks with lantern "views," finding lec-turing in the dark "joyous."[110]

But that summer, Katharine Coman was diagnosed with breast cancer. On her fortieth birthday, Katharine could only feel "forlorn.... Sinfully blue, but try not to make poor Katharine too miserable. Weary of this world... Am still lifting my head out of the clouds that still hang heavy about my foolish heart."[111]

Her friends Vida Scudder and Julia Eastman pointed her in a new direc-tion, though, taking her into Boston to the Boston Authors Club,[112] where she could listen to other writers discuss their book ideas, enjoy the stimu-lating energy of creative people beyond the campus, and think about her own writing projects.

Nevertheless, she was depressed: "Had to face the weariness of letters. When I'm not writing on Spain, I am doing nothing."[113] She did learn to play poker that Christmas at her brother Arthur's house in Portland, but then she tried an even better remedy.

Empowered by her international perspective and the camaraderie of her Boston writers, she would speak out on another war making headlines. In the South African Republic, English capitalists and the Dutch-descended Boers of the Transvaal region were fighting over an area rich in gold, diamonds, and oil.

Globe-trotting war correspondents like Winston Churchill used telegraph lines to get their daily reports of battles onto the front pages.[114] Initial Boer victories made South Africa "'Dark Africa' for the British,"[115] with the "terrible" slaughter of more than 6,000 British soldiers, and much criticism from within Britain and the rest of the world because "but for the reckless folly of Mr. Chamberlain and a few others, probably the war could have been averted."[116]

The new automatic handguns, smokeless powder, magazine-fed rifles, machine guns, hidden trenches, and aerial reconnaissance made people such as the Czar of Russia think of "the necessity of abolishing war [because] the task of attacking soldiery has become very grave."[117]

With blood being shed in the Boer War and Americans fighting the Philippine insurgency, both for materialistic gains, Katharine began publishing a series of remarkable antiwar poems. She wrote under the name of "James Lincoln," her ancestral name of Lincoln evoking America's past hope for peace.

Whether she was hesitant as a Wellesley faculty member to speak out on a controversial political question in her own name, or she felt a masculine name would be taken more seriously on international issues, "James" enabled her to write authoritatively on the horrors of war.

"James" was a like a close family member, a useful companion, and although she sometimes referred to him as her "son," he was more like the supportive and interesting husband she might have had in Theophilus or Oscar.

In her diary she recorded her excitement and humor over this new project: "Jay Lincoln is writing Transvaal lyrics.[118] ... My head still full of the Transvaal.[119] ... Have a mania for Transvaal rhymes.[120] ... Very much absorbed with Jay Lincoln and inclined to neglect Santiago and other saints.[121] ... Went into the Back Bay Post-office and engaged box 17 for my son Jay Lincoln.[122] ... visiting with Lincoln Jay all day.[123] ... Slipped in to Boston to start Jay Lincoln on his literary career. May be a staff to my age!"[124]

"Jay," not responsible for preparing and giving hours of college lectures, for evaluating hundreds of student papers, for supervising a growing English literature department, or for sitting through hours of stultifying college governance meetings, pulled her out of her depression.

Even when her classes started again, Katharine hung on to this new friend, fellow writer, lover, companion, and son: "Jay Lincoln grows restless. The College begins to close over."[125] "Blue as ever. Jay Lincoln will have nothing to do with me. College makes head and heart ache."[126] A "brief, bashful visit from my boy Jay Lincoln this evening."[127] "Poor Jay Lincoln has never had a letter. Grows dumb."[128]

In her antiwar poems Katharine could take a strong political stand and experiment with which voices and styles of poetry were the most persuasive. While she had always written patriotic poetry celebrating and encouraging her country, the poems "James" wrote showed that patriotism could also mean sharply questioning a nation's policies.

To Katharine's delight, "James" got published in *The Atlantic Monthly*.[129] His first poem, one of a pair of sonnets, described how he and his country have looked at Britain as a nation of high ideals and celebrated military history. Anyone who would "trust England" is advised to look at Nelson's column over Trafalgar Square with its "hieroglyph of DUTY" and at Gordon's statue near St. Paul's Cathedral celebrating "SACRIFICE" and think of England as a ship on a true course "shapen by the eternal stars."

However, his second sonnet replied to this lofty image of England by pointing out its current disillusioning shortcomings:

> But—God forbid!—if lust of yellow ore,
>> The pride of power, the trumpet's fanfaronade,
> Deforms your march of Progress to a raid,
>> And with Injustice stalking on before....

Watching Britain's "victory" in the Boer War, he wondered what would happen to the conscience of the world that it has "fostered well":

> We fear your victory, if, truth to tell,
> Your cause lack God. Though blood your arteries spill
> Is earth's most precious … if your own stroke should kill
> That great world-conscience you have fostered well?[130]

In his next poem, he asked simple questions, easy for any reader to grasp, pointing out the connections between the imperialism of Britain's Boer War and the United States' bloody ongoing battles in the Philippines:

REMARKS FROM UNCLE SAM

"I can't throw stones," sighed Uncle Sam,
    "I've built my own new house
—Imperial style, not pebble-proof—
    Of Philippino glass."

    ....

"Ain't we the Christian nations
    That head the march to Zion?
Ain't we the Christian nations
    That calculate to love
Our neighbors' countries as our own?
    The eagle and the lion
Will now walk out to luncheon
    Off the lambkin and the dove."[131]

In "An Anachronism" "James" wrote in the short clipped rhythms of tele-graphed war news to contrast the gentlemanly nineteenth-century manners of the Dutch and the English officers with the ugly reality of the monstrous weapons of twentieth-century warfare:

"Pray use my ambulance. Happy to lend,"
    Quoth General White, as if to a friend.
The Dutchman made a courteous bend.

"Burghers!" called Joubert [The Boer General]. "Blankets here
    And plenty of water! I sadly fear
These wounded British have need of cheer."
    Wide grinned the black-mouthed howitzers all
To see those queerest of enemies fall
    To pouring the balsam after the ball.[132]

In "Dundee" a messenger comes to tell a soldier's widow that her "wifely message" cannot "lull that soldier heart to rest, / While cannon shake the lea" before the poet turns to the reader and asks:

> O war! will gold repay us for
> Dundee, Dundee?
>> And if so rich the firstlings are
>> Of thy red-reaping scimitar,
>> How will thy granaries over-run,
>> Till shuddering stars and solemn sun
>> Tell God what things they see![133]

In "Prayers in Camp," "James" imagined the voices of the Boers at prayer: "We praise Thee for all Thy mercies... especially for the reverses / Befalling the British arms."[134] The Boers' prayers show they claim God's allegiance without seeing that both sides are guilty of violent slaughter:

> Chastise their greed and their vanity,
>> Their trespass against our rights,
> ....it's one thing to slaughter the Kaffir
>> And another to rob the Dutch.[135]

With grim humor "James" told the story of "A Veteran of Elandslangte," a soldier whose right arm is shot "four times through," but who can laugh: "'they dinna ken / I've the luck to be left-handed' [and] Kruger could have shot him then."[136]

In "Glory" Katharine used James's unsentimental voice to show that the high cost of a military promotion can be death:

> He had forgotten mother and fame,
>> His mind in a blood-mist floated,
> But when reeling back from carnage they came,
>> One told him: 'You are promoted!'
>
> ....

> Again he raged in that lurid hell
>> Where the country he loved had thrown him.
> 'You are promoted!' shrieked a shell.
>> His mother would not have known him.[137]

The following week Katharine experimented with another voice and point of view in "Puzzlehead," about a British soldier looking at a group of Boer soldiers on their knees in prayer trying to puzzle out, "What if Right makes Might, / Not Might makes Right,/ and God, the All or the Nought, / Is less extinct than we thought!"[138]

Confused, he asks:

> A prayer-meeting! What has that
> To do with a battle? Scat!
> Lyddite shell makes a queer amen.
> Was Jehovah joking then?[139]

Similarly, in "The Black Watch," a Scots soldier laments how the English have "trained us into their treasons, / And their withering welcome of lead / Might have been the best of reasons / Why another brigade had fled...."[140] Tragically, because the brave Scots have romanticized the battle culture of their own clans, they have followed their English generals to their death in twentieth-century warfare:

> But we Highlanders have our fancies,
>> Our glamour of old romances,
> And so we lie dying and dead.
>
> ....'Twas never an error
>> To follow a glorious chief.
>
> .... From dusk to dusk roars the battle,
>> Till the pulses cease in our wrists,
> The rifles muffle their rattle,
>> And our eyes are drowsy with mists.[141]

Katharine then "helped Jay on a sonnet,"[142] probably "Betrayed."[143] Perhaps she had in mind William Wordsworth's sonnet "Composed Upon Westminster Bridge, Sept. 3, 1802," which celebrated London at dawn—"Earth has not anything to show more fair: / Dull would he be of soul who could pass by / A sight so touching in its majesty"[144]—a century later she described a dawn when London awakes to the reality of the nightmare of sending men to fight a war over South Africa's gold and diamond riches:

> The nightmare melts at last, and London wakes
>> To her old habit of victorious ease.
> More men, and more, and more for over seas,
>> More guns, until the giant hammer breaks
> That patriot folk whom even God forsakes.[145]

The sonnet's final lines—

> But far beyond the fierce-contested flood,
>> The cannon-planted pass, the shell-torn town,
> The last wild carnival of fire and blood,
> Beware, beware that dim and awful Shade,
>> Armored with Milton's word and Cromwell's frown,
> Affronted Freedom, of her own betrayed![146]

—evoked two more of England's great poets: John Milton and Samuel Taylor Coleridge with their images of hell and a poet who speaks the truth.[147]

Katharine joked, "Darned Jay's blue stockings."[148] She was right to take care of him—he was an important catalyst for her growth, enabling her to speak out on world events through poetry.

V.

That same fall Katharine experimented with something else, playing golf on Wellesley's newly constructed nine-hole course, now the Nehoiden Golf Club, proudly noting her first attempt: "went boldly out to the golf grounds. Played over four links."[149] She enjoyed it enough to feel unhappy that correcting the proofs of her book on Spain kept her at her desk: "More proof, No golf."[150]

Soon she was back at it: "Went over the full golf course this afternoon."[151] Determined to improve, she got help with her shots, if not her terminology: "Had a golf lesson with Mr. Clarke this afternoon. Wish I could serve a ball like him."[152] She began to enjoy being a sportswoman, striding over the gently rolling course, a caddie in tow: "Played golf before [Academic] Council, with Willie Buckley for caddie. Quite the best fun out."[153]

Like many golfers, Katharine began to resent any activity that kept her off the course: "Lived through classes only to play golf, but had to leave the field for an At Home."[154] She resorted to an early English expression to express her dismay, or triumph, at shooting out of a sand bunker: "Had a fine golf game and went into the gravel pit. That was a gurly weird."[155]

She also left the campus more often for Boston activities that included men, confessing, "Ran away from Council to learn what Boston could tell me of ... the crafts ... Mr. Safford on patterns in household decoration."[156]

With her firsthand knowledge of Spain and her involvement in the Gulicks' Institute, Katharine kept abreast of America's relations with Cuba, uncharacteristically abandoning her summer writing projects to help Cuban women improve their English language skills at Harvard University. Becoming a temporary head of house at the university, she welcomed 1,300 Cubans, 40 percent of Cuba's public schoolteachers.

Good reviews of her book *Spanish Highways and Byways,* in which she had expanded her *Times* "Letters," began to arrive, as she happily noted in her diary, "Somewhat cheered after a long, stormy day by *Literary World* review."[157]

The Nation's praise was especially welcome, making up for its negative review of her American literature book. It praised her "rare insight into Spanish characteristics and life, and power of rendering that insight in exact and telling words.... delicious ...an oasis ...[written with] brightness and charm, ...lightness of touch, and the feeling of absolute truth in impression and rendering."[158]

Recognizing that it was a statement by a perceptive woman, doing what no American man had done, the reviewer called it a "a tribute to herself and her opportunities [because] she enjoyed an access to Spanish family and social life that falls to few birds of passage; and her knowledge of Spanish and her easy *camaraderie* carried her ... into converse with beggars and babies, nuns and pilgrims."[159]

With her "wildly independent (for a lone female) journey down the 'Silver Road' from Seville to Cadiz ... Miss Bates has known how to pass beyond towered cities and pageants to the people and the life working behind them and in them."[160]

But her day job of teaching and running a department was wearing her down. She now oversaw a department of nine professors and tried in vain to find pleasure in her classes: "Heavy presence of class work, five hours."[161] "Classes again, and, take them as you may, there is something absorbing and depressing about classes."[162]

She lamented that when she had been a student at Wellesley twenty years earlier, "the college girl ... came to college for professional training, expecting to earn her livelihood by teaching and so, with this definite end in view, worked steadily and closely.... [She might have been] stoop-shouldered ... and deficient in social ease, but she took her mind seriously."[163] In contrast, too many of Katharine's current students valued "youth, beauty, charm, [and] the genius for affairs," instead of cherishing learning.

And so, although she had barely recovered from that winter's ill health, Katharine began a new project that would reach younger students. While her more political friends took visible action to bring about change in factories, cities, and immigrant communities, Katharine, in her quieter way, took action by developing the imaginations, intellectual life, and social consciences of many generations of readers throughout the country.

When the publishing firm of Rand McNally commissioned her to do work for them, she mapped out her ideas: "Busy over Rand, McNally business. Copied my wise Suggestions and wrote poor Mr. Grover twenty-four pages."[164] She was the ideal person to write short introductory biographies and comments on British writers for their "Canterbury Classics," a series for school-age readers of important works illustrated with woodcuts in the William Morris Arts and Crafts style. With an eye to social and political issues, Katharine could choose which issues in their lives to emphasize.

To her young readers, she stressed John Ruskin's concern for "human welfare.... The hunger and dirt and ugliness in which many of England's poor had to live weighed upon his heart and conscience.... He wanted men to work together in business as friends, not against one another as rivals."[165]

This was work she enjoyed. "Came home from Ruskin seminary to sit before the fire, and read Ruskin far into the night."[166] He shared many of her own goals: "to help those who have eyes, to see the beauty of the earth; to help those have ears, to hear the moaning of the poor."[167]

Pleased with her work, Rand McNally offered her the job of general editor of their Canterbury Classics, and she harnessed her usual energy for it, noting, "A busy day, but found time to write the general introductions to Canterbury classics."[168]

She wrote to her young colleague Jeannette Marks that she had taken on this job in "the interest of more imaginative reading in the lower schools."[169]

The series appealed to educators worried by the huge influx of immigrant children. In the 1890s, three and a half million immigrants had come to the United States, and between 1900 and 1910, nearly nine million arrived. With her long interest in writing for the family market, Katharine made the classic tales with English roots accessible to the country's newest children. The series' steady payments and big market were also good for her morale and bank account.

VI.

Wellesley's new president Caroline Hazard was becoming a good friend to Katharine, and as an amateur poet, painter, and composer, used her office to help the college become part of Boston's literary and cultural circles.

With family money she built a stately Shingle-style President's House, Oakwoods, overlooking Lake Waban. Used to entertaining her Boston and Rhode Island friends at her Peace Dale estate, Caroline liked to welcome Wellesley's well-heeled guests into her new twenty-by-thirty-foot reception room, with its walls covered in Japanese paper and Oriental hangings.

There, Katharine met other women writers, many of whom had published alongside her in the *Transcript*. At one of her dinner parties Caroline honored author Alice Meynell on the night of her Author's Reading on the campus. She invited Katharine to join them along with popular Boston patron and hostess Annie Fields, widow of James T. Fields, as well as Sarah Orne Jewett.

Jewett, with her fiction about Maine women becoming very popular, wrote to Katharine later, "These must be charming days and very busy ones too at Wellesley: I like so much to remember my evening there with you and Miss Hazard and Mrs. Meynell."[170]

Such events encouraged Katharine to think about Hawthorne's centennial year, when publishers would bring out new editions of his work. The Crowell publishing house commissioned her to write introductions to their big 1902 edition of fourteen volumes of Hawthorne's works as well as to their smaller Popular Editions,[171] where she could guide readers with enthusiasm, humor, and authority to appreciate him. Taken together, her introductions are a short biography of Hawthorne's development as a writer, written from her perspective as a writer, critic, teacher, and woman.

Drawing on her own experiences, she could analyze an editor's treatment of a piece, its placement on a page, and its surrounding articles. She knew the importance of a book's appearance—the color and design of its cover, the size of its pages—as well as the difficulties faced by a writer challenging himself with each successive work attempted.

She set Hawthorne apart as a serious and accomplished American writer. Perhaps remembering her college visit to Longfellow's home, where Hawthorne had been a frequent guest, she knew that both writers were intent on creating a national literature, and both knew how much help one's mother, aunts, and sisters could be in supporting one's literary career. In these Hawthorne volumes, Katharine's introductions are unique among those of her contemporaries because of her thorough research and focus on women in Hawthorne's life and work.[172]

Of course she had been writing about women writers all her life, beginning with her student review of Elizabeth Barrett Browning's *Aurora Leigh*, and she began to write more commentaries on famous writers, male and female, as she put it, "Not strictly from the male perspective."[173] She called George Sand, the French woman novelist who led an unconventional but romantic life and scandalized the public by wearing men's trousers and smoking cigars, "a power in the development of the human race."[174]

Still coming to terms with living as an independent woman herself, Katharine understood Sand's happiness "at her midnight desk."[175] Like Katharine, Sand had to recover from an unhappy romance, and "after the first anguish of her experience … in the end, a source of wisdom and power to her—George Sand found her chief interest in theories of socialism and communism, in political movements, and in all phases of social reform."[176]

According to Katharine, Sand needed to find a channel where "the overflowing love of that mighty heart could pour itself without reproach or stint," a problem Katharine faced as well. She thought that Sand "had risen from the wreck of her romance to a new life for the state … to a more patient faith, a further-reaching hope, a more tenderly compassionate love for all humanity."[177] Perhaps she also could do that.

She spent the summer of 1902 with Katharine Coman, still suffering from cancer, in England, where they tried out a "motor-car, of all profanities…. Five breakdowns…. We let the Monster go snorting back without us."[178] At least their adventures would give her rich material for her travel book on England several years later.

But their trip was only a brief respite from depression and overwhelming work. She put more stress on herself by beginning an ambitious long-term scholarly research project on English dramatist Thomas Heywood, and moaned to her diary: "A busy day, — letters, examinations, graduate student, dinner, guests, and desk again. Who calls this living?... did my five hours and came home a total wreck."[179]

In her poem "April Fools"[180] she describes lovers who bear a romantic April heart through all the sultry, stormy circle of the year, a poem about painful love. Although Oscar may have seen her whenever he came to Boston, he had married Laura McAdoo in 1899. He may have been like the man with whom the poet Alice Carey fell in love. Katharine wrote of her that she "yielded her whole heart to a man who never came back to claim it. She trusted and waited, until she chanced, in a newspaper, upon the announcement of their marriage."[181]

She also kept in touch with Theophilus over the years since he had pressed his courtship in 1893. In May 1903, with Katharine Coman far away, "Mr. Root reappears. Lunched him at College … pleaded on piazza."[182]

After recovering his health, in 1900 he had become the minister of the small rural parish of Wood River Junction, Rhode Island, not far from the Hazards' Peace Dale. As a Harvard classmate observed, "Probably none smaller or more impecunious could have been found in New England…. [H]is salary was $600 a year when he could get it."[183]

This was hardly enough money on which to support a wife. But from his Rhode Island parish Theophilus could easily travel by train to Peace Dale, where Katharine had begun to spend more time, and to Wellesley. He also came to Boston to attend various alumni events over the years at Harvard. Two weeks after she listened to his pleas on the piazza, she recollected: "A beautiful drive, thro' delicious cool weather, to Concord (and back) for the Emerson Centennial."[184]

Two weeks later, she noted simply, "Mr. Root."[185]

However, Katharine Coman, who had been so persuasive that Katharine tell Mr. Root good-bye in 1893, returned from her travels and intervened again. "Katharine arrived this morning. Poor Mr. Root called this afternoon to be cannonaded with conversation."[186]

Even the arrival of a new collie puppy, Sigurd, a gift to the Katharines from Cornelia Warren, could not derail him. A week later, nothing had been resolved: "Hot. Went to Boston. Was at odds with poor Kathie [probably Coman] over my answer to Mr. Root's latest." [187]

During the month of July, Katharine tried, once more, to end their relationship, writing on August 1: "a long, heart-rending letter from Mr. Root, which must close all relations."[188] And the next day, "Wrote a letter which should put an end to Mr. Root's importunity."[189]

It did: "T. H. S. [the initials she had used once ten years before for him] at last returns my letters—wrapt in rose-leaves."[190]

Nevertheless, the next week, she "started down to the milliner's and ran into T.H.R."[191] A month later, it was "Mr. Root...—oh me!"[192] Unfortunately, she left no letters from him for posterity to see.[193]

Their romance over for the second time, they both poured their energies into their professional lives. He organized a series of over "fifty local interdenominational conferences on the study of the Gospel of John" that developed into the Providence, R. I., Conferences of 1903-04, where "many eminent preachers and scholars, for the most part personal friends of his, spoke."[194] He then edited the conference addresses,[195] and became known as "a scholar of wide learning and fastidious accuracy ... a preacher of great excellence [who] ... was acutely responsive to modern thinking, to modern methods, and essential needs of ... his community."[196]

Nevertheless, over the years, with mutual friend Annie Beecher Scoville in nearby Connecticut and Katharine making extended visits to the Hazard estate, she and Theophilus could easily have spent time together.

VII.

Americans continued to sing Katharine's song as one of several patriotic visions of America. But with the American flag now flying over the distant lands of Hawaii, Cuba, and the Philippines, how did it describe an imperialist nation?

In the 1899 Paris Peace Treaty, Spain had "relinquished" its sovereignty over Cuba, and "ceded" sovereignty over the Philippines to the United States.[197] European powers were ready to take over the Philippines, but the United States regarded itself as the sole possessor of a non-independent Philippines. The four-man Philippine Commission, which included General Dewey, wanted the United States to continue its rule to prevent "domestic anarchy and foreign intervention."[198]

American General Funston thought that "the Filipinos, although some are intelligent, are not yet capable, as a people, of self-government."[199] The American military should make "a steady, systematic advance which holds and rules the invaded territory and establishes there the authority of the United States."[200]

However, the Philippine leader General Emilio Aguinaldo had helped the United States gain military victory over Spain with the understanding that he would become the leader of an independent Philippines, so fighting in the Philippines grew increasingly bloody as the insurgency became a war.

Americans were divided about the future of these new territories. Expansionists argued that Providence had extended the borders of America's Manifest Destiny nation far beyond its shores: "'American' denotes a quality rather than a locality.... American interests and enterprise will not be turned back by the Pacific Ocean.... The Philippines are in the line of march of empire, and Providence has timed their coming to us to the exigencies of history. These new possessions ... open new fields for our civilization and our faith as well as for our trade.... We must educate them; we must civilize them; we must Christianize them."[201]

Opponents abhorred their belief that "trade follows the flag, that it is to be raised wherever there is opportunity, that once raised it is never to be hauled down and that all the territory over which it flies is the property of the United States, to be used for the advantage of those who have taken possession of it without regard to the rights or interests of the people who live in it."[202]

What was racist imperialism doing to America?

Katharine condemned her country's nightmare war in a scathing indictment of how an American soldier, indoctrinated to see the Filipinos as primitive little "brown men with spears," brags about his own bloodthirsty murders and cover-up lies:

We've set the torch to their bamboo town,
And out they come in a scampering rush,
Little brown men with spears,
Shoot!
Down they go in a crush,
Sickening smears,
Hideous writhing huddles and heaps
Under the palms and the mango-trees,
More, still more! Shoot 'em down
Like brown jack-rabbits that scoot
With comical leaps
Out of the brush.
No loot?
No prisoners, then. As for these—
Hush![203]

She ended her poem with a poignant image of the effect of such a war on America:

The flag that dreamed of delivering
Shudders and droops like a broken wing.

Silvery rice-fields whisper wide
How for home and freedom their owners died.[204]

Wellesley College brought in speakers such as the well-known Filipino patriot, Sixto Lopez, from a large, wealthy, prominent, and well-educated land-owning family. He had been secretary of the delegation sent to the United States in 1898 to discuss American recognition of Philippine independence.

To prepare for his talk, Katharine Coman had her Agora Club debate: "Resolved, That the Filipinos are capable of Self-government."[205] Ten nights after his talk at Wellesley, he argued at historic Faneuil Hall in Boston against America's establishment of concentration camps and hiring of mercenaries in the Philippines.[206] In spite of the March of 1901 capture of Filipino General Aguinaldo by the United States, the terrible battles continued.

Then, to the nation's horror, President McKinley was assassinated at the 1901 American Exposition at Buffalo, New York, by a man who wanted more economic and social justice for the laboring classes. With McKinley's death, Vice President Theodore Roosevelt, the most vociferous advocate of expansionism by any military means necessary, became President of the United States. As Ohio's Mark Hanna lamented, "Now look, that damned cowboy is President of the United States!"[207]

The American military had a policy of taking no prisoners alive and using the barbaric "water-cure" as an interrogation method. (A century later it would be called "waterboarding.") Many Americans, when they found out about this, were horrified, certain that it put their country on the wrong side of international law.[208] But to the US military brass, "water-cure" was an appropriate way to deal with the "uncivilized" Filipinos. In addition, Brigadier General Jacob Smith, wanting to turn the islands into "a howling wilderness," ordered the killing and burning of all Filipinos over ten years of age because they were capable of bearing arms.[209]

With the Philippine-American War causing some to advocate Filipino extermination,[210] in January 1902 Fiske Warren brought Lopez's sister Clemencia to Boston to educate Americans about how their government was imprisoning Filipino patriots such as her brothers.

In an eloquent address to the Massachusetts Woman Suffrage Association she expressed hope that her listeners would form a "more favorable opinion of the Filipinos," instead of imagining that they were "savages without education or morals."[211] She pointed out that while American women were striving to take part in their national life, Filipino women were striving for a national life to take part in.

As for war with the United States, Clemencia explained that her compatriots did not want to be governed by foreign lands, and suggested that American women "should take part in any investigation that may be made in the Philippine Islands...."[212]

She later conferred with President Roosevelt, who referred her letter to his Secretary of War. Apparently her actions bore fruit, although exactly what transpired that eventually resulted in her brothers' release is not known.[213]

On July 4, 1902, Independence Day, President Roosevelt declared the United States victorious in its war against the Philippines. But the tactic of moving thousands of innocent bystanders into concentration areas, so criticized by Americans when the Spanish General Weyler, "the Butcher," used it in Cuba, was now being used by the American military against the Philippine people.

Had imperialism turned Americans into the kind of oppressors it most criticized?

VIII.

As bloodshed continued in the Philippines in spite of Roosevelt's declaration, Katharine prepared her persuasive antiwar poetry to be published as a book.[214]

That fall she traveled more frequently into the evolving Boston literary scene, including to one Authors Club meeting at the home of Julia Ward Howe, poet of "Battle Hymn of the Republic," the rousing Civil War patriotic song.[215] Even thinking about her writing energized her, and when the Irish poet William Butler Yeats arrived in Boston, he sent Katharine back to work surrounded by "a strange inner music."[216]

She boldly spoke out against the strong unfairly conquering the weak as well as an "exclusively masculine point of view" when she wrote her introduction to Alfred, Lord Tennyson's long poem *The Princess,* which ridiculed women's intelligence and colleges.[217]

Galvanized by her travels and by the women speaking out around her, Katharine was ready to change the words of her 1895 "America." If the United States was going to rule other countries, it needed to remember its original values and start practicing them at home to be a model for its global possessions.

As Mark Twain sarcastically pointed out: "There must be two Americas: one that sets the captive free, and one that takes a once-captive's new freedom away from him, and picks a quarrel with him with nothing to found it on; then kills him to get his land.... we have debauched America's honor and blackened her face before the world.... we can have just our usual flag, with the white stripes painted black and the stars replaced by the skull and cross-bones."[218]

While some women thought that it should be women's job to heal the wounds of men's wars,[219] Katharine wanted to do more than that. In the previous decade the United States, like older nations, each with complicated cultures and alliances, had begun vying for political and moral dominance. She had changed as well, gaining a more global and historical perspective, traveling far beyond American borders—to Paris streets full of anti-Semitic rioting during the Dreyfus Affair, and to a defeated but proud Spain.

While her James Lincoln poetry protested against the bloody and perhaps needless Boer War caused by British and Dutch imperialistic agendas, now, with its wars against Spain and the Philippines, the United States was likewise asserting its military power for commercial gain in spite of the human cost.

Katharine agreed with such writers as Twain, Garland, and Howells, idealists who wanted peace, believed in internationalism, and thought that education could promote their cause.

The American flag had been used by both sides to symbolize their values. But after four years of war that seemed to have produced only death, battlefields began to seem less glorious to many Americans. With the nation torn apart at home by violent racism and anti-immigration nativists, it was time for Katharine to remind Americans of what their country's best self could be when they sang her words.

She had not used the word "brotherhood" at all in her 1895 poem, but in the years since, she had watched those around her working against class and race hostilities to promote brotherhood and community, writing, "Feast me no feasts that for the few are spread."[220]

Shared fellowship was a guiding concept in her family with her mother's generosity to the poor, in Henry Durant's dream for Wellesley College embodied in his hope that its graduates would "minister" to the world, and in the serious work of her closest friends—from Annie's teaching Indians at the Hampton Institute to Caroline Hazard's family creation of a benevolent community for their employees.

Oscar Triggs explained, "Democracy is a hope, a promise that evil is not necessary, that social conditions may be remedied, that poverty, disease, crime, cannot and shall not endure.... Brotherhood becomes really a question of national survival."[221]

The Eastern Anti-Imperialist Conference took the words of Abraham Lincoln as its motto: "'Those who deny freedom to others deserve it not for themselves, and, under a just God, cannot long retain it.'"[222]

Racism was still rampant in the United States, especially in the South, where slavery might have been abolished by the Civil War but Jim Crow laws and racial violence still threatened blacks. Race hatred was evident in the growing number of lynchings, like the ones in Mississippi where ten Negroes "were not charged with any crime, save that of alleged participation in a race conflict in which whites were quite as guilty as blacks."[223] In South Carolina, white men massacred a Negro postmaster and his family, and the issue was seen not as "white supremacy, but of law and order and the maintenance of civilization."[224]

Race questions had arisen even at Wellesley when African-American girls applied for admission. The faculty were divided, as Katharine noted: "Long [Academic] Council meeting on 'colored-girl' question."[225]

Katharine Coman promoted interracial brotherhood, one person at a time: when Wellesley accepted Harriet Rice, an African-American student, she befriended and mentored her. One of the first black women to graduate from a women's college, Rice later attended medical school and never forgot Coman's friendship and support, writing to her that the many small kindnesses "'received at your hands ... made a far more lasting impression in my young girlhood than many pages of history....'"[226]

Activist and "accomodationist" Booker T. Washington sent his daughter Portia to Wellesley, with the support of faculty like Coman. But when Portia left the college after only one year, the resulting public outcries showed strong opposition to racial integration.

Although Wellesley turned out to be Portia's first step in a distinguished musical career, the furor over her presence at the college showed how difficult it was to take a such a step.

Nevertheless, Katharine had watched Coman's untiring work for social justice.

Wherever she traveled, from Washington to Honolulu, Coman found Wellesley graduates, "groups of earnest women ... working for Negroes in the Black Belt, working for poor whites in Kentucky [mountains], working for ... foreigners [in] our great cities—Everywhere [a] sense of *non ministrari sed ministrare*, wise and efficient service."[227]

At the top of Pike's Peak in 1893, Katharine had been inspired to celebrate the beauty and patriotic history of America in spite of the terrible economic depression and the sectional and class conflicts tearing the country apart. She hoped that the shared American landscape and idealism could someday create a future nation of "nobler men" where "selfish gain" would no longer "stain" the "banner of the free."

In 1895 she had intended "America" as a patriotic poem when Americans had not yet found a song with a singable and appropriate melody that expressed their love for their nation. The tune for "My Country, 'Tis of Thee" was the melody for the British "God Save the Queen," and as Katharine noted, "the popular voice has never quite learned to sing" the "Star Spangled Banner."[228]

When composer Silas G. Pratt published Katharine's poem set to a melody he composed, it attracted "an unexpected amount of attention."[229] Americans wanted to have plenty of patriotic songs to celebrate their country in the years before and after the Spanish-American War, and President Roosevelt, with much ballyhoo, had recently raised the American flag above the Panama Canal, a waterway that would facilitate the growth of America's commercial and military power.

As Americans began to sing her poem to various melodies, they changed her words as they saw fit. And so finally, in 1904 Katharine "re-wrote it, trying to make the phraseology more simple and direct."[230]

But she did far more than simplify her language; she gave her poem a new theme. Americans could not wait for the "whiter jubilee" of her 1895 poem. They needed her prayer for brotherhood in new words as "fine" and "ample" as she could make them.[231]

"Halcyon" skies became "spacious," perhaps because they were no longer peaceful but needed to be large enough for lofty ideals. Her earlier "enameled plain" became "fruited," a bountiful garden created by hard-working farmers on otherwise barren land that could sustain a growing country.

Because she wanted Americans to see their nation as one enormous community whose borders stretched "From sea to shining sea," she changed the closing two lines of the first stanza to the words so famous today, extending her prayer that "God shed his grace on thee" by adding a second request: "And crown thy good with brotherhood / From sea to shining sea!" She asks God to augment His goodness with an even greater treasure, brotherhood, if America was to be a model for people beyond its shores.

Such a community of people should be America's valuable crown, the treasure beyond the material riches within the nation and with its global neighbors. By ending the first and final stanzas of her poem with those two lines, she ensured that they would be the climactic lines of the song, whether only the first verse or all the verses were sung, and thus swell with the greatest volume and remain in the singers' memories the longest.

Her revised "America" ran in *The Boston Evening Transcript* on Nov. 19, 1904.[232] The words below in boldface are Katharine's revisions:

O beautiful for **spacious** skies,

For amber waves of grain,

For purple mountain majesties

Above the **fruited** plain!

America! America!

God shed his grace on thee

And crown thy good with brotherhood

From sea to shining sea!

In the second stanza, Katharine kept her evocative image of the country's founding "pilgrim feet" marching through "wilderness," but altered the final three lines by adding another request to her prayer: that God correct, heal, and make whole the flaws of the nation, and make firm or strengthen its "self-control" and its freedom within the framework of its original rule of law.

In the heated discussions of American imperialism, many had thought that the United States needed to follow its Constitution and focus first on establishing and guaranteeing the rights of its own citizens before imposing itself on foreign territories, a principle she emphasized in her revisions:

O beautiful for pilgrim feet,

Whose stern, impassioned stress

A thoroughfare for freedom beat

Across the wilderness!

America! America!

God mend thy every flaw,

Confirm thy soul in self-control,

Thy liberty in law!

In her third stanza, Katharine added three lines stating her hope that God would "refine," or improve, America's gold, its material wealth, until its success be counted in its spiritual wealth, rather than in human riches or territory:

O beautiful for glory-tale
>> Of liberating strife,
When **valiantly,** for man's avail,
>> Men lavished precious life!
America! America!
>> **May God thy gold refine**
Till all success be nobleness
>> **And every gain divine!**

Her final stanza reminds its singers of the dream of national unity by patriots from George Washington to Abraham Lincoln, a dream evoked by the "alabaster" city of the Chicago fair. By changing the the final two lines of the song to repeat those in the first stanza, she emphasized how her country could become worthy of divine grace:

O beautiful for patriot dream
>> That sees beyond the years
Thine alabaster cities gleam
>> Undimmed by human tears!
America! America!
>> God shed his grace on thee
And crown thy good with brotherhood
>> **From sea to shining sea!**

The *Transcript* declared that she had written "the American national hymn … a thoroughly American production well-nigh perfect as poetry, and in the most exalted strain as politics. America has only to live up to the aspirations here breathed to realize its Golden Age,—the Golden Age of those idealists of late held in scant respect, the Fathers of the Declaration and the Constitution."[233] Her third stanza, "the most beautiful and exalted," uttered "the patriot's prayer and faith in America's perfectibility."[234]

She noted proudly in her diary, "*Transcript* commends my 'America.'"[235]

In her years of turmoil since 1893, with disappointing courtships by two idealistic and intense men, her humiliating experiences as an American woman in Spain, her work on American writers, and her emergence as a woman confident to speak out for women and others who didn't have a voice, Katharine had gained the knowledge, wisdom, and determination necessary to give the nation her poem.

Knowing what it was like to be marginalized and silenced, she wrote for those who had no voice, and she gave Americans a fresh and inspiring ideal of their country as an inclusive community.

The new words of her hope for the country became the song's dominant concept because she believed that "Americans are at heart idealists, with a fundamental faith in human brotherhood."[236]

They began to sing her new song to more melodies, including Samuel A. Ward's "Materna," the one we sing today.

Although women were still barred from most colleges, graduate schools, professional organizations, and professional careers including the ministry, as well as from powerful male social networks, to say nothing of from voting in and running in national elections, with her poem Katharine answered Harvard's President Eliot, showing him what a college-educated woman could do.

PART THREE

Creating a Global Community:

1905-1929

CHAPTER NINE

1905-1915
"NEW WOMAN OF EGYPT"[1]

I.

Although the *Transcript* praised her "America" as "well-nigh perfect,"[2] when Katharine tallied up her earnings for 1904 ("Salary = $2,000.00. Outside lectures = $30.00. Tutoring = $90.00. Royalties = $140.89. Editorial = $50.00. Literary = $390.31. Prose = $155.75, Verse = $77. James Lincoln = $157.56). Total $2701.20"),[3] she saw that she needed to find new writing projects to help pay for the construction of a family home that, with Arthur's financial help, her mother and sister would share with Katharine.

She was like her character, the impoverished Greek Professor Lane, with a study, much like Katharine's with a Homeric library and collection of Greek dramatists.[4] He fears that he will never be able to travel to the lands of his dreams, but, fortunately, he has a good friend who knows "what paltry salaries the university pays its professors—salaries that a first-class janitor would refuse,"[5] and gives Lane $10,000, saying, "'Make that trip ... you have been planning.... Start with the notion of taking a holiday, but be sure that some good work will come out of it.'"[6]

Caroline Hazard became that good friend to Katharine, taking her to Egypt and the Holy Land, an unforgettable journey that did yield "good work." New Women that they were, thanks to their determination and Caroline's wealth, they would travel independently of a tour group to see the storied lands.

Caroline had been cultivating a close friendship with Katharine, leading a college-wide celebration of her newly revised "America," and afterwards bringing her a bouquet of "pinks" and "persuasion."[7]

Because travel books, including her own on Spain, were selling well, Katharine planned two more. She would go for the summer with Katharine Coman to get material for a travel book on England illustrated with Coman's photographs and then join Caroline in Switzerland and travel on to Egypt and the Holy Land.

As their departure drew closer, Katharine spent more of her weekends in Rhode Island with Caroline. Nearby, at Wood River Junction, Theophilus was "steadily gaining in strength" and expected to be "stronger than ever."[8]

Before she left, Katharine cosigned the mortgage with Arthur for the new house and land in Wellesley on Curve Street, owing $2,000.[9]

After her summer in England, she joined Caroline and family members in Vevey, Switzerland. There she impressed Caroline's nephew, Leonard Bacon, a future poet, with her "long delightful talks about everything under the sun, about … the interpretation of a line of Shakespeare or legends about the thousand-year-old castles that crowned the vine-smothered hills."[10] He remembered thinking: "'This lady is thirty years older than I, and what a good time we are having!'"[11]

Caroline liked to travel in style, as Katharine joked with her mother. At the plush Hôtel Trois Couronnes on Lake Geneva, "Dinner is at half past seven and is quite an awful function, for which my gayest duds are by no means gay enough. We have about a dozen courses of strangely disguised viands—the pigeon pie served … in a pastry drum, with the Swiss flag flying from the lid."[12]

From Naples, Katharine, along with Caroline and the latter's maid, Miss O'Brian,[13] sailed for Alexandria, Egypt. She was astonished by her first view of how Eastern women were treated, noting that a nobleman "promenaded the deck constantly, a gentleman of highly cultivated and sensitive face, that surveyed us all serenely from under its red fez, but [his wife] only appeared on disembarking … a muffled, graceful figure, with the face veiled so that only the eyes could be seen." Once on land, the woman was put into "a closed carriage drawn by white Arabian horses."[14]

On "high seas," they sailed into the lovely crescent-shaped harbor of Alexandria.[15] Katharine had pictured Egypt in biblical stories, in *The Arabian Nights*,[16] in the "Cairo" exhibit at the 1893 Chicago Exposition, and in the Egyptian archeological treasures in Boston's Museum of Fine Arts. Now, she could see it in person.

In 1906, Cairo was emerging as a cosmopolitan international city, the largest city in Africa and in the Arab world, attracting such celebrities as Sarah Bernhardt and Arthur Conan Doyle, author of the Sherlock Holmes stories. To Katharine, it was a "jewel city clad in / Color and sheen!"[17]

They traveled twenty miles out to Giza, passing gray buffaloes and clay villages, to the exciting "silver outlines of a pyramid."[18] She enjoyed the "noisy, rollicking party of Turks there, galloping their donkeys up to the Sphinx … on their way to Mecca on the holy pilgrimage which every good Muslim tries to make once in his life."[19]

WATERCOLOR PAINTING BY CAROLINE HAZARD: THE PYRAMIDS

As she had done in Spain, France, German and Italy, Katharine learned a little of the local language, greeting her mother: "Nehârak laben! (May thy day be white as milk!)," and signing her letter, "'Al Allâh. (To God's care!) Your ever loving Egyptian."[20]

Their train ride south to Luxor was a "wonderful journey" through Arab villages shaded by palm trees along the muddy Nile through the vast desert and fertile land along its shores.[21] She was surprised by "a Turk with his family, consisting of three women and a lot of simultaneous children. He sat in one compartment by himself, smoking with much dignity, and his harem, if it was his harem, were all crowded into another."[22]

Outraged at this, the American women did a slow boil in their own compartment until eventually "Miss O'Brian went out into the aisle and told Hashem vigorously what she thought of trundling women about the country in chicken-coops, but Hashem was unabashed.

"'That's good way. That's all right. No, <u>not</u> too many. One his daughter, three his wives. Three wives all right.'"[23]

However much such practices disturbed her, though, Katharine soon imagined a new career for herself, confessing to her mother: "I long to be an Egyptologist and have a school of my own and go out into the desert and dig."[24]

Staying on the Nile in Luxor for six weeks, Katharine enjoyed waking up each morning in "a semi-tropical world, most strange and beautiful ... with strange birds ... chattering out in a garden of tropical flowers beneath a sky of the most dazzling blue."[25]

On Christmas Eve, the hotel gave their American and European guests a "remarkable Christmas dinner" and "quiet ball."[26] Katharine found the Russian princes, German barons, and the rest "excellently entertaining,"[27] and they celebrated the New Year "by a memorable trip on the Nile, the sunset an archangel's song."[28]

Beyond the entrancing Avenue of the Sphinxes, Katharine and Caroline entered the Temple of Luxor through huge pylons that stood sentry before the acres of hieroglyph-covered walls, columns carved to resemble stalks of papyrus and lotus plants with blossoms in bud and bloom, cartouches identifying ancient kings and queens, and obelisks, some still with their original brightly colored paint depicting the scenes of religious processions and episodes in the lives of the gods. It was "a great, enchanting playground."[29]

They made many visits to the extensive Temple of Karnak, dedicated to the Theban moon-god Khons, son of Ammon and Mut. Within its pylons, halls, and sanctuary loomed the great Temple of Ammon. Once they followed Baedeker's advice to see it when the moon was full because "moonlight adds a peculiar charm to a visit to the ruins there."[30] And so Katharine found it: "How pale the melancholy moonlight falls / On obelisk and column, cut with signs / Of perished pomps and silent rituals!"[31]

To explore the ancient treasures in the hills in the Valley of the Kings and Queens, they crossed the Nile, scared "to death,"[32] to the rocky hillsides honeycombed with burial sites of the Luxor pharaohs hidden below the surface. At the time of their visit, forty-one tombs had been discovered, two as recently as 1898. Treading down ancient staircases and through small passages into various chambers, they could see scenes painted on the walls of burial preparations for voyages into the underworld and afterlife.

They returned to "the Valley of the Shadow of Death, borne on Egyptian shoulders in the true Pharaoh fashion."[33] Nevertheless, Katharine saw Egyptian history as oppressive: "Pharaohs tyrannical in very death!"[34]

WATERCOLOR PAINTING BY CAROLINE HAZARD: THE COLOSSI

Below the mountains in Deir el-Bahri they saw the imposing mortuary temple of Hatshepsut, the woman who ruled Egypt for twenty-two years as regent for, and then senior co-ruler with, her nephew and stepson, Tuthmosis III. Fascinated, Katharine bought reproductions of her palace frescoes. Calling this female ruler a "New Woman of Egypt,"[35] this American New Woman planned to surround herself with these pictures in her new study.

After an exhilarating day at the races, where, "God had his right hand upon us,"[36] Katharine and Caroline left Luxor like heroes, "scattering piastres like snowflakes among the host of table-waiters, chambermen, porters, door-boys and the like who came flocking to see us off."[37]

They traveled south along the Nile, in "a wonderful journey thru' the desert"[38] to Aswan. With broad streets and whitewashed houses, Aswan was an important and prosperous city with its granite quarry, which had supplied centuries of Egyptian architects and sculptors. Located at the Nile cataracts and channels between African Nubia and Egypt, it was the starting point of caravan routes.

When Caroline looked for a "dragoman" to be their future guide, their old friend of the Luxor market, "Hassan Abdullah, as smiling, as black, as amiable and mendacious as ever," appeared.[39] "He told the surging crowd of dragomen [local guides] that we were his…. They fell back and we meekly acquiesced, letting Hassan — Mohammed A. says he takes hashish! — escort us to our hotel."[40]

Hashish or not, to Caroline he was like the butler of her childhood. He was "a man of sixty, keen and clever, who had begun life with Professor George Ebers, and had some real knowledge of archeological treasures."[41]

They settled into the Grand Hotel Assouan in "two pleasant rooms … high enough to overlook the tree-tops."[42] In the cool of the morning, Katharine listened "to the buzz of bees and the chirp of birds and the ceaseless chant of the Nile boatmen, who can't work without singing" and "now and then the snarl of a camel, indignant because somebody is climbing up his hump," a "most furious" sound, "equal to bears and lions."[43]

She had a divided skirt made for riding camels and donkeys, telling her mother, "It will not be long before I come up Curve street on a white camel,"[44] and Caroline found Cornelia's "spicy comments on our Egyptian experiences very entertaining."[45]

One day Katharine enjoyed a beautiful sail on a boat, probably a felucca with its distinctive lateen rig, a "brightly painted, green and red and yellow sail-boat,"[46] where, in spite of the stiff wind, the crew "trimmed their sail cleverly enough, our young Nubians, and pulled at their big, clumsy oars with a will. As soon as we had distanced a rival boat, they broke out into a barbarian yell, winding up, as the Nile boatmen usually do, with: 'Hip, hip, hooray! Very nice! Thank you!'

"Then our reis [chief], a handsome young black of twenty … pulled out a durabukka, the native drum which looks something like a water-jar with dried skin stretched across the mouth, and thrummed vigorously on that, singing a native song to which the other lads howled a chorus.

"The wind meanwhile was filling our sail and on we went merrily past Elephantine Island, where the Nilometer used to stand and mark the height of the risings of the river…. This island was strongly garrisoned with Roman troops, for it marked the southern-most boundary of Roman Egypt."[47]

She laughed at the irony of knowing that her "old torment, Juvenal the satirist, who's hard to translate, was packed off here from imperial Rome as prefect of the garrison, to punish him for his sharp-edged wit."[48]

Below Aswan, Katharine and Caroline traveled to "that wonder of wonders, Abu Simbel," where the mountain was "hollowed out with fifteen halls and chambers, all sculptured and brilliantly painted; the deepest of all, holding the four statues enthroned in a row of the three sun-gods and Ramses himself…. We … watched it from the deck till the last minute as we steamed away."[49]

Before they left Aswan, Katharine went by boat to see the island of Philae and its temples to Isis, the goddess of love and fertility. They had been mostly submerged when the dam near Aswan was completed in 1902. The Nile grew wider and deeper as she neared the dam, and "islands of these polished, sable, strangely-sculptured boulders peered up out of the water.

"And there, at last was Philae — the solemn beauty of its pylons, the graceful columns of the kiosk, the colonnades submerged to their capitals, perhaps the loveliest and at one time the most sacred of Egyptian temples sacrificed to modern engineering."[50]

Women had "come flocking from Greece and Italy for the mystic healing of Isis" to this most classical temple of elegant proportions below them. Katharine looked down "at beautiful reliefs and decorations gleaming pathetically up at us from under the water, and our rowers shoved us from shrine to shrine with oars set ruthlessly against exquisitely cut cartouches and the reproachful faces of Pharaohs and of gods. The drowned temple … looks pensive and appealing."[51]

She left "wondering if the chant of the boatmen who brought the tourists was the same as that of the boatmen two thousand years ago who brought the pilgrims."[52]

Katharine wanted to bring Egypt back to her new home, shopping enthusiastically, choosing all kinds of Egyptian items, and "reveling in the risky sport of bargaining for antiquities."[53]

At the time, tourists could acquire genuine and fake Egyptian antiquities at bazaars, on the streets and through dealers, robbers, and archeologists. She chose many treasures that celebrated female lives—a "wing of the Goddess of Truth ... from the doors of a tomb,"[54] and a Nubian girl's garment made "of strips of antelope skin and snail shells, smeared in castor oil for perfume ... from our boat on the Nile of the children themselves ... and an "Egyptian figure with child-Isis and Horus" even if they were not genuine.[55]

Although she was well aware of the illegalities, she couldn't resist: "the chief Luxor dealer, El Hagg Mohammed Moassed, — a great personage ... who has made so much money buying antiquities cheap from Arab grave-robbers and selling them dear to American tourists that he has built a glorious new mosque in Luxor...."[56]

She bought several such treasures, including an alabaster "(genuine) funereal urn from Egyptian tomb,"[57] and a dagger, "probably the product of one of the shameless 'Manufactories of Antiques,'" and a scarab.[58] Perhaps most amazing was her choice of a "Beaded Mummy Cloth – very valuable. Secured by dragoman for me. Probably genuine."[59]

II.

Katharine and Caroline then headed for the Holy Land of Christianity. Traveling through Goshen on the train, Katharine saw both a biblical land—"the ruins of the treasure-cities that Ramses the Great made the Children of Israel build for him"—and its people, "the characteristic Egyptian features ... a man in green gown and white turban ploughing with a camel and a bullock yoken together."[60]

On their way to Port Said, their train ran alongside the hundred-mile-long 1869 Suez Canal, connecting the Mediterranean with the Red Sea, where "great ocean steamers" sailed on the "narrow blue ribbon" of the "tight-fitting canal."[61] With nearly 3,500 vessels traversing it each year by 1900, it facilitated the increasing political and commercial interdependency of nations.

In the port of Haifa, they found a big "hubbub [when] the air was rent by the wild Oriental vociferations of the porters,"[62] and joined their fellow-passengers on deck— "Greek Church papas and Roman priests, glowering on one another, tourists of every European tongue, and a sprinkling of indignant Americans, for the boat was dirty to the point of filthiness, and the dinner was uneatable."[63]

Katharine proved to be an indestructible traveler. When their ship finally anchored, she was "passed down" a ladder to smaller rowboats and then "grasped by a strong brown arm and hustled on to a platform that seemed, at that moment six feet or more above that dancing boat. But, as the boat rose on the next wave, I felt a suggestive push and jumped desperately down into another strong brown clutch that thrust me like a parcel on to a seat."[64]

Then she had to clamber up to the top of the dock, where, before she had time to see how, she was "seized and vigorously boosted. I flung up my foot like a dancing-master toward that beam which it couldn't at all reach and flung up my hands toward the big brown arms reaching over from above, and in a minute more, doing my best to walk [up] the wall, I had been hauled up to the top of the pier."[65]

A few days later, she was jolting over primitive roads to dirty inns in Carmel and by the Sea of Galilee but began to feel connections between these New Testament lands and the Bible she and Caroline read, as she wrote her mother: "Tiberias, On the Sea of Galilee, Dearest Mamma: Here is your big-little girl actually looking out upon the sea and hills which Christ knew so well, — just now a sea grey with sudden wind—'And there rose a great storm of wind, and the sea beat into the ship.'"[66]

When she stood on its shore, Katharine could picture Jesus there.[67] With Caroline in charge, their pilgrimage was for the "uplifting of the soul."[68]

In Nazareth they went to "the one place" where she felt sure that Mary and Jesus had been, "the fountain known as Mary's Well…. I liked at Nazareth to think of Jesus as the Elder Brother, with James and Joses and Juda ??? and Simon and the little sisters trooping about Him."[69]

Back at the inn, Katharine hoped that her new grasp of the Gospels and Christianity would always remain with her, telling her mother, "Yet we were homesick already, as I think we shall always be in our hearts, for the lake and hills Christ loved…. I am sure you understand better than I can tell why we look back on those rainy days that we spent, half ill, in the hardly clean little inn of an extremely dirty town … as the best days of our pilgrimage. Although the cities that circled the lake in Christ's day are perished, although the very trees are cut down … one can realize the figure of 'the prophet of Galilee' who so loved these waters and these shores, far more vividly than elsewhere."[70]

At the top of a hill near Jericho, Katharine had a revelation:

> Above that dazzling road was a sky-arch of burning sapphire, and I could see, from where I sat, the Dead Sea already blue with distance, and its … hazy-purple mountains. It was an easy climb but brought me out on a summit where I seemed to stand against the sky, with all the world spread out before

me....— the mighty hill-barrier east of the Jordan, the blue line of the Dead Sea, and the great sweep of the plain, most of it brown and barren, but with shining green about Jericho....

It was still strange to realize that those further mountains walled the land of Gilead and the land of Moab, while the nearer crags, west of the Jordan, may have been the scene of the Temptation.... I could almost have seen Moses, if I had been standing on Pisgah....[71]

At the mountaintop, Katharine felt a divine presence, the biblical promise of God's love for His chosen people. Like her epiphany at the top of Pike's Peak in Colorado fourteen years before, her vision of a community blessed by a divine spirit enlarged and strengthened her faith. She would certainly need it in the years ahead.

Soon, however, on their rocky route over tribal territories not yet divided into the countries mapped out after World War I, Katharine slowly began to realize the dangers around her: "We met trains of camels and pack-mules, laden with produce for the port, donkeys on which men or women sat sideways, as one would sit on a bench, and Syrians of all sorts, but all distinguished by keen, gleaming eyes, very different from the patient look of the Egyptian fellaheen.... Many carried guns, and even the poorest peasants, with the smallest patches of tilled ground to guard, carried heavy staves."[72]

She had a startling story for her relatives at home: "There are old rock-tombs about, and I read a thrilling tale in one of my books, which I didn't tell Miss Hazard ... of how some travellers, thirty years ago, took refuge during a storm in one of these, and found it preoccupied by a party of half a dozen travelers who had started out a few days earlier— all with their throats cut!"[73]

Katharine had "noticed that, as in central Galilee, husbandmen and shepherds went around with guns slung over their shoulders and heavy staves in hand."[74] Near Jericho, she was alarmed by a Bedouin rider whose sword swung beside him: "At last it dawned on me that this was our armed escort whom Hassan had sent along to protect me!"[75]

With her "stout umbrella ... for a staff," as Baedeker's guidebook had suggested, when Katharine climbed to where she believed Jesus had given the Sermon on the Mount,[76] she wanted to sit and read the New Testament.

But her dragoman tramped "disconsolately about ... urging the descent.... he pointed out the black tents of the Bedouins in the sloping pastures below and said it would never do to let the dusk find us in their neighborhood.... So I contented myself with the Beatitudes, while Hassan, afraid I would read them aloud, edged off as far as possible.... I wanted to remain for hours, but I meekly followed Hassan, who took a tight grip of my arm."[77]

Nevertheless, on their trip Katharine was curious about the Muslim religion and went to see a "brilliant mosque, a great octagon crusted with marble slabs below, and porcelain tiles, in rich, harmonious colors, above. Even through that dark day it shone like an immense jewel. Around it like a frieze runs, in Arab fashion, an interweaving of Koran texts."[78]

In Acre she enjoyed the wonderful scene outside her carriage window, "where turbaned Moslems were selling all manner of cakes and sweetmeats, plying their trades in open shops or taking coffee and playing checkers at little tables in the market-place. Fishermen, with the colored cloth and camel's-hair ring for head-gear, were bringing up their slippery spoils from the sea."[79]

When they had to get out of the unwieldy carriage and walk, Katharine and Caroline found themselves "in a genuine Oriental bazaar, among donkeys, veiled women, gowned and turbaned Syrians, staring children, with the stalls on every hand [with] the gay stuffs of the East, silks, shawls, embroidered jackets, flowered veils, rugs, carpets, and all the gaudy trappings for horses and camels ... meat-stalls and the flat cakes ... heaps of golden oranges and green pistachio nuts ... pressed masses of dates and figs ... bright-colored drinks, cresses, cucumbers, water-pipes, tobacco, cigarettes, leather-work, copperware, daggers, coffee-cups and saucer, attar of roses, bracelets, anklets, necklaces, [and] red and yellow slippers."[80]

She was so entranced with a mother camel and her baby on spindly legs and with "the trains of desert camels sneezing at the sea" that she invested "in that necessity of Wellesley life, a camel-bridle."[81]

Katharine rejoiced in the variety of life around her: "The driver and passing children gathered me flowers, and I gave them candies, and watched the constant stream of camels, donkeys, peasants, pilgrims, priests, Jews, Moslems, Europeans, horses, cows, goats, sheep, saints and sinners, all glorified by the sunset."[82] It was a kind of global community.

Katharine traveled through Spain back to London and the British Museum, where she could roam through its vast displays of Egyptian statuary and tomb objects. Leonard Bacon remembered her there: "'I found her ... in England fresh from the vast experience of the Nile and openly glorying in her delicious and perennial capacity to run a little mad over a new interest, this time tomb-paintings of the 18th Dynasty."[83]

III.

She was still treated disrespectfully as a woman traveling alone. On her way from Egypt to Barcelona, she was ordered to pay additional money for a train seat she had already bought in the one compartment reserved for ladies. Despite her fluent Spanish, the men, all smoking, would not listen to her:

> I remonstrated in vain. Every seat was taken, and the corridors were filled with men standing.... I had five Spanish señores for room-mates, and their idea of comfort was to shut that carriage up as tight as a wedding-cake box and smoke all night. I disciplined them sternly with the window, opening it whenever they began to smoke. The air was mild, but they were sure it would be fatal, and coughed and scolded and pleaded. I didn't care a bit. When they were good and didn't smoke, I shut the window and resigned myself to suffocation, but when their surreptitious puffs began, I calmly opened the window again and made believe I was asleep, so they couldn't argue.
>
> 'It is a Russian Nihilist,' one said to the rest.
>
> 'It is a señora who wishes to kill the human race.'
>
> 'It is not proper that she should be travelling unprotected at night,' said another very severely.
>
> 'But it is we who need protection,' said another plaintively.
>
> I had to wake up and laugh at that, and I said: 'Gentlemen, when you have finished your smoke, I shall be happy to close the window.' And then they laughed a little, too, but rather ruefully and pitched their cigarettes out, but we kept up a pretty lively war all night.[84]

Such experiences only reinforced her idea for the unique travel book on England that she had been working on when she could manage it. Knowing Hawthorne's book on England, *Our Old Home*, very well, having written a new introduction to it, she decided that in her own travel book she would reply to him and show an England that included the many women silenced and ignored as travelers and chroniclers. Having had such a successful trip with Caroline, she had a newly confident storyteller's voice.

Hawthorne had advised travel writers to give "the emotions that cluster about [the scene], and, without being able to analyze the spell by which it is summoned up, you get something like a simulacrum of the object in the midst of them."[85] Katharine did that, describing her distinctive "cluster of emotions" while creating her unconventional *persona* of a female traveler in quest of English writers' lives.

Her book, *From Gretna Green to Land's End*, was an attractive armchair travel book illustrated with Coman's photographs. Its cover, especially the first edition's deep red background for the heraldic designs in gold leaf, suggested an authentic quest, and its enclosed pullout map invited her readers to join her.

Her tone is exuberant and welcoming to her readers, as she reveals how the English landscape comes alive to her as the home of poets, dramatists, and novelists.

Where Hawthorne ushers his readers into his "dusky and stifled" consular office in Liverpool,[86] Katharine welcomes her readers aboard her train as it rolls through northern England, asking them to imagine joining "us," herself and Coman, in their all-female compartment, a private space, comfortable for their imaginary guests.

Hawthorne had negative feelings about such journeys, but Katharine relished her adventures in the landscapes most associated with writers she loved. On her trip to the Lake District from the Border, Katharine's humorous and honest descriptions make her an appealing guide, as she recounts the difficulties of finding lodgings, of being "banged and clanged along a few miles of fairly level road" in a "motor-bus, of all atrocities."[87]

Although her Lake District, with its Wordsworthian "opalescent hills and silver meres"[88] was full of rain, her scholarly work on early English drama enabled her to see a significance in ceremonies which might have been overlooked by those like Hawthorne, without her training.

The two Katharines found it almost impossible to take charge of their transportation, having tried "an automobile scamper" across Staffordshire, where the driver had not listened to their directions or requests. Even in a cart, the women had wanted to drive themselves (both literally and metaphorically), "but the English hostlers, shaking their stolid heads, preferred that we should be driven."[89]

They had been lucky to find one "broad-minded butcher" who would trust them on short expeditions with a pony and cart, but they were not so fortunate near George Eliot's village of Nuneaton. There they had to engage a "victoria" pulled by a single horse for a shilling a mile, controlled by the reins of the male driver. Having never heard of "George Eliot," he could not understand the women's quest.

In her final chapter, Katharine identified with all adventurers, female and male, ending her journey in Cornwall, appropriately at the seacoast, long the launching-place of such explorers as Sir Francis Drake and Sir Walter Raleigh, a place "freshly discovered by each new lover of the moorland and the sea, of soft air and the play of shadows, of folklore and tradition, of the memory of heroes."[90]

From Gretna Green to Land's End created a new literary England. With wit and good humor, Katharine remodeled Hawthorne's England into a new "*Home*" for both male and female readers and writers.

The book earned her a whopping $900 when it was published,[91] and outdid Hawthorne's in popularity, going through at least five editions.

IV.

While Katharine had been enjoying fourteen months of travel and writing, her brother Arthur, while living in Portland, Maine, had been supervising the construction of her new house. The design of the tall brown Shingle-style house, built near the college campus and a train station, may have been based on the "House of the Seven Gables" described by Hawthorne in his novel.[92]

Now more successful than ever in her professional life, Katharine hoped to settle into it with her mother, her sister, and Katharine Coman. But problems started while she was miles away—"a hard letter from Arthur.... Wretched again over these home affairs and only half able to work. Life gets too difficult."[93] She worried about being in debt, having signed a $2,000 mortgage, and so decided to furnish it "as cheaply as possible."[94]

The house appeared to have been built facing the back of the property instead of the front, and the "hurly-burly" of the house kept up[95] when Katharine found that the wrong chairs had been delivered, the carpenters had left the cold-air pipe gaping, and bills were lost, but she at least enjoyed sleeping on the "leafy balcony."[96]

She named this home "The Scarab," a name that reflected her new sense of completeness and autonomy. She placed her small Egyptian scarab on the study mantel and put the large "Art Scarab" on the mantel of the larger parlor.

The scarab beetle, so beloved in Egypt, combines both male and female elements in its body, enabling it to reproduce itself. She saw it as an "emblem of immortality because it is forever climbing. In the spring the little scarabs climb up the banks of the Nile in order to deposit the egg in the sun."[97]

Now nearly fifty, Katharine was herself "forever climbing." She was a successful author, a well-known scholar—a woman who had family, friends, and successful work of her own. By October, she felt that her study was "falling into ordered beauty.... The Scarab begins to feel like home."[98]

Even so, she was still dreaming of Egypt, surrounded by her souvenirs. On a cold night in the study she could wrap up in her beloved steamer rug, "used on trip to Palestine and Egypt. Embroidered by Miss Hazard. (Names of ships and dates) Mediterranean color red; Atlantic yellow & Symbols for Egypt of the Lily and the Bee; Jerusalem cross."[99] Over the bookcase she hung the "pictures ... bought in Egypt—we framed and grouped them" and alabaster from the tomb of Osiris.[100]

THE SCARAB

On the second floor of the house in the sewing room she hung a picture of the "Holy Family travelling through Egypt."[101] Tiles with drawings of lions like the Assyrian tiles "in the British Museum" decorated the room she called "The Haven."[102] Nearby hung the "Cairo Tapestry" below the photograph of Muslims on their prayer rugs.[103] She draped the beaded mummy cloth under two of the paintings done by Caroline Hazard of Egyptian scenes.[104]

On one night that winter when Katharine hosted friends who wanted to see her Egyptian treasures, she and Hatshepsut welcomed them to her study where they popped corn over the fire for a "very enjoyable evening."[105]

To her young great-niece Elizabeth Olmstead, Katharine's house was "lovely ... full too of the treasures of her trips abroad ... a wing of Truth from an Egyptian tomb ... and colorful strings of ceramic and alabaster beads."[106]

Revitalized from her world adventures, she could finally create a settled domestic life for herself like that of many families. Students visited; her mother joined the mothers of her colleagues in social outings; her sister, now deaf, sewed, helped run the house, and typed her manuscripts; while a housekeeper, usually Irish or Swedish, did the hard work of housekeeping, got the meals on the table, and did the laundry. Katharine Coman, who had the large top attic floor to herself, helped with expenses.

These women were herded into line by the Scarab's male resident, the energetic and sociable collie, Sigurd, named for Golden Sigurd, "the shining hero of the Volsunga Saga."[107] He was a new experience for Katharine: "My first vivid sense of the comfort of having a dog smote me on the edge of a tired evening, when, trudging home from a long day in one of the Boston libraries, a sudden nose was thrust into my hand and a gleaming shape leapt up out of the roadside shadows in jubilant welcome."[108]

He was the child she would never have: if their "hurried days" had given them time "for the fine art of mothering" they "would have cherished a child instead of a collie, but Sigurd throve on neglect and saved us from turning into plaster images by making light of all our serious concerns."[109]

He was "a frolicsome bandit who knew of no better use for a mortar-board [the cap for an academic gown]—perhaps there is none—than to spin it around by its gilt tassel."[110] Every day at four o'clock, "we would drop pens, shut books and take Sigurd to walk, —a duty that he by no means allowed us to forget."[111]

The two professors read to him about famous dogs in history and in literature, and he herded them, "with ancestral art, jumping upon the deserter and gently pushing her back, or standing in the path to block her progress, protesting all the while with coaxing whines, with expostulary barks and with all manner of collie eloquence…. But when we both accepted his invitation to the lake [Waban], the three hundred acres of the college park hardly sufficed for his antics."[112]

Forced to stay indoors by winter storms, he "would pick quarrels with the rugs, scatter the pile of newspapers and dance a scandalous jig with that elderly, respectable Bostonian, *The Transcript*."[113]

"'When is a clutter not a clutter?' asked my mother, and answered her own conundrum: 'When Sigurd does it.'"[114]

He had a "piquant" game with her: While "he wagged his tail in ever wilder circles at her, [she] would wag her *Congregationalist* in exact mockery at him, until he would make a maddened leap and snatch that sacred sheet from [her] hand."[115]

Katharine's memoir, *Sigurd*, increased her fame. Albert Payson Terhune, popular creator of many fictional collies, including "Lassie," wrote to her: "Your book is a masterpiece…. It is a gem…. at every angle and every facet, your delineation is flawless."[116]

But her brother Arthur teased her: "You have made an interesting story which will appeal to a great many people and I am glad that I did not succeed in hanging Sigurd, otherwise this story would never have been written."[117]

Unfortunately, Katharine's life began to change when her mother's health grew worse.

Cornelia stayed engaged with life, writing to Arthur despite her weakened state: "I am much exercised about that line of ships going through the Straits of Magellan. I wish they [had] been equipped with wireless."[118] The ships were the "Great White Fleet," American battleships that Theodore Roosevelt sent around the world to show American military strength.

But by the end of January 1908, her "heart began to fail. The whole day, hour by hour, we lived in those failing breaths, —dear mama!"[119] The next day, "We went with her into the Valley of 'the Shadow,' even to the iron gates. She died at 1:30 in the hush of night, and life seems to hush with her."[120]

In her "Poems Account" notebook, Katharine simply wrote, "(Mother dies, but I cannot put sorrow into words as yet.)"[121]

Still "craving" her mother, she dreamt of her return:

A marble wall, illimitable, dumb,

   A blank of white! when lo, her own sweet face,

      With no more halo than the crispy lace

      I knew so well, from sudden casement smiled,

      —Her blithe, audacious self, infringing so

      With stolen peep Death's new punctilio,

      Breaking his code to reassure her child.[122]

Her mother was "merry to the last" on her deathbed when she "murmured quite triumphantly" the words in Spanish of the 23rd Psalm, which even Katharine could not remember.[123]

She stayed close to Cornelia's memory by finishing their joint project, a volume of translations, *Romantic Legends of Spain,* by the important Spanish poet, Gustavo Adolfo Becquer, and lamented, "If only Mother were here to be happy and skeptical over it!"[124]

Katharine's enlarged worldview also helped her recover. She wrote "The Sacrifice," an elegy for Dr. William Jones, an Indian ethnologist, who was slain in the Philippines.[125] Another of her poems was set to the tune of a Spanish hymn, and she turned to Spanish history for material, spending several days writing on Cuba.[126]

Becoming more newsworthy herself, she saw the humor when one Boston newspaper sent a reporter to the Scarab: "A <u>Post</u> reporter inflicts herself on my <u>At Home</u> and writes a bogus interview, — in consequence of which my mail is enriched by a letter from a jailbird."[127]

But she struggled, "pattering away at the library, Spanish questions, and all the old interests, but with little heart," working "dazedly, as if it were life, not death, that is shadow and dreams."[128] She tried to slog away at her research on Thomas Heywood, "never quite so tired of any book" as the one she was writing about him.[129]

Alone during the fall of 1910, still grieving for her mother and for Sophie Jewett, who had died suddenly the year before, with Katharine Coman away in Chicago being arrested "for the glory of the strikers' cause,"[130] and Caroline retired from the college presidency, Katharine fought her depression by once more joining her writing friends at a Boston Authors Club meeting in their new rooms.[131]

She used her pseudonym of James Lincoln to ask, "Why Not Marry a Suffragette?"[132] When her early mentor and friend Julia Eastman died, Katharine, "with aching heart," reread her books, reflecting on the life of a talented writer who, like herself, had had to devote too much of her creative energy to her school.[133]

Then in April 1911, Katharine received from Katharine Coman "the heart-shaking news that she must undergo surgery" for breast cancer.[134] She tried to sleep, "so as to be ready for Katharine's need.... The May is all about me, but I can't get it into my heart.... The world is full of bird-songs, but I cannot even work.... A long day at college ... but all the while there is a tolling in my heart.... Still working in a dream. Barely endured the seminar.... Took up classes again, tho' so weary from this strain of anxiety that I don't know Shakespeare from grosbeaks.... In desperate need of distracting my thoughts from Katharine's ordeal now so close."[135]

"Perhaps the hardest thing that I ever did was to come away and leave Katharine in her hospital room"[136] in Boston. After the surgery, she went into Boston to meet her "beautiful, sad, black-clad Katharine ... and bro't her home."[137]

At first, with "all the indicators" pointing to recovery,[138] they spent the summer in the mountains of New Hampshire. Relieved, Katharine returned to her writing projects, but, in Portland, when she looked through the scrapbooks of her poems, stories, and articles that Arthur had saved from newspapers and magazines, she "realized" that some were failures."[139]

When her September classroom called, Katharine tried to rally herself: "The college grind begins. It seems bare and uninteresting, but there is always Poetry.... A long weary day at College. With College callers all the evening. Such is the stuff of life."[140]

That fall she saw her book *America the Beautiful and Other Poems* published at last. She now called her "America" poem "America the Beautiful,"[141] and tightened up the wording in the first four lines of the third verse to praise the heroism of Americans who give their lives for their country:

> O beautiful for heroes proved
>> In liberating strife,
>> Who more than self their country loved,
>> And mercy more than life.[142]

Her poem was soon called "the most beautiful patriotic hymn we have."[143] As the United States continued to grow into a major world power, her words described the "heroes" that American soldiers would soon become.

V.

By 1912 "America the Beautiful" was being sung in a country very different from the rural village of her birth in 1859. Then the country had been on the verge of a bloody sectional civil war that threatened to destroy the nation. Now the country was full of big cities, big business, and global concerns. By 1900, twelve million immigrants had come to the United States, and according to the census of 1910, one out of every three American adults was either foreign-born or had one foreign-born parent.[144] Social and political progressives like Katharine wanted reforms that would help the country with a shrinking common cultural heritage begin to understand that heritage and put its ideals into action.

Political turmoil began swirling with the looming November presidential election. A few days after Roosevelt's return to national politics, Katharine argued that women in America should be able to help determine the future of their country by voting. Since she had to convince male voters of this, rather than identify herself as a female activist, she signed James Lincoln's name to "Ten Reasons Why a Woman [Should] Vote."[145] She would have to wait eight more years to vote in a presidential election herself.

Unable to speak through the ballot box, her Wellesley firebrand colleagues Vida Scudder and Ellen Hayes joined other protesters in Lawrence, Massachusetts, to support women mill workers in the violent Bread and Roses strike. When they gave speeches demanding better working conditions for the women, their public display of radical political views shocked some Wellesley trustees, who called for their dismissal from the college.

Katharine described Vida and Ellen's "indiscretion at Lawrence" as "generous"[146] and hoped that the socialist movement was working toward her own ideals. And so instead of dismissing her friends, she merely canceled Vida's "Social Ideals in English Literature" course for that year.[147] Katharine herself turned to her writing to change American minds, planning her next collection of poetry, *America the Dream*.

She also wanted young Americans to see how Roosevelt's desire for American imperial supremacy looked to its victims. Her next book, *In Sunny*

Spain, told the story of a young Spanish brother and sister whose father goes off to fight in the Spanish-American War. It sympathetically portrays children in the "enemy" country whose loving father becomes a victim of American military power and shows her young American readers how children in its conquered nations feel.[148]

Meanwhile, she watched Katharine Coman's cancer become worse, praying, "God help us!"[149] She helped her finish her book *Economic Beginnings of the Far West*, understanding how she had put portraits of women, family farm pioneers, and working-class miners, quoting their "racy touches of frontier speech," into American history. As Katharine knew, the "country was her document.... [and she] never lost her love and comprehension of the West...."[150]

In the *Transcript*, Katharine wrote that Coman's depictions of "Spanish and French explorers, of fur-hunters, missionaries, Mormons, gold-seekers, emigrant farmers, and ... adventurers into the great wilderness ... all told with the verve of a pioneer historian,"[151] far surpassed Theodore Roosevelt's *The Winning of the West*.

Roosevelt was then attempting to win the presidency by running as a third-party (Bull Moose) candidate against Republican William Howard Taft and Democrat Woodrow Wilson, a former president of Princeton University who had been chosen on the forty-sixth ballot by his party. With Republicans divided between Taft and Roosevelt, Wilson won a large majority of electoral votes but only 42 percent of the popular vote. He tried, unsuccessfully, to unify the divided nation in his inaugural address, stating, "Here muster not the forces of party, but the forces of humanity."[152]

Because Katharine Coman wanted to keep researching the reform causes she cared about so passionately, the Katharines planned another journey together that would enable Coman to investigate the difficult working conditions of women in various European countries.

Once abroad, they threw themselves into their travels before terrible news came from Wellesley. In March 1914, College Hall, the stately five-story center of the college, had burned to the ground.

Katharine imagined the scene through Sigurd's eyes, writing that he "had roamed [College Hall's] familiar corridors ... and ... he found the next morning a desolation of blackened walls and blowing ashes. If Sigurd could have counted the hundreds, he would have known that every girl was safe, but if he could have read in the papers of the quiet self-control with which, roused from their sleep to find the flames crackling about them, they had steadily carried through their fire-drill, formed their lines, waited for the word and gone out in perfect order, he would have been no prouder of them than he always was. Of course his Wellesley girls would behave like that."[153]

Sadly, only a month before their return, they learned that Sigurd had died. At his grave on Observatory Hill, Katharine remembered an ancient Greek sentiment, "'Thou who passest on the path, if haply thou dost mark this monument, laugh not, I pray thee, though it is a dog's grave. Tears fell for me.'"[154]

Soon, Coman's illness and the care she required "overwhelmed" Katharine.[155]

In the meantime, international political tensions were intensifying as Germany expanded its armaments and built its navy's power. In London, the Katharines watched the growing number of people demanding that women be allowed to have a say in Britain's military buildup. They went to a "militant" suffrage meeting, although they were too late to see the suffragists swim in The Serpentine.[156]

War clouds darkened in Europe with the assassination of Archduke Franz Ferdinand in June 1914 and Austria's ultimatum to Serbia on July 23. The Great War began when Britain responded to Germany's invasion of Belgium on August 4, 1914. British troops began landing in France, and Austria declared war: "The Thunder of Guns. Russia Mobilizes Her Millions," and "the great novelty of the war—the flying fighters" showed the newest weapons—airplanes.[157]

How would the United States respond? Wilson had run as a progressive candidate, promising to keep America out of European political entanglements, and Katharine wrote "To Our President," a sonnet in which she called him the "Hope of the Nations" and a "True Champion of Peace." She depicted the raging of the "war-storm" as "bleeding Christian armies, sudden foes / That slaughter in a fierce astonishment,"[158] in "view of ... the ever-deepening horror of the war news."[159]

The war spread, as the *Transcript* warned: "France Is Now Courting Italy. Allied Armies Getting Together in Belgium. Gathering in Force to Meet the Onslaught of the Kaiser's Armies."[160]

She responded by writing "Marching Feet," in which she voiced Americans' dread of the "desolation" of the war that pitted "nation against nation":

These August nights, hushed...

tremble with a strange vibration,

A sound too far for hearing, sullen, dire,

Shaking the earth....

We are haunted by a horror, a mistrust,...

Vaguely aware

...Of brooding thunders unbelievable,

Fierce forces that conspire

Against mankind....

We start awake;

... Our eyelids down, but still we feel the beat,

Dull, doomful, irretrievable,

Of Europe's marching feet

Enchanted, blind,

By wizard music led ...

To baths of blood and fire.[161]

American progressives warned that European alliances could force America to abandon its policy of isolationism. They also feared that Eastern banking and business interests would profit from America's involvement in the war at the expense of working men and women, especially those in the West. Besides creating sectional conflicts, the war could exacerbate class conflicts, with the workingman being the first having to sacrifice his life in Europe. Some progressives, perhaps like Katharine, simply believed that war's bloodshed might be avoided through negotiations.[162]

In August 1914, 1,500 black-clad feminists marched slowly down Fifth Avenue, afraid that a deadly war would elevate males as battling warriors, and so delay women's progress towards full human rights including suffrage. Jane Addams and others formed the Women's Peace Party to oppose the American military build-up.[163]

Even in suburban Wellesley, "No talk anywhere but of the war."[164] The *Transcript* told of 20,000 wounded in Austria and Hungary, and pointed out the war's effect on international commerce: "A wall of bayonets shuts off the imports of Europe. Armies march through fields and vineyards. Millions of industries and producers have suddenly turned into destroyers."[165]

With the world economy in chaos, the *Transcript* urged its readers to mobilize as part of a humanitarian war effort: "It is America's opportunity. We must feed and clothe the world.... WAR IS AMERICA'S OPPORTUNITY—GET BUSY!"[166]

A month later, Germany's army threatened to attack Paris: "Another Air Raid on the City of Paris.... Belgium Was Crucified and French Strongholds Were Sacrificed."[167]

Horrified, Katharine wrote "Fodder for Cannon," for the popular *Life* magazine, in the insistent rhythm of soldiers marching in rigid lines: "Bodies glad, erect / Beautiful with youth, / Life's elect,... Marching host on host.../ Manhood's boast..." before reminding her readers that the young men are marching to their end as food for guns:

> Hearts and brains that teem
>> With blessing for the race.
> Thought and dream,
>> Vision, grace,
> Oh, love's best and most,
>> Bridegrooms, brothers, sons,
> Host on host,
>> Feed them to the guns.[168]

Katharine felt that the "great war-shadow and the deep pain of Katharine's illness" had changed her life "to grief."[169]

The day after *Life* ran "Fodder for Cannon," the *Transcript* headlines were grim: "Germans Continue to Pound the Lines of Dunkirk. Also Violently Assail Allies on the Somme.... The Karlsruhe Has Sunk Thirteen British Ships. German Cruiser's Speed Allows Her to Evade Pursuing Ships."[170]

By December, Katharine was also watching the end come for her beloved friend: "Katharine goes to the very gates of death, and nothing else is real to me."[171] Then: "When I went in this morning at seven, Katharine raised her arms to me for help. I gave her what poor help I could till the end came quietly— thank God for that...."[172]

She wrote in her journal, "On January 11 my Darling goes free."[173] And a week later: "I don't know why this heart of mine should go on beating when Katharine's heart is ashes, but it does."[174]

She tried to stay close to her, writing, "I live with Katharine in spirit and sometimes, as tonight, can almost feel her smiling in my soul.... I have a little Paradise of my own, all walled in by kindness, a rose-garden where I live with Katharine's spirit."[175] She began to spend more time in Coman's large attic room, "Bohemia," where "tears and verses" relieved her heart.[176]

In the gloom, a new housekeeper, Mary Reddell, with a cheerful disposition and warm heart, began to restore order and harmony to the Scarab, now the place that would enable Katharine to do her most ambitious life work.

CHAPTER TEN

1915–1929
"SWEPT INTO THE MIGHTY CURRENT
OF THE TIMES"[1]

I.

Psychologist Erik Erikson defines the middle stage of adult growth as "generativity," a period when someone nurtures people and expresses ideas that will outlast him or her, creating a legacy for future generations. It is a good description of how Katharine spent her final years.

Not content to be simply the poet of "America the Beautiful," she began to use her Wellesley academic position, her national reputation as a poet, and her intriguing Scarab home to welcome and promote the next generation of American poets—including the unknown Robert Frost—poets who were inspiring, networking, and arguing with each other about poetry in twentieth-century America.

Longfellow wrote in 1824 that "the fear of poverty ... deters many gifted and poetic minds from coming forward into the arena,"[2] and many years later, Katharine was typical of poets whose poetry income was small because readers knew little of their work.

That situation began to improve in 1912, when Chicago's Harriet Monroe launched *Poetry: A Magazine of Verse* to publish new poets, award monetary prizes to them, and encourage new readers. She believed with Walt Whitman that great audiences help create great poets.[3]

Monroe rushed to publish her first issue of *Poetry* because she knew that William Stanley Braithwaite—the *Transcript*'s African-American poet and literary critic, an anthologist, and a friend of Katharine's—was about to publish his own *Poetry Journal* in Boston.

Their race heated up when the wealthy cigar-smoking eccentric and larger-than-life Boston Brahmin poet Amy Lowell climbed onto the *Poetry* bandwagon.[4] She declared herself an "imagist"—allying herself with the expatriate poet Ezra Pound in England, who encouraged poets to depart from traditional verse forms to write esoteric poems, often with phrases in a variety of foreign languages for a tiny audience of readers.

That spring Katharine herself finally had time to focus on new poetry, because, as she noted with relief, "After ten years or more, 'Old Heywood'"—her scholarly edition of two of Thomas Heywood's plays—"is at last getting into print."[5]

She began encouraging talented poets by hosting them at Wellesley, welcoming "our poet of Illinois," the exciting Vachel Lindsay, to "chant" to her "Poet's Class" before an evening meeting with him at the Authors Club in Boston.[6]

He was the current star in the world of poetry, famous for both his poems and his striking oral performances. With a poetic temperament of "a revivalist preacher poetically inspired," his poems were "a blend of speech and song, clattering but impassioned, that well expressed the hurtling energy of America."[7] One of Katharine's students remembered that he recited his poems to "the sound of bongo drums."[8]

Interested in how other poets tackled her own themes in their poems, and perhaps thinking about how to write about her beloved Katharine Coman, Katharine was so taken with Edgar Lee Masters, and his unusual long poem about a fictional village and its citizens buried in its cemetery, that one May afternoon she read aloud his entire *Spoon River Anthology* to her longtime friend and sister poet, Marion Pelton Guild.[9] Katharine had a good ear for new talent—*Spoon River* is still popular.

That spring she joined such other published poets as Helen Archibald Clark and Charlotte Endymion Porter (founders of *Poet Lore* magazine), Braithwaite, and Amy Lowell to discuss how they could organize a New England poetry club to reach new readers of new American poetry.[10]

Lowell refused to join unless she was made president. In spite of her bossy personality and imagist theories, the other members agreed, hoping that her fame, charisma, and wealth would help generate public interest in the club's poetry activities.

Katharine became vice-president of the club,[11] where "'her wise policies and spirit of cordial fellowship were of great service.'"[12] It was "for the purpose of friendly and artistic intercourse … with tea money payable in October,"[13] although its first meeting included a man "whose hair was filled with hay" in search of the Poultry Association.[14]

At one of its early meetings Katharine met the striking-looking Robert Frost. He was fifteen years her junior, with broad shoulders, dark hair, and blue eyes, shaded by bushy gray eyebrows.[15] Frost had been advised that attending the formation of such a club "would be an advantage" for him.[16] It was.

Six days later, he was "booked for a lecture at Wellesley"[17] because, like Katharine, he wanted to make poetry come alive for listeners when they heard the voice of the poet reading his poems aloud and talking about them.

He had spent three years in England, where he published his first two books of poetry, *A Boy's Will* and *North of Boston*.[18] Although the Poetry Society of America in New York City had welcomed him as "America's newest poetic discovery,"[19] he wanted Boston to be the center of his professional life.[20]

He had gone to dinner at Amy Lowell's Brookline, Massachusetts, mansion, and introduced himself to Braithwaite and *The Atlantic Monthly's* editor, Ellery Sedgwick,[21] who had already heard that he was "*a very*

ROBERT FROST

considerable figure indeed…. [S]ince Whitman's death, no American poet has appeared, of so *unique a quality*, as Mr. Frost."[22]

He began to attend the New England Poetry Club meetings with Katharine in the Back Bay homes and social clubs of its wealthy members. Lilla Cabot Perry, a poet and painter who had studied with Claude Monet at Giverny, hosted most of its "serious meetings" in the Fenway Studios, lofty spaces where Boston's growing colony of painters, sculptors, and writers worked and lived.[23]

There the club members entered the terra cotta–tiled grand foyer and climbed a double set of stairways to gather in Perry's studio.[24] As she wrote to Katharine, it had "the advantage of being so large (and two stories tall) that it does not get stuffy and also that it has an open fire so that any amount of smoking [probably by the men and Amy Lowell] does not matter."[25]

Members often gave each other's poems their first "hearings" at meetings,[26] and sometimes they wound up discussing pressing social problems, as they did when Robert Schauffler read a poem about young men arriving in the United States from a variety of countries, only to be reduced, in many cases, to one category, the "scum of the earth." His poem "launched a discussion on the immigration question,"[27] a pressing topic, with the increasing numbers of immigrants arriving in Boston during the war.

Katharine and her colleagues decided to rank the best poems heard at each meeting, and eventually members submitted their poems anonymously in order to have them evaluated with "meticulous criticism before the votes for the prizes."[28]

To help encourage college-age poets and readers, at one meeting the club welcomed the Harvard Poetry Society to join them to hear *Poetry*'s founder, Harriet Monroe. As Harvard student Robert Hillyer, later Katharine's good friend, recalled, Monroe "instructed us in our poetical duties, after which a few found courage to read verses.... Bravery before this pedagogy, lacking only its blackboard, was [bravery] indeed. We all felt as though we were going to be graded D-."[29]

Meanwhile, Katharine followed the news in each day's "Morning Paper" of more German battle victories and responded:

> *Carnage!*
> Humanity disgraced!
> .... Poison gases and flame
> .... Bayonet, bomb and shell!
>
> .... *Courage!*
> To gain their fiery goal,
> Some crumbling, blood-soaked knoll,
> How fearlessly they fling
> Their flesh to suffering....[30]

In May 1915, she heard the "awful" news of the "sinking by a German torpedo of the Lusitania.... All the world horrified over 'Lusitania Massacre.'"[31] With 128 Americans killed, many wanted the United States to declare war, but President Wilson and former President Taft resisted. Katharine agreed, writing, "The country is full of war talk, but I put faith in Wilson.... Italy is in the war.... Pres. Taft addressed us on <u>Peace</u> at College Commencement."[32]

Upset by more grim war news—Germany had captured Warsaw and Allied troops had landed at Salonika—at the end of December, Katharine bade goodbye to 1915: "Farewell year—…year of Europe's murderous agony,"[33] and asked,

> How long …
>
> Shall folk of the burned villages in starving, staggering throng
>
> Flee from the armies that, in turn, are mangled, maddened, slain,
>
> > Till earth is all one stain
>
> Of horror…?[34]

That year she gave permission for "America the Beautiful" to be published in social reformer Upton Sinclair's anthology, *The Cry for Justice: An Anthology of the Literature of Social Protest.*

II.

To find new audiences, poets like Katharine also hosted and gave readings on college campuses. The English poet John Masefield, later poet laureate of Britain, "read" at the Wellesley "Barn," then the largest space on campus, as her guest.

The next month she hosted Vachel Lindsay again for an evening reading. A week later, he returned unexpectedly to read to her from his new book "till nearly midnight,"[35] before reading to a "mob of girls" at the college.[36]

Although Frost had attended both Dartmouth and Harvard, he had never graduated from any college, so in order to appeal to colleges, he needed help from respected academics like Katharine, and wrote hopefully to her:

> My dear Miss Bates:
>
> If you *will* remember me for a lecture and reading at Wellesley when it can be thought of as being my turn. It's the colleges I look to…. Not everybody would be interested in my ideas…. but really I can be quite off-hand with them fetching them edgewise between poems as I read. All this is for when my turn comes—if it ever does come…. Thank you for your good words.[37]

Perhaps he wanted to reassure Katharine that he would be a better reader on stage than he had been when she heard him at Boston's College Club.

She had confided in a letter to a friend who would be on the platform with him at Wellesley, "I was a good deal concerned when I heard Mr. Frost read his poems, for the reading was evidently so difficult for him that I wondered how he would be able to keep it up for a continuous hour. I felt sure he would stand in need of an elder brother to fill in the pauses and cover up the embarrassments.

"I am writing tonight to suggest to Mr. Frost that any comments he cares to throw in on his principles of rhythm, view of realism, etc. would be most welcome. I see that he talks more easily than he reads. I only wonder that so sensitive a poet can bring himself to face an audience at all."[38]

Frost agreed to her suggestion, replying, "I think it might be a good idea for me to break the monotony of my reading by a little offhand talk on a subject not unrelated to my poems," and he asked her to choose several of the poems he would read.[39]

She was eager to help him. Like Katharine, he wrote in traditional poetic forms that originated in Greece and Italy, wanting to be called a "classical" poet, and happy that Pound had compared him to Virgil. Like her, he loved the great English ballads and the poetry of Shakespeare, Wordsworth, Tennyson, and Browning in Palgrave's popular *Golden Treasury*.

Believing with Wordsworth that poets should write in ordinary language as "men speaking to men,"[40] they had both grown up reciting and memorizing the poems of Longfellow, who had also wanted the sound of American voices in his poems. Frost had linked himself to Longfellow by entitling his first book of poems *A Boy's Will*, a phrase from Longfellow's poem "My Lost Youth," hoping that Americans who loved their Longfellow would see him as his descendant.

Perhaps remembering how Longfellow had complimented her poem in his Brattle Street home long ago, Katharine could pass his mantle as America's most popular poet on to Frost and help him through her friendship with the influential Braithwaite, because newspaper articles about new poets, reviews of poetry books, and coverage of readings and meetings drew crowds to their public readings.

Braithwaite was enlarging the number of poetry readers and book buyers with his *Transcript* articles. For decades the newspaper had published poems, such as Katharine's, daily, but he became its specialist and created his own

Anthology of Magazine Verse and Yearbook of American Poetry each year from 1913 until 1929 for the growing poetry market.

Frost wrote to Braithwaite, giving him good copy for his column. Impressed, Braithwaite publicized him in his articles "A Poet of New England: Robert Frost a New Exponent of Life" and "Robert Frost, New American Poet."[41]

Poetry was beginning to create a welcome round of social and professional events for Katharine. Wellesley alumna Eunice C. Smith gave money for formal "Poet Readings" on the campus, and Katharine arranged for Amy Lowell to read before an audience of seven hundred. Even more memorably, when Katharine hosted the imposing William Butler Yeats on the campus, and he forgot the lines of one his poems, "the whole college" prompted him and "he was so pleased."[42]

When the charismatic Lindsay returned to Wellesley, she noted: "Am entertaining Vachel at the Durant Guest House. Dinner for him this evening and party of Wellesley and Harvard poets later."[43] She later hosted him "in crowded Billings Hall to the overflow."[44]

Her Poetry Club began sponsoring large public readings for Frost and others at grandiose sites like Boston's Steinert Hall and the Hotel Vendome, the first building in Boston illuminated entirely by electricity.[45]

With growing fame, Katharine was flattered when Oberlin College gave her an honorary degree. In a humorous letter to her brother Arthur, who had helped pay for her trip out to Ohio, she described the ceremony:

> When ... President King ... addressed me ... assuring me that I was a 'discerning scholar' and that my books were of 'nationwide renown' and that my hymn, whose last stanza he recited, expressed etc. etc. etc.... I trembled along (it seemed a mile) past him to the two stalwart professors who put on my hood, all crimson and gold, [I was] applauded so long I had to rise and bow to hush it up.[46]

Encouraged, Katharine piloted a new course at Wellesley, "Twentieth Century Poetry"—English poets in the fall semester and American poets in the spring. Such courses sprang up in other colleges, and Frost soon profited from her groundwork that generated a demand for recent poems and their live poets in the college curriculum.

Eventually, as a "poet in residence," Frost could devote most of his time to writing, becoming one of America's greatest poets and paving the way for the next generation of professional poets.[47]

III.

In February 1916, Germans attacked the French citadel of Verdun near the German border, and the fighting there became the bloodiest of the war. Katharine followed the news with dread when her brother Sam's son, William, named for her father, received his medical degree from the University of Pennsylvania that spring, and began preparing to serve in France if the United States entered the war.[48]

Katharine worried that some Americans advocating war did so because they could profit financially from it, writing: "Heed! Take heed! / For by greed / Glory dies."[49]

Germany's attack the next year on an American ship persuaded many that it was time for the United States to declare war. In Massachusetts, the Bay State Regiments stepped up their defense of the coastline from German attacks by guarding arsenals and bridges.

Boston feared attacks everywhere. About fifteen miles from Wellesley, "spies" were caught digging on the grounds of Watertown's large armory.[50] People became suspicious of pro-Germans, German-Americans, and pacifists.

Wilson could delay no longer. On April 2, 1917, he asked Congress to declare war on Germany, for reasons of peace, democracy, and justice:

> The present German submarine warfare against commerce is a warfare against mankind.... We are glad ... to fight thus for the ultimate peace of the world and for the liberation of its peoples ... for the rights of nations great and small and the privilege of men everywhere to choose their way of life and of obedience.
>
> The world must be made safe for democracy. Its peace must be planted upon the tested foundations of political liberty.... for democracy, for the right of those who submit to authority to have a voice in their own governments, for the rights and

liberties of small nations, for a universal dominion of right by such a concert of free peoples as shall bring peace and safety to all nations and make the world itself at last free.[51]

Three days later, the *Transcript* reported Congress's vote: "Roll-call Amid A Tense Silence—Some Senators Answer to their Names in Voices Shaken by Emotion. Wilson Demands Billions—Army of 1,000,000 Men At Once."[52]

The news of the Senate's 82-6 vote to declare war on Germany made Katharine sick: "Too tired. Rather went to pieces. But feel swept into the mighty current of the times."[53] Then on April 6, the House of Representatives overwhelmingly passed the War Resolution that brought the United States into the Great War.

Boston was ready when "the news was flashed from Washington that the House had passed the war resolution, [and] guards at Boston pounced upon the German ships in port and seized them."[54] "War Has Begun. Seizure of Ships First Act of War. German Vessels Seized—Boston First to Carry Out the War Instructions of the Government—273 German Sailors Taken by Surprise."[55]

The President's proclamation made it clear that anyone suspected of spying for the Germans would be severely punished; the U.S. Attorney General advised: "Obey the law; keep your mouth shut."[56]

Once war was declared, Katharine rallied her readers to unite behind Wilson, praying in "Our President," "God help him! Ay, and let us help him, too, / Help him with our one hundred million minds / Molded to loyalty...."[57]

She gave her permission for all four verses of "America the Beautiful" to be published in the pocket-sized songbooks issued to American soldiers and sailors boarding ships for Europe. Many would carry it in their knapsacks onto the battlefields.

Katharine joined other Americans writing to pump up America's war effort in "The Vigilantes," a new publication. Its initial one hundred contributors included many famous names—novelist Hamlin Garland, poets Edwin Arlington Robinson, and Joyce Kilmer, who was later killed in the Second Battle of the Marne; artist Charles Dana Gibson; children's author Thornton W. Burgess; and journalist William Allen White—and before the war's end it had four hundred contributors.

Its logo incorporated a drawing of Paul Revere riding through Boston's streets to awaken patriots. It might have reminded Katharine that Longfellow had written "Paul Revere's Ride" during the Civil War to rally Americans to forget their differences and come together. Similarly, these modern "Vigilantes" were "A Non-Partisan Organization of Authors, Artists and Others for Patriotic Purposes" to "arouse the country to a realization of the importance of the problems confronting the American people" and to "awaken and cultivate in the youth of the country a sense of public service and an intelligent interest in citizenship and national problems."[58]

THE VIGILANTES

Former president Theodore Roosevelt contributed to their publications, and his friend Hermann Hagedorn, the son of German immigrants, wrote to Katharine to say that with suspicions against "hyphenated" Americans growing worse, he liked her poem "The German-American."[59] It describes a young man born in America of German parents who patriotically goes off to fight for his new country, although his "blood remembers / The old, enchanted ... Rhine." Hagedorn said that he would publish it immediately.[60]

Harvard men began to enlist in the Army, blending their "crimson" with the Army's "olive drab,"[61] and Robert Hillyer soon gave Katharine a vivid sense of the French battlefields. He was a rising star—his poems were published in 1917 in *Eight Harvard Poets* and his books, *The Wise Old Apple Tree in the Spring* and *Sonnets and Other Lyrics*, came out before he left for France.

After graduating from Harvard in 1917, he joined the famous American volunteer Norton-Harjes Ambulance Corps, funded partly by American novelists Edith Wharton and Henry James, which carried wounded soldiers to a French clearing station or field hospital, like the one where Katharine's nephew William would work as a surgeon.[62]

Katharine wrote letters each week to a Harvard poet, probably Hillyer, who was stationed near the Verdun area on the Western Front northwest of the Meuse River. He drove his ambulance—a primitive vehicle outfitted with a covered section that could hold a stretcher and some first-aid equipment—on narrow tires across muddy rutted roads often clogged with marching soldiers, convoys of open-sided five-ton camions, cavalry troops on exhausted horses, lumbering caissons, and exploding shell-fire and poisonous gas.

Hillyer's Harvard friends, writers e.e. cummings and John Dos Passos, also drove ambulances, and Dos Passos described what it was like:

Up the road a sudden column of black smoke rises among falling trees. A louder explosion and the cook wagon in front … vanishes in a new whirl of thick smoke. Accelerator pressed down, the car plunges along the rutted road, tips, and a wheel sinks in the new shell hole. The hind wheels spin for a moment, spattering gravel about, and just as another roar comes behind them, bite into the road again and the car goes on, speeding through the alternate sun and shadow of the woods.[63]

While one man drove the ambulance as best he could, his partner helped pick up wounded and dying soldiers to take to the clearing station.

Hillyer drove in one of the most dangerous areas around Verdun, called "Le Mort Homme" ("The Dead Man"), a shallow valley named for ancient bloody battles:

R. S. Hillyer

You walk up a deep roadbed to a hilltop;
The trees are splintered and the sun is gray,
Shells rip the cheese-cloth air, and curling gas
That smells of death, out of the lungs of death
Breathes; it is like the sap of slaughtered poplars
Rancid with spring, it is like the breath of old men
Who have been dead a long time but still breathe.
Shell by shell you note the approaching range,
[….]
Tread daintily among the rats and shell-holes,
Pick your way up the hill between the fragments
Of men and horses, let the blue gas curl.[64]

When the United States entered the war, new Wellesley College president Ellen Pendleton encouraged her students to become "more loyal citizens." In the morning, like all American soldiers, the students raised the flag to the tune of the "Star-Spangled Banner," but then they lowered it to Katharine's "America the Beautiful."[65]

Katharine wanted them to do more, rousing them to buy an ambulance in memory of her colleague, Sophie Jewett:

> The boys, splendid in their young courage and unselfishness, go out to war. And what of the girls? It is hard to be a girl these years…. You are looking for nothing so eagerly as for chances to help.[66]

> The American poets have sprung to the rescue…. Shall not one [ambulance] bear the name, precious in Wellesley memory, of Sophie Jewett? Two thousand dollars buys an ambulance and keeps it in commission for one year…. Who will help?[67]

With the crucial 1918 mid-term congressional elections coming up, Katharine advocated voting rights for women, arguing that Americans needed to be "one people" during the war, and that meant including women as voters since, as Red Cross nurses, they were already essential to the war. "Women," she wrote, "are tax-payers, patriots, workers for every national cause,—why not citizens?"[68]

In "The Purple Thread" she sympathized with the mothers who were sending their sons off to fight in the war:

> …proud mothers of beloved sons,
>
> To-day you send them forth to front the guns,
>
> Waving your boys farewell with smiles that pour
>
> Strength into their young souls.[69]

Keeping abreast of the writing of other war poets, Katharine reviewed *A Treasury of War Poetry: British and American War Poems of the World War* for *The Atlantic Monthly*.[70] In her own poems her strong images made the war's tragedies visible.

In her *Atlantic* poem "The Retinue," she pictured Archduke Ferdinand, thought to be responsible for the Great War, as a "captain of a mighty train, millions upon millions, / Armies of the battle-slain, hordes of dim civilians;

German ghosts who see their works with tortured eyes, the sorry
Specters of scared tyrants, Turks hunted by their quarry,
Liars, plotters red of hand,—like waves of poisonous gases
Sweeping through the Shadow Land the host of horror passes;

…

Like a moaning tide of woe, midst those pale battalions
From the Danube and the Po, Arabs and Australians,
Pours a ghastly multitude that breaks the heart of pity,
Wreckage of some shell-bestrewed waste that was a city.[71]

A drawing of Archduke Ferdinand leading a line of such ghosts illustrated her poem. It eerily anticipates John Singer Sargent's somber later painting "Gassed," commissioned by the British War office, of a line of khaki-clad soldiers, blinded by mustard gas, stumbling towards a clearing station.[72]

In "To Heavy Hearts" Katharine described the pain felt by families at home picturing the faraway soldiers in the dreadful trenches on Christmas Eve in 1917:

Hard is their Christmas in the aching trench,
Or in the listening darkness mounting guard,
Haggard with cold and sick with creeping stench.[73]

A worse nightmare was her image of a young man dying alone:

Somebody's boy, his young face gray,
    Lies where the shells, in demon play,
Fling up fountains of ruddy spray,
    Splinter and tear and toss.
Bleeding he waits on Death's wild whim.[74]

During her first "War-Christmas" she called the letters from "our soldier boys … precious beyond compare…. Letters to laugh over, cry over, crush / To the lips, our Christmas joys."[75] By then, she had another relative—Arthur's daughter's husband—on the battlefields. She lamented, "And now our boys are giving their glad lives for freedom and mercy. God help His world!"[76]

IV.

Although she never received any royalties for it, Katharine gave her permission for "America the Beautiful" to be widely published in hymnals, and songbooks for War Work Councils, National Service Committees, the Red Cross, and the Peace Foundation.[77]

However, because there was not yet an official national anthem, military bands often followed John Philip Sousa's lead and played "The Star-Spangled Banner" at a fast march tempo appropriate for wartime, rather than her song.

Nevertheless, many Americans did choose Katharine's stirring words to express their patriotism. Wellesley alumna Molly Dewson, a social reformer on her way to Paris's Red Cross war refugee bureau, wrote to her:

> We had reached France…. [a] boatload of two or three hundred persons with one idea—to help France—and a twinge of danger—the submarines—is enough to make any trip unusual…. A man from Colorado dug in his bag and snapped his electric torch on a little copy of [your song] so that [we] could sing every verse…. [We] sang it three times and it sounded very, very lovely to me on that top-heavy boat rushing along in the darkness with only the dim misty lights of the shore.[78]

Another fan of the song, "thrilled" and "impressed" with it, wrote to Katharine that he had sent a printed copy to "every member of the 17th department of the Massachusetts State Guard" (later part of the Yankee Division) and disposed of 1,000 copies of it to the "boys in camp and at sea" to be sung by them:

> The country owes you thanks for your fine inspiration…. One hundred visiting sailors sang your song the first time I heard it and their voices rolled it like a paean of glory through the great church. It is a fine thing to have written a song that could inspire such a response as theirs was.
>
> Thank you for your vision of America so inspiring … in these grave times.[79]

American troops were essential to the Allies' survival, and the New England Yankee Division, the 26th, was among those sent to the eastern edge of France occupying positions in French Lorraine.[80] When they shipped out from Boston, Katharine wrote: "Our hearts are with the ships / That bear our boys / Across the ocean for their stern crusade. / O terror unconfessed!... Our jealous hearts / Would guard them even from glory and from rest."[81]

They were being trained by French officers, but the American general Pershing insisted that his troops would fight in exclusively American units rather than be deployed where the French needed help in their own lines. Besides wanting an efficient English-language chain of command, American commanders hoped that decisive American victories would give the United States more leverage at the eventual peace negotiations.

A second draft call for 800,000 men hit Katharine hard, as she admitted in her diary: "Got amazingly tired, — less with my work than with the war."[82] Her poem "The Thrift Stamp" tells of how the war haunted her wherever she went.[83] And in "Darby and Joan Keep Their Golden Wedding" she told how the couple bought a Liberty Loan, a bond to support the war, for their anniversary gift to each other.[84]

She was glad to hear that the publishing firm of Dutton & Sons had her collection of poems about the war, *The Retinue*, in proof.[85] Her "war lyrics," she said, recorded how Americans changed "from consternation at the horror of war itself" to supporting it once they realized "the supreme issues involved."[86]

But she wondered how anyone could still write poetry "with that awful battle raging in France?"[87] Marshal Foch was named the Allied Supreme Commander to turn the tide of the war, and Katharine cheered: "On the keen jump all day, ending up with reading my war-poems ... at Phi Beta Kappa."[88]

A month later, her nephew William arrived in Chatel Guyon, in southeastern France, at the Army Hospital set up by the University of Pennsylvania. A surgeon, he was in constant danger from artillery, air raids, gas attacks, and rampant disease while treating hundreds of soldiers of various nationalities for wounds, shell fragments, gas, disease, and shell shock.[89]

The Youth's Companion ran her poem "Died of Wounds," whose title was a phrase used in the dreaded letters to surviving parents. Perhaps thinking of her own nephews, she described an American soldier with one leg and one arm amputated in a French hospital ward:

The chaplain wrote us of him, —how he lay

   A winsome boy in that long ward of pain,
Greeting the nurse with smiles day after day.
   ….

   An hour before he died, with rapid tread
   A famed French general came to that screened bed;

And there were tears upon the war-bronzed face
   As terse, crisp accents told of deeds well done,
—A message sped through streets of fire in race
   With death, a wounded comrade dragged from one
   Grim shellhole to another, fallen son

Of France, who thus her debt of love confessed.
   The general, stooping, kissed each pallid cheek
And pinned the *croix de guerre* upon the breast.
   The blue eye lightened, and the one hand, weak
   And groping, sought the cross.…

'Tell dad. He knew that when I went
   I was afraid that I would be afraid.'[90]

Katharine told her Boston readers how Wellesley women helped the war effort by knitting over 2,600 items, sewing garments for the Red Cross, and financing four ambulances in the war, so that among the college "treasures" was "a chipped and battered automobile plate, marked Wellesley College" from the first college-financed ambulance that served, from March 1915 to January 1917, "on some of the hottest fronts. Again and again it was so badly damaged, the second time by the shell fire of Verdun."[91]

WELLESLEY AMBULANCE IN FRANCE

After more battles, that first ambulance was "such a wreck that it had to be scrapped," and so a second ambulance took its place.[92] It was the Frances Warren Pershing Memorial Ambulance, given by Wellesley alums, especially the class of 1903, the class of General Pershing's late wife, Frances. Pershing, whom Katharine described as "Wellesley's illustrious son-in-law," wrote that the only ambulance that had reached him was the one from Wellesley, "on duty here at my headquarters and … of very great service."[93]

At the end of the summer of 1918, day by day, American troops fought hard in the battles of the Meuse-Argonne, near Verdun: "Pershing Advances 7 Miles Over 20 Mile Front. Captures Twelve Towns, 7000 Prisoners—Still Going Ahead."[94]

It was the news that Boston families hoped to hear: "At Last! Long Waited, Strategic—the Battle!—Everywhere German Defence Is Failing."[95] And the next day: "Rapid Advance By Yanks. Americans Overran First German Position in Few Hours."[96]

The Associated Press reporter traveling with the American army north-west of Verdun wrote that the enemy "first attempted to make a stand … but the Americans pushed ahead…. Dozens, and sometimes scores, of airplanes darted back and forth over the lines and engaged in daring combats above the moving columns."[97]

But it was not easy: "Yanks and French Plunging Forward. Germans Fighting Hard to Stop Americans from Advancing."[98] A few days later, Katharine exclaimed in her diary, "Bulgaria and her Victorious Enemies lay down arms at noon today. Christ be praised!"[99]

Although the Germans were "desperately resisting" the Americans, soon, "German Lines Giving Before Yank Pressure."[100] By now there were 1,800,000 American troops in the war, with the Yankee Division spearheading the charge around Verdun: "Yanks Strike Again.... Swarms of Prisoners Entering the Cages.... Yanks and British in Entire Control of Air ... Driving Germans Headlong.... Enemy's Center in Rapid Retreat."[101]

With "Anglo-Americans in Hot Pursuit," Germany began to bargain for peace with President Wilson.[102] But "Allies Scorn Truce.... Germany Must Be Made Powerless To Make War."[103] Another German offer of an armistice was refused, and Austria surrendered. American artillery was pounding the German front northwest of Verdun while the Italian army was crushing Germany at the Monte Grappa Front.

It was the final push: "Countless Prisoners. So Many they Block the Roads.... Dynastic Powers Crumbling to Dust.... German Position Hopeless."[104] Such news got printed "within range of the enemy's guns" so that aviators could quickly drop notices of Allied victories into the trenches of both American and German soldiers.[105]

Then the *Transcript*'s report that Germany was sending a delegation to negotiate an armistice caused "joyful outbursts" in Boston and New York City.[106] General Foch gave Germany seventy-two hours to reply to the armistice proposal and refused to halt the fighting. The truce terms "staggered" the Germans, making them realize how complete was the defeat of the Kaiser's Armies.[107]

As the deadline approached, "Whirlwind advances on a wide scale by American, French and British armies in France and Flanders mark the closing stages of the German debacle ... as if to force upon the German high command the imperative necessity of accepting the armistice terms."[108]

The Germans finally signed the armistice agreement at 5:30 a.m. on November 11, 1918, in a special railway carriage pulled off on a siding in a forest in France, but since it was not to go into effect until 11 a.m., officers commanded the soldiers to keep fighting.

> Along the American front awaiting the eleventh hour was like awaiting the arrival of a new year. All the batteries from Moselle to Sedan ... prepared for the final salvo.... The infantry were advancing, glancing at their watches.[109]

There were a few seconds of silence. "Then: 'Eleven o'clock! Fire!' The shells shot through the heavy mist. Then the war was over.

> There was a roar of cheering all along the miles of the line!
> Individual groups unfurled the Stars and Stripes, shook hands
> and cheered again.[110]

And on one hillside, a battalion of American soldiers, in stunned silence, staggered into formation and sang Katharine's "America the Beautiful." When she heard of it later, her eyes filled with tears.[111]

One *Transcript* reporter described the "gallant" Yankee Division's celebration that night as they:

> paraded in triumph through the pitiful ruined streets of
> Verdun.... Men of the 26th division, the Yankees, the men
> from [Fort] Devens, your brother and mine—these were the
> gallant American soldiers who figured more prominently in
> the 'peace' parade in Verdun, the most famous fort in the war
> ... as they marched round and round, headed by a bugle band,
> heralding the news that the armistice had been signed, that the
> fighting was over....
>
> Behind the buglers marched a shouting, singing and dancing
> column of French, American, Senegalese and Algerian soldiers
> and civilian celebrants keeping time with the downbeats and
> shouting: 'The war is over! Vive la France! Vive l'Amerique!'[112]
> The bell ringers pulled the bell ropes until they fell down from
> sheer exhaustion.[113]
>
> Surely the sons of New England who participated in this
> parade will never forget it nor forget what it means to the history
> of the world. There is no soil in the world more sacred
> than all these scenes are destined to become.[114]

A French general, watching an American doughboy raise an American flag over the damaged Verdun cathedral, said, "Those stars as they float in the breeze are like the stars in the Heaven, and those American boys who represent the stars are like messengers from Heaven who have well carried out their errand."[115]

That morning Katharine had boarded a train for Boston to join its boisterous celebration of the end of the "war to end all wars." Pealing church bells, clanging fire alarms, and fire-crackers had awakened the city "with a joyous start [of] noise—shouting, cheering, [and] blowing … horns."[116]

At 6 a.m. hundreds of men from the North End carrying American and Italian flags marched to their rousing Roma band.[117] At North Station, factory girls burst into patriotic songs, while in the big food warehouses of the Market District, white-frocked men boyishly slapped each other's backs, shouting "Peace, Peace."[118]

Quickly discovering how to make their engines sound like artillery, war workers at the great arms factories in South Boston commandeered trucks to drive into Boston, and circled around the city, adding to their numbers with each gyration, and carrying an effigy of the Kaiser on a stretcher.[119]

Charlestown Navy Yard workers, 2,000 strong, "swung out" with their marching band into downtown Boston, and soon workers from the outlying Watertown Arsenal, Quincy's Fore River shipyard, and the Victory shipbuilding plant, fell into step with them.[120]

High above the streets, office workers threw confetti onto hats, heads, and skirts below, and paper streamers wildly waved from lampposts and telephone wires. With great relief, Katharine could finally see and hear Boston overwhelmed with joy.

When two marching processions passed each other, they exchanged jokes and congratulations. Belgians swept up Winter Street behind their "Union Belge," their band loudly announcing "The Yanks Are Coming." Then, as they turned into Tremont Street, their tune became the rolling thunder of the French "Marseillaise." Italians marched down Beacon Street to the same tune. Several hundred Portuguese, "headed by a band of musicians in their working clothing," inspired others to sing and cheer.

That evening at the top of Beacon Hill, with the blackout precautions over, the State House dome was lit for the first time since the United States entered the war.

Before she boarded the train back to Wellesley, Katharine told a little group of Wellesley students that she was "writing an Armistice Day poem,"[121] perhaps one about the end of the war for which the *Transcript* had asked. That night at the college, her poem "The Throne That Endures" was read at the chapel service.[122]

V.

When the surviving troops returned home, many brought the dreaded influenza epidemic with them. It eventually killed more people than did the war, including some of those who welcomed them home. Katharine saluted the women who now risked their lives helping the sick and wounded men, praising their "holy heart of motherhood."[123]

She bade goodbye to the year: "1918: Peace—if it be peace. I feel great trust in Wilson, but the world is one huge problem. Only love can save us."[124]

Many Americans, including many of her colleagues at Wellesley, had opposed the United States' participation in the war.[125] Wellesley College trustees had expected faculty members to abide by regulations affirming loyalty to the nation, but some of Katharine's closest friends, like Vida Scudder, believed that restricting pacifist free speech violated the right of faculty to academic freedom,[126] and the U.S. Senate began to investigate them.

The trustees announced they would not reappoint Emily Balch because of her pacifist views, and Katharine hosted a "long" meeting of her supporters.[127] But Balch, who later would win the Nobel Peace Prize, was forced to leave Wellesley.

Throughout the country, mourning continued for the dead and wounded. In "Motoring through New England" Katharine wrote that, wherever she went, "up and down the street" families had hung symbolic service-flags, a blue star for a war survivor and a gold star for a dead serviceman.[128]

In January, Theodore Roosevelt, still grieving for his youngest son, Quentin, killed over Germany, died at the age of sixty. His death stunned her: "The whole country grieves for Roosevelt. I did not realize that I should miss him so."[129] As she thought about him, a "burning-hearted Patriot," she asked, "What race is now to run?"[130]

The war was incomprehensible to her.[131] She wrote that Americans, "Bewildered, drugged with horror," could not "realize what / A vast event here sets its crimson blot / On Time's worn vellum.... / Centuries must wane before this war that flings / Its wild alarm to the shaken stars / Is merged within the sum of mortal things."[132]

To Vida Scudder, the war "was not only a world event of the first magnitude; it was also an interior event to every one then living. No one emerged from those war years quite the same person as entered them."[133]

Wilson hoped the end of the war would be the first step toward world democracy, stating in his Proclamation to Americans on Nov. 11, 1918:

"Everything for which America fought has been accomplished. It will now be our fortunate duty to assist by example, by sober friendly counsel and by material aid in the establishment of just democracy throughout the world."[134]

At the first round of Paris peace negotiations in 1919, he was able to get the League of Nations Covenant from his Fourteen Points of Peace incorporated into the first section of the peace treaty.

Katharine, too, wanted to see this dream of world community realized, writing "Wild Weather," the first in her "Path of Brotherhood" poems:

> A great wind sweeps
>
> Across the world, hurling to heaps
>
> Of gilded rubbish crowns and thrones, mere gleam
>
> And flicker of dry leaves in its fierce path....
>
> May its wild wings
>
> Burst the old tanglement of things.[135]

When Wilson returned from the Paris talks to the United States by way of Boston in February, Katharine wrote song lyrics, "Welcome to Wilson, friend of man, / Who follows the gleam... / Of a dream, a dream / That shall save the world!"[136]

But the 1918 mid-term elections gave Republicans a majority in the Senate, the legislative body that needed to ratify the Versailles Treaty with its controversial provisions for the League of Nations. They did not want a treaty requiring each participating sovereign state to guarantee the political independence and territorial integrity of all member nations against outside aggression because they feared Americans could be committed to military action without Congressional approval.[137]

However, to Katharine, the war's brutality showed the necessity of preventing a future war, an ideal that she hoped a League of Nations could encourage. She listened to other war poets and hosted poet Robert Nichols, who was "heart-breaking" in showing what war does to boys.[138] That night she worked late on a lecture for her students on "Young English War Poets."[139]

On an exhausting cross-country tour to take his treaty ideas directly to the people, President Wilson suffered a serious stroke from which he never fully recovered. Nevertheless, Katharine continued to speak out for world community.

The Senate rejected the Versailles Treaty, and Wilson then vetoed a congressional resolution declaring an end to American belligerency because it was not on his terms. Katharine published "Idealists" to honor Wilson's ideas: "Deserted and betrayed today, / A million morrows come / To follow where you lead the way / And make the world a home."[140]

She aimed "The League, Yes or No?"[141] at newly nationally enfranchised American women. For the first time in her life, Katharine was also able to speak through her ballot, voting for Democrats James M. Cox for president and Franklin D. Roosevelt for vice president, as well as the state Democratic ticket, noting, "And was tremendously beaten, but proud of my side."[142] (The Republican who defeated Cox, Warren G. Harding, is today widely regarded as one of the worst presidents ever.)

Americans were now beginning to read firsthand accounts of the war's horrors and question its human costs. Dos Passos's character, the American ambulance driver Martin Howe, blames America's entry into the war on ignorance: "[Americans] don't know what [war] is. They are like children. They believe everything they are told…. they have had no experience in international affairs."[143]

Disillusioned by how the press created patriotic hysteria, Martin explains to a French soldier: "What terrifies me rather is their power to enslave our minds…. I shall never forget the flags, the menacing, exultant flags along all the streets before we went to war, the gradual unbarring of teeth, gradual lulling to sleep of people's humanity and sense."[144]

He doesn't like what his country has become: "America has turned traitor" to its idealism, he says. "Now we're a military nation, an organized pirate."[145] Other Harvard graduates such as e.e. cummings and Malcolm Cowley also felt the war had been fought in vain.[146]

Many agreed, such as the controversial English poet Siegfried Sassoon, whom Katharine hosted at Wellesley.[147] A decorated officer, he had thrown his war medals away to protest against "the political errors and insincerities for which the fighting men are being sacrificed."[148]

Challenging the romantic images of war and horrified by its inhumanity, Katharine kept working for Wilson's ideal of world community in spite of its declining popularity. She noted that her poem on Wilson, "in appreciation of our President, is praised so warmly by Mr. Sedgwick, tho' he thinks the <u>Atlantic</u> should print no more pro-Wilson material at present…."[149]

The next spring she helped get a motion of support passed for the League of Nations in one of her organizations,[150] and published "A Brotherhood of Nations" in the *Springfield Republican*.[151] President Harding proclaimed to Germany and the other Central Powers an official end to American hostilities in 1921, but Katharine continued to promote Wilson's ideas, creating a "special program" about him and writing reports for the Woodrow Wilson Foundation.[152]

Near the end of 1923, Harding announced that there would be no American support for the League. At Wilson's death, on Feb. 3, 1924, Katharine called his dream "white" but "pierced."[153] His hopes of the United States participating in an organization that would facilitate world cooperation and peace had been killed partly by America's increasing isolationism, an outlook alien to the kind of global citizen that Katharine had become. She knew that "wounds unhealed" could feel "no armistice."[154]

VI.

As more Americans sang "America the Beautiful," a committee requested that Charles H. Woodbury paint Katharine's portrait,[155] and a *Boston Herald* reporter interviewed her for their "Familiar Conversations with Literary Workers of Boston."[156] She enjoyed her time with other poets, especially Frost, welcoming him to her Shakespeare class, and calling him a "shining soul" after he had visited with her in the Scarab "from six to eleven" before his daughter Lesley began attending Wellesley.[157]

In June of 1920 Katharine thankfully passed on the chairmanship of the English Literature Department to Margaret Sherwood and dreamt of "a desk and my Corona [typewriter] and a clear conscience as I lock my door."[158] Without student papers to grade and time-consuming college committees to run, she could finally complete her *magnum opus*, a set of ambitious poems in memory of Katharine Coman.

Stimulated and fortified by the support of the poets she hosted—Frost, Lindsay, Yeats—and the members of the Poetry Club, she wrote the revolutionary *Yellow Clover: A Book of Remembrance*, in which she demonstrated to the "free verse" crowd how traditional poetry could break new ground with radical, even shocking, content.

She published it in the Easter season, a season of resurrection appropriate for her poem of her own rebirth as a woman and poet. Emphasizing that theme, she inscribed George Herbert Palmer's copy with the phrase "Easter Hope."[159]

Katharine wanted to convey Coman's warmth and "free and ample nature," as well as her religious faith, far stronger than Katharine's, which was the basis of all her work to reform the world on New Testament principles.[160] Her students had loved her energy and imagination when she took them on field trips inside Boston-area factories or donned a male judge's white wig to preside over campus debates on social issues.

**KATHARINE COMAN
IN COSTUME**

Eventually becoming Katharine's most intimate companion,[161] Coman had shown her how a woman professor could use her scholarly and creative work to challenge accepted attitudes towards women's social, economic, cultural, and gender roles. As a poet, Katharine had to find literary ways to convey Coman's belief in women's unlimited potential. So, in order to memorialize this pioneering woman properly, she took the traditional poetic structures used mainly by male poets to tell her story of female love and rescue with Coman as a Christ figure.

The reader first sees the symbol of their loving relationship down the edge of *Yellow Clover*'s ivory-and-sage-colored front cover, a chain of block-printed yellow clover designs that represents their intertwined lives.

Inside the cover, the reader sees an etched vignette of a youthful Coman as Katharine first saw her. Below is Katharine's bold epigraph in Latin, a quotation from lyric poet Horace that means, "What shame or limit should there be to grief for one so dear?" It was the question that Horace asked of Virgil at the death of a mutual male friend. It announces Katharine's intention to place her elegiac poems to Coman in the classical literary tradition where men often celebrated male friendship and love. Katharine will mourn her beloved companion in these forms but take what she wants from them to create her own female story.

After poems that describe their years of travel, work, and love together, Katharine concludes *Yellow Clover* with an extraordinary sonnet series, "In Bohemia," forty-nine sonnets in seven sets of seven sonnets each.

Because the last line of each sonnet is repeated in the first line of the subsequent sonnet, they are linked together verbally in a kind of circular structure called a corona, or crown, of poems so that their structure portrays the poet's traditional crown of "bayes" or laurel in the male elegy tradition. It also can suggest the crown of thorns worn by Christ Jesus at his crucifixion, appropriate to Katharine's portrayal of Coman in these poems as well as to their interwoven lives.

For male literary models, Katharine first drew on the pattern of "La Corona," seven interlocked sonnets by seventeenth-century poet John Donne in which he tells God that he wove his "crown of prayer and praise" in "low devout melancholie," hopeful that they would give him "A crowne of Glory, which doth flower always; / The ends crowne our works, but thou crown'st our ends." The drama of Donne's corona comes from its speaker's struggle to move from feeling isolated from God to feeling drawn to Christ's holy spirit by means of his poems. Katharine dramatizes her similar struggle and multiplies Donne's seven sonnets into forty-nine sonnets that surprisingly place Coman in Christ Jesus' role of giving salvation to a struggling poet.

For a secular model, Katharine turned to Tennyson's "In Memoriam," the elegiac poems he wrote in tribute to a male friend. While his poems consider the idea of immortality, their real subject, according to some critics, is the unfulfilled "same gender desire" of the mourner.[162] Echoing its title "In Memoriam" with "In Bohemia," she also follows its classical structure with her farewell to the departed traveler, her reminiscence of the departed beloved, and her funeral lament.

Christina Rossetti, the two women's favorite woman poet, gave Katharine models of two long sonnet sequences—one of fourteen sonnets about love and one of twenty-eight sonnets about desiring to please God while contemplating the death of loved ones.

Like these poets, Katharine first portrays the spiritual crisis of the survivor who feels abandoned by the beloved who has gone on to a higher level of existence. Coman's deep spirituality made Katharine fear that with her death, she had left her behind to move forward alone in her spiritual life. She worries that Coman has vanished, "quenched in darkness, like a shooting star." She can reach her only by trying to understand Coman's immortal life, a quest that becomes the plot of the sonnet series.

Katharine constructed her sonnets by dividing each fourteen-line sonnet into an octet, where she poses her doubts, and a sestet, in which she tries to answer them. With varied rhyme schemes, each sonnet is thus like a thought strung together with the other six sonnets of the section which then joins with the other sets to create the corona.

In the opening line of the first set of sonnets, she says to Coman, "I give you joy, my Dearest. Death is done." She then recalls painful details of her appearance (her withering hair, her "numb, forgetful hand," and her worn face in great pain from cancer) when she died. Katharine tries to feel happy that her friend's physical suffering is over but moves into what had been her room in "Bohemia" to try to remain with her.

Nevertheless, she feels that her companion has left her behind. In the second set of sonnets, she tries to feel joy for her, but it is the joy of human love, easily overcome by "lurking grief." She moves forward in the third section by realizing that it is Coman who still lives in spirit while it is she who is spiritually dead, "Bewildered past all pain, past all desire" since she will never again be able to enjoy Coman's human presence.

In the fourth section, she tries to bring her back by reminding Coman of her "dear-loved earth" and their travels together, but by the fifth section, Katharine realizes that Coman's new home in Paradise may be more wonderful than Earth's wildwood or a bungalow by "water's edge." She imagines the spirits of their departed friends and of Jesus surrounding Coman in her new home, and asks sadly,

> Have they no need of us who need them so?
>
> Do they never, of eternity grown weary,
>
> Long for the river-song of Time's onflow?
>
> Can one tree, even the Tree of Life, suffice?
>
> Do saints go gypsying in Paradise?

But seeing heaven as simply a different version of Earth gets Katharine no closer to her.

Finally in the sixth section, understanding that her "mortal vision" is not sufficient to reach Coman, Katharine rouses her own fragile faith, a "shipwrecked mariner, whose frail / Boat lurches while he leaps to caulk and bail, /

Make fast his water-keg with shred of rope, / Still searching, searching, dizzy eyes a-grope, / The blank of ocean for a saving sail," like Jesus' disciples, who need him to calm the seas and their fears. In spite of her doubts in God's power, her strong love for Coman encourages her to ask her to be her "interpreter" who can "pray / The prayer" that Katharine cannot.

Thinking of Coman as her intercessor enables Katharine in the seventh section to see her as a spiritual presence rather than a human one who has vanished. She recalls that when her "mortal beauty dimmed, the glow / Of spirit brightened...." Her vision of Coman as a Christ figure who will come to help her enables her to remember that there have been moments when she has indeed felt her spirit:

> Have I not sometimes felt your presence nigh?
> You said: 'I will not leave you comfortless.'

When she remembers this promise to her, which echoes Jesus' words to his disciples and his promise to come to those who believe in God, Katharine prays to Coman to "still shed blessing" on her. She feels that as a spirit, Coman can still hear her, teach her, and save her so that she can join her in eternal life.

The seven years since her death, symbolized by the seven sets of sonnets, have given Katharine time to learn from Coman:

> By seven springs has your far grave been grassed,
> And in my depth of sorrow are astir
> New powers, perceptions, joys, against my earth
> Up-pressing, secret agonies of birth,
> At bidding of their angel gardener:
> 'The Life Eternal! Let us hold it fast!'

In this last sonnet Katharine shows that as she did in life, so in death, Coman has helped her understand that their spirits cannot be separated from each other since they are both surrounded by God's "eternal radiance."

This idea finally brings peace to Katharine, who used to call Coman "Joy-of-Life." In the concluding line of the corona, which repeats its opening line, she can now give Coman "joy" because as a Christ-figure, Coman can continue to guide and lead her. When Katharine now says, "Death is done," repeating it from the first line of the corona, she means that she understands Coman's human death is meaningless because she has eternal life, and that her own death of the spirit is "done" because of feeling Coman's constant ministering presence in her life.

The formal success of Katharine's corona, celebrating the vitality, adventurous spirit, and abiding spiritual presence of their love, is also a celebration in traditional male poetic forms of Coman's exploration and success in traditional male territory. Like Horace, Katharine shows why no amount of grief was too much for an extraordinary person. Like Donne, she moves through despair at her religious doubts to a sense of reconciliation with Christian theology, but in the context of an intimate female human love that enables her to embrace a Christian one. Like Tennyson, she feels a sense of peace and the presence of her beloved at the elegy's conclusion, but her change is permanent, unlike Tennyson's, once she recognizes Coman's life in God that she has begun to share, at least in the poems.

Like Rossetti's, her sonnet series depicts a human love story in devotional imagery, but instead of becoming a bride of Christ, like Rossetti,[163] Katharine is saved by her beloved, a female Christ. Her literary memorial is a woman's crown, a corona. It symbolizes a crown of eternal life,[164] an "unfading crown of glory,"[165] which Katharine created on the pages of her book. Expanding the poetry of her male and female predecessors into a virtuosic display of her own creative powers, she wrote a dazzling and revolutionary tribute fitting for the woman so dear to her.

Yellow Clover, poetry for a woman by a woman, was Katharine's most original contribution to American literature. It joined Walt Whitman's same-sex themes in such poems as "Calumus," and Emily Dickinson's portrayal of female completeness in such poems as "Mine—by the Right of the White Election!"

One reviewer called the corona of sonnets "the most intimate lyric poetry... [a] passionate series to eternal friendship, immediate, unabashed, full-voiced...."[166] Another described *Yellow Clover* as "holy ground, so full of beauty and no lover of Miss Bates's work but must cherish it reverently."[167]

Braithwaite wrote that Katharine "sings poignantly in the higher altitudes of her passion; she sings wistfully through the underbrush of her emotional devotion to memories, and thus makes an elegiac pattern of many designs and fervors, of many textures and poignancies ... [concluding] with that magnificent portrait of the Friend, which is painted in a corona of sonnets" that "lovingly" evokes Coman's "keen spirit" and the "unfading radiance of its absence."[168]

That review must have pleased Katharine, who felt that she "could not attempt direct biography," but had "tried to get something" of her beloved Coman "into it."[169]

VII.

Katharine wrote to a friend, "We who are kept behind [when our] mates go on must hold all the closer together, for the world grows very lonely."[170] As she reached out to students, poets, and future readers, drawing them into what Scudder called "the magic circle of her presence,"[171] she began to further enlarge her legacy to her country.

With keen insight and determination, she championed, hosted, mentored, and taught more new and important American writers to the next generation of readers. Many of these were women, such as Willa Cather, soon to win the Pulitzer Prize for her novel *One Of Ours*. In 1913 Cather had published a novel that celebrates its female protagonist's creative powers: *O Pioneers!* Likewise, her novels *The Song of the Lark,* in 1915, and *My Antonia,* in 1918, portray gifted women and their success.

Poet Sara Teasdale complimented Katharine for her reviews of new writers: "What you say covers so much more than the book under consideration that it seems to get at the very spirit of poetry. It opens a door onto the great sunlit field of literature as a whole, and to point out to the writer of the minute the eternal horizon toward which he may travel…. [Yours is] criticism that builds up poetry."[172]

Teasdale understood that Katharine "built up" the poetry of her nation by helping readers appreciate its strengths and enlarging its boundaries to include the then little-known Emily Dickinson, regarded today as a literary giant.[173] She saw Dickinson's genius in Martha Dickinson Bianchi's 1924 edition of Dickinson's poems, letters, and biography, writing in the prestigious *Yale Review* that "the universe was hers" in her "lightning" phrases and "darting lines" that "sting imagination."[174]

Katharine both publicized and advised new poets like Mary Dixon Thayer, who appreciated her "spirit of generous sympathy," which enabled her to "hear the melody itself which, however imperfectly," she "was trying to sing."[175]

New American male writers interested Katharine too. She praised William Faulkner in *The Literary Review* and *The New York Evening Post*,[176] and after hearing Archibald McLeish lead a discussion on "The New Poetry" at the Poetry Club in Boston, she called him a "Young American Poet Whose Work Is Very Well Worth Watching."[177]

Of all her poet friends, she still valued Frost the most. Together they judged poetry contests and enjoyed talking about poetry. He wrote to her: "It seems a long time since we last encountered—Was it in the Mt. Holyoke poetry contests (as judges)? Do you get excited about free rhythms? ... I wonder if you don't get impatient with some people who give their sentiment divine against the being of a line between prose and verse. *I shall want to hear what you have to say.*"[178]

Frost biographer Lawrance Thompson wrote about her: "Always above jealousy ... was the unassuming Katharine Lee Bates, poet and professor, who had ... brought Frost to Wellesley College as often as she could."[179]

She enjoyed the visits that Frost and his wife made to her, hosting them in the fall of 1922 for his reading at the College and then at the Poetry Club in Boston: "Running two sets of guests, —the Frosts at the Guest House and [two others] here."[180] In the midst of the formal readings, "Mr. and Mrs. Frost spent the morning here in delightful talk. He gave a most successful reading this afternoon.... Their visit was a joy."[181]

Like Katharine, Frost knew it was important to find new ways to teach and encourage young poets. He supported the new Bread Loaf graduate summer school near Middlebury College in Vermont because he suspected "that we aren't getting enough American literature out of our colleges to pay for the hard teaching that goes into them."[182] He spent more than forty years at the school, Katharine taught there in 1922, and they both supported the development of the Bread Loaf Writers Conference.[183]

Frost went on to win four Pulitzer Prizes and forty-nine honorary degrees. He became so successful giving public readings after the early problematic ones that he "barded around" for nearly fifty years, first charging $50, then $200 to $300, and finally $1,000.[184]

When poet Seamus Heaney received the Nobel Prize for Literature in 1995, he said, "I loved Frost for his farmer's accuracy and his wily down-to-earthness."[185] Katharine would have agreed.

Although her heart disease was growing worse, she still loved sharing poetry. One graduate student recalled her "striking impression of a wholly unacademic personality [with her] lovely silvered head with the wayward streak of young dark hair, the keen, smiling brown eyes, and the motherly figure.... [and] Miss Bates's very way of taking poetry for granted as one of the major necessities of life.... It might have been her first adventurous year of teaching, instead of her forty-fourth."[186]

Another remembered "the surprising way in which she could awake knowledge one had not realized one possessed. As she talked or asked questions she seemed to tap unexpected reservoirs of information. One had never thought so clearly nor to the point. It was delightful and stimulating."[187]

When "some girls ... elected her course, hoping to learn how to write poetry, [with] a twinkle in her eye, she explained that though she could not teach us how to write poetry, she could definitely show us how to write clear, accurate prose."[188] Nevertheless, an aspiring student poet remembered that when Katharine read one of her "youthful verses," she said, "'It is almost a poem.' She showed me words were alive."[189]

She now taught her seminars at home in the Scarab, where her second collie, Hamlet, tried to "run" these Wednesday afternoon classes. As she told her old Falmouth friend Hattie Gifford: "These girls arrive at two ... and at four we usually pause for coffee and cake and then come back and work until half-past five. But often I am so absorbed in the thing we are doing that I forget to notice the hour [and] Hamlet comes bustling in exactly at one minute of four and plants himself in front of me with his paw upon my knee, gazing up with reproachful pleasing eyes—since the cake is the only part of the seminar that interests him—until I remember the hour."[190]

Katharine served "delicious homemade cakes and fragrant coffee" to her students on the cups and plates that she had bought in Oxford so long ago.[191] Gwendolyn Bossi, a student in her Modern Poetry class, remembered that around Katharine's "nice fire ... [her] idea was to have us read a lot of poems and remember them.... She was trying to inculcate in us the way to read poetry, to enjoy it.... You began to feel a respect for how the poem was put together."[192]

These students chose fifty of their favorite contemporary poems from her poetry periodicals, copying them out to make their own anthologies for her assessment. She wrote to Gwendolyn about her choices, which included poems by Edna St. Vincent Millay, Dickinson, and Frost: "You might better have called this White Magic, for all your selections ... have the bewitching quality [and] joyful reading. I hope you will keep the gladness of the poets about you all your life."[193]

To this student, Katharine seemed "a lovely, fun person—You would have loved to spend time with her.... She was a person of some magnitude ... [and] helped to entertain any bigwigs who came [to Wellesley].... She would have little patience with frippery, but she seemed up-to-date, modern."[194]

"I loved being in that class. I would never have read [the poems otherwise, but] you catch the interest that a teacher has in her subject."[195]

Katharine welcomed famous poets to the Scarab, "such a pleasant place to linger—the book-lined rooms, the study looking out on the 'jungle' where in early summer the laurel blooms so abundantly...."[196] She still was entranced by Walter de la Mare, "so fascinating" that she almost forgot his "waiting audience."[197] He sang Katharine's "praises" with fellow poets.[198] Edwin Arlington Robinson knew that she could see the "strength" of a poem he sent her.[199]

Like many of her guests, DuBose Heyward, later the author of *Porgy*, the source for *Porgy and Bess*, wrote to her: "You must let me thank you for the delightful experience that you gave me this week. I shall not soon forget Wellesley, and the fine response to my effort that came from your students."[200]

Katharine became "the patron and friend of all young poets," including one "who came at ten in the morning and stayed till ten in the evening."[201] George Woodberry excitedly looked ahead to his date with her, "Vive the 22nd!"[202] Robert P. Coffin wrote that he had "long wanted to make the acquaintance of the author of America the Beautiful."[203] He later called his visit to her "a red letter day in my life."[204]

Young poet Tucker Brooke wrote to her:

> I ... hasten to assure you of ... the special a pleasure which your kindness and that of your colleagues gave me.... I have never received more perfect, more delicate or more universal courtesy; and I ... count the twenty-five hours (nearly) which you permitted me to spend at Wellesley among my most treasured recollections.[205]

KATHARINE LEE BATES IN HER STUDY

Katharine wanted to know just how these young poets regarded "modern" poetry. One replied to her, "If being 'modern' means a break with the old masters of music and masters of thoughts that have wings, then I shall ... never be permanently of the 'modern' group.... The sort of poetry I should like to write … is the sort that creates an impression of life that is better than life ever can be, that has a symbolism and a dignity and a completeness … the kind of poetry you have written for many years!"[206]

She continued to enjoy her favorite Harvard poet: "Mr. Robert Hillyer — charming boy! — read his poems this afternoon, dined and met The Scribblers in Tower Court [a Wellesley dormitory] …."[207] He agreed that American poets should be experts at traditional verse forms, and she suggested to the Massachusetts Group of the American Literary Association that he be made one of their judges.[208]

As they worked together in the Poetry Club, Hillyer appreciated her mentoring this community of poets, confessing, "It is good to feel a part of such a fellowship — not only our own circle, but those who have been and shall come, — isn't it? Needless to say, your own generous friendship is to me one of the happiest of boons."[209]

Katharine was still a vital presence; one student recalled: "I have seen a dinner table full of people rouse to life at her arrival, or a roomful of people transformed by her entrance."[210] According to Caroline Hazard: "Her smallest party became a festival with the magic of her imagination."[211]

The Boston Authors Club applauded two lines from one of her poems as "the most poetical utterances of the last decade,"[212] and the Poetry Society of America article on her was sent to three million women's clubs members.

Her listeners marveled at her abilities, one writing, "Where do you get the strength to stand up before an audience like that and read such an admirable paper? And what a lot of work you must have put into it, when you have all those other things waiting to be done…. What charmed me about the paper was that you seemed to create an atmosphere, in which I really almost began to feel like an author myself."[213]

The Forum published a photograph of her "In her study at Wellesley College."[214] Now distinguished in her academic gown with her white hair piled on her head, Katharine stands in front of her crowded desk with its photo of Katharine Coman. She had come into her own as a woman who had something to say, proud to represent the best of women's education, and one who was leaving a legacy of making the voices of the best American writers heard for the generations to come.

VIII.

Nevertheless, she often felt "tired to a frazzle."[215] Her English Literature Department honored her with a special retirement dinner that filled her "with joy and sorrow … all so dear."[216] But at her desk, "the sudden tears fell."[217] She retired officially in June 1925. A few days later, her class of 1880, whom she called her own "veterans," greeted her for their forty-fifth class reunion.

She could finally take charge of all of her time and work endlessly at her writing. Nearly sixty-six, with her health growing weaker, she nevertheless was determined to steer her ship where she wanted.

She was still in demand as a poet, with one national magazine asking to see every poem before she sent it to any other publication.[218] As someone who could speak to and for the nation, she noted with satisfaction that *The Congregationalist* celebrated "the publication of America the Beautiful thirty years ago."[219] She was the guest of honor "for the sake of A the B" of the National Hymn Society.[220]

Gradually more housebound as heart trouble worsened, she spent more time corresponding with writers and fans throughout the world. Intensely interested in which poets were publishing what, she wrote review essays in which she could explain and educate her readers about new poetry.

The college poetry readings that she had helped establish were still going strong. She welcomed poet Lizette Woodrooth Reese, whose poems had run alongside hers so long ago in the *Transcript*.[221] When she heard the poet Alfred Noyes read his poems, she "liked the poet himself far better" than she expected to.[222]

On the eleventh anniversary of Coman's death, surrounded by "heather and pink roses and calendulas" from Vida and others, Katharine felt, "Peace and joy are surely here."[223]

She also may have continued to keep in touch with Theophilus. In 1920, during a "tremendous thunderstorm," her thoughts were "much with T.H.R.,"[224] who had treasured her letters enough to wrap them in rose leaves.

He attended his many Harvard class reunions in nearby Cambridge, and when she went to Vermont in the summers, she was not too far from Westmore, Vermont, a parish of three scattered villages of three hundred inhabitants, where he became minister in 1919.[225]

He was like her in many ways; both were true scholars, and just as she nurtured her students, he tended his congregations at the churches where he served.

A beloved pastor, he would be eulogized as always thinking of others, ever "contemplating some good he could do for his fellows, collectively and individually."[226]

To make his church truly the center of his community, he spent his last years collecting books for "The Pastor's Library," to be a gift to the town. He wanted Katharine in it. On the special bookplates he helped design for these books, he chose the Wellesley motto, and his Harvard classmate even referred to that phrase in his tribute to him: "Economic remuneration is no index of the worth of a Man of God, who came not to be ministered unto, but to minister."[227]

In the Scarab, Katharine's little household gathered around her, and thanks to the wonders of the radio from Arthur and the telegraph, she felt connected to the activities she loved, including her many former students, noting: "This evening we clad ourselves in our gayest kimonos and wine-colored slippers and attended the Symphony Concert by radio. New York Wellesley Club telegraph: '351 Wellesley women assembled send you loving greetings.'"[228]

The radio also connected Katharine with Jane Addams[229] and the President. She heard "Coolidge this evening over the radio delivering a very dull but virtuous address on Washington."[230] Seeing the humorous possibilities of radio, she wrote "Broadcast," which depicts flower bulbs listening "on the radio" for "Spring's dear steps."[231]

Surprisingly, she enjoyed listening to prizefights on the radio. As her friend Marion Burton recalled, Katharine "shuddered to think what the world would say if the author of 'America the Beautiful' died while hanging breathless over the outcome of a fight!"[232]

Like her mother, who had wished to hear from Roosevelt's Great White Fleet, Katharine excitedly anticipated Admiral Byrd's broadcast from the South Pole's "Little America": "To me that broadcast is the greatest marvel of a lifetime of marvels. I am speechless before the miracle of radio, by which one man can speak to millions over so many miles of frozen silence, and make all of them feel like one family around a single hearthstone."[233]

During the spring of 1926 she had happily noted: "Putting *The Pilgrim Ship* into shape for its voyage."[234] With her favorite theme of an explorer out to discover new territories, Katharine's poems were inspired by her own travels to Egypt and Palestine. But she chided herself, "It is high time that K.L.B. got well!"[235]

With no official melody, "America the Beautiful" was still sung to various tunes.[236] Her own favorite was by the Rev. W. W. Sleeper, pastor of the Wellesley

Congregational Church. However, she did not advocate any particular melody, not even "Materna," which had widely caught on, and that hampered its chances of being made the national anthem. In 1926 the National Federation of Music Clubs held a nationwide contest for an American-born composer to create a new melody for Katharine's famous words.[237] But even with 961 entries, no winner was chosen.

Although brimming with plans for future writing projects, Katharine knew her time was limited. In the spring of 1928, she "faltered" when she placed her beloved sister Jeannie's ashes beside their mother's grave,[238] and that autumn she wrote out an inventory specifying who should received the Scarab's special items after her death.[239]

In January 1929, the Poetry Society of America elected her a permanent member of their Council, "a representative body of the leading poets of the country."[240] She began constructing a little book of poems, "Midnight in Bohemia," twenty-eight leaves of typewritten poems, and eighteen blank leaves, "written during Miss Bates' last illness."[241]

Midnight had indeed come to Bohemia, the attic room, originally Katharine Coman's, and then Katharine's own writing studio. Its name suggested exotic lands, art, and individuality. It described the life that Katharine had created for herself, an unconventional life for a woman in 1929. Although she entertained guests, enjoyed her garden, and nurtured her relatives and friends in the domestic spaces and gardens of the Scarab, it was Bohemia, her creative workspace for poetry, where she had her "adventure of the spirit."

IX.

In Katharine's words, the tide was calling, and the anchors about to lift.[242] For this Cape Cod girl "rock'd in a clamshell" who had truly become an explorer and pathfinder for future generations of women and men, readers and poets, students and teachers, it was time for her final journey.

One day in March 1929, she asked to be driven slowly around the college campus.[243] The early spring campus held many memories: the gates she had come through as "Katie of '80," the hill where Mr. Durant's exuberant creation of College Hall had stood, the woodland paths around beautiful Lake Waban, the buildings where she hosted poets, and the Chapel, near the president's house, built by Caroline Hazard, at whose inauguration Katharine had heard

Harvard's president assert that women's "intellectual capabilities" were less than men's. As a New Woman, Katharine had been ready to reform American cities with settlement houses and then to skip faculty meetings to play golf.

An inspiring role model for her students of a woman who turned out generations of informed readers and writers, of teachers, especially of American literature, and shared her enthusiasm at the power of language, Katharine was a social activist, poet, scholar, literary critic, memoirist, travel writer, and, as all her guests could see, an enthusiastic globe-trotter.

As the car drove her back to the Scarab that day, she rode over the train tracks which had taken her on so many journeys—myriad trips to Boston's libraries and clubs, as well as to Chicago, Colorado Springs, and New York Harbor, the gateway to Europe.

On March 28, Katharine's longtime sister poet, Marion Guild, read her "At Last," a poem by Durant's friend John Greenleaf Whittier,[244] whom Katharine and her friends had excitedly welcomed to Wellesley years before. She had spent her career enlarging his field of American literature in her classes, her textbook, and her Poetry Club activities, as well as in championing the next generations of poets.

Fittingly, her friend's voice reading an American poem was the last sound Katharine ever heard before she died. When Wellesley learned the news of her passing, the flag on Tower Court, where College Hall had stood, "fluttered down and then rose to half-staff."[245]

She was memorialized at Wellesley and in Boston and her ashes buried in Falmouth. Tributes to her poured in. "T.H.R." was still thinking of her after her death, writing to Annie that for his Pastor's Library, he hoped she would write out by hand the words of "America the Beautiful" with Katharine's name over it.[246]

But before her death, Katharine had an extraordinary final vision of what her most famous poem could say to its millions of singers today.

Epilogue

"From Sea to Shining Sea"[1]

I.

At her song's anniversary in 1918, a few months before the end of the Great War, Katharine explained that its "hold ... upon our people, is clearly due to the fact that Americans are at heart idealists, with a fundamental faith in human brotherhood, — that faith for which our nation, in this crucial hour of history, stands ready to risk and suffer all."[2]

But after the war, many Americans feared the world was not more "safe for democracy," as President Woodrow Wilson had hoped, and wanted the United States to return to isolationism rather than search for a way of using diplomacy to forge a community committed to peaceful resolutions of international conflicts.

In her final public speech, Katharine answered them by explaining a new way that Americans could think of their world when they sing her song.

On cloudy and cold March 1, 1928, a year before her death, she made one of her final public appearances, at Mechanics Hall in Boston, a huge brick Victorian building with a turret and tall arched windows. It sometimes hosted indoor track meets, wrestling matches, dog shows, and a circus with elephants.

That day, public school superintendents from across the country came to celebrate Katharine. In spite of her heart trouble, she made the difficult climb to the stage: "two flights of stairs first—then thousands of people—was never so near toppling over on a platform...."[3]

J. M. Gwinn of the National Education Association announced to the hushed audience: "Now we are to have the singing of 'America the Beautiful.' As you know, the author is sitting on the stage. So that it may not interfere with the children's singing, I would suggest that you restrain your tendency to sing until the last stanza.

"It is a matter of considerable interest that this chorus of girls represents twenty different nationalities, all singing 'America The Beautiful.'"[4]

The chorus was like that organized by Charles W. Dimick, who welcomed Boston children to his downtown Lancaster Movie Theatre for free Saturday afternoon shows if they joined his chorus of nearly twenty nationalities, which always finished their programs with "America the Beautiful," because, he explained, the "children love that song, and ... they show it in their singing."[5]

After the chorus and audience sang Katharine's words that day, Gwinn introduced her as "a woman who stands out in Massachusetts as one of the great educational leaders, for many years a distinguished professor in Wellesley College. Her service has done much in bringing the young people from this land and those who come from foreign lands to our shores into a better understanding of American citizenship and the meaning of this country to them."[6]

In the vast hall the huge audience applauded her with a standing ovation. She thanked the children and the audience and told them: "It is not work to write a song, it is great joy.... During the thirty years since I wrote it, I have seen such a love for America...."[7]

Then she described how the country itself turned her into the poet of "America the Beautiful" who saw both its challenges and potential:

> It was thirty-five years ago ... in the year of the World's Fair, that I made my first journey to the far West. My first great thrill was at Chicago. I saw America in the making, and this lovely city turned all men into poets, realizing that against the smoke-stained, sin-stained city of the day there lay the possibility of some spiritual invention that should give us cities that were all beautiful.
>
> We went out and crossed the prairies and the farm lands and the richness of the farm lands and the great wheat fields impressed the memory of those poets, Pilgrims from East to West who were building at such cost the material prosperity of our country, and we came at last to the Rocky Mountains in all their majesty, and climbed at last the mystic height of Pike's Peak. It was during our brief stay there that summer, looking out over that great expanse, that the opening stanza was promoted in my mind.[8]

However, in spite of requests to lengthen her song, in 1928 she did not want to add a new stanza "to express international brotherhood,"[9] although she was in favor of the idea, because "the song is long enough already."[10]

But then Katharine described her bold vision of international brotherhood to help her country move forward out of the isolationist policies of the past into the future as a leader of a global community. In the ten years after American soldiers had sung "America the Beautiful" on the Verdun battlefields at the end of the Great War, she had come to understand how to encourage those who sing her song to see their world in a new way.

She said that when Americans sing her words, "From sea to shining sea," they should think of them as "applying from the Pacific to the Atlantic, around the other way, and all the states in between, and that will include all the nations and all the people from sea to shining sea."[11] It was time "to think anew and act anew," as Abraham Lincoln had said.[12]

She hoped that when Americans sing her words, they would think of themselves as connected to everyone "from sea to shining sea."

As a five-year-old child in the Cape Cod village of Falmouth, Massachusetts, Katharine had seen her widowed mother's grief at Lincoln's assassination. At his memorial service, when she recognized her mother's widow's shawl along with those of the other widows draping the church, she had felt connected to the nation beyond her village. There she understood for the first time that she was part of a larger community faced with coming together to heal after the Civil War, feeling the "nation's sorrow" her own sorrow.[13]

The determination of the Falmouth widows to show their patriotism and help their country heal from war had shown Katharine that even her mother, an impoverished and powerless woman who could not preach from a minister's pulpit, could find a way to bring her nation together. It was a powerful example for the girl who then helped America visualize its best self.

Shortly before his death, Lincoln counseled his country to come together to heal: "With malice toward none, with charity for all, with firmness in the right as God gives us to see the right, let us strive … to do all which may achieve and cherish a just and lasting peace among ourselves and with all nations."[14]

Katharine had devoted her life to those ideals, helping her country understand its identity as a community that was one part of a worldwide community. Her village of Falmouth and then the "Adamless Eden" of Wellesley College had given her models for the communities she helped create throughout her life—of students, of colleagues, of poets, of readers, and of all who love her song. She knew brotherhood was essential as an ideal for the nation, and she felt that international brotherhood could be symbolized by the "seas" that that reached around the globe from one coast of the United States to the other.

II.

When she died, Americans were still singing "America the Beautiful"—to several different melodies. Throughout the war, military bands had played John Philip Sousa's up-tempo version of "The Star-Spangled Banner." Then, after much lobbying by residents of Baltimore, Maryland, whose Fort McHenry was the site of the battle that inspired its words, Congress voted to make "The Star-Spangled Banner" the national anthem in 1931, two years after Katharine's death.

Nevertheless, many Americans have felt that "America the Beautiful" best unites the nation and should be made the national anthem. Although such attempts have been unsuccessful, as a prominent journalist has noted,[15] it has remained a song deep in the national psyche, one that permeates our culture, from detective Nancy Drew's mystery plots to James Taylor's performance during a recent World Series game to honor the first responders, survivors, and victims of the 2013 Boston Marathon bombing.[16]

Her words, a humble plea that God "shed His grace" on America and "crown thy good with brotherhood" have often been chosen in moments of national crises to pull Americans together in a shared vision of what is possible for the country.

One such moment occurred when the newly sworn-in President Lyndon B. Johnson first addressed a packed Congress a few days after John F. Kennedy's assassination. Johnson ended his speech by imploring all there to join together to help the traumatized and grieving country begin to heal.[17] In a voice filled with intense emotion, he quoted Katharine's prayerful words: "America, America, God shed His grace on thee, And crown thy good with brotherhood, From sea to shining sea." When he finished, many around him were in tears.[18]

"America the Beautiful" certainly fulfills what the (all-male) committee was looking for in a national anthem in 1861, when the Civil War began to tear the country apart. At that time, the prominent critic Richard Grant White had written that a true national anthem would "pervade" and "penetrate" and "cheer the land like sunlight." It would be "the national heart-beat set to music."[19]

Henry Wadsworth Longfellow wrote that great literature is "an image of the spiritual world ... of the internal, rather than the external."[20] Katharine portrayed that spiritual world of ideals through her writings grounded in the concrete external world of her trailblazing life.

Her legacy is best described in a passage she marked in her copy of the River Duddon sonnets by William Wordsworth. The only true memorial one can leave for future generations, he wrote, is "something from our hands" which has "power / To live, and act, and serve the future hour."[21]

Her immeasurable legacy is still with us. It is in generations of women college graduates, in students and teachers who have benefited from her classroom texts and innovative teaching style, in Americans who understand and appreciate their national literature, especially poetry, in urban "settlement houses," and in all those who love America and work for brotherhood.

She answered Longfellow's question, when he wondered in his poem "Possibilities" about who would speak to America as a poet after his death:

> Where are the Poets...?
>
> Perhaps there lives some dreamy boy, untaught
>
> In schools, some graduate of the field or street,
>
> Who shall become a master of the art,
>
> An admiral sailing the high seas of thought,
>
> Fearless and first and steering with his fleet
>
> For lands not laid down in any chart.[22]

She was that "dreamy boy ... sailing the high seas of thought, / Fearless and first and steering with his fleet / For lands not laid down in any chart" who launched her career from the shores of Cape Cod. She became an "American heroine" like the one she described while still a Wellesley student, "who will surpass all others ... of all women the most daring, intelligent, and forceful."[23]

As her mother's uncle said about Katharine, "Her father and his father, both ministers, would rejoice to see themselves outdone [by her]."[24]

Indeed, it is this daughter of a minister who, against all odds, still ministers to her country. Past generations of Americans learned about their nation when they recited Longfellow's poems in their own voices. Then, later at the public poetry readings Katharine fostered, they listened together to the voices of American poets like Robert Frost portraying their country.

Katharine called "America the Beautiful" her "gift" to the nation,[25] and today, when we blend our voices and hear each other sing her words, we honor her ideal of brotherhood "from sea to shining sea."

ACKNOWLEDGMENTS

During my years of researching and writing about the life and times of Katharine Lee Bates, I have greatly appreciated the help of many people.

I thank the descendants of Katharine Lee Bates's family—William Bates, Jr., the late Elizabeth Olmstead, and especially her daughter Elizabeth Bates Null—for their unflagging interest and generous loans of family documents. With their wit and energy, they were my personal link to Katharine.

My research would not have been possible without the financial and professional encouragement and support of Pine Manor College, which awarded me the Lindsey and Wean Sabbatical leaves and numerous research stipends. I also thank my faculty colleagues and student research assistants for their support. The travel fellowship from the North East Modern Language Association enabled me to do essential library and travel research in Colorado Springs with its "purple mountain majesties."

I thank the Falmouth Historical Society for its interest and its celebrations of Katharine Lee Bates's life, and for the assistance of its archivists. The Rev. Douglas K. Showalter helpfully shared his knowledge of the history of the First Congregational Church of Falmouth, and my Falmouth hosts Stephanie and Leonard Miele have given me much warm hospitality while sharing their knowledge of Katharine's Falmouth connections with me over the years.

For patient help during all my hours of researching in Wellesley College's extensive collection of Katharine's letters, diaries, scrapbooks, and publications, I thank its archivists, Ian Graham, Mary Yearl, and especially Wilma Slaight, for her invaluable suggestions of crucial documents.

In Colorado Springs, I appreciated the help of Ginny Kiefer, curator of Special Collections at the Tutt Library of Colorado College. Dave and Pat Dinsmore, Barbara Dutra-Silveira, Pete Frech, Dave Rickert, and Gordon Gray, as well as my "Rails to Trails" host Veronica Serna, all helped me understand Katharine Lee Bates's extraordinary summer of 1893 in Colorado Springs.

As I have written and revised various drafts of my manuscript, I have appreciated the supportive enthusiasm, encouraging suggestions, and helpful readings of my manuscript by John L. Idol, Jr., Kathleen Aguero, the late Lester M. Ponder, the late Andrew Bunie, Raymond P. Lee, Anne Hanford, and David E. Herder, who also accompanied me to Egypt and Verdun, France. I especially thank Robert M. Sprague for his ideas and cheerful assistance. I also thank my Boston Biographers group, historian Patricia Palmieri, Simon Winchester, and Lynn Sherr for their suggestions and encouragement.

For all her editorial help transforming my manuscript into a book, I thank Ruth Walker for her patience, thoughtful insights, and thorough editing. I appreciate Deborah Bloom's beautiful book cover design and Keith Arbour's excellent index. I thank Windy City Publishers, especially Ruth Beach and Dawn McGarrahan Wiebe, and I thank Jennifer Richards for her work as my publicist.

My family have all helped in many ways. It was my late mother, Sallie Clover Ponder, who introduced me to Katharine Lee Bates long ago when she proudly told me that a woman from her college had written "America the Beautiful." And over the years I have appreciated the loyal support of my sister, Constance Ponder Zubek.

I also thank my three daughters, Betsy Klimasmith, Kate Wilson, and Abigail Klima, for their years of interest in my work.

And I hope their children—Sophie, Zack, Natalie, David, Caleb, and Teddy—will help create a world that values brother and sisterhood, from sea to shining sea.

IMAGE CREDITS AND PERMISSIONS

I have made every effort to contact all copyright holders. If notified, I will be happy to rectify any errors or omissions at the earliest opportunity.

COVER DESIGN
by Deborah Bloom.
Inspired by a painting by Joseph Downs.

AUTHOR PHOTOGRAPH
by Ken Burg.

YANKEE DIVISION FLAG:
1987.121 National Color, 104th Infantry (World War I).
Courtesy Commonwealth of Massachusetts, State House Art Commission.

FIRST CONGREGATIONAL CHURCH, FALMOUTH
NOBSKA LIGHT, WOODS HOLE
Courtesy of the Falmouth Historical Society, Falmouth, Mass.

THE BATES FAMILY (WILLIAM, CORNELIA, ARTHUR LEE, SAMUEL LEE, JANE, AND BABY KATHARINE LEE BATES); KATHARINE LEE BATES (3); PAULINE DURANT; HENRY DURANT; ALICE FREEMAN (BETWEEN PILLARS, IN WHITE RUFFLE) AND STUDENTS; KATHARINE COMAN (2); VIDA SCUDDER; MARGARET SHERWOOD; SOPHIE JEWETT; CAROLINE HAZARD; THE BARGE IN FRONT OF COLLEGE HALL; COLLEGE HALL; COLLEGE HALL, CENTER COURT; COLLEGE HALL, LIBRARY; THE SCARAB; WELLESLEY COLLEGE AMBULANCE IN WORLD WAR I.
Courtesy of Wellesley College Archives.

HENRY WADSWORTH LONGFELLOW
c. 1880. Courtesy National Park Service, Longfellow House—
Washington's Headquarters National Historic Site.

ILLUSTRATION FROM "GOODY SANTA CLAUS ON A SLEIGH RIDE"
BY KATHARINE LEE BATES
Wide-Awake, v. 28 (Dec. 1888), 34.

ILLUSTRATION FROM *ROSE AND THORN* BY KATHARINE LEE BATES
New York: Thomas Nelson and Sons, 1901, Frontispiece.

"The Tower, Magdalen College"
Taken by Katharine Coman. *From Gretna Green to Land's End* by Katharine Lee Bates.
New York: Thomas Y. Crowell Company, 1907, 210-211.

Oscar Lovell Triggs
Courtesy of Special Collections Research Center,
the University of Chicago Library.

T.H. Root
HUD 285.25A
Courtesy of Harvard University Archives.

"The Columbian Illuminations," "The Southern Vista,"
"Eastern Veranda of the Woman's Building"
The Dream City: A Portfolio of Photographic Views. St. Louis:
N. D. Thompson Publishing Co., 1893, 67, 157, 103.

"Pike's Peak at Sunset—The Mountain Shadow in the Eastern Sky"
Harper's Weekly, Sept. 20, 1877, 768.

"Pike's Peak from Colorado Springs"
Harper's Weekly, June 11, 1892, 573.

Postcard from Spain
Owned by Katharine Lee Bates.
Gift to author from Elizabeth Olmstead.

"The Pyramids," "The Colossi," "The Sea of Galilee, Roman Fortification"
Watercolor paintings by Caroline Hazard.
Courtesy of Wellesley College Archives.

R.S. Hillyer
1917. HUD 317.870p
Courtesy of Harvard University Archives.

Robert Frost
Courtesy of Dartmouth College Library.

"The Vigilantes"
Publisher's design in *Fifes and Drums: A Collection of Poems of America at War*, 1917.
Image retrieved from https://en.wikipedia.org/wiki/The_Vigilantes#/media/
File:Fifes_and_Drums_Vigilantes_1917_The_Vigilantes.jpg.

NOTES

ABBREVIATIONS

In these notes, Katharine Lee Bates is referred to as KLB. Her papers are collected as the Katharine Lee Bates Papers, 3P, in the Wellesley College Archives (WCA) and Wellesley College Special Collections (WCSC), Wellesley College.

Specific items are referred to below by their box numbers. The following abbreviations are used for other important people and publications:

- ABS: Annie Beecher Scoville
- ALB: Arthur Bates
- CH: Caroline Hazard
- CLB: Cornelia Lee Bates
- ENH: Eben Norton Horsford
- ENN: Emily Norcross Newton
- KC: Katharine Coman
- LMH: Louise Manning Hodgkins
- RHL: Rose Hawthorne Lathrop, later Mother Mary Alphonsa Lathrop
- THR: Theophilus Huntington Root
- VS: Vida Scudder
- BET: *The Boston Evening Transcript*
- SSR: The *Springfield Sunday Republican*

PROLOGUE: "TEARS ON THEIR FACES"

1. Katharine Lee Bates, Excerpt of a typewritten note. Based on "Day after Thanksgiving, 1926" letter to her brother Arthur Bates, KLB Papers, Box 4. WCA. Thanks to Wilma Slaight, former Wellesley College archivist, for suggesting this document.

2. KLB, Diary, Nov. 7, 1918. KLB Papers, Box 4. WCA.

3. *Boston Evening Transcript*, Nov. 11, 1918.

4. As the Allied commanders worked on an Armistice acceptable to Germany, even rumors of peace sufficed to set off a premature New York celebration.

5. Stephen Erlanger, "War Resonates Anew on Hallowed French Ground." *The New York Times*, Nov. 10, 2011.

6. Robert Hillyer, "Dead Man's Corner, Verdun," from *Collected Poems* by Robert Hillyer, copyright 1961 by Robert Hillyer, copyright renewed 1989 by Francesca P. Hillyer and Elizabeth V. Hillyer. Used by permission of Alfred A. Knopf, an imprint of the Knopf Doubleday Publishing Group, a division of Penguin Random House LLC (all rights reserved), 216.

7. Frank Palmer Sibley, *With the Yankee Division in France*. Boston: Little, Brown and Company, 1919, 320.

8. *BET*, Nov. 12, 1918.

9. Sibley, 341.

10. *BET*, Nov. 11, 1918.

11. *BET*, Nov. 13, 1918.

12. KLB, Diary, Nov 11, 1918. Box 4. WCA.

13. Harriet Parke, Wellesley Class of 1920. Letter to the author, May 6, 1990. She wrote me that KLB was "a dear, *friendly and jovial person*—she was always stopping and talking to us as we walked on campus."

14. KLB, "'Died of Wounds'" in *The Retinue and Other Poems*. New York: E.P. Dutton & Co., 1918, 164.

15. *BET*, Nov. 11, 1918, 1.

16. *BET*, Nov. 11, 1918, 4.

17. *BET*, Nov. 11, 1918, 5.

18. Ibid.

19. *Boston Globe*, Nov. 11, 1918.

20. *BET*, Nov. 11, 1918.

21. Ibid.

22. Ibid.

23. Parke.

24. KLB, Excerpt.

25. KLB, "America the Beautiful," in *America and Beautiful and Other Poems*. New York: Thomas Y. Crowell Company, 1911, 3-4.

26. KLB, Excerpt.

27. Richard Grant White, *National Hymns: How They Are Written and How They Are Not Written—A Lyric and National Study for the Times*. New York: Rudd & Carleton, 1861, 70, 75.

CHAPTER ONE: 1859-1871-"ROCK'D IN A CLAM SHELL"

1. KLB, Letter to ABS, July 29, 1883. Box 19, Folder 781. Beecher Family Papers (MS 71). Manuscripts and Archives. Yale University. (Hereinafter "Beecher Papers.") Katharine wrote, "your infancy was not rock'd, like mine, in a clam-shell."

2. First Congregational Church of Falmouth of the United Church of Christ, *Two Hundredth Anniversary, 1708-1908*. First Congregational Church of Falmouth, Massachusetts, Oct. 11-13, 1908. Privately printed, 45.

3. Dorothy Burgess, *Dream and Deed: The Story of Katharine Lee Bates*. Norman: The University of Oklahoma Press, 1952, 8, 11.

4. Quoted in (the Rev.) Lewis F. Clark, *Discourse Occasioned by the Death of Rev. William Bates*. Boston: J. E. Tilton and Company, 1859, 19.

5. First, *Two*, 45.

6. Quoted in Clark, 19.

7. Dorothea Lawrance Mann, "Katharine Lee Bates, Poet and Professor," originally published in *BET* and reprinted in booklet format, n.d., 7. Loaned to me by Elizabeth Olmstead.

8. Douglas K. Showalter, e-mail correspondence with the author, May 29, 2010.

9. Clark, 27.

10. Ibid.

11. Burgess, 11.

12. Ruth Sterling, "Memories of Old Falmouth: The Parsonage Children." *Falmouth Enterprise*, August 19, 1955, 2.

13. Arthur Lee Bates, "A Few Recollections." Handwritten family memoir, 1937, 123. Courtesy of Elizabeth Olmstead.

14. Burgess, 15.

15. Elizabeth Olmstead, personal interview, 1995.

16. ALB, "Few," 127, 129.

17. KLB, inscription in *The Dramatic Works and Poems of William Shakspeare*, Vol I. New York: George Dearborn, Publisher, n.d. Courtesy of Elizabeth Olmstead.

18. Burgess, 7.

19. KLB, "The Rest Is Silence," in *America the Beautiful*, 182-183.

20. Quoted in Burgess, 57.

21. ALB, "Few,"128.

22. ALB "Few," 129.

23. Sterling, "Memories," 1.

24. KLB, "Falmouth" (also called "My Falmouth."). *The Stratford Monthly*. n.d.

25. Theodate Geoffrey, "Suckanesset." Falmouth: The Falmouth Publishing Co., Inc., 1930 (copyright 1928, 1930 by Dorothy G. Wayman), 67-68.

26. KLB,"The Falmouth Bell," in *America and Beautiful*, 39-41.

27. First, *Two*, 60.

28. First, *Two*, 61.

29. Sterling, 8.

30. First, *Two*, 46. This was ten more men than its quota.

31. Douglas Showalter, *Chapters on the History of the First Congregational Church of Falmouth, Massachusetts of the United Church of Christ* (unpublished draft), 42, quoting First, Church Register, Dec. 30, 1864.

32. Bruce Chalmers, "Falmouth: A Retrospect," in Mary Lou Smith, ed., *The Book of Falmouth*, The Falmouth Historical Commission, 1986, 14.

33. *BET*, April 12, 1865.

34. *BET*, April 14, 1865.

35. *BET*, April 15, 1865.

36. Ibid.

37. *Boston Daily Advertiser* special dispatch to the *BET*, April 15, 1865.

38. KLB, "When Lincoln Died." *The Youth's Companion*, April 27, 1922, and later reprinted in KLB, *America the Dream*. New York: Thomas Y. Crowell, Publishers, 1930, 107-109. Subsequent quotations in the paragraphs following are also from this poem.

39. KLB, "The Falmouth Bell."

40. KLB, "When Lincoln."

41. KLB, "The Falmouth Bell."

42. KLB, Undated Diary, 1866, 79. KLB Papers, Box 2. WCA. Katharine's spelling has been retained in quoted passages. Later in her life she would become interested in the Indian rights movement. When at Wellesley College, both as a student and later as a professor, she heard many chapel talks by activists in the movement that sought justice for the Indians being pushed west, forced into reservations, or killed during much of her adult life. Later she wrote a moving and distinctive poem, "Indian Bearers," in which she describes how the "palefaces" imposed their way of life on the Indians and their land. Written atypically in the first person, as if she is the wronged Indian speaking, Katharine suggests her deep compassion for the people familiar to her from her childhood.

43. KLB, "The Flower of Chivalry." *SSR*, n.d., l883.

44. Elizabeth Olmstead, "Katharine Lee Bates: Scholar, Patriot, Poet." Unpublished manuscript for talk at the Wellesley Historical Society.

45. ALB, "Few," 139.

46. Samuel Eliot Morison, *The Maritime History of Massachusetts, 1783-1860*. Boston: Northeastern University Press, 1979, 295-299.

47. ALB, "Few," 126.

48. Ibid.

49. Ibid.

50. Ibid.

51. Geoffrey, 104.

52. Sterling, "Memories," 8.

53. Ibid.

54. KLB, Letter to ABS, July 29, 1883.

55. Geoffrey, 99.

56. ALB, "Few," 127.

57. Sterling, "Memories," 8.

58. KLB, "Falmouth."

59. Sterling, "Parsonage," 16.

60. Sterling, "Parsonage," 11.

61. Sterling, "Parsonage," 15.

62. KLB, "Falmouth."

63. KLB, "When Cap'n Tom Comes Home," reprinted in Leonard Miele, *Voice of the Tide: The Cape Cod Heritage of Katharine Lee Bates*. New Bedford, Massachusetts: Spinner Publications, 2009, 97.

64. ALB, "Few," 142.

65. Ibid.

66. ALB, "Few," 123.

67. Burgess, 24.

68. KLB, Undated Diary, the first pages, and Burgess, 3.

69. KLB, Undated Diary, July 11, 1866. Although this entry is dated 1866, Burgess states (p. 3) that the diary was given to her "about 1868."

70. ALB, "Few," 157.

71. KLB, Diary, Dec. 22, 1866.

72. ALB, "Few," 158, 157.

73. KLB, Letter to ABS, Aug. 31, 1884. Box 19, F. 783. Beecher Papers.

74. KLB, Diary. On her juvenile writing, see Miele.

75. KLB, Miscellaneous letters, poems, report cards, and "Weekly Journal" juvenilia. Falmouth Historical Society Collections, Gift of Cecelia Bowerman Fuglister. The Bates family still treasures these report cards.

76. KLB, "Lydd," in *The Retinue and Other Poems*, New York: E.P. Dutton and Company, 1918, 82.

77. ALB, "Few."

78. Ibid.

79. Ibid.

80. Burgess, 163.

81. This pin was exhibited by the Falmouth Historical Society with the note: "Topaz pin surrounded by pearls given to Elizabeth Keith Olmstead (her great-niece) by KLB. Originally contained hair of Joshua Bates in place of the topaz."

82. KLB, "Rebecca and Abigail" in *Fairy Gold*, 185-189. Letter to Harriet Gifford, May 5, 1916. Falmouth Historical Society Collections.

83. CLB, Letter to KLB, Aug. 8, 1864. KLB Papers. Box 22. WCA.

84. KLB, Diary, Feb. 24, 1866. Box 2.

85. KLB, Diary, Aug. 15, 1866.

86. KLB, Diary, March 10, 1866.

87. KLB, Diary, Dec. 1, 1866.

88. KLB, Diary, Sept. 20, 1866.

89. Gaston Bachelard, *Poetics of Space*. Boston: Beacon Press, 1994 (orig. pub. 1964).

90. KLB, "An Autobiography in Brief of Katharine Lee Bates." Plymouth, Mass.: Enterprise Press, 1930. KLB Papers, 3P, Box 1, WCA.

91. Ruth Sterling, "As I Remember Katharine Lee Bates." *Cape Cod Compass*, 1959 (Vol. 12), 29.

92. ALB, "Few," 124.

93. KLB, "Falmouth."

94. KLB, "The Falmouth Bell."

95. KLB, "Autobiography."

96. KLB "Miriam's Choice." *SSR*, July 30 and Aug. 6, 1882.

97. KLB, "The Rest Is Silence," in *America the Beautiful,* 182-183.

98. First, *Two*, 44.

99. KLB, "When Lincoln."

100. Chalmers.

101. KLB, "Farewell to England," in *America the Dream*, 34.

Chapter Two: 1871-1880–"Katie of '80"

1. In Grantville, Massachusetts, then part of West Needham; Grantville is now part of Wellesley Hills.

2. Florence Morse Kingsley, *The Life of Henry Fowle Durant*. New York: The Century Co., 1924, 173.

3. Ibid.

4. This Bible is in the WCA.

5. KLB, Manuscripts, Sept. 23, 1917. Box 15. WCA.

6. Margaret Shackford, "College Hall." WCA.

7. He was a partner in their private banking firm, Welles & Co. Paris. Margaret E. Taylor and Jean Glasscock, "The Founders and the Early Presidents," in Jean Glasscock, ed., *Wellesley College 1875-1975: A Century of Women*. Wellesley, Massachusetts: Wellesley College, A Centennial Publication, 1975, 2.

8. Grace Harris Hubbard, Wellesley Class of 1885. "Wellesley College 1922." WCA.

9. KLB, Manuscripts, October 3, 1909, 6-7, Box 15. WCA.

10. Details of the ceremony and all quotations are from Glasscock, 7-9.

11. Glasscock, 9.

12. KLB, Manuscripts, October 3, 1909, 7.

13. Quoted on iv of Glasscock.

14. Patricia Palmieri, *In Adamless Eden: The Community of Women Faculty at Wellesley.* New Haven: Yale University Press, 1997, 14.

15. Taylor and Glasscock, 2.

16. Kingsley, 107.

17. Kingsley, 43.

18. Frances Knickerbocker, "Sarah Alden Bradford Ripley," in *Notable American Women, III.* Cambridge: The Belknap Press of Harvard University Press, 1971, 163-165.

19. John McAleer, *Ralph Waldo Emerson: Days of Encounter.* Boston: Little, Brown and Company, 1984, 47, quoting Henry Thomas and Dana Lee Thomas, *Living Biographies of Great Philosophers*, 249.

20. Knickerbocker, 164.

21. Kingsley, 42.

22. As Palmieri points out, this was a typical pattern among the first generation of Wellesley College students.

23. KLB, "Reflections," *The Wellesley Magazine*, Vol. II, No. 1 (Oct. 14, 1893), 2.

24. There had been so many applications at the opening in 1875 that there were between two and three hundred qualified applicants who had been turned away. Students who could not pass the exams had to do additional preparatory work on the campus.

25. Peter Fergusson, James F. O'Gorman, and John Rhodes, *The Landscape and Architecture of Wellesley College.* Wellesley, Massachusetts: Wellesley College, 2000, 33, 45.

26. Details are from Edward Abbott, "Wellesley College," *Harper's New Monthly Magazine.* August 1876, Vol. LIII, 321-322.

27. Details of the interior of College Hall come from Fergusson, 29-44, and Ellen Gow, letter to "My Dear Sister," Sept. 25, 1875. WCA.

28. Wellesley College *Calendar*, 1876-1877.

29. Details of the early campus come from Fergusson, 1-10.

30. Sarah Searing, "Reminiscences of Wellesley in 1883." KLB, 3P, Autograph letters, Box 23. WCA.

31. Quoted in Kingsley, 199.

32. Ibid.

33. Ibid.

34. Kingsley, 252.

35. Abbott, 325.

36. Henry Wadsworth Longfellow, "A Noble Institution," letter to H. F. Durant, Oct. 29, 1879. Unpublished; privately printed. WCA.

37. Abbott, 325.

38. Ibid.

39. Margaret Sherwood, "Wellesley College." Typewritten article about Wellesley College, 1914, 2. Margaret Sherwood papers, WCA.

40. Abbott, 325.

41. Ibid.

42. KLB, Manuscripts of Speeches, October 3, 1909, Box 15. WCA.

43. Abbott, 328.

44. Gow, 2.

45. Quoted in Kingsley, 251.

46. KLB, "Correspondence," 53-54.

47. Class History of 1880, 6C/ 1880, 21-22. WCA.

48. KLB, "Reflections," 3.

49. Glasscock, 35.

50. KLB, "The Wellesley Vision." *The Wellesley College News Magazine Supplement*, Vol. XXIV (April, 1916), 16.

51. Food information is from Hubbard.

52. Helen Lefkowitz Horowitz, *Alma Mater: Design and Experience in the Women's Colleges from Their Nineteenth-Century Beginnings to the 1930s*, 2nd Edition. Amherst: University of Massachusetts Press, 1993, 51 and 54.

53. Abbott, 328.

54. Quoted in Kingsley, 262.

55. KLB, "Wellesley Watchwords," in *The Wellesley Magazine,* October 15, 1892, 2-3.

56. KLB, "Vision,"16.

57. KLB, "Vision," 17.

58. Taylor and Glasscock, 15.

59. Hubbard.

60. Kingsley, 216, quoting a letter of Miss Sarah F. Whiting, professor of physics, Wellesley College.

61. Kingsley, 256.

62. Kingsley, 321.

63. Wellesley College *Calendar*, 1878-9, 68.

64. Abbott, 329.

65. Taylor and Glasscock, 9.

66. Quoted in Kingsley, 263.

67. KLB, "Watchwords," 9. However, forty-five years after her graduation she recalled "how torn" she was by his demands: "'I loved his poetic side, but his fanaticism drove me out of church and theology for all time." Taylor and Glasscock, 17.

68. Horowitz, 12.

69. Kingsley quoting Durant's "The Spirit of the College," 238-239.

70. KLB, "Watchwords," 3; "A Forgotten Pageant." *BET*, July 22, 1911.

71. KLB, "Vision,"16-17.

72. KLB, "Watchwords," 5.

73. KLB, "A Forgotten."

74. Gwendolyn Bossi Henson, personal interview with author. July 27, 1993, in East Orleans, Massachusetts.

75. KLB, "Watchwords," 6.

76. Kingsley, 309-310.

77. Mary Russell Bartlett, "The History of the 'O. P.'" *The Wellesley Prelude*, Vol. I, #27 (April 26, 1890), 382.

78. KLB, "A Forgotten."

79. KLB, "A Forgotten." All quotations in this episode come from this article.

80. Ibid.

81. Ibid.

82. KLB, "Watchwords," 2.

83. Bartlett, 382.

84. KLB, "The Sea Father," in *BET*, n.d., KLB Scrapbook 1876-1885, Box 19, WCA.

85. Van Wyck Brooks, *The Flowering of New England, 1815-1865*. New York: E.P. Dutton and Company, 1936, 214.

86. William Dean Howells. Autograph letter signed W. D. Howells to "Miss Bates," March 11, 1879, Boston. Wellesley College Special Collections.

87. Horace, "Epistle to the Pisones," trans. by Norman J. De Witt, in *Criticism: Major Statements*, 4th edition. Ed. by Charles Kaplan and Wiliam Davis Anderson. Boston: Bedford/St. Martin's, 2000, 84-95.

88. Anonymous Review, KLB Scrapbook 1876-1885, Box 19, WCA.

89. KLB, "A Forgotten."

90. William Dean Howells, *Literary Friends and Acquaintances*. New York: Harper and Brothers Publishers, 1900, 179-181.

91. Howells, *Literary*, 191.

92. Howells, *Literary*, 190. Andrew and Elizabeth Craigie occupied it from 1791 to 1819.

93. Longfellow National Historic Site (LNHS) website. "Occupants."

94. KLB, "A Forgotten."

95. Howells, *Literary*, 183.

96. Howells, *Literary*, 184.

97. Henry Wadsworth Longfellow, *Poems and Other Writings*, ed. J. D. McClatchy for The Library of America. New York: Literary Classics of the United States, 2000, 811-12.

98. Ibid.

99. Quoted by James Mellow, *Nathaniel Hawthorne and His Times*. Boston: Houghton Mifflin Company, 1980, 34.

100. Brooks, 167.

101. LNHS website. "Study," quoting Robert Ferguson, September 1864, from Carlisle, England.

102. Howells, *Literary*, 198-199.

103. Longfellow, *The Song of Hiawatha*, in *Poems*, 278.

104. See photograph from LNHS in Charles Calhoun, *Longfellow: A Rediscovered Life*. Boston: Beacon Press, 2004, Plate 21.

105. Howells, *Literary*, 196.

106. LNHS website, "Study"; the chair was presented on Feb. 27, 1879.

107. Ibid.

108. I thank Anita Israel, archivist at the Longfellow National Historic Site, for this idea. July 14, 2009.

109. Burgess, 42.

110. Longfellow had written his own poem about sleep, "Curfew." In *Poems*, 55-56. Thanks to Rob Velella for this information.

111. Howells, *Literary*, 201.

112. Longfellow, "Table-Talk" in *Poems*, 798.

113. Howells, *Literary*, 184.

114. Horowitz, 51.

115. Searing, 6.

116. Ibid.

117. Kingsley, 319-320.

118. KLB, "Watchwords" 4-5.

119. Class History of 1880, 121.

120. Class History, 122.

121. Ibid.

122. KLB, Uncatalogued Material, April 29, 1880. WCA.

123. Henry Wadsworth Longfellow, "Possibilities." *The Poetical Works of Henry Wadsworth Longfellow: With Numerous Illustrations*. Boston: Houghton, Mifflin and Company (The Riverside Press), 1885, 300.

Chapter Three: 1880-1885–"A Little Money, a Little Fame"

1. "I have a little money, a little fame, a little goodwill up and down the street, and a profession that gives my intellectual activities and my human sympathies equal play," from KLB, "The Red Tassel." *SSR*, Nov. 9, 1884.

2. Wellesley College Calendar, 1879-80, WCA.

3. KLB, "Autobiography."

4. KLB, "The Schoolroom." Unpublished manuscript. KLB, Manuscripts of Verse: 1870-1923, Box 15. WCA.

5. KLB, Letter to Mary Sheldon (Barnes), Feb. 14, 1881. KLB, Box 5. WCA.

6. Its tuition, $325 per school year, quite an unusual monetary investment for a girl's education, meant that Dana Hall students were from families who could afford to send their daughters to a new preparatory school in hopes of improving their chances of being admitted to Wellesley College. It was more expensive than Katie Bates's $250 annual tuition at Wellesley College had been.

7. Appendix to Wellesley College *Calendar*, 1889-91.

8. Winifred Lowry Post,*"Purpose and Personality": The Story of Dana Hall*. Wellesley, Massachusetts: Dana Hall School, 1978, 6.

9. KLB, "The Beginnings of Dana Hall." *Our Town*, June 1899, 3.

10. KLB, "Beginnings," 4.

11. KLB, *Sigurd Our Golden Colllie and Other Comrades of the Road*. London: J.M. Dent & Sons Ltd., 1921, 63.

12. KLB, "Beginnings."

13. KLB, Letter to LMH, July 1, 1885. KLB Papers, Box 6. WCA.

14. Elizabeth Keith, "Katharine Lee Bates and the Scarab." *St. Nicholas*, January 1931, 218.

15. Gamaliel Bradford, *Early Days in Wellesley*. Wellesley: Wellesley Historical Society, 1928, 8; and Elizabeth Hinchliffe, *Five Pounds Currency, Three Pounds of Corn: Wellesley's Centennial Story*. Wellesley: Town of Wellesley, 1981, 51. However, even when I went to Wellesley College in the 1960s, we referred to the stores and ice-cream parlor we could walk to as "The Vil."

16. Hinchliffe, 51.

17. Joseph Fiske, quoted in Hinchliffe, 50.

18. Bradford, 17.

19. KLB quoting Julia Eastman in "Julia Eastman." *BET,* Jan. 2, 1911.

20. Ibid.

21. Quoted in George S. Merriam, *The Life and Times of Samuel Bowles,* Vol. 2. New York: The Century Co., 1885, 391.

22. Merriam, 393.

23. Richard B. Sewall, *The Life of Emily Dickinson.* New York: Farrar, Straus and Giroux, 1980, 471.

24. Ibid.

25. Quoted in Merriam, Vol. 2, 333, 334.

26. KLB, "The American Heroine." *BET,* July 21, 1879.

27. KLB, "A Story of Christmas Eve." *SSR,* Jan. 1, 1882.

28. Ibid.

29. Ibid.

30. She had already published "Mother Time's Family" in *SSR,* with a similarly capable female figure, since Father Time is nowhere to be seen.

31. William Dean Howells, "A Call For Realism," reprinted in *The Rise of Silas Lapham, A Norton Critical Edition.* New York: W.W. Norton & Company, 1982, 500.

32. KLB, "An Odor of Violets." *SSR,* April 24, 1881.

33. Nevins, "Bowles (1826-1878)," 519. Bowles's son continued his father's active interest in state and national politics, influencing public opinion about the future of the United States.

34. KLB, "Miriam's Choice." *SSR,* July 30 and Aug. 6, 1882.

35. Barbara Miller Solomon, *Ancestors and Immigrants: A Changing New England Tradition.* Cambridge: Harvard University Press, 1956, 101. While Boston was beginning to absorb many non-Anglo groups of immigrants during this period, Jews were still a small minority of the population.

36. KLB, "Miriam's."

37. Although Bates may have found this to be the case at this particular temple, such casual behavior is not typical in a Reform service.

38. Sewall, 363.

39. However, Bates was unlikely to have known much about Emily Dickinson until the first volume of her poetry was published in 1890.

40. KLB, Letter to ABS, July 29, 1883. Beecher Papers.

41. KLB, "The Unknown Tongue." *SSR,* Aug. 19, 1883.

42. KLB, Letter to ABS, Aug. 31, 1884.

43. KLB, Letter to ABS, Dec. 24, 1883. Box 19, F. 781. Beecher Papers.

44. KLB, Introduction to the "Lenox Edition" of *Hawthorne's Romances, Vol. VII, A Wonder Book for Boys and Girls.* New York: Thomas Y. Crowell, 1902, viii.

45. For a good discussion of this genre, see E. F. Bleiler, ed., *Eight Dime Novels.* New York: Dover Publications, Inc., 1974.

46. Bleiler, vii.

47. KLB, Letter to ABS, Aug. 6, 1885. Box 19, F. 795. Beecher Papers.

48. Ibid.

49. Ibid. Lyman Abbott may have had an even closer connection to Annie Scoville through her Beecher relatives. From 1876 to 1881 Abbott co-edited the *Christian Union* with Annie's grandfather Henry Ward Beecher, and Abbott replaced Beecher in 1887 as minister of the Plymouth Congregational church in Brooklyn. Abbott continued to edit the *Christian Union* after its name was changed in 1893 to the *Outlook*, selecting Hamilton Mabie as one of its associate editors. Mabie, then a frequent speaker at Wellesley College, would become another of KLB's editors and mentors, especially with her textbook, *American Literature.*

50. Herbert A. Kenny, *Newspaper Row: Journalism in the Pre-Television Era.* Chester, Connecticut: The Globe Pequot Press, 1987, 3.

51. Edward Everett Hale, *Lend A Hand.* Boston: J. S. Smith, 1887.

52. *BET,* Nov. 10, 1853.

53. In April 1884.

54. Joseph Edgar Chamberlin, *The Boston Transcript: A History of Its First Hundred Years.* Boston: Houghton Mifflin Company, 1930, 162, 166.

55. Chamberlin, 208.

56. Kenny, 210, 176.

57. When she had first appeared in the *Transcript*'s "Brilliants," her poem "To a Friend" headed the group of poems. Her name was the only one of the poets' to be printed in all uppercase letters. Only Thoreau is remembered today, but for his prose, not his poetry.

58. A sampling of poets from another group of "Brilliants" shows the high caliber of poets that readers expected to find in this feature. The poetry of such New England favorites as Henry Wadsworth Longfellow, John Greenleaf Whittier, Lucy Larcom, and Oliver Wendell Holmes, all at least one generation older than Katharine, was what the readers of the *Transcript* were used to and enjoyed.

59. *BET*, Jan. 28, 1882.

60. D. Lothrop & Company was the name of his publishing house.

61. KLB, "Julia Eastman." *BET*, Jan. 2, 1911.

62. Post, 4.

63. "Notice" in *Paper World,* in KLB's Scrapbook, 1876-1885, Box 19. WCA.

64. Ibid.

65. Clipping from a Portland, Maine, newspaper in KLB's Scrapbook 1876-1885. Box 19. WCA.

66. Neither the notice from the *Transcript* nor that from the *Congregationalist* gives a date or place of publication in KLB's Scrapbook 1876-1885, Box 19, WCA.

67. Clipping from KLB scrapbook, from *BET,* n.d.

68. KLB, Letter to ENN, May 9, 1883. KLB, Box 7. WCA.

69. KLB, "The Red Tassel." *SSR*, Oct. 5, 1879.

70. She wrote graciously to her new department head at the College that the Misses Eastman were "exceedingly kind, as always" and that their friendly relations had been strengthened, rather than weakened, by her move. Letter to LMH, July 1, 1885. KLB, Box 6. WCA.

71. KLB, Diary, 1898-1911: Nov. 29, 1899. Box 3. WCA.

72. Frank Luther Mott, *A History of American Magazines.* Cambridge: Harvard University Press, 1938 and 1957, Vol. 4, 11.

73. Quoted in Palmieri, n. 29, 278.

Chapter Four: 1885-1890 – "New Lines of Thought and Purpose"

1. KLB, Letter to ABS, May 18, 1888. Box 20, Folder 793, Beecher Papers.

2. KLB, Letter to ABS, June 30, 1885. Box 19, Folder 785, Beecher Papers.

3. Ibid.

4. KLB, Letter to ABS, July 18, 1885. Box 19, Folder 785, Beecher Papers.

5. KLB, Letter to LMH, July 1, 1885. KLB. Box 7. WCA.

6. Ibid.

7. Wellesley College *Calendar* for 1876 and 1885.

8. Hubbard.

9. Ibid.

10. According to Harvard's President Eliot—quoted by George Herbert Palmer, *The Life of Alice Freeman Palmer*. Boston: Houghton Mifflin Company (The Riverside Press, Cambridge), 1910, 118.

11. Caroline Hazard, "To the Girls of the Alice Freeman House," Peace Dale, R. I., November 22, 1916, 2.

12. Hazard, 1, 2.

13. Hazard, 1.

14. Freeman had been Katharine's senior class advisor at Wellesley.

15. Palmer, 157.

16. KLB, Letter to Gertrude Bates, Nov. 27, 1885. The original letter is owned by Katharine Holland and was transcribed by Elizabeth Bates Null, and I thank them for its use. Elizabeth Bates Null is the granddaughter of the expected baby mentioned in the letter.

17. KLB, Letter to LMH, Nov. 19, 1886. (3P: KLB Letters to LMH, 1885-1889), KLB, Box 6. WCA.

18. Mary Hazlett, Letter to KLB, June 10, 1908. KLB Papers, Box 8. Uncatalogued. WCA.

19. KLB, ed., *Coleridge's Ancient Mariner*. Boston and New York: Leach, Shewell and Sanborn, 1889, 26.

20. KLB, *Coleridge's*, 28.

21. KLB, *Coleridge's*, 26-29.

22. Lillian Corbet Barnes Long, "Katharine Lee Bates, A Memory," written as a letter to Phi Sigma, September 21, 1945, 1- 3. WCA. (Phi Sigma: Katharine Lee Bates.)

23. Palmer, 165.

24. Searing, 7.

25. Vida Scudder, *On Journey*. New York: E.P. Dutton and Company, 1937, 86-87.

26. Scudder, *On Journey*, 96.

27. Scudder, *On Journey*, 103.

28. Scudder, *On Journey*, 107-108.

29. Ibid.

30. Scudder, *On Journey*, 109.

31. "Women at Cambridge and Oxford," *BET*, July 18, 1887.

32. Scudder, *On Journey*, 110.

33. *BET*, Jan. 1, 1886.

34. "Labor Troubles," *BET*, Feb. 9, 1886.

35. "Labor Troubles," *BET*, Jan. 18, 1886.

36. "Labor Troubles," *BET*, Feb. 1, 1886.

37. "Labor Troubles," *BET*, Jan. 18, 1886.

38. "Who and What the Knights of Labor Are," *BET*, Jan. 1, 1886.

39. Ibid.

40. Events are mentioned in the *Wellesley Courant* for the year.

41. *Wellesley College President's Report,* 1888.

42. *BET*, March 1, 1886.

43. KLB, Letter to ABS, Dec. 14, 1887. Box 20, Folder 789, Beecher Papers.

44. KLB, Letter to Gertrude Bates, Nov. 27, 1885.

45. KLB, Letter to ABS, Jan. 12, 1888. Box 20, Folder 790, Beecher Papers.

46. Ibid.

47. KLB, Letter to ABS, Jan. 14, 1888. Box 20, Folder 790, Beecher Papers.

48. KLB, Letter to ABS, Jan. 19, 1888. Box 20, Folder 791, Beecher Papers.

49. KLB, Letter to ABS, Jan. 28, 1888. Box 20, Folder 791, Beecher Papers.

50. KLB, Letter to ABS, Feb. 13, 1888; Box 20, Folder 791, Beecher Papers.

51. Col. Thomas Wentworth Higginson was a writer widely read in periodicals, whose "Letter to a Young Contributor" in *The Atlantic Monthly* of April 1862 led to his long correspondence with Emily Dickinson.

52. KLB, Letter to ABS, Feb. 14, 1888. Box 20, Folder 791, Beecher Papers.

53. KLB, Letter to ABS, March 6, 1888. Box 20, Folder 792, Beecher Papers.

54. *BET*, April 3, 1888.

55. KLB, Letter to ABS, May 18, 1888. Box 20, Folder 793, Beecher Papers.

56. Scudder, *On Journey,* 110.

57. Ibid.

58. KLB, Letter to ABS, May 18, 1888. Box 20, Folder 793, Beecher Papers.

59. KLB, *Rose,* 7.

60. KLB, *Rose,* 8.

61. KLB, *Rose,* 9, 10.

62. KLB, *Rose,* 10.

63. KLB, *Rose,* 12.

64. KLB, *Rose,* 13.

65. KLB, *Rose,* 19.

66. KLB, *Rose,* 16, 20.

67. KLB, "Lesson No. 6 of a Course in Creative Reading." Ed. Robert Emmons Rogers. Cambridge, Mass.: Institute of Current Literature, College House, Harvard Square, 1927, 17.

68. KLB, "Lesson," 5.

69. KLB, "Lesson," 21.

70. KLB, *Rose,* 272.

71. KLB, *Rose,* 273-274.

72. KLB, *Rose*, 273.

73. KLB, *Rose*, 273-274.

74. KLB, *Rose*, 274.

75. KLB, *Rose*, 275.

76. KLB, *Rose*, 277.

77. KLB, *Rose*, 44.

78. KLB, "Lesson," 21.

79. KLB, "Lesson," 23.

80. KLB, *Rose*, 175.

81. KLB, *Rose*, 67.

82. KLB, Letter to Edith Tufts, Aug. 28, 1888. KLB papers unprocessed, *Courant* letters, WCA.

83. *The Wellesley College Courant, College Edition*, October 12, October 19, November 3, 1888.

84. KLB, Letter to ABS, Sept. 6, 1888. Box 20, Folder 794, Beecher Papers.

85. KLB, Letter to Edith Tufts; no date, probably Dec. 20-24, 1888. KLB papers unprocessed, *Courant* letters, WCA.

86. KLB, Letter to ABS, Misdated April 2, 1888: should probably be 1889. Box 20, Folder 793, Beecher Papers.

87. KLB, Letter to LMH, July 4, 1889. KLB Papers. Box 7. WCA.

88. KLB, Letter to Edith Tufts, July 3, 1889. KLB papers unprocessed, *Courant* letters, WCA.

89. KLB, "Goody Santa Claus on a Sleigh Ride." *Wide-Awake*, December 1888 (v. 28), 38.

90. KLB, Letter to ABS, Nov. 10, 1888. Box 20, Folder 795, Beecher Papers.

91. M.C. Hazard, editor, Congregational Sunday-School and Publishing Society. Letter to KLB, Jan. 15, 1889. KLB Papers, WCA.

92. KLB, Letter to ABS, Jan. 17, 1889. Box 20, Folder 795, Beecher Papers.

93. *BET*, Jan. 1, 1886.

94. R. Gordon Kelley, ed., *Children's Periodicals of the United States*. Westport, Conn.: Greenwood Press, 1984, xxx.

95. KLB. *Hermit Island*. Boston, D. Lothrop & Company, 1890, 7-8, WCA.

96. Although there are no scenes comparable to those of sweatshop labor in New York tenements, one character, Mr. Grafton, has gotten wealthy in Colorado Springs from the difficult labor of the men down in his mines, and is too loud and too money-conscious. In the end, Yorke decides to "undertake literary labors in earnest" in New York City (312), knowing, like his creator, that he had to push forward with his writing and take it seriously to be a professional success.

97. KLB, Letter to LMH, Aug. 22, 1889, KLB Papers. Box 7. WCA.

98. Eben Norton Horsford, Letter to LMH, July 9, 1888. ENH Papers. Box 10. WCA.

99. KLB, Letter to LMH, Spring, 1890. No date on letter. KLB Papers, Box 7. WCA. It was published as part of the *Students' Series of English Classics* by Leach, Shewell, and Sanborn in 1890.

100. *BET*, April 4, 1890, 1. I thank my Pine Manor College research assistant Melanie Gaffney for her help with this research. "The Ideal" was in *The Wellesley Prelude*, Vol. I, No. 31 (May 24, 1890), 433-434.

101. "The Ideal" appears in KLB, *America the Beautiful*, 59-60.

102. Returning to the allegorical portrait of an abstract subject like that in her poem "Sleep," she similarly used a demanding traditional poetic form to contain the long rhythmic lines that convey the urgency in the voice of the poem's speaker.

103. KLB, Letter to LMH, April 15, 1890. KLB Papers. Box 7. WCA.

104. Richard C. Cabot, Letter to KLB, Nov. 18, 1890. KLB Papers; Unprocessed material transferred from Special Collections 10/12/81 [box 2] 1X (ALS to: Katharine Lee Bates, also to Mrs. George Burgess about Miss Bates's work. WCA.)

105. KLB, *The Ideal and Other Poems, 1887-1895* in a leather-bound volume of handwritten manuscripts. Box 15, WCA.

106. KLB, Letter to LMH, No date. Incomplete letter from the spring of 1890. KLB Papers. WCA.

CHAPTER FIVE: 1890-1893–"THE LOVE-LIGHTS BURN FOR YOU"

1. KLB, "Heart of Hearts." *The Century*, February 1892, and in KLB, *America the Beautiful*, 149.

2. *Across the Atlantic* is the title KLB gave to this first travel diary. Papers of KLB. Diaries (1890), "Across the Atlantic," May 22, 1890. Box 2. WCA.

3. KLB, *Across*, June 3, 1890. WCA.

4. She was already beginning to notice the difference in the way that women were treated in Britain—Scottish boys were not much help to their mothers in "this woman-working land." KLB, *Across*, June 5, 1890.

5. Letters to her family, June 23, 1890, Edinburgh, Box 4. WCA.

6. KLB, *Across*, June 19, 1890. WCA.

7. KLB, *Across*, June 26, 1890. WCA.

8. KLB, *Across*, Oct. 6, 1890, WCA.

9. Although she had never enjoyed her required Bible classes, when she visited Wells Cathedral, she met a Bible scholar already well known to her, as she wrote her mother, probably amused: "The Dean is Dr. Plumptre, whose work on the Hebrew prophets I have used so much in Bible teaching at Wellesley."

10. KLB, Letters to her family, Aug. 24, 1890. Box 4. WCA.

11. KLB, *From Gretna Green to Land's End: A Literary Journey in England*. New York: Thomas Y. Crowell Company, 1907, 343.

12. Papers of KLB, Letters to her family, July 6, 1890. Box 4. WCA.

13. KLB, *Across*, July 14, 1890. WCA.

14. KLB, Letters to her family, Sept. 7, 1890. WCA.

15. KLB, Letters to her family, Sept. 14, 1890. WCA.

16. KLB, Letters to her family, Sept. 28, 1890. WCA.

17. KLB, *Across*, July 16, 1890. WCA.

18. KLB, Letters to her family, Aug. 24, 1890. Box 4. WCA.

19. KLB, Letters to her family, Sept. 7, 1890. WCA.

20. She had gone there to see Dante Rossetti's altar painting and William Morris's stained glass windows. KLB, *Across*, Sept. 24, 1890, WCA.

21. While 138 Walton Street is sometimes given as her address, her application forms for the Bodleian Library list her address as 143 Walton St. Personal letter to me from S. R. Tomlinson, Assistant Librarian of the Bodleian Library, July 1, 1993.

22. KLB. ALS to her family (1890): Oct. 26, 1890, WCA.

23. Ibid.

24. Ibid.

25. Ibid.

26. Ibid.

27. KLB, *From Gretna*, 210.

28. KLB, Letter to her family, Nov. 4, 1890. Box 4. WCA.

29. KLB, Letters to her family, Oct. 19 and Oct. 26, 1890. Box 4.WCA.

30. KLB, Letter to her family, Nov. 4, 1890. Box 4. WCA.

31. KLB, Letter to her family, Oct. 12, 1890. Box 4. WCA.

32. KLB, Diary, Oct. 19, 1890. Box 2. WCA.

33. KLB, Diary, Oct. 25, 1890. Box 2. WCA.

34. Ibid.

35. KLB, Letters to her family, Nov. 16, 1890. Box. 4. WCA.

36. KLB, Letters to CLB and her family (1890): Dec. 10, 1890. Box 4. WCA.

37. KLB, Letters to her family (1890): Oct. 26, 1890. Box 4. WCA. Annie is referred to as "Nan" in these letters. Katharine did use the china for many years when she hosted students and friends, and they are still handed down in her family.

38. KLB, Letter to her family, Nov. 23, 1890, WCA.

39. KLB, Diary, Nov. 30, 1890. Box 2. WCA.

40. Edward C. Alden. *Alden's Guide to Oxford*: Oxford: Alden & Co., Ltd., 1922, 133, 135.

41. KLB, Letter to her family, Nov. 23, 1890. Box 4. WCA.

42. KLB, Diary, Oct. 30, 1890. Box 2. WCA.

43. KLB, Letter to her family, December 26, 1890. Box 4. WCA.

44. KLB, Letter to CLB and her family, Dec. 10, 1890. Box 4. WCA.

45. Ibid.

46. KLB, Letter to CLB, December 2, 1890. Box 4. WCA.

47. KLB, Diary, Dec. 11, 1890. Box 2. WCA.

48. KLB, Diary, Dec. 23, 1890. Box 2. WCA.

49. Similarly, in a later letter, Katharine wrote to her mother and sister that while she liked *all* the young men, they seemed young to her. Letter to CLB, April 12, 1891. Box 4. WCA.

50. KLB, Letter to CLB and her family, Dec. 28, 1890. Box 4. WCA.

51. Ibid.

52. Marion Pelton Guild. Letter to Ellen Pendleton. RE a life of Mrs. Durant. 2 ALS to Ellen Pendleton. 1917 February 22 Wellesley [Mass.], 1936 February 15 West Roxbury, Mass. Accompanied by typescript of "Notes for the Possible Use of Mrs. Durant's Possible Biographer."

53. She may not have realized what one of her closest friends, Marion Pelton Guild, explained later, that in her undergraduate days she had been regarded "in high quarters as a heretic of questionable influence, however gifted and beloved. So largely did her shy defenses of ready and delightful humor conceal the intensity of spiritual life which was behind them. The early estimate had been very slow to change. Katharine had not been invited back to Wellesley College to teach until five years after her graduation, "and then by special allowance, contrary to the church membership statute. [However], during the six years which followed, her scholarly thoroughness, her exceptional gifts as a teacher, and her essential nobility of character, all supplemented by her personal charm, had won her an honored place among her associates."

54. KLB, Letter to CLB and her Dec. 23, 1890. Box 4. WCA.

55. KLB, Letter to CLB and her family Jan. 1, 1891. Box 4. WCA.

56. KLB, Letter to CLB, Dec. 30, 1890. Box 4. WCA.

57. KLB, Letter to her family, July 27, 1890. Box 4. WCA.

58. Originally, women had been asked to sit at the two tables set aside for them.

59. Quoted in P. R. Harris, "The Reading Room." London: The British Library Board, 1986, 25.

60. KLB, Letter to CLB and her family, Jan. 1, 1891. Box 4. WCA.

61. KLB, *Across,* July 24, 1890. WCA.

62. KLB, Letter to her family, July 27, 1890. Box 4. WCA.

63. KLB, Letter to CLB and her family, Jan. 1, 1891. Box 4. WCA.

64. KLB, "A Norman Lady." The *Chatauquan,* January 1891. Scrapbook: 1886-1894. Box 19. WCA.

65. KLB, "Woman as Scholar." The *Chatauquan,* April 1891. Scrapbook: 1886-1894. Box 19. WCA.

66. Ibid.

67. KLB, Letter to her family, 1890-1891: Jan. 1, 1891. Box 4. WCA.

68. KLB, Diary, March 6, 1891. Box 2. WCA.

69. Burgess, 88-91.

70. KLB, Letters to Andrews through Hazard. Letter to Katharine Coman, February 28, 1891. Box 5. WCA.

71. Ibid.

72. KLB, Letter to CLB, Feb. 21, 1891. Box 4. WCA.

73. KLB, Letter to CLB, Feb. 16, no year; probably 1891. Box 4. WCA.

74. KLB, Letter to her family, May 27, 1890. (Letter was probably misdated and actually written in 1891.) Box 4. WCA.

75. KLB, Letter to her family, "Tues. Eve," n. d. [spring, 1891, before April 12]. Box 4. WCA.

76. KLB, Diary, April 7, 1891. Box 2. WCA.

77. Ibid.

78. She wrote with relief to her sister that her bodily functions, including her monthly periods, had returned to normal, something she clearly worried about for whatever reason, about which we can only speculate. KLB, Letter to Jeanne Bates. May 7, 1891. WCA.

79. KLB, Letter to CLB, April 19, 1891. Box 4. WCA.

80. KLB, Travel Diary, Oxford 1890? -91? May 30, 1891. Box 2. WCA.

81. KLB, Diary, July 2, 1891. Box 2. WCA.

82. KLB, Diary, April 17, 1891. Box 2. WCA.

83. Fiona MacCarthy, *William Morris: A Life for Our Time.* New York: Alfred A. Knopf, 1995, xii.

84. KLB, Diary, May 2, 1891. Box 2. WCA.

85. MacCarthy, 588.

86. KLB, Letter to CLB, Aug. 19, 1891. Box 4. WCA.

87. KLB, Letter to CLB, June 29, 1891. Box 4. WCA.

88. KLB, Travel diary, Oxford, May 30, 1891. Box 2, WCA.

89. Ada S. Woolfolk, *The Wellesley College Annals,* 1890-91, 2. 6, WCA.

90. KLB, Letter to LMH, Sept. 12, 1891, Box 7. WCA.

91. KLB, "Sophie Jewett, Poet." *The Wellesley Magazine,* Vol. 18, #2, (Nov. 1, 1909), 48.

92. Scudder, *On Journey,* 123-124.

93. Frances E. Lord, Acting President, *Wellesley College President's Report*, 1891. Boston: Frank Wood, Printer. (This report notes that 259 students elected English literature; 195 elected German.) English literature courses were not required. WCA.

94. KLB, "The Women's Colleges of Our Country." *American Agriculturist,* January 1892, in Scrapbook 1886-94, 52, KLB Papers, Box 19. WCA.

95. Ibid.

96. Article in *The Wellesley Prelude,* June 25,1892, Vol. III, p. xxxvi.

97. KLB, Commencement Dinner Speech, June 21, 1892. In Box 15, Folder, "Manuscripts of Speeches." WCA.

98. Ibid.

99. Ibid.

100. Ibid.

101. *BET*, Oct. 8, 1890.

102. *BET*, April 3, 1891.

103. *BET*, July 2, 1891.

104. *BET*, July 8, 1891.

105. *BET,* Jan. 17, 1890.

106. *BET*, April 3, 1891.

107. *BET*, July 3, 1891.

108. *BET*, Oct. 8, 1890.

109. *BET*, Jan. 3, 1891.

110. Ibid.

111. *BET*, July 7, 1887.

112. *BET*, Jan. 2, 1890.

113. From 1880 to 1890, the population of school-age children in Boston had increased by 25 percent, although the *Transcript* said that the public schools accommodated them, perhaps expressing the view of business owners who saw in the immigrants possible non-union workers willing to work for lower wages than native-born union members (July 10, 1891). In the spring of 1891, the *Transcript* reported, "The tide of Irish emigration is unabated," and predicted record numbers in the months ahead (April 6, 1891).

114. *BET*, Jan. 5, 1886.

115. *BET*, July 1, 1891.

116. *BET*, Jan. 2, 1890.

117. *BET*, July 6, 1891.

118. *BET*, Jan. 18, 1890.

119. *BET*, Jan. 1, 1891.

120. *BET*, April 3, 1891.

121. Kevin Phillips, *Wealth and Democracy: A Political History of the American Rich.* New York: Broadway Books, 2002, 3.

122. Charles W. Eliot, president of Harvard, quoted in Phillips, 305.

123. Phillips, 306.

124. Ibid.

125. Quoted in Phillips, 307. Direct taxation was proposed for those with incomes above $1,000 to help everyone else, and although a law would be created in 1894 to establish a tiny federal income tax on the top percentiles of income, it would be struck down in 1895.

126. KLB, May 1905 in 7B, Alumnae Biographical Files, Bates, Katharine Lee, 1880 (Part I). WCA.

127. Vida Scudder, "The College Settlements Movement." *Smith College Monthly*, May 1900, 447.

128. Editorial in *The Wellesley Magazine*, November 1892, 90-91.

129. Scudder, "The College," 453.

130. Ruth Bordin, *Alice Freeman Palmer: The Evolution of a New Woman*. Ann Arbor: University of Michigan Press, 1993, 254, quoting Alice Freeman Palmer to George Herbert Palmer, October 21, 1892, Wellesley Typescripts.

131. Erik Larson, *The Devil in the White City: Murder, Magic, and Madness at the Fair That Changed America*. Illinois: Crown, 2003, 182.

132. He was probably Daniel Sheldon Rodman, a minister who had graduated from Yale Theological Seminary and been ordained but then was "dismissed." He nevertheless had become a principal of Young Ladies Seminary in Montclair, New Jersey, until 1882, when he moved to Wellesley.

133. KLB, Letter to ABS, Sept. 6, 1888. Box 20, Folder 794. Beecher Papers.

134. KLB, "Insecurity." *BET*, May 9, 1892. Also in *America the Beautiful*, 154. When KLB pasted a clipping of this poem into *The Ideal and Other Poems,* the volume she compiled for KC, she wrote "Written at Oxford," WCA. Perhaps this poem was inspired by Triggs but applied to THR as well.

135. KLB, "Heart of Hearts." *The Century*, February 1892 and in KLB, *America the Beautiful,* 149. I have quoted its wording as originally published. Although she did include a clipping of this poem in a little volume of her poems, *The Ideal and Other Poems,* from 1887 to 1895, which she later gave to Katharine Coman, we do not know for whom it was written.

136. KLB, "When It Befortunes Us." *The Literary Northwest*, January 1893, and *America the Beautiful*, 151-152.

137. KLB, "To Truth," in *The Chatauquan*, September 1893; in *America the Beautiful*, 87-88; and copied by KLB into *The Ideal and Other Poems* from 1887-1895, which she later gave to Katharine Coman. She told her that she had written this poem in Oxford in the spring of 1891.

138. Oscar was divorced in 1907.

139. Although there were few chances for the cloistered Wellesley girls to meet young men, popular Glee Club concerts could sometimes be attended by family members. Lizzy became its president, and Katharine sometimes wrote the words to songs it commissioned. Born in 1861, Lizzy's brother Theophilus had spent his childhood in Western Massachusetts, in the area where Katharine's Lee relatives lived. Like Katharine's ancestors, Theophilus's ancestors on both sides of his family had come from England in the early 1600s. His father, Oliver Dean Root, had graduated from Harvard Medical School and died of yellow fever during the Civil War.

140. THR, "Class Lives," *Harvard College Class of 1885*, page 4 of the typescript transcription from the manuscript, Harvard University Archives.

141. THR, "Class Lives," *Harvard College Class of 1885*, 5, Harvard University Archives.

142. THR, "Class Lives," *Harvard College Class of 1885*, 10, Harvard University Archives.

143. After graduating from Wellesley College with Katharine in 1880, Lizzy too had first become a teacher.

144. KLB, Letter to ABS, March 26, 1888. Box 20, Folder 792. Beecher Papers.

145. It was with the help of Wellesley College graduate Amy Stimac, then a librarian at Pine Manor College, that I tracked down THR, after years of searching for his identity, via his articles in *The Biblical World,* which he sent to KLB.

146. On small blank spaces she recorded her daily feelings in a few brief phrases—Sunday, Jan. 22, 1893: "'Love.' Dined at Freeman." Jan. 29: "'Love.' Call from Anna Walkson." On Feb. 2 she received a book from Oscar, noting that she would write him about it, and recorded "'Love'" again on Monday, Feb. 6. Her reference to "Love" may be a short title for her poem "Were Love but True," which she published in July 1893, or her poem "Love," and, in either case, it could refer to either Oscar or "T. H. R."

147. KLB, "Valentine." *The Independent*, Feb. 9, 1893, and *America the Beautiful*, 151.

148. Her diary shows her despair, after the deaths of Lothrop and Horsford, over her romantic turmoil and impending loss. On Saturday, February 11, 1893: "Went out to Dorchester for Sunday. Met little Cherokee." Dorchester, part of Boston, was then still somewhat of a Yankee enclave with several Congregational churches where Theophilus or Oscar could have been. The "little Cherokee" may have been a new love interest of Oscar's—possibly Laura McAdoo. (KLB, Feb. 11, 1893. All diary references for the spring of 1893 are from KLB Papers, Box 3, Diaries: 1893-97, 1894. Box 4. WCA.)

149. KLB, Diary, March 2, 1893. Box 4. WCA.

150. KLB, Diary, March 3, 1893. Box 4. WCA.

151. KLB, Diary, March 21, 1893. Box 4. WCA.

152. KLB, Letter to ABS, Feb. 29, 1888. Box 20, Folder 792. Beecher Papers.

153. KLB, Diary, April 4, 1893. Box 4. WCA.

154. KLB, Diary, April 16, 1893. Box 4. WCA.

155. KLB, Diary, May 20, 1893. Box 4. WCA.

156. KLB, Diary, May 21, 1893. Box 4. WCA.

157. KLB, Diary, May 14, 1893. Box 4. WCA.

158. KLB, June 4, 1893, Diary, 1893-97. WCA. Hamlin Garland, "Under the Lion's Paw," *Main-Travelled Roads*. New York: Harper Brothers (The Arena Publishing Company), 1891, 143.

159. William Cronon, *Nature's Metropolis: Chicago and the Great West*. New York: W.W. Norton & Company, 1991, 283.

160. Cronon, 41.

161. Cronon, 341.

162. Leo J. Harris, "The Search for Marian Shaw" in Marian Shaw, *World's Fair Notes*. N.P: Pogo Press, 1992, 81.

163. Richard J. Storr. *Harper's University: The Beginnings*. Chicago: The University of Chicago Press, 1966, 26.

164. Bordin, 245.

165. Harper had envisioned the University of Chicago running its own Press with his journal as one of its publications.

166. Bordin, 228. She may well have encouraged Katharine to go to Chicago and Colorado.

167. On May 27, 1893, she probably heard her feminist colleague Professor Ellen Hayes describe the Chicago Fair in her talk at Wellesley on the Women's Congress at the Chicago Fair.

168. June 22: "Began lecture V." June 23: "[Lecture V] went slowly. Stupid subjects." June 24: "Still find lecture tough whittling." June 26: "Lecture again." June 27: "Finished last lecture and took to the typewriter at Newton Highlands." June 29: "Finished re-visions of type-copy."

169. KLB, Diary, June 21, 1893. Box 4. WCA. She misspelled "Alumni," perhaps showing that her mind was on her day, not on correct Latin.

CHAPTER SIX: 1893–"AN ENCHANTED SUMMER"

1. KLB, Diary, June 30, 1893. Box 4. WCA.

2. Ibid.

3. KLB, Diary, July 2, 1893. Box 4. WCA.

4. KLB, "America the Beautiful." *The Journal of the National Education Association*, December 1928.

5. *Harper's Weekly*, Sept. 29, 1877, 768.

6. Colorado Summer School of Science, Philosophy, and Languages, "Prospectus," 1893, 17. Folder: "Curriculum—Summer School, Colorado College—1874-1959," Special Collections, Tutt Library, The Colorado College.

7. KLB, "America" (NEA).

8. KLB, Letter to her class reunion book, 20 years later. WCA.

9. Giuseppe's Restaurant pamphlet, acquired June 1999.

10. KLB, Diary, July 4, 1893. Box 4. WCA.

11. Quoted in John S. Fisher, *A Builder Of The West: The Life Of General William Jackson Palmer*. Caldwell, Idaho: Caxton Printers, 1939, 161.

12. Quoted in Fisher, 162.

13. Quoted in Fisher, 162, 163.

14. Quoted in Fisher, 164.

15. Quoted in Fisher, 173.

16. Quoted in Fisher, 203.

17. See Marshall Sprague, *Newport in the Rockies: The Life and Good Times of Colorado Springs*. Athens, Ohio: Ohio University Press, 1961, 1987 revision, 20.

18. Palmer was interested throughout his life in literature and arts.

19. Richard Harding Davis, "The West From a Car Window VIII: The Heart of the Great Divide." Illustrations from photographs by W.H. Jackson. Harper's Weekly, June 11, 1892, 571.

20. Quoted in Sprague, 18.

21. KLB, "America" (NEA).

22. Quoted in Fisher, 178.

23. This is my surmise.

24. *Colorado Springs City Directory, 1894*, 203.

25. Fisher, 215.

26. Sprague, 19.

27. *City Directory*.

28. KLB, "America" (NEA).

29. Sprague, 107-8.

30. Sprague, 109.

31. KLB, Diary, July 6, 1893. Box 4. WCA.

32. KLB, Diary, July 7, 1893. Box 4. WCA.

33. KLB, Diary, July 8, 1893. Box 4. WCA.

34. KLB, "Manuscripts of Verse: Notebook," 65, 66. Box 15. WCA.

35. KLB, "America" (NEA).

36. My thanks to Glen Eyrie historian Len Froisland for giving me a private tour and to his sister Betty as well for information about the Palmers and Glen Eyrie.

37. *Colorado Springs Gazette,* July 23, 1893.

38. KLB, "Westering Heart." *Yellow Clover.* New York: E.P. Dutton & Company, 1922, 57.

39. KLB, "A Mountain Soul." *America the Beautiful,* 173-174.

40. Polly King Ruhtenberg and Dorothy E. Smith, *Henry McAllister: Colorado Pioneer.* Freeman, South Dakota: Pine Hill Press, 1972, 22, 42.

41. Robert D. Loevy. *Colorado College: A Place of Learning 1874-1999.* Colorado Springs: Colorado College, 1999, 32.

42. Loevy, 32, quoting E.P. Tenney, *The New West: As Related To The Christian College,* 3rd. ed. Cambridge, Mass.: Riverside Press, 1878.

43. Loevy, 34, quoting from Burgess and Draper, *The First Congregational Church of Colorado Springs, Colorado,* 17.

44. Colorado Summer School, "Prospectus," 1893, 6.

45. Colorado Summer School, "Prospectus," 6-7.

46. Colorado Summer School,"Prospectus," 8.

47. July 16, 1893.

48. Colorado Summer School "Expenditures." List of Faculty Salaries (1893). Folder: "Curriculum,— Summer School, Colorado College—1874-1959," Special Collections, Tutt Library, The Colorado College. Katharine received $130, ranking in payment below only President Andrews of Brown University, who was a lecturer and the keynote speaker ($147), and Professor Rolfe, who received $135 for the same number of lectures, only five dollars more than Katharine, a woman half his age, received.

49. Dr. Ely was paid $85.00, Dr. Bemis $60.00, and Katharine Coman $64.00.

50. *Gazette,* Aug. 7, 1892.

51. Sprague, 69-70.

52. *Gazette,* July 17, 1893.

53. Quoted from Nov. 5, 1893, 1, in Carl Ubbelohde, Maxine Benson, and Duane A. Smith, *A Colorado History* (Seventh Edition). Boulder, Colorado: Pruett Publishing Company, 1995 (1965, 1972, 1995).

54. Wyoming granted women the vote earlier, but through the state constitution.

55. Colorado Summer School, "Prospectus," 13.

56. July 28, 1893.

57. *Gazette,* July 5, 1893.

58. *Gazette,* July 12, 1893.

59. *Gazette,* July 8, 1893.

60. *Gazette,* July 15, 1893.

61. *Gazette,* July 16, 1893.

62. *Gazette,* July 20, 1893.

63. *Gazette,* July 21, 1893.

64. Ibid.

65. KLB, Diary, July 17 and July 19, 1893. Box 4. WCA.

66. KLB, Diary, July 21, 1893. Box 4. WCA.

67. July 19, 1893.

68. KLB, "America" (NEA). All subsequent quotations of her memories in are from this account.

69. KLB, Diary, July 21, 1893. Box 4. WCA.

70. Today the Summit House is justly famous for its special doughnuts made according to its own traditional recipe and its sweet and dark hot chocolate, both of which I enjoyed in my visit, courtesy of my local hosts.

71. KLB, "America" (NEA).

72. Ibid.

73. Longfellow, *The Song of Hiawatha*, in *Poems*, 144-6.

74. Ibid.

75. Ibid.

76. KLB, Telegram to CLB, July 22, 1893.

77. KLB, Diary, July 22, 1893. Box 4. WCA.

78. KLB, Diary, July 26, 1893. Box 4. WCA.

79. *Gazette*, July 23, 1893.

80. July 26, 30; Aug. 1, 1893.

81. She could have read about it later in the *Gazette*.

82. *Gazette*, July 30, 1893.

83. Quoted in the *AAA Colorado-Utah Tour Book*. Heathrow, Florida: AAA Publishing, 1998, 34. Roosevelt traveled by train on the Short-Line Railroad, which followed the old stagecoach road.

84. *Gazette*, July 7, 1892.

85. KLB, "America" (NEA).

86. "Tour the Famous Mollie Kathleen Gold Mine" (brochure). Cripple Creek, Colorado: Gold Mine Tours, Inc. (n.d.).

87. Judith Reid Finley, *Time Capsule 1900: Colorado Springs A Century Ago*. Colorado Springs: Pastwords Publications, 1998, clxxxi.

88. Loevy, 20-23.

89. KLB, Diary, July 30, 1893.

90. *Gazette*, July 29, 1893.

91. If Katharine continued to follow Colorado news after her return East, she would have learned that these two "Wests"—Cripple Creek and Colorado Springs—were locking horns in a heated labor conflict. The following winter, a five-month strike would involve President Slocum of Colorado College and become famous for demonstrating the strengths of American democracy on the frontier.

92. He gave his talk to the American Historical Association at the Fair and later published it in the "Proceedings of the State Historical Society of Wisconsin," December 14, 1893.

93. KLB, "Autobiography."

94. This poem, "America," was published in *The Congregationalist*, July 4, 1895.

95. KLB, "America" (NEA) and Diary, Aug. 15, 1893. Box 4. WCA.

CHAPTER SEVEN: 1893-1897-"ON THE KEEN JUMP ALL DAY"

1. KLB, Diary, August 31, 1894. Box 4. WCA.

2. KLB, Diary, August 7, 1893. Box 4. WCA.

3. KLB. "Ruby Heart." Published July 19, 1894; no place of publication given in KLB's Scrapbook (1886-1894). Box 19. WCA.

4. KLB, Diary, Box 4. WCA.

5. KLB, Diary, Oct. 23, 1893. Box 4. WCA.

6. KLB, Diary, Oct. 25, 27, and 29, 1893. Box 4. WCA.

7. KLB, Diary, Nov. 6 and 7, 1893. Box 4. WCA.

8. KLB, Diary, Nov. 18, 1893. Box 4. WCA.

9. He later explained it was "owing to overwork for a number of years preceding." Theophilus Huntington Root, entry in the Harvard College Report of the Class of 1885, 49. Harvard University Archives.

10. Ibid.

11. KLB, Diary, Jan. 3, 1894. Box 4. WCA.

12. KLB, Diary, March 21, 1894. Box 4. WCA.

13. Mary Kavanaugh Oldham Eagle, ed., *The Congress of Women, Held in the Woman's Building, World's Columbian Exposition, Chicago, U.S.A., 1893* (conference proceedings). Philadelphia and Chicago: S.I. Bell & Co., 1894, 26.

14. Eagle, *Congress,* 27.

15. As reported by Jeanne Madeline Weimann, "A Temple to Women's Genius: The Woman's Building of 1893," in *Chicago History,* Vol. 6, No. 1 (Spring 1977), 23.

16. Stanley Appelbaum, *The Chicago World's Fair of 1893: A Photographic Record.* New York: Dover Publications, Inc., 1980, 69.

17. Jeanne Madeline Weimann, *Fair Women.* Chicago: Academy, 1981, 239.

18. Circular of "A Preliminary Prospectus," September 1891, quoted in Weimann, *Fair,* 393.

19. Weimann, "A Temple," 28-30.

20. Weimann, *Fair*, 391.

21. Rose Hawthorne Lathrop as quoted in Patricia Dunlavy Valenti, *To Myself a Stranger*, Baton Rouge, Louisiana: Louisiana State University Press, 1990, page 123, quoting from James J. Hennesey, *American Catholics: A History of the Roman Catholic Community in the United States*, New York: 1981, 191.

22. Halsey C. Ives, Introduction to *The Dream City: A Portfolio of Photographic Views.* St. Louis: N. D. Thompson Publishing Company, 2.

23. Quoted in Weimann, *Fair*, 26.

24. Ives, 99, 116.

25. The booklet, "World's Columbian Exposition, 1893, Wellesley College, Wellesley, Mass.," in "Chicago Wellesley Club" Box, WCA.

26. Addams, Jane, *Twenty Years at Hull-House with Autobiographical Notes.* Ed. by Victoria Bissell Brown. Boston: Bedford/St. Martin's, 1999, 30-31.

27. "Living Among the Poor," *The Boston Herald*, History of Denison House, Carton 1: Miscellaneous Clippings, 5, [45]. The Schlesinger Library, Radcliffe College.

28. KLB, Diary, June 30, 1894. Box 4. WCA.

29. KLB, Diary, June 30, 1894. Box 4. WCA.

30. KLB, Letter to her sister, July 6, 1894. Box 4. WCA.

31. KLB, Letter to CLB, July 8, 1894. Box 4. WCA.

32. Burgess, 114.

33. KLB, Letter to CLB, July 16, 1894, Oxford, England. Box 4. WCA.

34. KLB, Letter to CLB, July 17, 1894. Oxford, England. Box 4. WCA.

35. KLB, Letter to CLB, August 12, 1894. Box 4. WCA.

36. KLB, Letter to CLB, July 8, 1894. Wytham. Box 4. WCA.

37. KLB, Diary, Aug. 31, 1894. Box 2. WCA.

38. Ellen Louise Hill, Letter to KLB, no date. Unprocessed KLB papers, WCA.

39. KLB, "Knowledge Versus Feeling," *Poet-Lore*, v. 6, pp. 383, 386.

40. KLB, Letter to CLB, July 29, 1894. Box 4. WCA.

41. KLB, Letter to Samuel Bates, Aug. 19, 1894. Box 4. WCA.

42. *BET*, Dec. 23, 1893, 1.

43. *BET*, Dec. 30, 1893, 1.

44. "The Business Outlook," *The Congregationalist*, Feb. 8, 1894, 45.

45. *The Congregationalist*, Jan. 4, 1894, 31.

46. KLB, Letter to her family (n.d.), summer 1894. Box 4. WCA.

47. See *Modern Art*, 1:3 (October 1893) and David F. Burg, *Chicago's White City of 1893*. Lexington: University of Kentucky, 1976, 62.

48. See Weimann, *Fair*, 287-289, for further discussion of this statue's history.

49. Larson, 207, 222.

50. Larson, 222-223.

51. Frontispiece of program for "America," the show that KLB attended in Chicago. Harvard Theatre Collection, Harvard University Archives.

52. "America," frontispiece.

53. "America," 4.

54. Barbara Barker, "Imre Kiralfy's Patriotic Spectacles: 'Columbus, and the Discovery of America' (1892-1893) and 'America' (1893)." *Dance Chronicle*, Vol. 17, No. 2 (1994), 169.

55. See Barker, 149-178; for production details, 168-173.

56. Barker, 173.

57. Ibid.

58. KLB, "1893." *The Independent*, January 1894.

59. *The Congregationalist*. July 19, 1894, 71.

60. R.W. Gilder, Letter to KLB, May 8, 1894. Box 24. WCA.

61. Ibid.

62. KLB, "Festivals in American Colleges for Women: At Wellesley" in *The Century*, Vol. XLIX.—56, 441.

63. KLB, "Festivals," 441-442.

64. The class cheer and the Wellesley call both remain alive and thriving in my own Wellesley experience.

65. KLB, "English at Wellesley College," *The Dial*, Oct. 16, 1894, 221.

66. In *The Congregationalist*, Sept. 5, 1895, 336.

67. In *The Congregationalist*, Sept. 5, 1895, 335.

68. Ibid.

69. In *The Congregationalist*, Sept. 5, 1895, 335, 336.

70. *The Congregationalist*, Feb.7, 1895, 214.

71. *The Wellesley Magazine*, December, 1894, 163.

72. Kate Douglass Wiggin, Letter to KLB, Sunday, Nov. 11, 1894. Unprocessed KLB papers, WCA.

73. Ibid.

74. KLB, Letter to ABS, Dec. 30, 1894. Box 20, Folder 801, Beecher Papers.

75. The wife of astronomy professor David Peck Todd, Mabel had been at home in Amherst having an affair with Emily's married brother Austin while her husband was leading Katharine's expedition up Pike's Peak in 1893.

76. William Michael Rossetti, Letter to KLB, Nov. 13, 1894. Wellesley College Library Special Collections.

77. Ibid.

78. Eulogy of Francis Hovey Stoddard, at time of retirement, 1914. New York University, Elmer Holmes Bobst Library Archives.

79. Francis H. Stoddard, Letter to KLB, Sept. 25, 1920. Uncatalogued. WCA.

80. KLB, Diary, Dec. 25, 1894. Box 2. WCA.

81. KLB, Letter to ABS, Jan. 23, 1895. Box 20, Folder 801, Beecher Papers.

82. Newspapers and magazines typically ran poems and articles appropriate to the holidays and anniversaries near their publication dates.

83. *The Congregationalist*, July 4, 1895, 1.

84. *The Congregationalist*, July 4, 1895, 17.

85. White, 18.

86. White, 23, 65.

87. White, 70.

88. White, 72, 74.

89. White, 143, 147.

90. White, 144.

91. White, 75.

92. KLB, "Literature in Relation to Life." *The New Cycle*, February 1895 (Vol. VIII, No. 8), 479.

93. KLB, "Literature," 480.

94. See Marc Leepson's *What So Proudly We Hailed: Francis Scott Key, A Life*. New York: Palgrave Macmillan, 2014, 67-69.

95. KLB, Diary, July 4 and 5, 1895, Box 4. WCA.

96. H. H. Furness, Letter to KLB, March 27, 1895. Uncatalogued. WCA.

97. KLB, Diary, Aug. 15, 17, and 18, 1895. Box. 4. WCA.

98. KLB, Diary, Sept. 10, 1895. Box 4. WCA.

99. Burgess, 124.

100. KLB, Diary, Sept. 20 and 21, 1895. Box 4. WCA.

101. KLB, Diary, Dec. 17, 1895. Box 4. WCA.

102. KLB, Diary, Oct. 26, 1895. Box 4. WCA.

103. KLB, Diary, Oct. 31, 1895. Box 4. WCA.

104. KLB, Review of *College Girls*. *The Wellesley Magazine*, Jan. 18, 1896 (Vol. IV, No. 4), 184.

105. Ibid.

106. Frances Albert Doughty, "The College Woman in Literature." *The Critic*, Oct. 5, 1895 (No. 711), 210.

107. KLB. Diary, Jan. 17, 1896. Box 4. WCA.

108. KLB, Diary, Jan. 30, 1896. Box 4. WCA.

109. KLB, Diary, Feb. 1, 1896. Box 4. WCA.

110. KLB, Letter to Miss Ward, March 11, 1896. Letters to Miss Ward. Box 22. WCA.

111. KLB, Diary, March 19, 1896. Box 4. WCA.

112. KLB, Diary, March 20, 1896. Box 4. WCA.

113. KLB, Diary, March 21, 1896. Box 4. WCA.

114. KLB, Diary, March 25, 1896. Box 4. WCA.

115. KLB, Diary, April 9, 1896. Box 4. WCA.

116. KLB, Letter to Miss Ward, April 10, 1896. Letters to Miss Ward, KLB Papers, Box 22. WCA.

117. KLB, Diary, April 13, 1896. Box 4. WCA.

118. KLB, Diary, May 3, 1896. Box 4. WCA.

119. KLB, Diary, May 4, 1896. Box 4. WCA.

120. Moses King, *The Back-Bay District and Vendome.* [Boston: no publisher given], 1880, 7, 31.

121. KLB, Diary, March 31, 1896. Box 4. WCA.

122. Margaret Sherwood, *A Puritan Bohemia.* New York: Macmillan & Sons, 1896, 11.

123. Sherwood, *Puritan* 12, emphases mine; 27.

124. Sherwood, *Puritan*, 40.

125. Sherwood, *Puritan*, 89.

126. Sherwood, *Puritan*, 90.

127. Sherwood, *Puritan,* 161.

128. KLB, Diary, Jan. 11, 1896. Box 4. WCA.

129. Feb. 7, 1896. See a summary of his talk in *Poet-Lore*, Vol. VIII (June, 1896), 361.

130. KLB, Diary, Nov. 2, 1895. Box 4. WCA.

131. KLB, Diary, Oct. 7, 1895. Box 4. WCA.

132. KLB, Diary, Oct. 11 and Oct. 14, 1895. Box 4. WCA.

133. KLB, Diary, Oct. 17, 1896. Box 4. WCA.

134. KLB, Diary, Nov. 9, 1895. Box 4. WCA.

135. It was at 11 St. James Avenue.

136. King, *Back-Bay*, 7, 31.

137. KLB, *American Literature.* New York: Macmillan, 1898, 134, 133.

138. By 1889. "A Studio of Her Own: Women Artists in Boston, 1870-1940," brochure for exhibition of the same title at the Museum of Fine Arts, Boston (Aug. 15-Dec. 2, 2001).

139. Walter Muir Whitehill. *Boston: Portrait of a City.* Photographs by Katharine Knowles. Barre, Massachusetts: Barre Publishers, 1964, 15. The swan-boats have been operating since 1877.

140. Amy Lowell, *The Complete Poems.* Boston: Houghton Mifflin Co., 1955, 21.

141. RHL, Letter to KLB, Nov. 16, Wellesley Hills. Unprocessed Katharine Lee Bates papers, WCA. No year is listed on this letter, but her biographer, Patricia Dunlavy Valenti, thinks that Rose might have been in Wellesley Hills between 1894 and 1896.

142. RHL, Letter to KLB, Jan. 18, Wellesley Hills, Mass. Unprocessed Katharine Lee Bates papers, WCA. No year is listed; see above on dating.

143. *BET*, Feb. 18, 1896 (n. p.). In KLB Scrapbook 1894-1899, p. 103. Loose. Box 21. WCA.

144. Her talk was on Feb. 10, 1896. *The Wellesley Magazine*, March 1896 (Vol. IV, #6), 346.

145. RHL, Letter to KLB, May 5, Wellesley Hills. Unprocessed Katharine Lee Bates papers, WCA. No year is listed; see note above on possible date.

146. KLB, "To Mother Mary Alphonsa Lathrop." *The Congregationalist*, July 23, 1926. (Typed transcription is from p. 103 of scrapbook 7, Box 21, WCA.)

147. Manning Hawthorne to KLB, Nov. 23, 1928, Bowdoin College, Brunswick, Maine. Unprocessed KLB papers. WCA.

148. KLB, *American Literature*, v.

149. KLB, *American Literature*, 336.

150. KLB Diaries, Dec. 28, 1896; Jan. 1, 1897; Jan. 4, 1897; Jan. 23, 1897; Feb. 18, 1897; July 14, 1897; July 18, 1897; Aug. 26, 1897. Box 4. WCA.

151. KLB, Diary, Sept. 8, 1897, Box 4. WCA.

152. KLB, Diary, Sept. 10, 1897, Box 4. WCA.

153. KLB, Diary, Sept. 20, 1897, Box 4. WCA.

154. KLB, Diary, Sept. 21, 1897, Box 4. WCA.

155. There were only three academic literary history textbooks and two combination anthologies-commentaries by university professors before she published her book.

156. KLB, *American Literature*, 10 and 2.

157. KLB, *American Literature*, 2.

158. KLB, *American Literature*, 8 and 31.

159. KLB, *American Literature*, 78.

160. KLB, *American Literature*, 86.

161. Brander Matthews. *An Introduction to the Study of American Literature*. New York: American Book Company, 1896, 9.

162. Lawrence J. Oliver, "Theodore Roosevelt, Brander Matthews, and the Campaign for Literary Americanism." *American Quarterly*, Vol. 41, #1 (March, 1989), 96.

163. KLB, *American Literature*, 38.

164. KLB, *American Literature*, 80.

165. KLB, *American Literature*, 85-86.

166. KLB, *American Literature*, 105.

167. KLB, *American Literature*, 115.

168. KLB, *American Literature*, 260. I thank Laurence Buell of Harvard University for pointing out her importance in this regard to me.

169. Ibid.

170. KLB, *American Literature*, 264.

171. KLB, *American Literature*, 265.

172. KLB, *American Literature*, pages 199, 198.

173. KLB, *American Literature*, 201.

174. Ibid.

175. KLB, *American Literature*, 202.

176. Ibid.

177. KLB, *American Literature*, 128.

CHAPTER EIGHT: 1898-1904–"AND CROWN THY GOOD WITH BROTHERHOOD"

1. KLB, "America." *BET,* Nov. 19, 1904, 19.

2. See Oliver, 34, for Matthews's and Oliver's opposition to "New Women." See Oliver, 79, on Brander's refusal to let women attend his literature classes or be elected to the National Institute/Academy of Arts and Letters.

3. Review of KLB's *American Literature,* no author, date, or place of publication. In "Papers of KLB—Reviews of Miss Bates's Publications: undated, 1901-30," Box 17. WCA.

4. Review of KLB's *American Literature. The Nation,* March 10, 1898 (Vol. 66, No. 1706), 193.

5. Theodore Roosevelt, "On American Motherhood." March 13, 1905, speech given in Washington, D.C., before the National Congress of Mothers.

6. Ibid.

7. Albert S. Cook, to Letter to KLB, Jan. 12, 1897. Box 24. WCA.

8. A. H. Tolman, Letter to KLB, Jan. 18, 1897. Unprocessed KLB Papers. WCA.

9. See Burgess, 124.

10. Katharine Coman,"Concepcion Arenal, the Reformer," in *The Wellesley College News,* May 1914, 9.

11. *BET,* Feb. 17, 1898, 1.

12. *BET,* Feb. 28, 1898, 1.

13. *BET,* March 3, 1898, 1.

14. *BET,* March 8, 1898, 1.

15. *BET,* March 8, 1898, 1.

16. *BET,* March 14, 1898 1.

17. *BET,* March 14, 1898, 12.

18. Financial interests of United States investors in Cuba favored such a settlement. The insurgents in Cuba wanted President McKinley to recognize an independent Cuba so that they could float a contingent loan, and the American representatives of "Spanish-Cuban" bonds wanted the United States to guarantee the payment of the debt incurred by Spain on account of Cuba. If Spain lost her "valuable" colonies in a war, it would be unable to repay this debt incurred to American investors. Other countries were pressing for peace for the same reason.

19. KLB, Diary, March 28, 1898. Box 4. WCA.

20. *BET,* March 31, 1898, 9.

21. KLB, Diary, April 3, 1898. Box 4. WCA.

22. *BET,* April 7, 1898, 7.

23. KLB, "Let Me Be Blessèd for the Peace I Make." *BET,* April 18, 1898.

24. KLB, Diary, April 11, 1898. Box 4. WCA.

25. *BET,* April 13, 1898, 7.

26. *BET,* April 15, 1898, 1.

27. KLB, Diary, April 16, 1898. Box 4. WCA.

28. *BET,* April 20, 1898, 7.

29. KLB, Diary, April 23, 1898. Box 4. WCA.

30. *BET,* April 26, 1898, 1.

31. KLB, Diary, May 3 and 4, 1898. Box 4. WCA.

32. KLB, Diary, April 30 and May 8, 1898. Box 4. WCA.

33. See Evan Thomas, *The War Lovers: Roosevelt, Lodge, Hearst, and the Rush to Empire, 1898*. New York: Little, Brown and Company, 2010, 178.

34. *BET*, May 3, 1898, 1.

35. KLB, Diary, May 6, 7, 8, 1898. Box 4. WCA.

36. *BET*, May 7, 1898, 1, and May 9, 1898, 1.

37. *BET*, May 21, 1898, 1.

38. *BET*, May 23, 1898, 1.

39. *BET*, June 16, 1898, 1.

40. Quoted in G. J. A. O'Toole, *The Spanish War*. New York: W.W. Norton & Company, 1984, 386. Also see Stephen Kinzer, *The True Flag: Theodore Roosevelt, Mark Twain, and the Birth of American Empire*. New York: Henry Holt and Company, 2017.

41. *BET*, June 21, 1898, 1.

42. KLB, Diary, May 5, 1898. Box 4. WCA.

43. KLB, Diary, May 7, 1898. Box 4. WCA. Perhaps as a backup plan, if travel in Spain was impossible, she began taking Italian lessons.

44. KLB, Diary, June 22, 23. 1898. Box 4. WCA.

45. *The Congregationalist*, July 7, 1898 (Vol. 83, #27), 7.

46. *The Congregationalist*, July 7, 1898 (Vol. 83, #27), 10.

47. *The Congregationalist*, July 28, 1898 (Vol. 83, #30), 107.

48. Quote from the *New York Evening Post* in *The Congregationalist*, Aug. 4, 1898 (Vol. 83, #31), 147.

49. *The Congregationalist*, Aug. 4, 1898 (Vol. 83, #31), 162.

50. Ibid.

51. KLB, Letter to CLB, Aug. 12, 1898. Box 4. WCA.

52. KLB, Letter to CLB, Sept. 23, 1898. Box 4. WCA.

53. KLB, Diary, Sept. 28, 1898, Box 4. WCA.

54. KLB, Letter to CLB, Oct. 31, 1898. Box 4. WCA.

55. KLB, *Spanish Highways and Byways*. New York: The Macmillan Company, 1900, 353.

56. KLB, Letter to her mother, Oct. 31, 1898. Box 4. WCA.

57. KLB, *Spanish Highways*, 353.

58. KLB, Letter to CLB, Nov. 28, 1898. Box 4. WCA. She replied to her mother's fear of Catholics: "As for the convent, they never offer me any food there, but they wouldn't poison me, any more than I would poison them." Jan. 1, 1899. Box 4. WCA.

59. KLB, Diary, Dec. 31, 1898. Box 4, WCA, and Burgess, 129.

60. KLB, *Spanish Highways*, 1.

61. KLB, Diary, Jan. 17 and 18, 1899. Box 4. WCA.

62. KLB, Diary, Jan. 19 and 20, 1898. Box 4. WCA.

63. KLB, Diary, Feb. 3, 1899. Box 4. WCA.

64. KLB, "On the Spanish Frontier," *The New York Times*, Feb. 12, 1899, 7.

65. Ibid.

66. Ibid.

67. *The Congregationalist*, July 14, 1898, 40.

68. KLB, *Spanish Highways*, 22.

69. KLB, *Spanish Highways*, 22 and 23.

70. KLB, *Spanish Highways*, 27, 31-32.

71. KLB, Letter to CLB, Feb. 26, 1899. Box 4. WCA.

72. Ibid.

73. KLB, *Spanish Highways*, 33 and 34.

74. Ibid.

75. KLB, *Spanish Highways,* 35-36.

76. KLB, *Spanish Highways*, 38.

77. Headlines in *The New York Times*, April 23, 1899.

78. KLB, Diary, March 29, 1899. Box 4. WCA.

79. KLB, *Spanish Highways*, 73, 74.

80. KLB, *Spanish Highways,* 77.

81. KLB, *Spanish Highways*, 55-56.

82. KLB, *Spanish Highways*, 57.

83. KLB, *Spanish Highways*, 52.

84. KLB, *Spanish Highways*, 124, 125.

85. KLB, *Spanish Highways*, 131.

86. Ibid.

87. See, for example, the account of a lynching in Illinois, which "cannot rebuke her fellow-citizens in the South for their crime against law and humanity." *The Congregationalist*, Nov. 17, 1898 (Vol. 83, #46), 709.

88. KLB, *Spanish Highways*, 91.

89. KLB, *Spanish Highways,* 93, 95.

90. KLB, *Spanish Highways*, 147.

91. KLB, *Spanish Highways*, 148.

92. KLB, *Spanish Highways*, 151.

93. KLB, *Spanish Highways*, 152.

94. KLB, *Spanish Highways*, 157-8.

95. Henry Loewenthal, Letter to KLB, May 16, 1899, *The New York Times*. Papers of KLB, America the Beautiful: General letters, WCA.

96. Rojas, Julio, Letter to KLB, May 15, 1899. Box 22. WCA.

97. See note appended to this letter: KLB Papers, Letters from various people, May 15, 1899, WCA.

98. KLB Papers, Letters from various people, June 11, 1899, WCA.

99. KLB, "A Private." *New England Magazine*, July 1899. (No pages available.)

100. Quoted in Oliver, 106.

101. KLB, *Spanish Highways*, 1.

102. Franklin Ware Davis, "Today in 'Manana' Land." *The Boston Sunday Journal*, Dec. 3, 1899, n.p. In KLB Scrapbook 1894-1899. Box 19. WCA.

103. George H. Palmer, Letter to CH, March 6, 1899, 1DB5, Caroline Hazard Papers. Box 4. WCA.

104. Rev. A. E. Dunning, "The Inauguration of Wellesley's New President." *The Congregationalist,* Oct. 12, 1899 (Vol. 84, #41), 522.

105. Ibid.

106. "A Record of the Exercises Attending the Inauguration of Caroline Hazard, Litt.D., as President of Wellesley College, 11 October, MDCCCXCIX." Cambridge: The Riverside Press, 1899, 17.

107. Ibid.

108. "A Record," 20.

109. KLB, Diary, Oct. 19, 1899. Box 4. WCA.

110. KLB, Letter to Mary Woolley, Jan. 13, 1904. Box 8. WCA.

111. KLB, Diary, Aug. 13, 14, 1899. Box 4. WCA.

112. KLB, Diary, Nov. 27, 1899. Box 4. WCA.

113. KLB, Diary, Dec. 3, 1899. Box 4. WCA.

114. During Katharine's first winter back from Spain, Professor Silas M. Macvane lectured at Wellesley on "England and the Transvaal" early in December 1899, and Frederick W. Holls described "The Peace Conference at the Hague," which brought activists from many countries opposed to war together and focused public attention on the general fear of and opposition to war. But three months later, the Anglo-Boer War began in Africa, an event that both disillusioned and energized those who had believed in the goals of the Peace Conference.

115. *The Congregationalist,* Nov. 9, 1899 (Vol. 84, #45), 682.

116. *The Congregationalist,* Dec. 28, 1899 (Vol. 84, #52), 1006; Dec. 21, 1899 (Vol. 84, #51), 962, 960.

117. *The Congregationalist,* Jan. 11, 1900 (Vol. 85, #2), 44.

118. KLB, Diary, Dec. 18, 1899. Box 4. WCA.

119. KLB, Diary, Dec. 21, 1899. Box 4. WCA.

120. KLB, Diary, Dec. 22, 1899. Box 4. WCA.

121. KLB, Diary, Dec. 28, 1899. Box 4. WCA.

122. KLB, Diary, Dec. 29, 1899. Box 4. WCA.

123. KLB, Diary, Dec. 31, 1899. Box 4. WCA.

124. KLB, Diary, Jan. 2, 1900. Box 4. WCA.

125. KLB, Diary, Jan. 4, 1900. Box 4. WCA.

126. KLB, Diary, Jan. 5, 1900. Box 4. WCA.

127. KLB, Diary, Jan. 6, 1900. Box 4. WCA.

128. KLB, Diary, Jan. 8, 1900. Box 4. WCA.

129. KLB, Diary, Jan. 18, 1900. Box 4. WCA.

130. KLB, "To England." Originally published in *The Atlantic Monthly* but quoted here from the book compilation KLB made from many of these antiwar poems: James Lincoln, *Relishes of Rhyme.* Boston: Richard G. Badger, The Gorham Press, 1903, 11-12.

131. KLB, "Remarks from Uncle Sam," originally published in *SSR* on Jan. 22, 1900, but quoted here from Lincoln, *Relishes,* 14.

132. KLB, "An Anachronism," originally published in *SSR* but quoted here from Lincoln, *Relishes,* 44.

133. KLB, "Dundee," originally published in *SSR* on Feb. 6, 1900, but quoted here from Lincoln, *Relishes,* 21.

134. KLB, "Prayers in Camp," originally published in *SSR* on Feb. 6, 1900, but quoted here from Lincoln, *Relishes,* 16.

135. Ibid.

136. KLB, "A Veteran of Elandslangte," originally published on Feb. 17, 1900, but quoted here from Lincoln, *Relishes*, 23.

137. "Glory," originally published in *BET* on Feb. 21, 1900, but quoted here from Lincoln, *Relishes*, 18.

138. KLB, "Puzzlehead," originally published in *SSR* but quoted here from Lincoln, *Relishes*. 17.

139. Ibid.

140. KLB, "The Black Watch," originally published in *BET* after Feb. 26, 1900, but quoted here from Lincoln, *Relishes*, 28.

141. KLB, "The Black Watch," 28-29.

142. KLB, Diary, March 22, 1900, Box 4. WCA.

143. KLB, "Betrayed." Originally published in *The New England Magazine* in July 1900, but quoted here from Lincoln, *Relishes*, 52.

144. Wordsworth describes the city in all its pastoral beauty at daybreak:

"This City now doth, like a garment, wear
The beauty of the morning; silent, bare,
Ships, towers, domes, theatres, and temples lie
Open unto the fields, and to the sky;
All bright and glittering in the smokeless air."

Katharine may also have hoped her readers would think of another Wordsworth sonnet, "The World Is Too Much With Us; Late and Soon," which laments England's "getting and spending," which causes Englishmen to "lay waste" their "powers," seeking riches.

"Shall not Great England work her will on these,
The foolish little nations, and appease
An angry shame that in her memory aches?"

145. KLB, "Betrayed," from Lincoln, *Relishes*, 52.

146. Ibid.

147. Her images of a landscape ravaged by the fire and blood of war evoke Milton's images of Hell in *Paradise Lost*. A personified Freedom, so valued by Puritan John Milton, is now a "dim and awful Shade," like visions of corpses from Shakespearean tragedy, as Freedom has been tragically "betrayed" by the English nation that sent men to die to accomplish its imperial takeover of the rich land of the Boers in Africa. Katharine's speaker's words, "Beware, beware," echo the words of Coleridge's famous poetic bard in "Kubla Khan," who has the power to tell the truth.

148. KLB, Diary, Oct. 14, 1900. Box 4. WCA.

149. KLB, Diary, Oct. 4, 1900. Box 4. WCA.

150. KLB, Diary, Oct. 8, 1900. Box 4. WCA.

151. KLB, Diary, Oct. 20, 1900. Box 4. WCA.

152. KLB, Diary, Oct. 26, 1900. Box 4. WCA.

153. KLB, Diary, Nov. 2, 1900. Box 4. WCA.

154. KLB, Diary, Nov. 6, 1900. Box 4. WCA.

155. KLB, Diary, Nov. 7, 1900. Box 4. WCA. "Gurly" means ill-humored or evil in Old Scottish, and "weird" means fate or destiny, so she voiced an expression of vexation and irritation, perfect for having shot her ball into a bunker.

156. KLB, Diary, Nov. 16, 17, 20, 21, 1900. Box 4. WCA.

157. KLB, Diary, Dec. 5, 1900. Box 4. WCA.

158. "An American Woman in Spain." *The Nation*, April 11, 1901 (Vol. 72), 300.

159. Ibid.

160. Ibid.

161. KLB, Diary, March 12, 1901. Box 4. WCA.

162. KLB, Diary, May 22, 1901. Box 4. WCA.

163. KLB, "The College Girl of the Period." *BET*, June 14, 1902, n. p.

164. KLB, Diary, May 13, 1901; see May 12 and Feb. 19, 1901, as well. Box 4. WCA.

165. KLB, ed., *The King of the Golden River or the Black Brothers: A Legend of Stiria*. New York: Rand McNally & Company (Canterbury Classics), 1903, 69.

166. KLB, Diary, Dec. 3, 1901. Box 4. WCA.

167. KLB, *The King*, 70-71. By the end of 1901 she had also edited *The Eve of St. Agnes and Other Poems*, selections of John Keats's works with her comments.

168. KLB, Diary, Dec. 13, 1901. Box 4. WCA.

169. KLB, Letter to Jeannette Marks, Dec. 16, 1901. Box 7. WCA.

170. Sarah Orne Jewett, Letter to KLB, ALS, New York, June 8, no year. WCSC.

171. Crowell republished the introductions Katharine had written earlier to make the set known as the Lenox edition of *Hawthorne's Romances*. See footnote 7, p. 215, of my essay in *Hawthorne and Women: Engendering and Expanding the Hawthorne Tradition*. Ed. John. L. Idol, Jr. and Melinda M. Ponder, Amherst: University of Massachusetts Press, 1999.

172. Having made a personal connection with Hawthorne's daughter Rose by corresponding with her and inviting her to Wellesley College, Katharine then shone her spotlight on Hawthorne's mother, aunts, sisters, sister-in-law, and wife, correctly finding that they each made important contributions to his developing career as a writer, especially when the chips were down, and fame had not yet come. She also recounts how his wife, Sophia, enabled him to have the time and space (money and a new study) in which to write *The Scarlet Letter*, the book that made him a best-selling author. But other women were important too, as Katharine shows, describing how the careers of such women as Margaret Fuller, Hannah More, Elizabeth Barrett Browning, Harriet Beecher Stowe, and the Cary sisters touched Hawthorne's. And see my book, *Hawthorne and Women*.

173. KLB, ed. Tennyson's *"The Princess."* New York: American Book Company (Gateway Series), 1904, 7.

174. KLB. "George Sand: A Sketch," in *The Booklovers Reading Club: The World's Great Women Novelists*. Philadelphia: The Booklovers Library (Course XX: Booklovers Reading Club), 1901, 55.

175. KLB, "George Sand," 67.

176. KLB, "George Sand," 65.

177. KLB, "George Sand," 65-66.

178. KLB, Diary, Aug. 30, Sept. 2, and Sept. 3, 1902. Box 4. WCA.

179. KLB, Diary, Jan. 28, 1903. Box 4. WCA.

180. Published in *Booklovers' Library* in April 1903, n. p.

181. KLB, ed. *The Poems of Alice and Phoebe Cary*. New York: Thomas Y. Crowell, 1903, xviii and xxix.

182. KLB, Diary, May 12, 1903. Box 4. WCA. I think it possible that she saw him on May 23 and 24, 1900, when she went to New Haven, Connecticut: "Beautiful drive all about East Rock."—Diary, WCA. Root took up his pastorate in nearby Wood River Junction in July 1900.

183. The Rev.Walter Folger Greenman writing in the Harvard College Class of 1885 50th Anniversary Report, pages 200 and 202, Harvard University Archives.

184. KLB, Diary, May 25, 1903. Box 4. WCA.

185. KLB, Diary, June 9, 1903. Box 4. WCA.

186. KLB, Diary, June 25, 1903. Box 4. WCA.

187. KLB, Diary, July 1, 1903. Box 4. WCA.

188. KLB, Diary, August 1, 1903. Box 4. WCA.

189. KLB, Diary, August 2, 1903. Box 4. WCA.

190. KLB, Diary, Oct. 13, 1903. Box 4. WCA.

191. KLB, Diary, Oct. 20, 1903. Box 4. WCA.

192. KLB, Diary, Nov. 20, 1903. Box 4. WCA.

193. I have found no trace of those letters, and since she destroyed most letters from Katharine Coman before she died, I believe she destroyed other letters as well.

194. Greenman, 200.

195. It sold 3,000 copies. Greenman, 201.

196. Greenman, 200.

197. This is pointed out in Canning Eyot, *The Story of the Lopez Family*. Manila, Philippines: Platypus Publishing, 2001 (originally published in Boston, 1904), 135. I thank Wilma Slaight of the Wellesley College Archives for this source.

198. *The Congregationalist*, Nov. 9, 1899 (Vol. 84, #45), 682.

199. *The Congregationalist*, Oct. 19, 1899 (Vol. 84, #42), 558.

200. Ibid.

201. Ibid.

202. Ibid.

203. KLB, "The Pity of It," in *America the Beautiful*, 1911, 30. I thank Leonard Miele for calling my attention to this poem.

204. Ibid.

205. Reported as held on Jan. 26, 1901, in *The Wellesley Magazine*, March 1901, 328.

206. Martin Green, *The Mount Vernon Street Warrens*. New York: Charles Scribner's Sons, 1989, 157.

207. Quoted in George Brown Tindall and David E. Shi, *America: A Narrative History*. New York: W.W. Norton & Company, 1992, 300.

208. Paul Kramer. "The Water Cure." *The New Yorker,* Feb. 25, 2008. See http://www.newyorker.com/magazine/2008/02/25/the-water-cure.

209. O'Toole, 394-95; Richard E. Welch, Jr., *Response to Imperialism*. Chapel Hill: The University of North Carolina Press, 1979, 40-42.

210. Eyot, *Lopez Family,* 22.

211. Clemencia Lopez, "Women of the Philippines," in *The Woman's Journal*, June 7, 1902. Retrieved from http://www.boondocksnet.com/wj/wj_19020607.html. In Jim Zwick, ed., *Anti-Imperialism in the United States, 1898-1935*. http://www.boondocksnet.com/ail98-35.html (Nov. 6, 101). And see Zwick's foreword to Eyot, *Lopez Family,* for a detailed account of Fiske Warren's involvement with the Lopez family.

212. Clemencia Lopez, "Women of the Philippines," in *The Woman's Journal*, June 7, 1902. Retrieved from http://www.boondocksnet.com/wj/wj_19020607.html. In Jim Zwick, ed., *Anti-Imperialism in the United States, 1898-1935*. http://www.boondocksnet.com/ail98-35.html (Nov. 6, 101).

213. Eyot, *Lopez Family,* 26-28, 30. This account names Cornelia Warren, "whose sympathy and counsel were all that Mr. Cortelyou's reply was not," as Clemencia's "kindly hostess," 27.

214. KLB, Diary, July 11, 1903. Box 4. WCA. She donated a copy of her *Relishes of Rhyme* to the Athenaeum on November 16, 1903, inscribed from "The Author," although it remained filed under "Lincoln" until I identified it as being by Katharine.

215. KLB, Diary, Nov. 7, 1903. Box 4. WCA.

216. KLB, Diary, Dec. 1, 1903. Box 4. WCA.

217. KLB, ed. *Tennyson's "The Princess."* New York: American Book Company (Gateway Series), 1904, 7.

218. Mark Twain, "To the Person Sitting in Darkness," February 1901, quoted by the Hispanic Division, Library of Congress, in *The World of 1898: The Spanish-American War*, retrieved from http://www.loc.gov/rr/hispanic/1898/twain.html.

219. *The Wellesley News*, No. 7, April 1901, 379.

220. KLB, "The Fellowship." *Everybody's Magazine*, Jan. 19, 1904, n. p.

221. Oscar L. Triggs. *Browning and Whitman: A Study in Democracy.* New York: Macmillan & Co., 1893, 107 and 122.

222. Quoted in E. Berkeley Tompkins, *Anti-Imperialism in the United States: The Great Debate, 1890-1920.* Philadelphia: University of Pennsylvania Press, 1970, 152, from *The New York Post*, "Special Anti-Imperialist Supplement."

223. *The Congregationalist*, March 30, 1899 (Vol. 84, #13), 445.

224. *The Congregationalist*, April 27, 1899 (Vol. 84, #17), 595.

225. KLB, Diary, Oct. 13, 1899 and Oct. 20, 1899. WCA.

226. Quoted in Palmieri, 170, letter from Harriet Rice to KC, June 1913. Unprocessed KC Papers, WCA.

227. KC, "Lecture: Contract Labor in Hawaii. Notes." In KC Papers, WCA.

228. KLB, *American Literature*, 105.

229. KLB, "America the Beautiful, A History of the Hymn by the author Katharine Lee Bates written for the Boston Athenaeum, 1918." Courtesy of the Boston Athenaeum Special Collections.

230. KLB, "America the Beautiful" (Athenaeum), 3.

231. She had begun thinking about revising it as early as 1902, about the time she had been writing her introduction to Hawthorne's *The Blithedale Romance*, the story of how a group of idealists try to form and live in a community dedicated to achieving the common good. She wrote that she wished Hawthorne had given "so pure a dream ... a finer and ampler memorial." KLB, Introduction to *The Blithedale Romance*, vol. 9 of *Hawthorne's Romances*. New York: Thomas Y. Crowell, 1902, xxi. I thank John L. Idol, Jr., for suggesting this idea to me.

232. Published with commentary in *BET*, Nov. 19, 1904, 19.

233. Ibid.

234. Ibid.

235. KLB, Diary, Nov. 19, 1904. Box 4. WCA.

236. KLB, "America the Beautiful" (Athenaeum), 6.

CHAPTER NINE: 1905-1915–"NEW WOMAN OF EGYPT"

1. KLB, "Certain Contents of the Scarab," House Inventory, compiled in October 1928. Box 2. WCA.

2. *BET*, Nov. 19, 1904.

3. KLB, Diary. Box 2. WCA.

4. KLB, under James Lincoln, "Superannuated." *The Atlantic Monthly* (Vol. 95), June 1905, 759.

5. KLB, under James Lincoln, "Superannuated," 764.

6. KLB, under James Lincoln, "Superannuated," 766.

7. KLB, Diary 1898-1911, Feb. 22, 1905. WCA.

8. Theophilus Root, Class Notes Harvard College Class of 1885 Report for 1905, p. 82 of Record Book. Harvard University Archives.

9. KLB, "Certain Contents."

10. Quoted in Burgess, 150-151.

11. Ibid.

12. KLB, Letter to CLB, Sept. 30, 1906. Box 4. WCA.

13. Caroline described her as "an excellent trained nurse … who for the sake of the experience was travelling as my maid." In fact, though, Miss O'Brian's nursing skills came in handy, because Caroline was ill during parts of the trip. Caroline Hazard, *A Brief Pilgrimage in the Holy Land*. Boston: Houghton Mifflin Company, 1909, v.

14. KLB, Letter to CLB, Dec. 21, 1906. Box 4. WCA.

15. KLB, Diary, Dec. 17, 1906. Box 4. WCA.

16. KLB, Diary, Dec. 18, 1906. Box 4. WCA.

17. KLB, "Cairo," in *America the Beautiful*, 219.

18. KLB, "The Delta," in *America the Beautiful*, 219.

19. KLB, Letter to CLB, Dec. 21, 1906. Box 4. WCA.

20. Ibid.

21. KLB, Diary, Dec. 20, 1906. Box 4. WCA.

22. KLB, Letter to CLB, Dec. 21, 1906. Box 4. WCA.

23. KLB, Letter from Palestine, #6, Letters to various people from Palestine, 1907. Box 4. WCA.

24. KLB, Letter to CLB, Dec. 21, 1906. Box 4. WCA.

25. Ibid.

26. KLB, Diary, Dec. 24 and 25, 1906. Box 4. WCA.

27. KLB, Diary, Dec. 29, 1906. Box 4. WCA.

28. KLB, Diary, Jan. 1, 1907. Box 4. WCA.

29. KLB, Diary, Jan. 5, 1907. Box 4. WCA.

30. Baedeker, Karl. *Egypt Handbook for Travellers*, Fifth Revised Edition. London: Dulau and Co., 1902, 184.

31. KLB, *America the Beautiful*, 220.

32. KLB, Diary, Jan. 14, 1907. Box 4. WCA.

33. KLB, Diary, Jan. 31, 1907. Box 4.WCA.

34. KLB, "The Valley of the Tombs of the Kings," in *America the Beautiful*, 220.

35. KLB, "Certain Contents."

36. KLB, Diary, Jan. 4, 1907. Box 4. WCA.

37. KLB, Letter to CLB, Feb. 11, 1907. Box 4. WCA.

38. KLB, Diary, Feb. 8, 1907. Box 4. WCA.

39. KLB, Letter to CLB, Feb. 11, 1907. Box 4. WCA.

40. KLB, Letter to CLB, Feb. 11, 1907. Box 4. WCA.

41. Hazard, v-vi.

42. KLB, Letter to CLB, Feb. 11, 1907. Box 4. WCA.

43. Ibid.

44. Ibid.

45. KLB, Letter to CLB, Feb. 24, 1907. Box 4. WCA.

46. Ibid.

47. Ibid.

48. Ibid.

49. KLB, Letter to CLB, March 12, 1907. Box 4. WCA.

50. Ibid.

51. Ibid. If only Katharine could have joined me, one hundred years later, on Philae, to see its buildings, which were moved to a nearby island when the new Aswan Dam was built in 1964.

52. KLB, Letter to CLB, March 12, 1907. Box 4. WCA.

53. KLB, Diary, Jan. 3, 1907. Box 4. WCA.

54. KLB, "Certain Contents."

55. Ibid.

56. KLB, Letters from Palestine, #1, KLB Papers, Letters to various people from Palestine 1907. Box 4. WCA.

57. KLB, "Certain Contents."

58. Ibid.

59. Ibid.

60. KLB, Letters from Palestine. Letters to various people from Palestine 1907. Box 8. WCA.

61. KLB, Letters from Palestine, #1. Letters to various people from Palestine 1907. Box 8. WCA.

62. Ibid.

63. Ibid.

64. KLB, Letters from Palestine, #2, March 23, 1907. Letters to various people from Palestine 1907. Box 8. WCA.

65. Ibid.

66. Ibid.

67. See KLB, in *America the Beautiful,* 223.

68. KLB, Letters from Palestine, #2, March 23, 1907. Letters to various people from Palestine 1907. Box 8. WCA.

69. KLB's Letters from Palestine, #3, March 25, 1907. Letters to various people from Palestine 1907. Box 8. WCA.

70. KLB, Letter to CLB, March 14, 1907. Box 4. WCA.

71. KLB, Letter from Palestine, #10. Letters to various people from Palestine 1907. Box 8. WCA.

72. KLB, Letter from Palestine, #3, March 25, 1907. Letters to various people from Palestine 1907. Box 8. WCA.

73 KLB, Letter from Palestine, #7. Letters to various people from Palestine 1907. Box 8. WCA.

74. Ibid.

75. KLB, Letter from Palestine, #10. Letters to various people from Palestine 1907. Box 8. WCA.

76. KLB, Letter to CLB, March 14, 1907. Box 4. WCA.

77. Ibid.

78. KLB, Letters from Palestine, #9. Letters to various people from Palestine 1907. Box 8. WCA. Her description is of the Mosque in Jerusalem.

79. KLB. Letter from Palestine, #6. Letters to various people from Palestine 1907. Box 8. WCA.

80. Ibid.

81. Ibid.

82. KLB, Letter from Palestine, #11. Letters to various people from Palestine 1907. Box 8. WCA.

83. Quoted in Burgess, 150-151.

84. KLB, Letter to CLB, May 20, 1907. Box 4. WCA.

85. Nathaniel Hawthorne, *Our Old Home, Centenary Edition of The Works of Nathaniel Hawthorne,* ed. William Charvat, et al. Columbus: Ohio State University Press, 1962, Vol. 5: 259.

86. Hawthorne, *CE* 5: 9.

87. KLB, *Gretna Green,* 31.

88. KLB, *Gretna Green,* 50.

89. KLB, *Gretna Green,* 138.

90. KLB, *Gretna Green,* 335.

91. KLB, Poems Account Book. "Undated Diaries." Box 4. WCA.

92. The house was designed by William Brainerd, who had designed Arthur's house in Portland, Maine. Architectural historian Alice T. Friedman believes Hawthorne's House of the Seven Gables in Salem, Massachusetts, was a model for the house ("Hiding in Plain Sight," *Home Cultures,* Vol. 12, #2, 1-28, 2015). I do not agree with her other points.

93. KLB, Diary, Aug. 1 and 2, 1907. Box 4. WCA.

94. KLB, "Certain Contents."

95. KLB, Diary, Aug. 30, 1907. Box 4. WCA.

96. KLB, Diary, Sept. 17, 1907. Box 4. WCA.

97. KLB, "Certain Contents."

98. KLB, Diary, Oct. 1 and Oct. 2 1907. Box 4. WCA.

99. KLB, "Certain Contents."

100. Ibid.

101. Ibid.

102. Ibid.

103. Ibid.

104. Ibid.

105. CLB, Letter to ALB, Jan. 3, 1908. I thank Elizabeth Bates Null for sharing this letter with me.

106. Elizabeth Olmstead, "Katharine Lee Bates: Scholar, Patriot, Poet." Ms. of talk at Wellesley College, courtesy of Elizabeth Bates Null. Olmstead wrote that "the scarab has now been authenticated and assured the place of honor."

107. KLB, *Sigurd,* 21. Their friend and Denison House patron Cornelia Warren had given them Sigurd.

108. KLB, *Sigurd,* 23.

109. KLB, *Sigurd,* 30.

110. KLB, *Sigurd,* 31.

111. KLB, *Sigurd,* 35.

112. KLB, *Sigurd,* 147-148.

113. KLB, *Sigurd,* 152.

114. KLB, *Sigurd,* 183.

115. KLB, *Sigurd,* 193.

116. Quoted in Burgess, 204.

117. ALB, Letter to KLB, Dec. 26, 1919. I thank Elizabeth Bates Null for sharing this letter with me.

118. CLB, Letter to ALB, Jan. 3, 1908. I thank Elizabeth Bates Null for sharing this letter with me.

119. KLB, Diary, Jan. 20, 1908. Box 4. WCA.

120. KLB, Diary, Jan. 21, 1908. Box 4. WCA.

121. KLB, Poems Account Book, January 1908.

122. KLB, "The Rest Is Silence," in *America the Beautiful,* 183.

123. KLB, Letter to Sara Teasdale, Jan. 21, 1927. Box 8. WCA.

124. KLB, Diary, Sept. 4, 1908. Box 4. WCA.

125. KLB, "Sacrifice." *The Chicago Daily News*, May 21, 1909, n.p.

126. KLB, Diary, June 5 and June 27, 1909. Box 4. WCA.

127. KLB, Poems Account Book, June 1909.

128. KLB, Diary, Nov. 1 and Nov. 3, 1909. Box 4. WCA.

129. KLB, Poems Account Book, December 1909.

130. KLB, Diary, Nov. 8, 1910. Box 4. WCA.

131. KLB, Diary, Dec. 2, 1910. Box 4. WCA.

132. KLB, Diary, Dec. 15, 1910. Box 4. WCA.

133. KLB, Poems Account Book, December 1910.

134. KLB, Diary, April 26, 1911. Box 4. WCA.

135. KLB, Diary, May 11, 15, 16, 17, 18, 24, 28, 1911. Box 4. WCA.

136. KLB, Diary, May 31, 1911. Box 4. WCA.

137. KLB, Diary, May 30, 1911. Box 4. WCA.

138. KLB, Diary, June 1, 1911. Box 4. WCA.

139. KLB, Diary, Sept. 11, 1911. Box 4. WCA.

140. KLB, Diary, Sept. 19 and 27, 1911. Box 4. WCA.

141. KLB, *America the Beautiful.*

142. KLB, *America the Beautiful,* 3.

143. Article in the *Kansas City Times*, Nov. 29, 1912, quoting Walter Rauschenbusch's book, *Christianizing the Social Order.* My thanks to Keith Arbour for this information.

144. David M. Kennedy, *Over Here: The First World War and American Society,* Twenty-Fifth Anniversary Edition. New York: Oxford University Press, 2004, 11 and 29.

145. KLB, Diary, Feb. 26, 1912. Box 4. WCA.

146. KLB, Diary, March 4, 1912. Box 4. WCA.

147. See Palmieri, 131-132.

148. KLB, *In Sunny Spain with Pilarica and Rafael.* New York: E.P. Dutton and Company, 1913.

149. KLB, Diary, June 5, 1912. Box 4. WCA.

150. KLB, "The Growth of a Book," *BET*, Oct. 12, 1912.

151. Ibid.

152. Quoted in Tindall and Shi, 966.

153. KLB, *Sigurd,* 210.

154. KLB, *Sigurd*, 213.

155. KLB, Poems Account Book, July and August 1914. WCA.

156. KLB, Diary, April 20, 1914, and April 26, 1914. Box 4. WCA.

157. *BET*, Aug. 8, 1914.

158. KLB, "To Our President" in *The Retinue and Other Poems*, New York: E.P. Dutton & Co., 1918, 10.

159. KLB, Diary, Aug. 8, 1914. Box 4. WCA.

160. *BET*, Aug. 10, 1914.

161. KLB, "Marching Feet," *The Retinue*, 7-8.

162. See Kennedy, 21-23.

163. See Kennedy, 30.

164. KLB, Diary, Sept. 15, 1914. Box 4. WCA.

165. *BET*, Sept. 15, 1914.

166. Ibid.

167. *BET*, Oct. 22, 1914.

168. KLB, "Fodder for Cannon," in *Life*, Oct. 22, 1914, n. p.

169. KLB, Diary, Oct. 24, 1914. Box 4. WCA.

170. *BET*, Oct. 23, 1914.

171. KLB, Poems Account Book, December 1914. WCA.

172. KLB, Diary, Jan. 11, 1915. Box 4. WCA.

173. KLB, Poems Account Book, January 1915. WCA.

174. KLB, Diary, Jan. 18, 1915. Box 4. WCA.

175. KLB, Diary, Jan. 22 and 25, 1915. Box 4. WCA.

176. KLB, Diary, March 28, 1915. WCA.

CHAPTER TEN: 1915-1929–"SWEPT INTO THE MIGHTY CURRENT OF THE TIMES"

1. KLB, Diary, April 5, 1917. Box 4. WCA.

2. "The Literary Spirit of Our Country," in *Longfellow: Poems*, 794, 795.

3. See *Dear Editor: A History of Poetry in Letters: The First Fifty Years, 1912-1962* ed. by Joseph Parisi and Stephen Young. New York: W. W. Norton and Company, 2002, 23.

4. *Dear Editor,* 26, 42.

5. KLB, Diary, April 26, 1915. Box 4. WCA.

6. She also hosted a luncheon at the Scarab for him before a reception at her Phi Sigma college society house and dinner with the Scudders. KLB Diary, Feb. 18, 1915. Box 4. WCA.

7. Ernest Sutherland Bates, "Nicholas Vachel Lindsay" in *The Dictionary of American Biography*, Vol. VI, edited by Dumas Malone. New York: Charles Scribner's Sons, 1933, 20.

8. Marion Burton, Wellesley Class of 1917, "Memories of Katharine Lee Bates." *Encore*, Winter 1976, 17 (from Alumnae Biographical Files, WCA).

9. KLB, Diary, May 6, 1915. Box 4. WCA.

10. The meeting was in May 1915.

11. Burgess, 185.

12. Quoted in Burgess, 185.

13. "A History of the New England Poetry Club, 1915-1931," 7, Boston Public Library. Courtesy of the Boston Public Library/Rare Books.

14. "A History," 6.

15. Jeffrey Meyers, *Robert Frost: A Biography*. Boston: Houghton Mifflin Company, 1996, 172, 38.

16. Thompson, Lawrance. *Robert Frost: The Years of Triumph, 1915-1938*. New York: Henry Holt, 1970, 141.

17. Robert Frost, Letter to Harold G. Rugg. *Selected Letters of Robert Frost*, ed. Lawrance Thompson. New York: Holt, Rinehart and Winston, 1964, 175.

18. Ezra Pound reviewed his first book of poems, *A Boy's Will*, in Monroe's *Poetry*. His next book, *North of Boston*, was also published in London, but after Amy Lowell's review, American editions of his books were soon in the works.

19. *Selected Letters of Robert Frost*, 153.

20. When a student at Harvard, Frost had visited the home of George Herbert Palmer and his late wife, Wellesley's Alice Freeman Palmer, and he renewed his acquaintance with Palmer.

21. Robert Frost, Letter to Sidney Cox. *Selected Letters of Robert Frost*, 154.

22. Edward Garnett, Letter to Ellery Sedgwick, April 24, 1915, in *Selected Letters of Robert Frost*, 169-170.

23. "A History of the New England Poetry Club," 9.

24. Ibid.

25. Lilla Cabot Perry. Letter to KLB, Oct. 14, n.y. WCA.

26. "A History," 8.

27. "A History," 9. The meeting was in January 1916.

28. "A History," 21.

29. "A History," 10.

30. KLB, "The Morning Paper" in *The Retinue*. 14-15.

31. KLB, Diary, May 7, 8, 11, 1915. Box 4. WCA. In "The Babies of the Lusitania" she described the Germans who would always hear the voices of "Drowned babies from the sea." (*Life*, June 8, 1916, n. p.)

32. KLB, Diary, May 24, June 15, 1915. Box 4. WCA.

33. KLB, Diary, end of 1915. WCA.

34. KLB, "How Long?" *The Retinue*, 24.

35. KLB, Diary, Feb. 22, 1916. Box 4. WCA.

36. KLB, Diary, Feb. 24, 1916. Box 4. WCA.

37. Robert Frost. Letter to KLB, Oct. 21, 1915. WCSC.

38. KLB, Letter to Nathan H. Dole, Nov. 30, 1915. The original is held in the Rare Books collection of the Boston Public Library; a copy is in WCSC. Courtesy of the Boston Public Library.

39. Robert Frost, Letter to KLB, Dec. 28, 1915. WCSC.

40. Meyers, *Robert Frost*, 71-72.

41. They appeared on April 28, 1915, and May 8, 1915, according to Thompson, *Letters*, 158.

42. Interview of the author with Gwendolyn Bossi Henson, July 27, 1993.

43. KLB, Diary, Feb. 5, 1919. Box 4. WCA.

44. KLB, Diary, April 18, 1922. Box 4. WCA.

45. Katharine heard Frost read at the Vendome in January 1916.

46. Quoted in Burgess, 189-190.

47. See Meyers, 309, 151 *ff*. Amherst College, then a small Massachusetts men's college, invited Frost to give a reading from his first three books, and after seeing his success on the stage, they offered him a job. As Professor of English, he would teach only two courses of his own choice each term (not the standard three), and could miss class any time to give readings at other colleges. This special position for a poet eventually became a poet-in-residence position for Frost in 1921 at the University of Michigan until his return in 1923 to Amherst. Later he took similar positions at Harvard and Dartmouth, which gave him both income and free time to write and travel.

48. He served at Penn Medicine's Hospital Unit, Army Base Hospital #20.

49. KLB, "War Profits." *The Retinue,* 49-50.

50. *BET*, March 27, 1917.

51. Wilson's April 2, 1917, War Message to Congress. Retrieved from http://wwi.lib.byu.edu/index.php/Wilson%27s_War_Message_to_Congress

52. *BET*, April 5, 1917. Of those, 500,000 would be conscripted. Two million more would be conscripted later.

53. KLB, Diary, April 5, 1917. Box 4. WCA.

54. *BET*, April 6, 1917.

55. Ibid.

56. Ibid.

57. Published in *The Christian Endeavor World*, April 12, 1917, n. p.

58. Hermann Hagedorn for the Executive Committee, Letter to KLB, May 2, 1917. Uncatalogued. WCA. They also worked "vigorously for preparedness; mental, moral and physical" and "for Universal Military Training and Service under exclusive Federal control, as a basic principle of American democracy."

59. Published May 17, 1917; no place of publication or page given in scrapbook. WCA. The Vigilantes included this poem in their *Fifes and Drums: A Collection of Poems of America at War* (New York: George H. Doran Company, 1917), a book "presented to the public in the belief that men and women in every corner of the Union will find reflected in them some of the love and aspiration they themselves are experiencing for their re-discovered country." They also wanted readers to see that in their "re-discovered country" children of immigrants should be respected for fighting against the country of their parents (Foreword to book).

60. Hagedorn.

61. *BET*, April 6, 1917.

62. It had been created in 1914 by Richard Norton, son of Harvard professor Charles Eliot Norton. French millionaire banker H. Herman Harjes's money enabled the fleet to grow to 300.

63. John Dos Passos, *One Man's Initiation: 1917*. London: Aegypan Press, 1917, 70.

64. Robert Hillyer, "Variations on a Theme." *Collected Poems* by Robert Hillyer, copyright 1961 by Robert Hillyer, copyright renewed 1989 by Francesca P. Hillyer and Elizabeth V. Hillyer. Used by permission of Alfred A. Knopf, an imprint of the Knopf Doubleday Publishing Group, a division of Penguin Random House LLC (all rights reserved), 216, 121.

65. Palmieri, 237.

66. KLB, "Sophie Jewett Memorial Ambulance" (short version). Box 17. WCA.

67. Ibid.

68. KLB, Letter to the Editor of the *Lewiston Journal*, Aug. 9, 1917, WCA.

69. KLB, "The Purple Thread." *The Outlook*, Sept. 5, 1917, n.p.

70. KLB, Diary, June 20, 1917. Box 4. WCA. Her review of *A Treasury of War Poetry: British and American War Poems of the World War,* compiled by George Herbert Clarke, was published in *The Atlantic Monthly* in August 1919.

71. It is the title poem in her book *The Retinue and Other Poems*, 1-3.

72. KLB, "The Retinue." *The Atlantic Monthly*, October 1917.

73. KLB, "To Heavy Hearts." *The Retinue*, 59-61.

74. KLB, "'Somebody's Boy,'" *The Retinue*, 169.

75. KLB, "Our First War-Christmas," *The Retinue*, 59.

76. KLB, Diary, Dec. 31, 1917. Box 4. WCA.

77. KLB, Poems Account Book, January 1918, and "America the Beautiful" (Athenaeum).

78. Molly Dewson, Letter to KLB, Dec. 3, 1917. Printed in "The Old Kit Bag," *Wellesley College News.*

79. William A. Hart, Letter to KLB, March 20, 1918. WCA.

80. *BET*, March 7, 1918.

81. KLB, "Our Hearts Are With the Ships." *America the Dream*. New York: Thomas Y. Crowell Company, 1930, 153.

82. KLB, Diary, March 7, 1918. Box 4. WCA.

83. KLB, "The Thrift Stamp." *War-Thrift*, March 16, 1918.

84. KLB, "Darby and Joan Keep Their Golden Wedding." No place of publication, March-April 1918.

85. KLB, Diary, March 14, 1918. Box 4. WCA.

86. KLB, Preface, *The Retinue*, xii.

87. KLB, Diary, March 29, 1918. Box 4.WCA.

88. KLB, Diary, April 17, 1918. Box 4. WCA.

89. Letters from his son, William Bates, Jr., to the author, Aug. 12, 2011, and Aug. 8, 2012. Later promoted to a major, the elder William was rotated in and out of field hospitals near the front lines of Soissons, Fismes, St. Mihiel, Verdun, Argonne, Toul, Chateau Thierry, Froidos, and Chaligny. I thank the younger Bates for providing this information on Aug. 10, 2012.

90. KLB, "Died of Wounds." *The Youth's Companion,* Oct. 3, 1918.

91. KLB, "Wistful Wellesley Does Her 'Bit.'" *BET*, Sept. 11, 1918, with notation on the clipping, "(Editor's title; not mine)."

92. Ibid.

93. Ibid.

94. *BET*, Sept. 27, 1918.

95. Ibid.

96. Ibid.

97. Ibid.

98. Ibid.

99. KLB, Diary, Sept. 30, 1918. Box 4. WCA.

100. *BET*, Sept. 30 and Oct. 1, 1918.

101. *BET*, Oct. 8, 9, and 10, 1918.

102. Ibid.

103. *BET*, Oct. 14, 1918.

104. *BET*, Nov. 1, 1918.

105. Ibid.

106. *BET*, Nov. 7, 1918.

107. *BET*, Nov. 9, 1918.

108. Ibid.

109. *BET*, Nov. 12, 1918.

110. Ibid.

111. KLB, Excerpt of a Typewritten Note.

112. *BET*, Nov. 12, 1918.

113. Ibid.

114. Ibid.

115. James T. Duane, "Dear old 'K.'" Boston: no publisher, 1922, 157.

116. *BET*, Nov. 11, 1918.

117. The Roma band still carries on the tradition today, playing World War I songs in Boston area parades.

118. As described in *The Boston Globe*, Nov. 11, 1918.

119. *BET*, Nov. 11, 1918, 4.

120. Ibid.

121. Parke.

122. Back at Wellesley, "The College paraded this evening. The Truth [or Throne] that Endures read at service." KLB, Diary, Nov. 11, 1918. Box 4. WCA.)

123. Published in KLB's Christmas card, 1918.

124. KLB, Diary, end of 1918, WCA.

125. Katharine understood their beliefs, calling pacifists "Freedom's crusaders." KLB, "The New Crusade" in the *St. Louis Times*, originally published in *The New York Times*, May 9, 1917, n. p.

126. See discussion of this in Palmieri, 235-244.

127. KLB, Diary, May 20, 1919. Box 4. WCA.

128. KLB, "Motoring through New England." *The Youth's Companion*, Feb. 13, 1919.

129. KLB, Diary, Jan. 7, 1919. Box 4. WCA.

130. KLB, "Roosevelt" in *BET*, Oct. 22, 1919.

131. KLB, "The Roll of Honor." *Good Housekeeping*, January 1909. Also, "The World War" and "A Frosted Bush in the Sun" in *Contemporary Verse*, February 1919.

132. KLB, "The World War," *America the Dream*, 178.

133. Palmieri, 235, quoting Scudder, *On Journey*, 278.

134. As reported in the *BET*, Nov. 11, 1918.

135. Published in the *BET*, Nov. 23, 1918. In her diary she said that she wrote it on Nov. 12, 1918. Box 4. WCA.

136. Its music was by Robert Armstrong. Published in *The Boston Globe*, Feb. 24, 1919.

137. See Kennedy, 348-363.

138. KLB, Diary, April 11, 1919. Box 4. WCA.

139. KLB, Diary, April 12, 1919. Box 4. WCA. She was glad to speak to the young soldiers returning from the war to her town of Wellesley with her poem "Welcome" for the May 24, 1919, celebration of "Our Soldier Boys."

140. KLB, "Idealists." *The Springfield Union*, Oct. 31, 1920.

141. KLB, "The League, Yes or No?" *The Chicago Daily News*, Oct. 27, 1920.

142. KLB, Diary, Nov. 2, 1920. Box 4. WCA.

143. Dos Passos, 106.

144. Dos Passos, 108.

145. Dos Passos, 109.

146. Kennedy, 218-230.

147. KLB, Diary, April 28, 1920. Box 4. WCA.

148. Quoting from Sassoon's public statement of protest, in Jon Stallworthy, *Great Poets of World War I: Poetry from the Great War*. New York: Carroll and Graf Publishers, 2002, 69.

149. KLB, Poems Account Book, December 1920. She noted that she had written "Shining in Darkness, in a terza rima stanza," the form used by Dante in the *Divina Commedia*.

150. KLB, Diary, April 1, 1921. Box 4. WCA.

151. KLB, "A Brotherhood of Nations" in the *Springfield Republican*, Dec. 26, 1921.

152. KLB, "Special Program for Woodrow Wilson." *The Townsman*, Jan. 14, 1922. And see her diary, March 12, 1922: "Spent almost the whole day over my first Woodrow Wilson Foundation reports." Box 4. WCA.

153. KLB, "February 3, 1924," in *America the Dream,* 195.

154. KLB, "The Star of Courage." *The Christian Endeavor World*, Oct. 1, 1925.

155. Burgess, 206.

156. Published on April 12, 1920.

157. KLB, Diary, April 13 and 24; Dec. 15 and 16, 1917.

158. KLB, Letter to Mrs. Milner, April 14, 1922. Uncatalogued. WCA. She had expected to retire then, but found it financially necessary to continue teaching, although often only one four-hour course at the Scarab, until 1925.

159. It was published in 1922. Palmer's copy is at Wellesley College. See my essay, "Gender and the Religious Vision: Katharine Lee Bates and Poetic Elegy," in *Seeing Into the Life of Things: Essays on Religion and Literature*, edited by John L. Mahoney. New York: Fordham University Press, 1998, 171-194.

160. Emily Green Balch, "Katharine Coman: Biographical Sketch." *The Wellesley College News*, April 1915, 2-7. Vida Scudder, "Religious Life." *The Wellesley College News*, April 1915, 21-22.

161. For discussions of such relationships as "Wellesley" or "Boston" marriages, see Palmieri, 137-42; Helen Horowitz, 188-91; Lilian Faderman, *Surpassing the Love of Men* (New York: Morrow, 1981), 147-230. For a discussion of *Yellow Clover* in the context of a romantic lesbian relationship, see Judith Schwarz, "*Yellow Clover*: Katharine Lee Bates and Katharine Coman." *Frontiers* 4, 1 (1986), 59-67.

162. Christopher Craft, "'Descend and Touch, and Enter': Tennyson's Strange Manner of Address." In *Homosexual Themes in Literary Studies*, ed. by Wayne R. Dynes and Stephen Donaldson. New York: Garland, 1992.

163. Anthony H. Harrison, "Christina Rossetti and the Sage Discourse of Feminist High Anglicanism." In *Victorian Sages and Cultural Discourses: Renegotiating Gender and Power,* edited by Thais E. Morgan. New Brunswick: Rutgers University Press, 1990, 87-104.

164. I Cor. 9:25.

165. I Pet. 5:4.

166. Annie Kimball Tuell, Review of KLB, *Selected Poems*. No date or place of publication. Reviews of Miss Bates' Publications, undated, 1901-30. Box 17. WCA.

167. Mann, 24.

168. William Stanley Braithwaite, "A Poetic Vision of Katharine Coman." *BET*, May 27, 1922.

169. KLB, Letter to Elizabeth Kendall, July 16, 1921. Letter owned by William Bates, Jr.; at the Falmouth Historical Society.

170. Ibid.

171. VS, Letter to Marion P. Guild, March 30, 1930. Scudder papers, Box 18. WCA.

172. Quoted in Burgess, 216-217.

173. She and Howells were among the few who had praised the first posthumous versions published in the 1890s.

174. KLB, Review of *The Life and Letters of Emily Dickinson* and *The Complete Poems of Emily Dickinson*, both by or edited by Bianchi, in unnamed magazine and in *The Yale Review*, January 1925, Vol. 14, 398, 399.

175. Mary Dixon Thayer, Letter to KLB, Nov. 21, 1925. Uncatalogued. WCA.

176. She wrote about Faulkner's poetry in *The Literary Review* in March 1925.

177. KLB, "Young American Poet Whose Work Is Very Well Worth Watching." *The Literary Review*, June 6, 1925, n. p.

178. Robert Frost, Letter to KLB, Oct. 8, 1919. In Thompson, *Letters*, 242. Italics mine.

179. Thompson, *Robert Frost,* 204.

180. KLB, Diary, Oct. 21, 1922. Box 4. WCA.

181. KLB, Diary, Oct. 23, 24 and 25, 1922. Box 4. WCA.

182. Robert Frost, Letter to Wilfred E. Davison, Dec. 19, 1920. Quoted in Thompson, *Robert Frost*, 161. The conference takes its name from nearby Bread Loaf Mountain.

183. "Middlebury College Bread Loaf Writers' Conference," on wysiwyg:38/http://www.middlebury.edu/-glwe/history/html. Founded in 1926, it hosted Frost for twenty-nine sessions and continues today. Nearby Middlebury College was where Katharine's grandfather had been president.

184. Meyers, 181.

185. Seamus Heaney, "Crediting Poetry." Nobel Prize lecture, delivered Dec. 7, 1995, quoted in *The Boston Globe*, Aug. 31, 2013.

186. Eva Phillips Boyd, "Katharine Lee Bates, Poet-Teacher." *The English Journal*, June 1931, Vol. XX, 456.

187. Mann, 14.

188. Alice Bradford Chapman Belden, "Memories." Wellesley Class of '23 Reunion book, June 1993, 25.

189. Margery Metheny Curry in the Wellesley Class of '23 Reunion book, June 1993, 72.

190. KLB, Letter to Harriet Gifford, n.d., Falmouth Historical Society.

191. Eva Phillips Boyd, "Katharine Lee Bates, Poet-Teacher." *The English Journal*, June 1931, Vol. XX, 457.

192. Gwendolyn Bossi Henson, Wellesley Class of 1923. Personal interview with the author, July 27, 1993, in East Orleans, Massachusetts.

193. KLB, Letter to Gwendolyn Bossi, n.d., Falmouth Historical Society.

194. Henson.

195. Ibid.

196. Mann.

197. KLB, Diary, Nov. 14, 1924. Box 4. WCA.

198. Norreys Jephson O'Conor, Letter to KLB, Nov. 5, 1924. Uncatalogued. WCA.

199. Edwin Arlington Robinson, Letter to KLB, Feb. 5, 1922. Uncatalogued. WCA.

200. DuBose Heyward, Letter to KLB, April 18, 1921. Uncatalogued. WCA. The next year she sent him the New England Poetry Club's anthology as a gift to his South Carolina poetry society.

201. Mann.

202. George E. Woodbury, Letter to KLB, Nov. 7, 1921. Uncatalogued. WCA.

203. Robert P. R. Coffin, Letter to KLB, Aug. 6, 1927. Uncatalogued. WCA.

204. Robert P. R. Coffin, Letter to KLB, Oct. 30, 1927. Uncatalogued. WCA.

205. Tucker Brooke, Letter to KLB, May 12, 1918, WCA.

206. Coffin, Oct. 30, 1927.

207. KLB, Diary, Oct. 31, 1922. Box 4. WCA.

208. KLB, Letter to Nixon Waterman, March 18, 1924. Uncatalogued. WCA.

209. Robert Hillyer, Letter to KLB, n.d. Uncatalogued. WCA.

210. Mann.

211. CH, "K.L.B." Caroline Hazard Papers, WCA.

212. William Dana Orcutt, Letter to KLB, March 24, 1924. Uncatalogued. WCA.

213. Gamaliel Bradford, Letter to KLB, Feb. 4, 1921. Uncatalogued. WCA.

214. KLB, "Great Lovers." *The Forum*, May, 1925.

215. KLB, Diary, April 7, 1923. Box 4. WCA.

216. KLB, Diary, May 22, 1925. Box 4. WCA.

217. KLB, Poems Account Book, May 1925. Box 4. WCA.

218. Burgess, 215.

219. KLB, Poems Account Book, June 1925. WCA.

220. KLB, Diary, Nov. 15, 1925. Box 4. WCA.

221. KLB, Diary, Nov. 10, 1925. Box 4. WCA.

222. KLB, Diary, Dec. 8, 1925. Box 4. WCA.

223. KLB, Diary, Jan. 11, 1926. Box 4. WCA.

224. KLB, Diary, Sept. 13, 1920. Box 4. WCA.

225. W.F.G. (the Rev. Walter Folger Greenman), "Theophilus Huntington Root." In the Harvard College Class of 1885 50th Anniversary Report, 201. Harvard University Archives. Served by three railroad lines, the area drew summer vacationers from Boston and New York. Attracted to its beautiful landscape, near Lake Willoughby, "the Switzerland of America," they augmented its population considerably.

226. "Rev. T. H. Root." Obituary in the *Orleans County Monitor,* April 19, 1933.

227. W.F.G., 202.

228. KLB, Diary, Jan. 23, 1926. Box 4. WCA.

229. KLB, Diary, Jan. 24, 1926. Box 4. WCA.

230. KLB, Diary, Feb. 22, 1926. Box. 4. WCA.

231. In *The Christian Science Monitor,* March 15, 1926.

232. Marion Burton, "Memories of Katharine Lee Bates." *Encore*, Winter 1976, 17.

233. Quoted in Earl Marlatt, "They Still Remember," *World Horizons,* April 1939, 18.

234. KLB, Diary, March 18, 1926. Box 4. WCA.

235. KLB, Diary, March 21, 1926. Box 4. WCA.

236. She acknowledged that it was most often sung to Samuel Ward's "Materna" melody, the melody we sing today. One Sunday in March 1913, Katharine had gone to church and heard Mr. Hamilton "play the four versions of <u>America</u> Ditson is publishing." In her 1918 "History," she notes that four other popular tunes for her poem are by Will C. Macfarlane, Clarence G. Hamilton, W. W. Sleeper, and Wiliam Arms Fisher.

237. See Lynn Sherr's *America the Beautiful: The Stirring True Story Behind Our Nation's Favorite Song* (New York: Public Affairs, 2001), 66-69, for a detailed account of this contest.

238. KLB, Letter to ALB, June 8, 1928. I thank Elizabeth Bates Null for showing me this letter.

239. KLB, "Certain Contents."

240. Curtis Hidden Page, Letter to KLB, Jan. 10, 1929. Uncatalogued. WCA.

241. KLB, "Midnight in Bohemia," 1929. The book was presented to Mrs. Charles L. Young, a member of Katharine Coman's family, who presented it to Wellesley College, July 1940. WCSC.

242. KLB, "Farewell to England." *America the Dream*, 34.

243. Burgess, 221.

244. Burgess, 222.

245. Ibid.

246. T.H. Root, Letter to ABS, Sept. 8, 1930 (incorrectly dated in the Yale Archives as 1893, long before Root was in Vermont). Box 27, 39002042285883, Group 71, Series I, Folder 1262. Beecher Papers.

EPILOGUE: "FROM SEA TO SHINING SEA"

1. KLB, *America the Beautiful*, 3-4.

2. KLB, "America the Beautiful" (Athenaeum).

3. KLB, Diary, March 1, 1928. Box 2. WCA.

4. "America the Beautiful: Singing by School Children and Greetings by the Author, Katharine [*sic*]Lee Bates," *Department of Superintendence Official Report*, Boston, Massachusetts, Feb. 26-March 1-1928, 139.

5. Harry Irving Shumway, "Dimick Lets the Children Help Him Run His Movie House," n.p., n.d. WCA.

6. "America the Beautiful: Singing," 139.

7. Ibid.

8. "America the Beautiful: Singing," 140.

9. Ibid.

10. Ibid.

11. Ibid.

12. Abraham Lincoln, the 1862 Annual Message to Congress.

13. KLB, "When Lincoln," 109.

14. Abraham Lincoln, the Second Inaugural Address, 1865.

15. See Sherr, 81-93.

16. Taylor sang it during the seventh inning stretch of Game 2 on Oct. 24, 2013.

17. Robert A. Caro, *The Passage of Power*. New York: Alfred A. Knopf, 2012, 432-33. I thank David E. Herder and Raymond P. Lee for suggesting this passage to me.

18. Ibid.

19. White, 75, 71.

20. Henry Wadsworth Longfellow, "Kavanagh, A Tale," in *Poems*, 755.

21. William Wordsworth, *The Poetical Works of William Wordsworth,* Cambridge Edition. Boston: Houghton Mifflin Company, 1982. KLB's marked copy of Wordsworth is in the Special Collections of the Wellesley College Library.

22. Longfellow, "Possibilities."

23. KLB, "The American Heroine." *BET*, Monday, July 21, 1879, 4.

24. James Davies Butler, Letter to Cornelia Bates, Sept. 30, 1903. I have regularized its punctuation. I thank Elizabeth Bates Null for sharing this letter with me.

25. "America the Beautiful: Singing," 140.

INDEX

100-1, 180; tours westernmost Europe 103; promoted to full Professor 104; reads English miracle plays 106; heads English Literature Department 106

Suffers deaths of supporters Lothrop and Horsford 112; friendship with Root (see Root, Theophilus); suffers depression (see Depression); prepares for Colorado Summer School 118; sees Niagara Falls 119; teaches at Colorado Summer School 130-1; tours Pike's Peak 134-6; tours Cripple Creek 137-9; second visit to England 151-3; promotes women writers 159; as 'New Woman' 160, 164, 167-8, 277; keeps "Poems Account Book" 163, 230; edits *Merchant of Venice, Midsummer Night's Dream* 163.

Rents room in Boston 166; writes on American literature 168-72; sabbatical in England, France, Spain (1898-99) 173, 175, 180-8, 212; uses pseudonym "James Lincoln" (see Lincoln, James/Jay); takes up golf 196-7, 277; writes on Hawthorne 200; summers in England (1902) 201; revises "America" 206-7, 209-12; summers in England, visits Switzerland and Italy (1906), 215; tours Egypt (1906) 214, 215-21, and Holy Land (1906) 221-4.

Has house ("The Scarab") built 227-8; returns to Europe with Coman 234; helps found New England Poetry Club 240; starts course on 20th-century poetry 245; her portrait painted 262; ceases to chair English Literature Dept. 262; heart disease worsens 270, 274; formally retires from Wellesley 274

Bates, Katharine Lee (discrete written works):

"America" xv, xvi-xvii, 120, 122, 136, 141-4, 156, 161, 202, 206, 207, 208, 232, set to music 209, 212, retitled "America the Beautiful" 232, 233, 243, 247, 250, 252, 257, 262, 271, 274, 275-6, 277, 279-84; *America the Beautiful and Other Poems* 232; *America the Dream* 233; *American Literature* 168-72, 174; "An Anachronism" 193; anti-war poems 191-6, 203-4, 206, 207; "April Fools" 201

Ballad Book 85-6; "Ballad of Three Sisters" 37; "Betrayed" 196; "The Black Watch" 195; "A Brotherhood of Nations" 262; "Classical Class of '80" 29; "Darby and Joan Keep Their Golden Wedding" 253; "Died of Wounds" xiv, 253-4; "Dundee" 194; *English Religious Drama* 163; "Fate" 57; "Fodder for Cannon" 237; *From Gretna Green to Land's End* 226-7; "The German-American" 248; "Glory" 194-5

"Heart of Hearts" 111-2; *Hermit Island* 84-5; "Home, Let Me Go" 14; "The Ideal" 86-7; "Idealists" 261; "In Bohemia" (sonnet series) 263-8; *In Sunny Spain* 233-4; "The League, Yes or No?" 261; "Let Me Be Blessèd for the Peace I Make" 177; "Luckless Tommy" 14; "Marching Feet" 235-6; "Midnight in Bohemia" 276; "Miriam's Choice" 51-2

"Path of Brotherhood" poems 260; *The Pilgrim Ship* 275; "A Plea for Rhymesters" 57; "Prayers in Camp" 194; "A Private" 187; "The Purple Thread" 250; "Puzzlehead" 195; "The Red Tassel" 60-1; "Remarks from Uncle Sam" 193; *The Retinue* 250-1, 253; *Romantic Legends of Spain* (transl.) 231; *Rose and Thorn* 71-9, 84, 101-2; "Ruby Heart" 146

"The Sacrifice" 231; "The Schoolroom" 46; "The Sea Father" 37; *Sigurd* 230; "Sleep" 37-9, 43, 53; "Slumber Fairies" 56; *Spanish Highways and Byways* 197-8; "A Story of Christmas Eve" 49-51; "Sunshine" 56; "Ten Reasons Why a Woman [Should] Vote" 233; "Three Newton Girls on Vacation" 37; "The Thrift Stamp" 253; "To Heavy Hearts" 251; "To Mother Mary Alphonsa Lathrop" 169; "To Our President" 235, 247; "To Truth" 113

"The Unknown Tongue" 53-4; "Valentine" 115; "A Veteran of Elandslangte" 194; "Weekly Journal, Falmouth Grammar School" 14; "When Lincoln Died" 7-8, 18; "Why Not Marry a Suffragette" 232; "Wild Weather" 260; "Woman as Scholar" 102; *Yellow Clover* 262-3, 267; "Young English War Poets" (lecture) 260

Bates, Samuel (KLB brother) 1, 3, 6, 10, 13, 19, 91

Bates, William (KLB father) 1, 2, 3, 5, 7, 9-10

Bates, William (KLB nephew) 246, 253

"Battle Hymn of the Republic" (Howe) 148, 206

Beecher, Henry Ward 53, 96

Bemis, Edward W. 131, 137

Bennett, Martha 47

Bernhardt, Sarah 152

Bianchi, Martha Dickinson 268

Bible 9, 21, 136, 171, 202, 215, 231, 263

Biblical World, The (periodical) 118, 146

Bierstadt, Albert 41, 135

Billings, Hammatt 22

Blackmore, William 124

About the Author

MELINDA M. PONDER is a graduate of Katharine Lee Bates's Wellesley College and received a M.A. in American Studies and a Ph.D. in English and American Literature from Boston College. She has published numerous articles and given many talks and interviews on Katharine Lee Bates, and has published two books on Nathaniel Hawthorne as well.

Born in Indianapolis, Ponder now resides in Cambridge, Massachusetts. She is Professor of English Emerita at Pine Manor College in Chestnut Hill, Massachusetts.